Monetary Policy and Practice

Monetary Policy and Practice

A View from the Federal Reserve Board

Henry C. Wallich
Board of Governors of the Federal Reserve System

LexingtonBooks
D.C. Heath and Company
Lexington, Massachusetts
Toronto

Library of Congress Cataloging in Publication Data

Wallich, Henry Christopher, 1914–
Monetary policy and practice.

1. Finance—United States—Addresses, essays, lectures. 2. Monetary policy—United States—Addresses, essays, lectures. 3. International finance—Addresses, essays, lectures. 4. United States—Economic policy—1971– —Addresses, essays, lectures. 5. Board of Governors of the Federal Reserve System (U.S.)—Addresses, essays, lectures. I. Board of Governors of the Federal Reserve System (U.S.) II. Title.
HG181.W28 338.973 81–47648
ISBN 0–669–04712–0 AACR2

Published simultaneously in Canada

Printed in the United States of America

International Standard Book Number: 0–669–04712–0

Library of Congress Catalog Card Number: 81–47648

To the memory of my brother Walter

Contents

Acknowledgments

My debt of gratitude is as diverse as the chapters in this book. I owe thanks to my assistants at the Board who gathered data, and to the members of the Board's staff who contributed them; to Steve Axilrod, Jim Kichline, Ted Truman, Joe Coyne, and others who commented on the papers; to my colleagues on the Board and the Board's staff for discussion and criticism; to Gail Veenstra and others who typed the material; to Laura Rubin for processing the manuscript; and to my wife Mable for general forebearance. I must reserve responsibility for all errors.

Introduction

The chapters in this volume are a by-product of seven years on the Federal Reserve Board. I joined the Board in 1974, at the time of the first oil shock, the first surge of inflation into the double digits, and the beginning of the second term of Arthur Burns. Events since that time have occasioned many speeches and papers of which this selection is a small part.

Since I am my own speechwriter, I have no grounds for surprise when someone asks why I spend evenings and weekends on this unremunerated activity. I believe that the central bank needs to speak up. Today silence is not the best monetary policy, even though one may believe that in the days long gone, when closed-mouthed central bankers made a mystery of monetary policy, the policy made was probably better. The Federal Reserve has many critics. Although it is the most economics-oriented government agency, with the largest staff of economists in the government, it is by no means the fair-haired child of the economics profession. Monetarists blast the Fed because the aggregates grow too fast, Keynesians because they grow too slowly. Monetary policy seems to be an easy matter that any professor with a couple of graduate students could handle, but the Fed somehow appears unable to manage it. I have tried to show the great technical complexities, the pulling power of competing objectives, and the severe limits on our knowledge of how things really work. If I am sure of one thing, it is that there are no simple answers and no mechanical panaceas.

Not all positions taken, suggested, or explored in these chapters represent Federal Reserve views. One of the advantages of writing out one's talks is that one discovers what one thinks. It is a wholesome discipline to work through a problem and to put ideas one has had into some order, and to test their consistency. Speaking in public is an opportunity to check one's thinking against that of others, learn from their comments, and perhaps move the subject forward a little.

Program chairmen can be very helpful in this process if they have interesting ideas for new topics or leave the selection to the invited speaker. When, in February, a chairman asks for a talk to be delivered in September, he can, of course, only be offered some such topic as "current problems of . . ." Wise chairmen in any event bear in mind Mark Twain's strategy as a speaker, who reportedly said that he charged only half as much for a topic chosen by him than for one set by the sponsor, although "in either case, of course, the talk will be the same."

The subjects of the chapters reflect very broadly some of the major concerns of the Fed, although they are by no means a full sample. The range of functions of the Fed has increased markedly in recent years. To its historic responsibilities for monetary policy and bank supervision has been added a mass of consumer regulations. Meanwhile, the traditional supervisory functions have expanded by activities pertaining to bank-holding companies, foreign banks, and nonmember banks and thrifts.

Each Board decision is, of course, participated in by all seven Board members, to the extent they are in town, implying a wide range of topics with which each member must be reasonably familiar. In a sense, seven persons are doing the work of one. However, there are specializations, except that all Board members are involved in monetary policy. My own special function is the international area, which is reflected by the relatively large number of chapters in this volume concerning the international monetary system, the Euromarkets, and international-lending activities.

Board members are appointed for a term of fourteen years. This gives each of them a continuity of service that is relatively rare in the federal government, other than, of course, the enduring and very powerful bureaucracy. The legislator's purpose presumably was to provide for stability in the conduct of monetary policy, in addition to shielding Board members from political pressures. My experience from the first half of my term is that this purpose has been achieved. Outside critics of the Fed have asserted that the Board follows the election returns and also seeks to influence the elections by manipulating monetary policy. I have not been aware of anything of this sort. But such charges seem to me to make it all the more desirable that Board members go on record with their views. That is desirable also to make the continuity of their point of view more visible and effective.

Not all board members, to be sure, serve out their full fourteen-year terms, and some, therefore, are appointed to unexpired portions of such terms. In the seven years I have been on the Board, I have had seventeen colleagues. During that time there were three chairmen as well as five Under Secretaries of the Treasury for Monetary Affairs, the administrative official with whom I have the greatest overlap. Fourteen years is a long time to be asked to stay in Washington in the anonymous obscurity of the Federal Reserve Board, at a pay less than that of a vice-president of Citibank. One must save before coming on the Board, or hope to recoup after leaving. In either case, the job is like J.P. Morgan's yacht—if you have to ask what it pays, you cannot afford it.

The wide range of concerns with which the Board must deal makes for good relationships among the members. After voting on opposite sides of one issue, one is likely to find oneself on the same side on the next. The issues dealt with in this book indicate the opportunities for such shifting combinations. I have learned something from all my colleagues, although I would not, of course, hold any of them responsible for any of my views.

The individual chapters in this volume, written at different times, reflect the gradual evolution of the subject as well as my views. I have made no changes in any of them other than to eliminate the usual expression of appreciation for the chance to address each particular audience. If from time to time my judgment was at fault, or my projections in error, it seemed better to let that speak for itself than to paraphrase it by pretending that my reasonable expectations were disappointed by the unreasonable course of events.

Inflation

I have placed a selection of chapters on inflation at the beginning of this book because inflation at last has been recognized as the main threat to our economy. My own professional concern with the subject goes back to a time when inflation was still regarded by many as on balance beneficial to the economy and at worst a minor nuisance. My earliest brush with the subject was an experience as a 9-year-old boy in Germany arriving at the city swimming pool. The price of admission at that time was 150 trillion Reichsmark, that is, the economic equivalent of 15 new pfennigs. My mother, who had not fully kept up with hyperinflation, gave me one note for 100 trillion and another for 5 trillion, instead of 50. When I arrived at the pool with this inadequate liquidity, I was not allowed in. I used to believe firmly that this kind of thing could not happen here, and I still believe it to be utterly unlikely, but I am no longer quite so sure.

Inflation always has appeared to me in part at least as a moral problem, transcending economics. Inflation is a form of cheating. It also has seemed to me that economists have had a great deal to do with paving the way for the inflation we are now experiencing. The first two chapters make those points. The deceptions, distortions, and miscalculations resulting from inflation are examined at an accounting level in a subsequent chapter.

One of our great errors has been to believe that fuller employment could be lastingly achieved by tolerating some stable rate of inflation. The notion of the Phillips Curve, embodying this idea, was probably the most disastrous misapplication of Keynesian doctrines in the postwar years. One of the chapters in this section examines how trying to ride the Phillips Curve was bound to carry us to ever-higher levels of both inflation and unemployment.

A technique of dealing with inflation, unorthodox but I believe promising, that I had some share in developing under the title of tax-based incomes policy (TIP), concludes this section. A penalty tax would be levied on the income of firms granting excessive wage hikes. TIP is an idea whose time may never come, after the failure of the Carter administration to attempt introduce it in the form of "real-wage insurance." There is nothing much wrong with TIP except that it is equally unpopular with business and labor. To me that seems to indicate that it is a reasonably even-handed approach. If we do not bring inflation down by some orthodox combination of monetary policy, fiscal policy, and reduction in price-raising government actions, the chances are that instead of going with a market-oriented device like TIP we shall find ourselves enmeshed in antimarket wage and price controls.

Monetary Policy

Monetary policy is the most important function of the Federal Reserve, although it by no means absorbs the largest part of the Board and Federal Open Market Committee (FOMC) members' working time. The published voting record indicates that my views have not always been identical with what eventually was decided. But dissent does not imply dissension. The organization is very cohesive. Disagreements do not often surface in public and certainly not in my public speeches. Nor does the published voting record fully portray degrees of difference of opinion in Board and FOMC discussion. Unlike in the Congress and even in some administrations, there is a strong tendency, after a debate, to close ranks, to "make it unanimous." This supports the organization on the outside and good working relationships on the inside.

One of the chapters in part II examines some aspects of the decision-making process. Most of the others deal with monetary policy techniques and their gradual evolution. As inflation has mounted, the Federal Reserve has moved increasingly in the direction of control of the money supply and away from efforts to control interest rates. As several of the chapters indicate, I regard this as an appropriate policy, but not because I believe that control of the money supply is a panacea or that there is some mysterious causal relationship running directly from the money supply to output and prices. The transmission mechanism that connects money supply with output and prices works through interest rates in the broadest sense, including rates of return on equities and physical assets, and perhaps even on human capital. These rates of interest and return encourage or discourage spending and saving and so guide the economy. In times of high inflation, unfortunately, there is no sure way of knowing whether any given nominal rate is high or low in real terms, particularly if tax deductibility is taken into account. Following a money-supply target and reducing it over time seems a better procedure under the circumstances. The last chapter in this section explores the limitations of this approach.

International Monetary Problems

It is in the international area where some of the greatest changes in monetary economics have taken place during the last decade—from a regime of normally fixed exchange rates to one of normally floating rates. To document the reasons for my own reluctant change of mind in this regard I have added several older chapters reflecting my earlier belief in the virtues of fixed exchange rates.

The change took place in the context of a massive decline in U.S. world power and influence. There was a similar decline in the sense of responsibility for the functioning of the world monetary system that had been characteristic of American monetary policy in the earlier postwar period. Floating replaced that sense of responsibility with something approaching economic nationalism, and the chapters included here bear reluctant witness to that.

Meanwhile enough concern has built up over the unpredictability and extreme movements of floating rates to endow my initial skepticism concerning them with some credibility. There seems to be no other alternative at this time, however, certainly not in the presence of high and internationally divergent rates of inflation. Monetary policy in the United States, however, has been little affected by the transition from one exchange regime to another. It now operates free from the constraint that dollar convertibility used to impose. As one of the chapters indicates, I believe that this does not free us from balance-of-payments discipline and that a dose of that discipline is in fact a good thing.

International Banking and Finance

The Euromarkets, and their implications for central banking, are a relatively recent development. Chapters in part IV trace the main themes. One issue is whether the Euromarkets create money. This question is now being answered by the Federal Reserve through the inclusion in its monetary aggregates of Eurodollars held by U.S.-resident nonbanks. Another question is whether the Euromarkets pose some great threat, the more awesome because it is so hard to be precise about it, to world financial stability and solvency. These fears have been largely reduced to their real content. We are dealing with a new banking system that bears watching and that is being watched by its regulators. Do Eurobanks take excessive risks in lending to developing countries, and are some of these countries getting themselves into unsustainable debt positions? One must concede that the possibility exists; the answer is one of reasonable proportions and rates of growth.

For central bankers, issues like these pose new questions with regard to their role as a lender of last resort. If banks lend from countries where they are not chartered to countries where they are not located and in currencies not of either country, which central bank is to give support, in a liquidity crisis, to which banks? These problems have been threshed out by central bankers, and some of their discussions are reflected in part IV.

The Euromarkets represent the effort of commercial bankers to escape from the controls and regulations to which they are subject at home. Total escape from control is undesirable. On the other hand, the action of the bankers is a wholesome reminder to regulators that they must not overdo. Some forms of control eventually may be placed over the Euromarkets, too, but if that is accomplished it should be recognized that there are further escapes open to banks—such as into securities or nondeposit types of funds. Into such areas, regulators probably will be able to pursue them only after some calamity demonstrates the inappropriateness of a totally unregulated use of other people's money.

Several of the chapters pursue these lines of thought. The involvement of banks with developing countries, especially in Latin America, also has given me the opportunity to return to an old interest.

Banking

Three themes are the principal concerns of the chapters in part V: (1) the overregulation of banks and the directions in which they might be allowed to escape from it, (2) the mounting problem of capital adequacy, and (3) the damage done by inflation to bank earnings.

Bank regulation has given the United States a banking system that is unique in the world. The McFadden Act maintains a system of many very small banks; this system is more vulnerable than one consisting mainly of larger banks. The Act may have had more to do with the depth of the 1930s depression, which was greatly intensified by bank failures, than any other single cause. Today the tight regulation of banking activities encourages a proliferation of nonbanks to expand into the financial field. The banking regulators are in danger of doing to the banks what the Interstate Commerce Commission did to the railroads.

Inflation and low earnings have caused bank capital in large banks to fall behind assets and deposits. Low prices for bank stocks make it difficult to raise new capital. One of the chapters asks whether 100-percent insurance of bank liabilities, in lieu of the present limited insurance, could be the answer. It concludes that the inherent risk of total government domination of the banking industry may be too high a price to pay for this solution. The regulators must choose, in some degree, between imposing capital ratios on banks, at the possible cost of hobbling the banks' ability to finance the economy, and worrying about what could become an endless erosion of capital ratios.

Banks have tried to meet their capital problem by increasing their earnings and holding down their dividends. Many bankers congratulate themselves on their seeming success in raising the return on book value from its former 10 to often 15 percent or more. The chapters in part V point out that a good part of these earnings are illusory. The banks' capital is largely invested in paper assets and shrinks with inflation. Allowing for that shrinkage, bank profits are far less than they seem. This realization, unwelcome to bankers and regulators alike, seems to be dawning gradually on both.

Investments and the Stock Market

Any moderately successful economist must eventually face up to the problems of investment, in personal practice if not in theory. After dealing with portfolios for many years, I became an early believer in the dart-throwing theory of stock selection. Occasional doubts about the random-walk character of the stock market nevertheless are reflected in the chapters in part VI that deal with extreme market fluctuations. When the larger part of present discounted value reflects income to be received after many years, why should a current event like even a major recession cause such wide fluctuations, implying a radical revaluation of the distant future?

More recent pieces reflect mounting frustration about the difficulty of maintaining investment capital in the face of inflation. At the investment level, the present inflation has been a process of redistribution of wealth from the stockowner to the homeowner. Even so, several of the chapters express astonishment that investment advisers could consider an interest rate approximately equal to the rate of inflation as a return preferable to the going return on stocks for any but the tax-exempt investor. The damage done to the investor and saver is seen as part of the syndrome of consumer orientation in the American economy and of mounting antagonism to producer-saver interests.

Economic Growth

Central bankers are not precluded from an interest in economic growth. The first chapter in part VII, to be sure, is a carry-forward from *Newsweek* columns written during the great debate over the limits to economic growth during the early 1970s. In my subsequent incarnation as central banker, the immediate limits of growth had to be perceived, not so much in terms of resource constraints as in terms of capacity limitations. The rate of noninflationary growth open to the United States probably had been overestimated for years, and our policies had been excessively expansionary. To allow for a somewhat higher degree of slack in the economy, painful as it is, could be seen as an essential condition of making progress toward price stability and resumption of growth. During the 1970s, there was, of course, great resistance to such a policy.

The means to achieving a higher rate of noninflationary growth, on the other hand, have always been available. More investment and more productivity are the most immediate although not sole remedies. In the early 1970s this led to a debate over the existence of a capital shortage, of which the second chapter in part VII is an example. It was an early and by no means rare supply-side position, with the emphasis on corporate more than individual tax reform. The suggestion for disallowing part of the deduction for interest paid by corporations, compensated by an overall reduction in the corporate tax rate, was designed to help improve the excessively debt-heavy structure of corporate finance. It would seem no less appropriate when mounting inflation premiums have driven up interest rates, causing the tax system to sanction, in effect, tax deduction of the economic equivalent of debt amortization.

Political Economy

Much of the economic policy is technique. But some of it also is political economy, although not in a party-politics sense. The chapters in part VIII take up some of these aspects. Especially prominent is the concern with increasing consumer orientation and neglect of the requirements of production in the American economy. This has manifested itself in our tax policies, which have largely protected the consumer against the tax consequences of inflation but have allowed these consequences to be fully visited on the producer. Underdepreciation of business plant and equipment, thanks to a historic cost base and taxation of illusory inventory profits, are cases in point at the corporate level.

Consumer credit has been encouraged by full deduction of inflationary interest rates for tax purposes, as well as by regulation. Saving has been discouraged by holding down interest rates through Regulation Q and by the taxability of the inflation premium where higher interest rates were attainable. Environmental, health and safety, and consumer-protection regulations, desirable in principle, have been administered without regard to cost.

But, as other chapters argue, there has also been progress. We are not locked into some immutable social evolution but can make our choices. We may move into an increasingly business-oriented society, but there is a role for social responsibility of corporations. If we recognize both our strengths in making a free society work and our weaknesses as social engineers and economic planners, we can be confident about our future as a nation.

Part I
Inflation

1 Honest Money

As you prepare to arise from this seat of learning, the years of intake end, and the moment of output is at hand. You may well suspect that you will never know so much as you do now. For a while, you may feel like those great minds who forget more in a year than some learn in a lifetime. Education, after all, is what remains when all the detail has been forgotten. And if you find yourselves close to some leader of business or government, you may be contributing to great achievement. Nothing is impossible to the man with a competent assistant.

At this time, you are presumably looking at your future role in the world in the broadest possible sense, including a moral sense. Today I would like to talk to you about one aspect of your future that has a moral dimension, although it is technically an economic problem. I mean the breakdown in our standards of measuring economic values, as a consequence of inflation. Nothing that is stated about dollars and cents any longer means what it says. Inflation is like a country where nobody speaks the truth. Our failure to deal effectively with inflation results largely from our failure to regard it as a moral issue.

Inflation as Deceit

Inflation introduces an element of deceit into most of our economic dealings. Everybody makes contracts knowing perfectly well that they will not be kept in terms of constant values. Everybody expects the value of the dollar to change over the period of a contract. But any specific allowance made for inflation in such a contract is bound to be speculation. We do not know whether the most valuable part of the contract may not turn out to be the paper it is written on. This condition is hard to reconcile with simple honesty.

If our contracts were made in terms of unpredictably shifting measures of weight, time, or space, as we buy food, sell our labor, or acquire real estate, we would probably regard that as cheating, and as intolerable. Yet the case is much the same when we are dealing with monetary values.

Nor are we dealing with small differences between promise and performance. At the going rate of inflation of about 8 percent, a year at a leading

---

This is the text of a speech given at Fordham Graduate School of Business in New York City on June 28, 1978; it was published in: *Federal Reserve Readings on Inflation*, February 1979, pp. 1–12; *Federal Reserve Bank of Dallas Voice*, August 1978, pp. 1–4; and *Electric Perspectives*, no. 4 (1978), pp. 28–32.

college that today costs $7,000 will cost $32,630 by the time your children approach college age. If you buy an average home, by the time your present life expectancy ends, your heirs could sell it for almost $2.5 million. Of course, the only sure thing about these calculations is that they will not materialize. Inflation is not stable, nor is it predictable. But I hope the illustrations make their point.

The moral issues posed by inflation go beyond what I consider deceit. Inflation is a means by which the strong can more effectively exploit the weak. The strategically positioned and well organized will gain at the expense of the unorganized and the aged. Because inflation is unpredictable, its effects also cannot be predicted and safeguarded against.

Inflation is a means by which debtors exploit creditors. The interest rate may contain an inflation premium, but when you consider that it is taxable to the creditor and tax deductible to the debtor, the scales obviously are ill-balanced. The small saver, moreover, by law is not even allowed to obtain an adequate inflation premium. Interest-rate ceilings on savings deposits see to it that he will be a sufferer from inflation. The unpredictability of inflation, again, makes any inflation premium a speculation.

In the eyes of economists and of government, inflation becomes a means of exploiting labor's "money illusion," that is, its supposed failure to anticipate inflation correctly. The device through which this mechanism operates is the well-known "Phillips Curve," that is, the alleged tradeoff between unemployment and inflation. It is believed that labor will respond to a seemingly large wage offer that subsequently is eroded by inflation. If labor fails to notice the trick, it will keep working for less than it really had demanded, and employment will be higher. A government pretending to serve a nation's interest by, say, misinforming the people about its military plans would be harshly taken to task. Why should trading on the people's money illusion be regarded any differently?

As it happens, the attempt to trade on money illusion has backfired, because labor turned out not to be money blind. Mounting inflation was increasingly perceived, and as it came to be perceived, to accelerate. In consequence, we got both high inflation and high unemployment. Deceit revealed and rejected nevertheless remains deceit.

Business accounting is made deceptive by inflation. Inventory profits and profits due to a depreciation schedule that does not take adequate account of replacement costs grossly exaggerate true earnings. The government permits a remedy for the former—through last in, first out (LIFO)—but not for the latter. The effects on profits of a firm's net debtor or creditor position are ignored. Taxes and dividends are paid from profits that may not exist or, if they can be shown to exist by appropriate accounting adjustments, are not backed up by cash flows. In addition to misleading the stockholder and the public, these conditions push firms into higher leveraging. Business thus becomes more speculative.

Meanwhile, planning ahead becomes more difficult for business. Investment lags because long-term commitments involve risks that inflation makes incalculable. The need to guard against these unknowable risks compels both parties to any transaction, buyer and seller, employer and employee, lender and borrower, to introduce a risk premium into his pricing. Each must demand a little more or offer a little less than he would under noninflationary conditions. That reduces the range of possible bargains and the level of economic activity. Fewer jobs, less output in the private sector are the results.

Inflation also undermines the honesty of our public policies. It allows the politician to make promises that cannot be met in real terms, because as the government overspends trying to keep those promises, the value of the benefits it delivers shrinks. A permissive attitude toward inflation, allowing the government to validate its promises by money creation, encourages deceitful promises in politics.

Inflation Threatens the Market System, Property, and Democracy

Finally, inflation becomes a means of promoting changes in our economic, social, and political institutions that circumvent the democratic process. Such changes could be forced upon a reluctant nation because inflation may end up making the existing system unviable. One instance is the diminishing ability of households to provide privately for their future. Personal savings, insurance, pension funds all become inadequate. Money set aside in any of these forms for old age, for sickness, for education could be wiped out by accelerating inflation. One may indeed ask whether it is not an essential attribute of a civilized society to be able to make that kind of provision for the future. But that is not the point I want to stress. Rather, I want to emphasize that the increasing uncertainty in providing privately for the future pushes people seeking security toward the government.

Today, the best hedge against inflation is to be retired from the federal government. That guarantees a reliably indexed pension that may outgrow the pay of the job itself. Social security is the next best thing, although at a much lower level. Every other form of pension, even if indexed, is exposed to the risk that the employer, or the private sector as a whole, may not be able to perform. A government pension is riskless, short of a strike at the Bureau of Engraving and Printing.

A similar trend toward bigger government threatens at the level of productive enterprise. Inflation, as I have noted, distorts corporate accounting and cash flows. It creates liquidity and profitability problems. Strong firms become less strong, less strong firms become marginal. Dependence on and eventually absorption by government may be the ultimate outcome. Countries like Italy and Great Britain are already on their way to this solution.

In the United States we have not yet reached that condition, although the increasing passage of the railroads into government hands is a danger signal. But the role of government nevertheless has expanded as the private sector has retreated before the impact of inflation. Mounting regulation, tax burdens, and other impediments, of course, have also contributed their part.

Not long ago it was taken for granted that at full employment the private sector should be strong enough to produce a surplus in the federal budget. It was expected, in other words, that the inherent impulses of private consumption and especially investment would generate a level of aggregate demand sufficient to absorb capacity output. Today this has become very doubtful. Capital formation is too weak, consumption too low, to generate enough demand to sustain the economy at full employment without the crutches of a federal deficit.

We might be able to change this by appropriate tax reform that would stimulate investment. We could adopt policies that would cut down our enormous trade deficit that is sucking purchasing power out of the country. But inflation is an obstacle on either of these courses. Tax reform is unlikely to call forth large-scale business investment so long as inflation beclouds the outlook. Policies to improve the trade balance will avail little if inflation reduces our competitiveness.

Thus, by one route or another, inflation creates a vacuum in the private sector into which the government moves. By making the performance of the economy inadequate, inflation is likely to induce expanded government activity. The same result may follow if inflation leads to the imposition of wage and price controls. Indeed, if enduring controls were imposed, which I do not expect, our market economy would be on the way out. Of the three great dimensions of our society—private rather than public ownership, decision making by the market rather than by central planning, and democracy rather than authoritarianism—private ownership and market decision making will then be in retreat. No one can say how long, under such conditions, a shift also in the third dimension, away from democracy and toward authoritarianism, can be avoided.

The Sources of Inflation

What can be done? Before we look for remedies, we must examine the causes. Inflation is like cancer—many substances are carcinogenic, and many activities generate inflation. The sources of inflation can be diagnosed at several levels. The familiar debate about the sources of violence provides an analogy—do guns kill people? Do people kill people? Does society kill people? Some assert that money, and nothing but money, causes inflation—the "guns-kill-people" proposition. Some assert that the entire gamut of government policies—from deficit spending to protectionism to minimum wage to farm price supports to environmental and safety regulations—causes inflation: the "people-kill-people" proposition. Some argue, finally, that it is social pressures, competition for the national product, a revolution of aspirations, that is at the root—the "society-kills-people" proposition. The first view holds primarily responsible for inflation the central bank, the second the government in general, the third the people that elect and instruct the government.

In addition, time preference, the social discount rate, enters into the equation. Inflation usually is the final link in a chain of well-meant actions. The benefits of a tax cut, of increased public spending are felt within a few weeks or quarters. The penalty in terms of inflation, may not come until after a couple of years or even later. Inflation is the long-run consequence of short-run expediencies. Life, to be sure, is a succession of short runs, but every moment is also the long run of some short-run expediency of long ago. We are now experiencing the long-run consequences of the short-run policies of the past. These consequences are as unacceptable as rain on weekends and just as easy to change. If we continue to meet current problems with new short-run devices, the bill will keep mounting.

We will not defeat inflation if we always take the short view. We will then always find that the cost of fighting inflation is always too high, the short-run loss of output and employment too great. We shall find ourselves ignoring inflation, in the hope that it will somehow not grow worse. That is pure self-deception. Cancer ignored does not become stationary, and neither does inflation. Inflation ignored accelerates.

A Plan for Action

A long view is needed on inflation. It is a view very different from that of the politician, who is under enormous pressure to do quickly something that looks good. Harold Wilson said that in politics one week was a long time. More charitably, the pressure is until the next election. If the people will not instruct their elected representatives to do the things that are needed to end inflation, if they turn them out of office because the remedies take time and are temporarily painful, we will keep getting a little more employment and output now at the expense of much more unemployment and loss of output later. And we will get more inflation all along the way, down to its ultimate consequences.

We need to make the ending of inflation our first priority. That must be our overall policy. In the current circumstances, to implement it, we need to take a number of steps, some of which I shall list here.

1. We need to recognize that we are currently very close to full employment and accordingly must slow down the growth of the economy, gradually but firmly, to its long-term rate of 3.25 to 3.5 percent.

2. We must limit the pending tax cut to what is needed to offset the effect of inflation on income brackets, perhaps of the order of $10 billion.

3. We must work to bring the budget deficit for 1980 below $40 billion.

4. Monetary policy must prevent increases in money growth that would fuel inflation and must gradually bring the growth of the monetary aggregates down to levels commensurate with the real growth rate of the economy.

5. We must stop adding to inflation by government actions such as protectionism, regulation, farm price supports, minimum-wage increases, and high government-construction costs.

6. We must promote competition, through antitrust action, and productivity, through tax changes that stimulate investment.

7. We must maintain as strong a dollar internationally as our balance of payments will permit.

8. We would be wise to adopt an incomes policy that employs the tax system and the market mechanism, free from the taint of wage and price controls, commonly referred to as TIP.

The president's program of voluntary deescalation of price and wage increases deserves everybody's support. But in our highly competitive environment, voluntary sacrifices on the part of labor and business have their limitations. We should view the program as a supplement to, not a substitute for, a comprehensive anti-inflation program.

If inflation is a moral problem, we require a moral solution; that is, a recognition that public policies have led to serious inequities affecting people in different and unequal ways and a commitment to new policies that will correct the cumulative distortions and contribute to desired economic progress. The policies I have proposed require taking a long-run view of inflation. Nothing will stop inflation overnight, and in the short run the gains will always seem dearly won. But without such a long-run approach, the damage will mount, and the ultimate costs will escalate.

You, as you assume your roles in the productive sector of our nation, are in a better position than anyone to take such a long-run view. You have nothing to gain from the expedients of the past. You have a lifetime interest in the honest, noninflationary, productive performance of the American economy.

Economists and Inflation

Few economists, disagree as we may on many issues, today would quarrel with the proposition that our profession has much to be modest about. Many of our forecasts have gone wrong. Some of the laws and rules of economics on which we used to rely seem to have lost their dependability. Much of our advice has been less than helpful, and we failed to come up with good solutions for urgent problems.

Inflation more than any other problem has been the prize exhibit for the failure of conventional economic wisdom. Inflation today is widely regarded as the nation's number-one problem. In this talk, I propose to inquire into the attitude of economists with respect to inflation and into the remedies that they propose. The short answer, I regret to report, will be that mainstream or "orthodox" economists in the past have only too often been very little concerned about inflation, have contributed much to bringing it about, and have limited their policy advice to finding difficulties for every solution. These attitudes, which, of course, I would not impute to any individual economist, are deeply rooted in the history of economics and in present concepts and values of mainstream doctrine. I shall begin, therefore, with a look at history.

Taking Money for Granted

During much of recorded history, monetary disorder of one form or another has been the common lot of mankind. In the early days, familiar examples included instances of gold, silver, and copper coins minted, reminted, debased, and clipped by sovereigns or their subjects. This was followed, later on, by paper currency circulating at varying depreciated values, with occasional major inflations and sometimes total loss of value. Gradually, techniques were discovered to make money a more reliable means of making payment and of storing value. Central banks were created, monetary rules established, and norms developed to control the financial conduct of governments. Gold convertibility and balanced budgets played major roles in securing these arrangements. With the aid of such principles, countries came to have monetary systems much as they came to have transportation systems, which were reasonably reliable and could be expected to keep prices stable.

This chapter is the text of a speech given at Boise State University on October 22, 1979; it was published in: *Forbes*, December 10, 1979, pp. 117 and 120.

A new generation of economists forgot, if indeed they ever knew, the difficulties that their predecessors had experienced in arriving at a serviceable monetary system. They began to take the existence and proper functioning of the system for granted. They expected it to be able to take any amount of strain and abuse, through overexpansion, through violation of the built-in safety features, through diversion to purposes for which it had not been designed. The gold standard was cast out as a "barbarous relic." Reserve requirements against central-bank liabilities, designed to limit the monetary issue, were dropped. Limitations on government deficits were pooh-poohed. Warning signals flashed by incipient inflation were overridden.

All this could and did happen because mechanically the monetary system continued to function, even though its effects on production, employment, and prices often were very different from what they were expected to be. The need for repairs and maintenance was ignored. As a result, we have today a monetary system that is highly vulnerable and frequently unstable.

Removing the Veil of Money

Taking the monetary system for granted is not the only way in which economists have been trapped by their own past successes. A good part of classical economics was concerned with removing prevailing popular misconceptions, such as that money constitutes wealth. This came to be known as removing "the veil of money." The realization spread that the basic concern of economists had to be with production and employment, that, as Adam Smith put it, the wealth of a country is the product of its labor, and that prices are simply tickets stuck on real objects, whose relationship to each other, but not their absolute level, mattered for welfare. That is the intellectual vantage point from which an economist can say, with sovereign disdain, that it makes no difference whether wages are $10 a day and the price of bread 50 cents, or $100 a day with bread at $5. In an abstract sense, that is right. But the economist is wrong if he or she ignores the problems of the transition from the first price level to the second, popularly known as inflation.

The Supposed Benefits of Inflation

Inflation is something that can be engineered. At one time, it was fashionable to argue that engineered inflation could serve as an engine of economic growth. If businessmen borrowed heavily from banks to build factories, prices would tend to go up and consumption would be restrained. This would free some of the economy's output for investment. But output would grow faster as the new capacity came on stream. In the long run, therefore, everybody would benefit.

More recently, it has been the Phillips Curve that has served to justify the advocacy of inflation. It was argued that unemployment would be less if some inflation were tolerated. Labor would be promised a wage increase in excess of its productivity gains, and this would increase the willingness to take jobs. The wage gain in excess of productivity, to be sure, would be eaten up by inflation so that labor would always get less than it had bargained for. But output and employment would increase, benefiting all, and labor was expected not to notice the deceit.

These gimmicks and devices have largely been relegated to the history of doctrines. The proposed techniques to employ inflation for constructive purposes do not work, because wages move quickly in response to changing prices, leaving no margin for the businessman or woman to invest and no reduction in unemployment except of the most transient sort. People have exchanged their money illusion for rational expectations. The result is inflation.

Micro Consequences of Inflation

The preoccupation of many economists with the macro effects of inflation—employment, output, price level—was facilitated and encouraged by the difficulty of coming to grips with its micro effects. The principal question here, of course, is who benefits and who gets hurt. That question does not have an obvious answer. It is easy to say that people on fixed incomes or pensions get hurt, and that creditors are hurt while debtors benefit. But that does not pinpoint any particular individual or firm as a gainer or loser from inflation. How well an income receiver keeps up with inflation may depend on conditions in the industry or on the forcefulness of the labor union. Whether a pensioner really loses depends on whether the pension is indexed. Moreover, most men and many women are also producers, and what benefits them under one hat may hurt them under the other. Finally, one family may have all its assets in the form of a home while another many have nothing but fixed financial claims.

The most extreme instance of victimization by inflation—a retired consumer with an unindexed pension and all assets in fixed claims—may be quite typical. But his opposite number—a worker in a profitable industry affiliated with a powerful union and owning a home on credit—does not seem particularly satisfied with his present lot either.

The principal conclusion economists have been able to draw from a study of the micro effects of inflation is that one cannot generalize. A person relatively well positioned may quickly find himself pushed in the opposite direction, through loss of job, retirement, changes in the fortunes of firm or union, or changes in legislation concerning indexing. The abiding fact is a pervasive insecurity as people become increasingly uncertain about their future position in this game.

Neutral Inflation

This difficulty of generalizing about the micro impact of inflation makes it convenient for the economist to focus on overall effects. When we cannot say who will gain and who will be hurt, the easiest conclusion is that on balance gains and losses will wash out. From a sufficiently high level of abstraction, the economist can claim that inflation is neutral with respect to welfare. It is simply a process of random redistribution of income and wealth. It differs in this respect from burglary, which, like inflation, is a form of redistribution not provided for by law but which, in the nature of things, may be presumed to redistribute from the upper- to the lower-income brackets. If inflation is widely referred to as "the cruelest tax," it is, unlike death and other taxes, a highly uncertain one.

Expected Inflation

Economics, it has been said, is simple but not easy. One perfectly legitimate way of making economic analysis a little easier is to assume that market participants have perfect foresight. Firms and households so endowed will make decisions, given their circumstances and prospects, that economists can predict. The analysis will be free from the confusion that would be introduced by people making mistakes about the future.

A modest subcase of perfect foresight is perfect foresight with respect to inflation only. Firms and households could easily be endowed with such foresight if the government were to announce a given rate of inflation and stick to it.

Some interesting conclusions follow from this assumption. In such an economy, everything could be expected to become indexed. All prices would rise by the general rate of inflation, plus or minus any individual increases or declines that particular products like wheat, steel, television sets might experience. Wages would rise by the rate of inflation plus whatever would be the particular increase in each industry in the absence of inflation. Interest rates would contain an inflation premium, and so forth. In fact, in this fully indexed economy everything would be the same as in a noninflationary economy except that people would hold less money, assuming that the government cannot find a way of indexing currency and demand deposits.

From this hypothetical construct it is only a modest step, at least for an economist, to postulate an economy where inflation has become stabilized de facto without specific government edict and to argue further that this is the very economy in which we are now living provided the government would just take its hands off the inflation. The economist thus is enabled to conclude that the best thing for government is to ignore inflation. That will spare us the agony of wringing it out of the system.

In some respects, reality is sufficiently close to this construct to give it a superficial plausibility. Many wage contracts have cost-of-living adjustments (COLAs); interest rates contain an inflation premium; many public though few private pensions are indexed; many rent contracts have index clauses. Three things mainly are misleading about this picture.

First, few individual households or firms can be sure that their particular wage, product, price, interest, and so on will move with inflation. To know that this will happen on average is no assurance of survival.

Second, the government cannot really give assurance of a stable rate of inflation. Most of the beneficial effects that are claimed for inflation derive from accelerating rather than stable inflation. Most of the pressures that lead to inflation in the first place make for acceleration as time goes on. If the government did not have the strength to stop inflation when it was mild, how will it be able to hold it to a constant rate once it has become more virulent? Thus the notion of a stable rate of inflation, in the absence of government counteraction, is an illusion.

Finally, the picture of a fully indexed economy at the going rate of inflation is spoiled by the presence of numerous institutional and legal arrangements. Incomes raised by inflation move into higher tax brackets, and the tax system so far is not indexed. Interest received and paid, even though it contains an inflation premium, is fully taxable and tax deductible, respectively. The inflation premium, therefore, has a different value to taxpayers in different brackets. Increases in the price of assets, such as homes or equities that result purely from inflation, are nevertheless taxed as capital gains. Corporate profits are altogether distorted by inflation. In short, we do not have a fully indexed system with a stable rate of inflation. The government probably could not produce a stable rate if it tried, and the risk exposure of individuals and firms would remain high even if some overall inflation rate were stabilized.

The Lesser Evil

It would be unfair to accuse economists of ignoring altogether the evils of inflation. Now that early cries of "wolf" have revealed themselves as not unjustified, inflation is being seen more clearly as a dangerous cancer than in the past when only a few voices were crying about it in the wilderness. But while economists now predominantly regard inflation as an evil, many of them share with politicians the habit of always regarding it as the lesser of any two alternative evils. Bringing it down incurs the risk of a loss of output and of employment. Hence it is better not to fight it too hard. If holding inflation down means to forego some intrinsically desirable budgetary expenditure, it is always tempting to go for the expenditure. If anti-inflationary measures threaten to lose some particular block of votes, it is always cheaper to salvage the votes and hope that the inflation will not materialize.

In particular, inflation very urgently poses the choice between the short run and the long, and I do not see economists generally, as they ought to, coming out unambiguously in favor of the long run. Inflation confronts us with the choice between accepting a moderate amount of pain now or a much larger amount later on. The longer it is allowed to run, the more damaging it becomes, and the harder it will be to get it out of the system. As uncertainty mounts, businesses continue to go slow on investments. Output capacity lags, and so do available jobs. Consumer spending becomes increasingly speculative as people try to buy ahead to beat inflation. Consumer demand thus becomes increasingly unreliable as a basis for business expansion. All this argues for action that will strengthen the economy for the long run, even at some cost in the short run.

The Lure of "Potential"

Fighting inflation energetically may mean that the economy for some time may have to run below "potential." This does not mean a permanent recession, but it probably does mean less rapid growth than would be possible if the economy were in good health. The prevailing cult of potential makes it very difficult for many economists to accept such a solution. This attitude gives potential a much more precise meaning that it deserves. The maximum that the economy can produce is not a well-defined number. If we were all prepared to work nine hours a day instead of eight, obviously potential would rise dramatically. If, on the other hand, we cannot produce even at some seemingly moderate rate without overheating and threatening to destroy the economy, that potential obviously is not really within reach. Finally, if by mishandling the economy we reduce the rate of investment and slow the rise of productivity, we are assuring ourselves a future output level well below the potential that a higher rate of investment and productivity could have attained. Lamenting the loss of potential output keeps us from effectively acting against inflation.

International Complications

Our permissive attitude toward inflation reaches out into the international field. The old system of fixed exchange rates broke down largely because countries were unable or unwilling to keep their inflation under control. The new system of floating rates was advertised as permitting every country to enjoy the rate of inflation that it preferred. Now we find that a system of widely differing national rates of inflation produces large fluctuations in currencies, which threaten to undermine our liberal system of international trade and investment. Freedom to choose one's preferred rate of inflation, an objective once dear to economists, has turned out to be a snare and delusion.

Conclusion

If it is true, as Keynes said, that the world is ruled by little else than the ideas of economists and political philosophers, economists must accept a heavy responsibility for the inflation and all its consequences that we now endure. Economists have downgraded the ancient anti-inflationary safeguards such as a balanced budget. They have greatly overstated their ability to manage the business cycle. The cult of growth and maximum exploitation of potential has undermined stability. The attempt to trade inflation against unemployment, on the theory of the Phillips Curve, has been the most disastrous analytical and practical mistake in economics of the last twenty years. If economists had to run for reelection every two years, such policies would be understandable. For tenured academics who see the future stretching endlessly before them, this disregard of the long-run consequences of short-run expediencies is hard to understand.

A new generation of economists is now emerging that seems to see value in stability. It will take time until that value is universally recognized in my profession. Max Planck, the formulator of the quantum theory, once said that physics made progress from funeral to funeral. One would hope that with the evidence of past error so clearly before us, and in the interest of our own survival, we might progress faster in economics.

Inflation and Accounting

Profit Adjustments

Everyone knows that profits are distorted by inflation and how very difficult it is to come to grips with this phenomenon. The simplest cases are, of course, inventory and fixed assets. Accounting for inventory on a first-in, first-out (FIFO) basis and accounting for fixed assets and their depreciation on an original-cost basis both overstate "capital sustaining or economic" profits.

In its national-income accounts, the Department of Commerce now makes allowance for these defects by referring to "operating profits." For example, in the third quarter of 1977 profits before taxes and before adjustment for inflation amounted to $174 billion or 9.1 percent of gross national product (GNP). Operating profits after making the Department-of-Commerce adjustments were 15 percent lower, equal to only 7.8 percent of GNP, a figure that historically is very low. Although the accounting and tax systems do not reflect this, the stock market does.

Moreover, the Department of Commerce makes its adjustment on the basis of straight-line depreciation and 90 percent of Bulletin-F useful lives. If fixed assets were depreciated at a more accelerated rate or were assigned shorter useful lives than those used in the Department-of-Commerce adjustments, underdepreciation resulting from inflation would turn out to have been even more severe.

Incidentally, the Department-of-Commerce adjustments are, of course, conceptually analogous to those required by the Securities Exchange Commission (SEC) for its 10-K reports. There, a statement has to be made about replacement costs of inventories and fixed assets. That statement can serve as a means of approximating the impact of inflation, but it falls far short of a complete evaluation.

These misstatements of profits have far-reaching effects on the economy. They interfere with the expansion of plant and equipment, with the progress of the recovery, and ultimately with the ability to create jobs. Perhaps the most critical difficulty in the present expansion is that businessmen are hesitant to make commitments for new capital spending. At least one of the reasons for this is the profit picture. That is, although profits seem to be close to their historic percentage of GNP, when inflation adjusted they are much less.

This chapter was originally presented on November 11, 1977, before a meeting of the Mid-Atlantic Council of the National Association of Accountants, Arlington, Virginia.

Devices for Compensating Profits Distortion

Some ad hoc devices that help to cope with the inflation problem do exist in our accounting system. Firms can value their inventories on the basis of last in, first out (LIFO). I am always surprised, however, to find that relatively few firms have shifted from FIFO to LIFO. Based on a 1976 survey of six-hundred firms taken by the American Institute of Certified Public Accountants, about 50 percent of the firms were using LIFO in 1975, compared to about 25 percent in 1973. Those firms that continue to use FIFO induce a larger degree of overstatement in profit determination.

Underdepreciation based on original cost can be compensated to some extent by accelerated methods of depreciation, by shorter Bulletin-F lives, and by availability of the investment tax credit. However, these are not adequate substitutes for a more comprehensive inflation adjustment.

General-Price-Level Accounting

More sophisticated methods of dealing with inflation in the accounts of a company have been suggested. One is so-called general-price-level accounting (GPLA), which was proposed by the Financial Accounting Standards Board (FASB) in their much discussed draft, "Financial Reporting in Units of General Purchasing Power," issued December 31, 1974. Although it has been applied in a tentative way by many firms, it now seems to be quiescent.

Moreover, I find GPLA potentially misleading. The key to GPLA is to revalue nonfinancial assets and equity by the rate of inflation without regard to the changing prices of individual assets. Doing this leads to the firm's net-monetary-asset position; a company is either a net debtor or a net creditor. During inflation, a company then benefits from a net-debtor and suffers from a net-creditor position.

When these GPLA adjustments are made, some very interesting results are obtained. A staff economist at the Federal Reserve Bank of Boston recomputed the domestic profits of nonfinancial corporations, which in 1975 were $102 billion. When adjusted by GPLA methods, profits were reduced to $68 billion. Of that amount, moreover, only $44 billion were operating profits. Some $24 billion were profits resulting from a negative net-monetary-asset position, reflecting the fact that the corporate sector as a whole is a net debtor. These profits are of little value to the firm because they are not cash profits. No dividends, no taxes can be paid from them. If such profits were made the basis for tax liabilities, or, by internal corporate decision, the basis for dividend payments, the company would soon find itself in trouble. For example, Con Edison was quite profitable by GPLA standards on the day the company cut the dividend. Thus, GPLA seems to me a dubious way of adjusting for inflation. There is one area where I believe it has applicability—the banking system. To this aspect I will revert later.

Current-Value Accounting

Current-value accounting (CVA) is another form of adjustment for inflation. CVA emphasizes the present value of assets and the way they may have appreciated or depreciated over time. This again is a noncash adjustment. It focuses on the value of assets and liabilities and the way in which they may have changed rather than on cash flows.

The same economist at the Federal Reserve Bank of Boston found that the 1975 profits just mentioned, $102 billion before adjustment, rose to $146 billion when adjusted to CVA methods. One reason for this is that when inflation strikes, interest rates rise. When interest rates rise, the market values of bonds that are already outstanding fall. By CVA standards, this decline in bond values represents a profit to the issuer.

Because of inflation, for example, a 4½ percent bond issued by a company years ago may now be selling at 70 in the market. The company could buy the bond at a profit of 30 cents on the dollar, and add that to its profit account. However, the last thing probably that a company would want to do during inflation is to issue short-term debt to buy in long-term debt. In fact, the company probably would be very glad that it had that old debt outstanding. But this noncash item goes to swell total profits by CVA methods.

Pushed to an extreme, if a company were in really bad shape, and its bond depreciated severely, the CVA method would suggest mounting profits. If tax liability were based on these profits, the company could go into receivership. This kind of current-value accounting, therefore, would not be a helpful procedure to adjust corporate profits for the effect of inflation.

For a test of a sensible approach to the adjustment of profits for inflation, look at the stock market. The market is not fooled by phony profits. Any accounting system trying to adjust for inflation ought to reflect the judgment and the verdict of the market. It ought to produce a stated level of profits approximately equal to what the market seems to think is the level of profits. During 1974 and 1975, stocks were very low. Many enterprises were selling at large discounts from book value. Those years, of course, were a period of maximum impact of inflation on profits. The market seemed to say that, in 1974–1975, profits were exceptionally low.

Bank Profits

Of particular interest is the problem of bank profits during inflation and how to deal with it from an accounting point of view. Banks differ from other corporations in that nearly all their assets are monetary. Therefore, it seems to make sense to apply a general price index to the valuation of bank assets and bank liabilities, as GPLA does. When both assets and liabilities are mostly in money, the value of money as measured by either the consumer price index or the wholesale price index or the GNP deflator does become meaningful. It is clear, therefore, that general-price-level accounting seems to be most nearly applicable to banks.

Let us look at the structure of a bank's balance sheet. All its assets are monetary, except the building it may own, which is usually a small part of a bank's assets. Its liabilities, by definition, are monetary. It also has equity capital. Typically bank equity capital amounts to from 6 to 10 percent of total assets. The value of the building, if any, normally is substantially less than the equity. Thus, banks typically are net creditors. Their monetary assets exceed their monetary liabilities. And a net creditor is, of course, a loser in inflation. Banks are natural losers in an inflation.

Bankers may think that their profits are adequate because they make 10–13 percent on capital after taxes, of which they pay out only one-third to one-half in dividends while retaining the rest. But GPLA indicates that the truth, as far as accounting can reveal it, is otherwise. In 1974, banks actually paid out in dividends more than their GPLA-adjusted earnings. In two other years, 1973 and 1975, their earnings barely exceeded dividends.

Banks paid taxes, however, on unadjusted earnings. Therefore, when relating bank taxes to adjusted earnings for those years, the rate turns out to have been twice its reported value. Meanwhile the GPLA-corrected rate of return on equity for the period has been of the order of 3–5 percent, instead of a reported 10–12 percent.

Taxes and dividends are real. Profits are an accounting phenomenon. What inflation is doing to banks is a form of decapitalization.

Another aspect of banking during inflation reflects certain losses caused by inflation. The problems of the Real Estate Investment Trusts (REITs) have to do at least in part with inflation and rising interest rates.

Let me turn to another aspect of the banking system under inflation. Although it has to do perhaps as much with losses as with inflation, many of these losses have been produced by inflation. In particular the problems of the REITs in good part have been caused by inflation and rising interest rates and also, of course, by ill-conceived projects.

One possible way of dealing with the accounts of a bank is to apply current-value accounting and to require a bank to write down to market instantly its weak loans. Suppose a bank owns bonds that it has bought at par. Meanwhile the bonds have gone down to perhaps seventy. Should the bank write off that depreciation immediately even though presumably the bonds will eventually be paid off at par? A current-value accounting system says write "it off now." And if that were done, capital might have been reduced and the bank might have to be closed.

Applying this technique to the banking system can have drastic consequences. It carries us back to the conditions of the 1930s when examiners did something similar. They went into the banks, looked at the bond portfolios, which sometimes were well below cost, and made those banks write off such bonds. Many banks were closed in consequence. In 1938, the bank supervisory agencies concluded that this was not a good system. The examiners were instructed to give the banks time to work out some of their depreciated assets or to wait until they recovered. This involves the risk, to be sure, that a bank may carry an asset too long at book value instead of making proper adjustments on its books for a probable loss.

There are good reasons nevertheless for proceeding as we have been doing since 1938, letting a bank postpone a write-off if there is the prospect of collecting at maturity—based on considerations that are implicit even in the "Conceptual Framework" of FASB. I refer to the theory of risk diversification. That theory says that assets that move independently in price, so that one asset may improve while another deteriorates, are helpful in limiting risk exposure. Risk increases when all a bank's assets depreciate at the same time.

Therefore, when banks diversify their assets, and it turns out that some assets do well and some do less well, they are following that portfolio philosophy. Their assets then should be looked at as a portfolio, rather than as individual pieces. If any one of them does badly, it need not be written off immediately but should be given a chance to work out. Otherwise diversification would become very difficult. A bank could then only focus on the safest assets. A diversified portfolio instead allows a bank to take somewhat larger risks on individual assets. Such a strategy does, of course, require acceptance of the prospect of losses on some of the higher-risk assets. If those losses are compensated by better performances of other assets, the overall performance of the portfolio will be superior. In a well-put-together portfolio there almost inevitably will be some losses just as there will be some successes. The accounting system should make it possible for the bank to carry these assets temporarily rather than to write them off immediately.

Inflation Premia in Interest Rates

Let me turn to another problem that inflation poses for savers, for investors, and, therefore, for accountants—the treatment of the inflation premium that the market has built into interest rates. We all understand that an 8 or 9 percent interest rate is not a normal economic rate. The "real" interest rate has been estimated to be in the range of 3 percent. The rest is inflation premium. If inflation proceeds indefinitely at a rate of 5–6 percent, then a bond bearing 8- or 9-percent interest provides an inflation premium just enough to cover the inflation loss to the investor.

But this investor must be nontaxable to get an adequate benefit from the inflation premium. For a pension fund or for Yale University, a 5 or 6 percent inflation premium takes care of the depreciation of the purchasing power of a bond in an ongoing 5–6 percent inflation. It becomes in effect a continuing repayment of capital, the remaining value of the debt being reduced (by inflation) in real terms. A taxable investor who pays, say, 50 percent tax on his 8 percent interest, has 4 percent left after tax. After 5 or 6 percent inflation the real return to this investor is negative.

The reverse is true from the side of the debtor, who might be a corporation or a homeowner. To the debtor, the 8 percent interest is tax deductible. The 5 percent inflation premium, in effect a repayment of principal, is part of the deductible amount. The government thereby helps the debtor and hurts the creditor. Since inflation by its nature hurts the creditor and helps the debtor, we hardly need the government, with its tax laws, to add to the difficulty. But that is exactly what happens. The government, by insisting on taxability and tax deductibility of the inflation premium intensifies the effect of inflation.

This, incidentally, also further intensifies the inflation itself. A firm paying an interest rate of 8 percent presumably builds that interest rate into its price, treating it as a cost. Actually, what it is doing is to charge to the customer part of the amortization of its debt, by raising its price. Inflation thus accelerates.

Cost of Capital

These cost distortions are at least matched by further distortions that relate to to the cost of capital. As mentioned earlier, for a taxable debtor the real interest rate may be negative. That would suggest that capital would be cheap to a corporation. However, that is not so. The cost of capital to a corporation is a composite of interest cost and the cost of equity capital. The cost of equity is represented not so much by the income that needs to be earned on new issues, which today are infrequent. It is determined mainly by the equity that is outstanding and by what has to be earned on it to induce the stockholder to hold his stock at the going price. Today, in the face of a low real interest rate, the cost of equity nevertheless is very high. This is implicit in the price/earnings ratios observable in the stock market, which are very low. A price/earnings ratio of 6, where years ago one might have seen one of eighteen, means that the cost of equity capital to that corporation has become 16.7 percent when earlier it was 5.6 percent. Since much the biggest part of total new financing is by means of equity, including, of course, retentions, the dominant element in the cost of capital is in fact the cost of equity capital. Its very high cost today outweighs the low cost of debt. The overall cost of capital, therefore, is high. This is another reason why today business investment is sluggish.

Inflation is at the bottom of this high cost of capital. It is inflation that the market responds to when it lowers the multiples. Recent experience has shown that rising expectations of inflation adversely affect stock prices. The causal chain seems to run from higher inflation to higher interest rates to lower stock prices and from higher inflation to lower operating profits after taxes to lower stock prices. The distortions that, as we have seen, enter into the economic calculus through these various channels, enhance the adverse effects of inflation.

Capital-Gains Taxation

Let me supply one last instance of the impact of inflation on accounting that promises to become relevant if one of the tax-reform proposals that have been about should attract further attention. It has been proposed to tax capital gains at ordinary rates, with no allowance to be made for inflation in evaluating these capital gains. This is being argued despite the fact that for many investors the value of their stock mainly reflects past inflation. In real terms, that is, in constant dollars, such holdings often show little gain or even a loss.

The justification given for this deliberate disregard of the effects of inflation is one that does not stand up under analysis. It is argued that no inflation adjustment should be made for investors because none is made under the tax system for other income receivers. People who earn income from employment likewise are exposed to higher taxes as inflation raises them into higher tax brackets. If no adjustment is made for this (as a matter of fact, periodic tax cuts to offset the shift into higher tax brackets frequently are proposed), there also should be no adjustment for the inflation effect on capital gains. I think this is a profoundly wrong argument.

This can be seen easily when one traces through what is the effect of inflation on a taxpayer with employment income and one with only investment income. Suppose the taxpayer with employment income has the median family income of about $14,000. Assume, for simplicity, 10 percent inflation. If all prices and incomes adjust perfectly, this raises the taxpayer to $15,400. Suppose a second taxpayer with $14,000 investment income. If everything adjusts perfectly to inflation, including dividends, that investment income will go from $14,000 to $15,400. For both taxpayers taxes increase equally, by something more than 10 percent, reflecting the progressivity of the tax structure. But this is true only if the taxpayer receiving only investment income does not make any portfolio changes. If, as in this example, everything adjusts perfectly to 10 percent inflation, he will have unrealized gains (over and above his initial position) of 10 percent of his portfolio. Let us suppose that, at a 5 percent yield, his $14,000-income-implied initial assets are $280,000. Inflation raises these by 10 percent to $308,000. He has a nominal profit of $28,000, and, if he realizes this, he now pays capital-gains tax. The taxpayer has had no real gain at all. Even if he paid at less than ordinary rates, he would be worse off than the taxpayer whose income is from employment. He would have suffered a loss in real terms. It is clear, therefore, that no inequity would be involved in making an inflation adjustment for capital gains even if none were made for ordinary income. Failure to make such an adjustment would convert the capital-gains tax into a capital levy with further damage to capital formation and investment incentives.

This chapter has covered a random assortment of instances in which inflation distorts nominal magnitudes. It is up to the accountants to find ways of dealing with these problems. The techniques described go part of the way, but some of them do not even go in the right direction. Better approaches are needed. This, I think, is the conclusion at which one must arrive from the point of view of the accounting profession in the face of a continuing inflation.

There is a broader conclusion, however. That conclusion is that inflation probably cannot be coped with fully by accounting techniques. Inflation damages the economy no matter how profits, taxes, values of assets and liabilities are restated. The only way to avoid the damages, and to get back to more meaningful accounting data, is to put an end to inflation itself.

Stabilization Goals: Balancing Inflation and Unemployment

Unemployment and inflation are grave social ills; both capable, unless resolved, of changing our economic and perhaps political system. Between the two ills, moreover, there is only a very limited tradeoff. In the longer run, there is no tradeoff; indeed, they may tend to move in the same direction, if not at exactly the same time.

This last proposition is easier to defend today than it was twenty and even ten years ago when I first tried to argue it. That period spans the life and some might say the death of the Phillips Curve, probably the most important innovation in macroeconomics since Keynes. Today, the defense of the proposition that there is very little tradeoff—and that only transitory—between unemployment and inflation can fall back on the theoretical framework surrounding the "natural rate of unemployment," on "rational expectations," and on a growing body of empirical research. It can fall back also on the experience of the last dozen years. This experience has refuted the formerly widespread view that accelerating inflation is unlikely to occur without a continuously declining unemployment rate and would do little real damage if it did.

If ever there existed a meaningful tradeoff, it rested on workers' and employers' expectation that higher inflation would soon be reversed. Once experience ceased to validate that expectation, money illusion was bound to vanish quickly. With money illusion dissipating any tradeoff will occur only along a Phillips Curve shifting nearly concomitantly with changes in the rate of inflation.

Even a Phillips Curve that is vertical in the long run does not adequately explain present high and apparently stubborn levels of both unemployment and inflation. For most industrial countries, unemployment today seems to be above what one might suppose to be its natural rate. Yet inflation has moved to extraordinary high levels and is declining very slowly, if at all. Many special reasons can be adduced—oil-price increases, food shortages, raw-material scrambles, errors of monetary and fiscal policy, uncompetitive wage and price behavior, exchange-rate fluctuations. However, I believe that a more systematic pattern is discernible.

Inflation and unemployment have moved up together because a short-run

---

I am indebted to David Lindsey for many helpful comments, to Daniel E. Laufenberg for statistical and other assistance, and to numerous associates for criticism. Errors are mine. This chapter was originally published in *The American Economic Review: Papers and Proceedings of the Ninetieth Annual Meeting of the American Economic Association, December 28–30, 1977,* May 1978, pp. 159–164.

Phillips Curve that shifts over time in response to variations in inflation rates implies realized tradeoffs that change in accordance with the stage of the business cycle. When the economy expands, the curve traced out by unemployment and inflation becomes steep—much inflation must be accepted for a given reduction in unemployment. When the economy contracts, the curve traced out becomes flat—little reduction in inflation is accomplished for a given rise in unemployment. Where previously we recognized downward inflexibility of the level of wages and prices, today we are beginning to recognize diminishing downward flexibility of the rate of wage and price increases. Movements on the short-run Phillips Curve, in other words, are not reversible.

The upward zigzagging of inflation and unemployment has been aggravated by the stop-go character of anticyclical policy. In the United States as in various other countries, policy has moved back and forth between fighting inflation while ignoring mounting unemployment and fighting unemployment while ignoring mounting inflation. It is only recently that a more moderate approach has gained ground, seeking to reduce both evils simultaneously.

The net result has been the tracing out of a positively sloping relation between unemployment and inflation. The rough contours of this path for the United States are visible in table 4–1 showing periods of increasing and decreasing rates of unemployment and inflation. The cyclical movements outlined in table 4–1 are the result in considerable degree of policy measures, even though the precise consequences of those measures may not always have been adequately foreseen. This at least seems true of the United States, although not necessarily of other countries, where cyclical fluctuations often are imported. Could it then be argued that if no measures ever were taken to halt inflation, unemployment would never have to rise?

This would be tantamount to saying that continuously accelerating inflation might be indefinitely sustainable. Historical evidence indicates that it is not, and that hyperinflation in any event produces recession and unemployment. Even in the absence of acceleration, with inflation simply fluctuating around a high level, mounting unemployment ultimately seems unavoidable on present evidence. The reason is that inflation has shown itself to be adverse to investment and hence threatens a mounting imbalance between capital stock and labor force. In the United States, the growth of the capital stock clearly has not kept pace with that of the labor force. Full employment, by almost any definition, today would require operating the economy at rates of capacity utilization far in excess of historically noninflationary limits.

Thus, there seem to be three causal sequences through which inflation ultimately raises rather than reduces unemployment: (1) policy measures designed to curb inflations; (2) acceleration toward hyperinflation in the absence of such less than accommodative policy measures; and (3) disincentives to investment and reduction in the capital stock relative to the labor force.

In recent years, the economics profession seems to have modified its eval-

Table 4–1
Periods of Increasing and Decreasing Rates of Inflation and Unemployment (Four-Quarter Moving Averages)

Rate of Inflation[a]		*Rate of Unemployment*	
Decreasing	*Increasing*	*Decreasing*	*Increasing*
1960(I)–1961(I)			1960(I)–1961(III)
2.1 0.6			5.4 6.5
	1961(I)–1962(IV)	1961(III)–1962(IV)	
	0.6 2.1	6.5 5.3	
1962(IV)–1964(I)			1962(IV)–1963(IV)
2.1 1.3			5.3 5.4
	1964(I)–1966(IV)	1963(IV)–1967(II)	
	1.3 3.7	5.4 3.6	
1966(IV)–1967(II)			1967(II)–1967(IV)
3.7 2.5			3.6 3.7
	1967(II)–1970(I)	1967(IV)–1969(II)	
	2.5 5.6	3.7 3.3	
1970(I)–1972(II)			1969(II)–1971(IV)
5.6 3.8			3.3 5.8
	1972(II)–1975(I)	1971(IV)–1973(IV)	
	3.8 11.1	5.8 4.7	
1975(I)–1976(IV)			1973(IV)–1975(IV)
11.1 4.7			4.7 8.3
	1976(IV)–1977(III)	1975(IV)–1977(III)	
	4.7 5.6	8.3 7.2	

[a]The rate of inflation is a four-quarter moving average of the annualized percent change in the GNP deflator.

uation of the relative welfare loss from inflation and unemployment. In other words, in economist's perception, the indifference curve relating inflation and unemployment became flatter as the Phillips Curve became steeper. Estimates of the loss from inflation have been raised while those of the loss from unemployment have been lowered. In the higher estimate of the loss from inflation, abandonment of the assumption of perfectly anticipated inflation has played a role. The useful analytical tool, like other forms of perfect foresight, has no reliable counterpart in the real world. The evidence so far seems to indicate that inflation will not be correctly anticipated.

Moreover, even in a world where inflation is correctly anticipated, making the correct adjustment to inflation could prove to be very difficult. Governments, indeed, will make every effort to prevent correct adjustment by insisting on original-cost depreciation, on capital-gains taxes based on nominal rather than inflation-corrected values, on tardy adjustment of tax brackets, on interest-rate ceilings, and on treating the inflation premium in interest rates as if it were income or an expense item, just to name a few of the roadblocks thrown up on the highway to adjustment to inflation. Official statements of the need and intention to bring down inflation have a similar effect.

Inflation therefore does affect real variables—the level and distributions of income and wealth, relative prices, investment, growth, and employment.

Furthermore, even in the unlikely event that rational expectations were to lead to unbiased anticipations of inflation, this does not guarantee systematic avoidance of real effects. Markets and institutions may not permit wealthholders to obtain the inflation premia they would like to have. Borrowers may not want to pay a nominal rate equal to the real rate plus the inflation premium. Alternative assets may not be available that would provide an adequate inflation-adjusted return. In that case it does not help the wealthholder who correctly perceives future inflation to "demand" such a return. The same problem could occur in the labor market.

Moreover, the contracting parties—employers and employees, lenders and borrowers—may not feel completely sure of their expectations. Each may therefore want to charge their counterpart a risk premium. This means that supply and demand functions, adjusted for the respective risk premia, will be shifted inward and will intersect only at a lower volume of transactions than they otherwise would.

Finally, any change in the rate of inflation, even if correctly anticipated for the future, after it has become effective will leave a residue of old contracts that cannot be adjusted and that give rise to redistributive gains and losses. One has to mount to a dizzying level of abstraction to lose sight of these individual consequences of inflation.

Moreover it is fanciful to discuss inflation in terms of perfect anticipations, however qualified. The fact that the *U.S.* government issues thirty-year bonds callable only after twenty-five years at about 8 percent does not imply that the government expects twenty-five years of inflation at about 5 percent—it is simply a sensible act of risk diversification on the part of a debtor. If inflation were firmly expected by government or the private sector to continue at some constant rate, forces would come into being causing it to accelerate. That, I fear, are our prospects today. The essence of inflation is uncertainty.

This means that under conditions of inflation, the ordinary uncertainties attached to individuals' income and wealth are greatly increased. The variance or risk term in utility function rises. Since the variability of inflation has been shown to be positively related to its rate, risk rises with inflation and utility falls.

While the costs of inflation have been accorded increasing weight in professional opinion, the opposite has been the case with respect to unemployment. The costs of unemployment generally have been evaluated at two levels: the macroeconomic loss of total output, and the microeconomic financial and morale loss to those experiencing unemployment. The macroeconomic loss presumably exceeds the sum of the micro losses thanks to the various compensation schemes that redistribute the impact.

The perception of loss of potential output attributable to unemployment is being reduced by the shift that has been taking place in the definition of the full employment level of unemployment. At one time, a plausible definition of full employment seemed to be the equality of unemployment and job vacancies. Today, the natural rate of unemployment seems to find increasing acceptance as the measure of full employment. The latter definition obviously leads to a lower level of potential output and hence a lower loss attributable to a given level of unemployment.

Additional doubts can be raised, moreover, about the concept of "potential output" as such. It rests heavily on arbitrary institutional limitations, such as the forty-hour week and mandatory retirement at age 65. Today we seem to be in the process, with a minimum of fanfare, of raising the retirement-age limit. Should we recompute past potential and compute the loss from not removing the limit earlier? Some dissatisfaction with the eight-hour day, too, seems to be indicated by the heavy movement of women into the labor force, some of which may reflect dissatisfaction with the earnings that husbands bring home from their eight-hour stint. What would potential be, and how much output would we be losing, if the workweek were forty-two or forty-five hours?

At the micro level, too, the cost of unemployment is coming to be seen in a more measured perspective. A considerable part of unemployment today is viewed as search activity, that is, as voluntary. Although far from painless, the benefits from search must be weighted against the micro costs of unemployment. Insofar as job search leads to better matching of skills and jobs, it produces gains also at the macro level.

In addition the economic cost of unemployment to the unemployed individual is perceived to be less disastrous than it has often been presented to be. Much unemployment is that of secondary earners in a household. Unemployment compensation is more adequate. Together with food stamps, tax deductibility of the benefits, savings on transportation, on meals away from home, and on clothing, unemployment "income" may come close, in many cases, to offsetting the wages lost to the individual. Any induced extension of unemployment status must then also be viewed as voluntary.

The transient character of much unemployment also is more clearly perceived. "The unemployed," for the most part, are not a fixed group like "the aged," but more nearly like "the sick." The composition of the unemployed part of the labor force is more clearly seen: unemployment is much lower among heads of households and particularly married males than among women and particularly teenagers. This fact, incidentally, also limits potential output from a given unemployed labor force—during an expansion, markets for skilled labor will tighten faster than labor markets in general.

All told, unemployment in liberal discourse is losing its role as a successor to sex among the Victorians—as an utterly obscene and unacceptable part of the human condition.

If inflation were thought to be costly mainly because it causes unemployment, and if unemployment itself were judged to be less costly than had earlier been thought, the issue of balancing the two would lose much of its portentousness. Such a misconception could arise from defining the respective "costs" in too narrowly economic terms. There is more to an economic system than the production of *GNP*. Indeed it can be argued that the most significant impacts of unemployment and inflation fall outside the area of determination of income and wealth.

In particular it is easy to overrate the importance of any loss of aggregate income and growth resulting from the joint and several impacts of unemployment and inflation. Income per capita has tended almost to double in each generation. Does anyone argue seriously that earlier generations were substantially less happy than ours? That the 1950s or 1920s were periods of widespread distress? That one hundred years ago, at an income per capita about one-tenth of today's in real terms, Americans lived in misery?

There have been enormous gains, of course. But they have principally consisted in the elimination, or at least reduction, of extreme conditions of poverty, and hardly from major gains in the sense of well-being of the average household. Growth has brought satisfaction probably because it has given income receivers a rising rather than simply a higher living standard. And growth, of course, has not resolved the dissatisfaction arising from the iron law of rank: for everyone who gains satisfaction by rising in the scale of income, wealth, or other forms of prominence, there must be another who has lost satisfaction by moving down.

If unemployment and inflation were to continue at high levels, the principal individual and social welfare losses would not come from income foregone. Nor need they come from diminishing satisfaction through a slower rate of growth, since it is at least conceivable that growth might continue at about the rate of the past, albeit on a lower path. The principal loss, it would seem to me, would take the form of a lowered quality of life, in the form of heightened uncertainty, sharper social conflicts, great injury to some individual life patterns, and mounting hostility to the economic and political institutions that would be held responsible. Persistent unemployment and inflation are forms of pollution of the social environment.

Unemployment directly affects a relatively small number, but with considerable intensity. High turnover increases this number and softens the impact, as does improved compensation. However, in certain groups—not so much regional or occupational as age and racial, such as black teenagers—the condition with all its consequences is becoming endemic. Affected individuals and groups are in danger of moving outside the mainstream of society and becoming altogether alienated.

Little seems to be known about the consequences of this condition for the attitudes of those affected. A good deal has been said about the views and feelings of the unemployed, much of it derived primarily, one must assume, from introspection by overemployed economists. Given the paucity of objective studies, one may guess that plain hostility to the system must be at least as frequent a reaction as loss of personal dignity, frustration, and functional disturbances.

Inflation hits directly a much larger number than does unemployment, but generally far less severely and in many cases indeed with positive effects on income and wealth. Uncertainty, however, is bound to be pervasive under inflation. Partial indexation merely raises the risk of the unindexed remainder. The ability to provide for the future, an essential attribute of a civilized society, evaporates. Inflation, which early on had been thought to discourage saving, does nothing of the sort—in all major countries savings rates rose as inflation accelerated. Full protection of these savings can be offered only by government, to the extent it chooses to do so through indexation of social security, civil-service pensions, and at some future point perhaps indexed bonds.

Some concluding remarks on policy seem in order. The standard prescription against inflation derived from the natural rate of unemployment analysis is to allow the unemployment rate to remain above the natural rate for some time. To the extent that, by design or default, this prescription has been employed, it has so far given poor results. This experience reflects the view expressed earlier, that when inflation is on the way down, the short-run Phillips Curve becomes quite flat.

A type of action that would simultaneously reduce unemployment and inflation is the family of tax-oriented incomes policies (TIP). Numerous versions of TIP have been proposed. Restraint can be exerted through tax penalties, or through tax bonuses. It can be exerted against wages only, on the well-validated assumption that prices are closely tied to wages, or against both wages and prices. Applicability can be compulsory or voluntary. The taxes used can be the corporate income tax, or a payroll or sales tax. The principle is always the same. There are no mandatory controls. Market forces continue to govern. If a firm wants to concede a high wage increase, for whatever reason, it is free to do so, provided the tax is paid. Only the balance of bargaining power is shifted in favor of restraint.

The principle of TIP is to internalize to the wage and price setter the inflationary externalities he creates. The effect would be to break into the present spiral in which inflation moves forward mainly by its own momentum. The result should be not only a decline of inflation, but also an opportunity for lower unemployment. The Phillips Curve or, if one prefers, the natural rate of unemployment, would have been moved toward lower levels of unemployment.

There are difficulties to be overcome, both technical and political. In the light of the high social costs of unemployment and inflation, I regard the effort as eminently worthwhile. Those who do not share the view expressed here that these are the principal costs of those twin evils but are primarily concerned about their economic cost, or who continue to believe in the existence of a meaningful tradeoff between them, should find the proposal no less convincing.

Tax-Based Incomes Policies

This chapter presents my views on the subject of tax-based incomes policies (TIP). Among the several versions of TIP that have been under discussion, I will focus on the approach colloquially referred to as the "stick approach," on which Professor Sidney Weintraub of the University of Pennsylvania and I have collaborated since 1971. The stick version of TIP seeks to restrain inflation by imposing a tax on employers granting excessive wage increases. There is no interference with the forces of the market: employers who, for some reason, wish to raise wages substantially, can do so; TIP, therefore, in no way involves wage and price controls.

Various other forms of TIP have been proposed, especially the "carrot" approach, which rewards employers and employees for maintaining moderation in wage increases. A few comments on the differences between the two approaches will be made later. I would like to stress, however, that what counts at this time is the general principle rather than the specifics. What needs to be examined now is whether any form of TIP can contribute to restraining inflation rather than whether one or the other version may be preferable.

If other well-functioning weapons against inflation were readily available, there would be no need to discuss TIP. It is because the orthodox methods work slowly that a device such as TIP, despite its obvious inconveniences, deserves consideration at this time.

Fiscal and monetary policy, the orthodox weapons against inflation, so far have not been successful in winding it down. This does not mean that they would be without effect in the long run. Nor do I believe that the cost of applying them, measured against realistic alternatives, would be as high as is sometimes believed. The alternative to successfully combating inflation is not a constant rate of inflation. We do not have the choice between doing something about inflation and leaving it alone. Left alone, it will accelerate. This is because inflation increases the degree of uncertainty with which all participants in the market must cope. Thus business, labor, borrowers, and lenders will all tend to inject mounting insurance premia into their wage, price, and interest-rate behavior to guard against the contingency of higher inflation. Inflation itself tends to generate accelerating inflation unless effectively restrained. Accelerating inflation, however, means sure recession sooner or later. The cost of

---

This chapter was originally presented on May 22, 1978, before the U.S. Senate Committee on Banking, Housing, and Urban Affairs, Anti-Inflation Hearings, Washington, D.C.

letting inflation run, therefore, is higher than even a costly form of restraining it.

TIP, moreover, should not be viewed as an outright alternative to monetary and fiscal restraint. In 1971, wage and price controls were viewed as such an alternative, and fiscal and monetary policy accordingly turned expansive. I do not believe that TIP could offset the consequences of excessively expansive monetary and fiscal policies. Some restraint by use of these traditional tools will continue to be needed.

Nevertheless, an appropriate combination of TIP and the standard tools of fiscal and monetary policy offers great promise for the longer run, once the present inflation has been wound down. TIP, continuously employed, would exert continuous restraint on wages and prices. This means that fiscal and monetary policies could be somewhat more expansionary once reasonable price stability has been restored. TIP would tend to reduce the noninflationary rate of unemployment. Whatever the level of unemployment consistent with reasonable price stability (or a constant rate of inflation), the restraints imposed by TIP would tend to make it somewhat lower. Fuller utilization of resources and larger output would thus become possible. The payoff to a successful effort to wind down inflation would thus become very large over time.

Distinctive Features of Carrot and Stick Approaches

Both the carrot and the stick approaches rest on the well-documented fact that prices follow wages. Numerous researchers have arrived at that conclusion. At the same time, of course, prices influence wages, although the relationship is less close. There are other cost factors that often are claimed to be responsible for inflation—high profits, high interest rates, monopolistic practices, high prices of food, of oil, and the depreciation of the dollar. Although at times each of these does exert an effect, the main factor governing prices nevertheless is wages. With about 75 percent of national income representing compensation of labor, it could not be otherwise. All other elements, although at times possibly significant, are bound to be small by comparison. Therefore, restraint of wages means restraint of prices. Labor does not lose from wage restraint. Whatever it gives up in the form of higher wage increases, it can expect to get back in the form of lower price increases.

Such unchanging real-wage gains as wages and prices decelerate is all that the stick approach offers. The carrot approach offers that, plus the benefits from a tax bonus. The stick approach operates by shifting the balance of bargaining power between management and labor. The carrot approach breaks into the wage-price cycle by providing a tax bonus for wage earners—and possibly price setters—conditional on wage and price restraint.

There are further differences inherent in the two approaches. One difference is implicit in the fact that adherence to a carrot scheme can be made voluntary but also would probably have to be made universally accessible. The stick approach would have to be mandatory but could be limited to a group of the largest firms. Another difference would result if the carrot approach were so formulated as to require meeting accurately a wage guideline on penalty of losing the carrot. The stick approach proposes the penalty to be scaled to the degree of overshooting of the guideline. Finally there is the fact that thanks to its voluntary character and availability of a reward the carrot approach should be more readily acceptable while the stick approach avoids a revenue loss and may even yield additional revenues.

Form of Tax under Stick Approach

A penalty in the form of an increase in the corporate income-tax rate, equal to some multiple of the excess of a wage increase over a guideline, is one of several options.[1] It would have the advantage of relative difficulty of shifting the burden to consumers. It would have the disadvantage, on the other hand, of uneven impact between capital-intensive and labor-intensive firms. Also, it would not be applicable to firms with losses, although such firms are perhaps less likely to grant excessive wage increases. The difficulty of applying an incomes-tax penalty to unincorporated business, nonprofit institutions, and governments would not weigh heavily if TIP is applied only to a limited group of large corporations.

Disallowance of an excess wage increase for corporate tax purposes would be a second option. It has the advantage of simplicity and of having been on the statute books on prior occasions. Its main disadvantage is greater shiftability.

A payroll tax offers a third option. Against the advantage of simplicity of administration stands the fact that it appears to penalize labor when the purpose of the tax is to exert pressure on management.

The Guideline

The setting of a guideline for nonexcessive wage increases is not as critical a decision within the TIP framework as is sometimes argued. The consequences of a relatively high guideline can be compensated by more severe penalties for overshooting. The likelihood that a relatively low guideline will be frequently overshot can be compensated by a more moderate penalty. The concern that a guideline will become the minimum rather than the maximum should be largely allayed by the favorable effects of a guideline on wage setting in smaller firms, unincorporated businesses, and other employers that probably would not be covered. The guideline should embody the well-known principle that nationwide rather than industrywide or firmwide productivity gains are the proper standard for wage increases. The guideline would be the sum of this long-term nationwide productivity trend and an amount, such as one-half of the going rate of inflation, that would allow for the fact that inflation must be wound down gradually rather than overnight. At the present time, this sum might be 5.5 percent, reflecting 2 percent for productivity and 3.5 percent for inflation. The guideline would have to be reset periodically, perhaps annually, at lower levels ideally, until wage increases equal productivity gains.

If prices follow wages, as can be expected, labor would not suffer from accepting a moderate guideline, even if, at the original rate of inflation, this guideline seemed to leave no room for real-wage increases. As inflation decelerates, real-wage gains will be restored to their normal level, that is, on average equal to average productivity gains.

Costing the Wage Increase

To establish the tax consequences of overshooting the wage guideline, exact costing of a bargaining agreement including all types of fringes, is necessary. This requires measuring the total increase in compensation, including pensions, medical benefits, cost-of-living adjustments, improvements in working conditions, and others. It also becomes necessary to determine the increase per employee, or per hour worked, or per hour worked in each differently paid employee category. In all probability, the best approach would be an index of increases covering all employee categories, weighted by hours worked.

For both types of calculation—total increase in compensation, and the percent increase for a given firm—there are well-established precedents. The Internal Revenue Service continually has to deal with the question of what constitutes compensation and what does not. From the experience of the Council on Wage and Price Stability and before it that of the Pay Board, which administered wage controls during Phase Two, the problems involved in costing out a percentage increase are familiar. They are not simple, but they would yield to careful writing of regulations. The task would be made easier if the number of firms to be covered is limited. It would be eased also by the fact that small differences between taxpayers and the IRS would have only small consequences in terms of the penalty to be assessed under a graduated penalty scheme.

If a surcharge on the corporate income tax is employed as the tax "stick," the unit for which the wage increase must be computed clearly must be the parent corporation, rather than particular subsidiaries or plants. This means that a number of bargaining units may be involved, with different wage settlements. The fact that in such a situation management would be impelled by TIP to resist all wage increase demands, both high and low, is not a disadvantage, however. Wage restraint, to the extent possible, should be applied with equal strength at all margins.

Coverage

Conceptually, TIP can be applied to all employers, including unincorporated business, nonprofit institutions, and governments. Penalties other than the corporate income tax would, of course, have to be employed for some of these. In practice, limiting applicability to the largest thousand or two-thousand firms seems preferable from an administrative point of view. The largest one-thousand firms alone cover about 26 percent of all nongovernmental payroll employees. These firms also are the pattern setters for wages so long as the economy is not overheating. The existence of a guideline should help uncovered employers restrain the demands confronting them.

Narrow coverage would reduce a number of troublesome administrative problems. Among these are problems of new firms, and of merging or splitting firms.

One possible defect is inherent in narrower coverage. The closeness of the relation of prices and wages may diminish if coverage is incomplete. A loosening of this linkage could, of course, occur in special circumstances. A manner of dealing with it is outlined in the next section.

Restraining an Increase in Profits

In nationwide averages, prices move with wages. Under some circumstances, the link may loosen. Some of these instances are not capable of being remedied. For instance, a decline in productivity, a rise in oil prices, and the consequences of a drop in the dollar are real phenomena that affect the availability of goods. They are bound to affect real wages. This is not the case, however, of a loosening of the linkage of wages and prices that is reflected in a change in profit margins. In the unlikely event that deceleration of wages should fail to be followed by deceleration of prices without any of the noted factors present, profit margins would widen. The share of profits in GNP, in that event, would rise as a consequence of wage restraint.

This contingency could be guarded against by changing the corporate-profits-tax rate in such a way as to restore the after-tax share of profits to its previous level. To eliminate the influence of purely cyclical factors, some benchmark for the profit share based on historical relationships might be established. A tax designed to hold profits down to this share could be regarded as an excess-profits tax on the profits of the entire corporate sector. It would fall on corporations with high and low earnings. It would probably have a very moderate impact, thereby avoiding the familiar drawbacks of an excess-profits tax geared to the profits of particular enterprises. Given the close historical link between wages and prices, this corporate sector excess-profits tax probably would rarely, if ever, be triggered. But its existence would serve as a protection against an adverse shift in the distribution of income.

Revenues

Neither the penalty tax on excess wage increases nor the corporate-sector excess-profits tax are intended to raise revenue although they may do so. Any revenue that does accrue could be employed to reduce income taxes. The amounts raised by the penalty tax depend, of course, on the level at which the guideline would be set and on the penalty rate on overshooting these guidelines. The objectives in setting rates should be not the raising of revenue, but the optimal functioning of TIP.

Note

1. These and many other technical aspects are examined by Richard E. Slitor in a report, ''Tax-Based Incomes Policy: Technical and Administrative Aspects,'' prepared for the Board of Governors of the Federal Reserve System.

Part II
Monetary Policy

The Free Market and Monetary Policy

A discussion of the free market and monetary policy, in a French context, may suitably begin by taking a long look back. Nearly 130 years ago, a young man began his career in banking in Paris. From notes and letters he left, it is apparent that people at that time were much concerned about the survival of capitalism. Some sixty-odd years later, that young Paris banker, who meanwhile had become my grandfather, was writing his memoirs. They are full of concern about the threat of socialism, mounting taxes, diminishing return on capital. Those apparently were the preoccupations of bankers and businessmen in what we now look back to as a Golden Age. Almost three-quarters of a century later, the same concerns are still with us. They seem to have achieved a higher degree of urgency. But the principal fact that can be deduced form this footnote to history is, I believe, that after all these years filled with fears and forebodings, our economic system is still, in its basic principles, intact.

The system has demonstrated a degree of durability that presumably would have surprised some of its early observers, practitioners, and critics. I believe it is fair to say that it has been durable because it has been flexible. Not only has it produced enormous increases in income and wealth and has raised living standards many times, but it has also responded to many criticisms that were made of it. We may take for granted that one condition of its survival will be continued ability to adapt to change and to take account of legitimate criticism. It will not do to take credit for past flexibility and resist future change.

Supporters and Critics

I would like to examine where we stand and with whom we stand. There is no clear direction in which developments are moving. Economic freedom is advancing on some fronts, but on many others it is being driven back. The market system is gaining new supporters while old opponents continue their attacks. New demands are made on it as old demands are satisfied. In this struggle, support and opposition come from many sides, and these need to be carefully analyzed. There are opportunities for forming alliances in support of a free economy if the objectives of each group of supporters are correctly understood. By meeting new needs, by attracting new supporters, the vitality of the system can be renewed and sustained. Flexibility is essential to that end.

This chapter was originally presented on June 14, 1979, before a meeting sponsored by the Association pour l'Etude des Problèmes Economiques et Humains de l'Europe, Paris, France.

The essence of the market system is the belief that economic affairs should be guided as much as possible by the free interplay of supply and demand based on individual initiative rather than by the political process depending on a powerful government.

The market system is seen by some primarily as an efficient mechanism of production that makes optimal use of the economy's resources. It is seen by others as providing an opportunity for individual self-expression and initiative, a system of incentives and penalties, which they prefer to a collectivized society. It is seen by still others as a form of insurance against the dangers of an overbearing government that could destroy individual freedom and democracy. And it is seen by many, of course, as a source of comfortable privilege and a sheltered existence. More specifically, what kind of support can the market system hope to elicit and from what supporters?

The market system will have the support of businessmen, but not always their undivided support. If the system is to be more than a source of privilege, if it is to carry conviction, businessmen must accept the challenges it poses for them. They must be prepared to take risks, and they must be serious about competition. They must be consistent in their frequently voiced view that the government should keep its hands off business, even when business faces problems that could be more painlessly met with government intervention and support.

The market system can attract support from citizens and politicians who have observed that decision making by the political process is more difficult than decision making through the market. In the market, decisions are made implicitly, with a minimum of conflict. The political process creates confrontations—proposals must be stated overtly and must be voted up or down. Everybody must stand up and be counted. If these pressures become very heavy, democracy may suffer in the end.

Support for the market system may come also from the many who are disenchanted with governments' fumbling efforts to solve problems. For many years, the line of least resistance in the face of any problem has been to seek a solution through government. Government more often than not has been more than ready to take on any challenge, because that has meant more power. But government has not solved the great economic problems of our day—of inflation, unemployment, instability, and poverty. Some of these problems, on the contrary, are of the government's own making. Skepticism of and disenchantment with government today provide important support to the market system.

Intellectuals, and especially economists, also find new attractions today in the market system. Since the Great Depression, most economists have favored solutions of problems through government, have identified with government, and have in that way pushed back the market system. But the failures of government have given them much to be modest about with regard to their own discipline. The simple prescriptions of big government spending and easy money no longer seem persuasive. Meanwhile, the lessons of their discipline demonstrate to economists the virtues of a market economy. Although many noneconomists seem to believe that free competition in open markets creates chaos, economists know that competition means order. It is only in competitive markets that economic analysis permits predictions of how much will be produced and at what price. In markets that are infected with monopoly, many outcomes are possible and none is sure. Likewise, it is only when firms seek to maximize profits that predictions concerning their behavior and their achievements can be made in economic theory. Once that assumption is given up, uncertainty takes over.

Finally, the computer has helped economists to discover and document the virtues of the market. Thanks to the computer, it has become possible to study the response of producers and consumers to changing prices, wages, and interest rates. Innumerable studies of markets at a macro or micro level have demonstrated that market participants react to price changes. Supply and demand respond and come into balance. Government efforts to interfere with the price mechanism, like private efforts, lead to imbalances in the market and to inefficient use of resources. For economists, these observations are major factors in favor of the market system.

There exist the makings, therefore, of a broad base of support for the market system. This support not only can be drawn from the ranks of those directly interested in it as producers but also can be recruited from a much wider range of individual interests and intellectual positions. Nevertheless, the market system is questioned by many because of its identification with profits. Profit, in the eyes of many, represents inequality, exploitation, and injustice. Two responses can be made by the supporters of the market. One is to point to the functional role of profit, as a test of business performance, as a reward to effort, and as a source of funds for investment and growth. In recent years, when growth of productivity has become so inadequate in the United States, the need for more investment and therefore profits has gained growing acceptance. Accordingly, references to "obscene" profits seem to have become less frequent.

The other response is a more broadly based participation in profits. If more people owned shares in businesses, there would be fewer complaints about excessive profits. In the United States, most members of the privately employed labor force indirectly are shareholders through their participation in pension funds; this fact incidentally refutes the view that profits go only to the rich. But outright stock ownership by the broad public has severely diminished in recent years, ironically because profits have not been sufficient to keep the price of common stocks from falling.

Government Intervention

But the principal damage that is done to the market system does not originate from intellectual criticism. It derives from very practical efforts to interfere with the system in one way or another. Interference has come from many sources—on behalf of particular producer interests, on behalf of political constituencies, through demands for larger government benefits, on behalf of consumers, and, ultimately, in pursuit of objectives often intrinsically desirable, such as environmental protection, that are largely unrelated to economic objectives.

Let me give a few examples. There are the familiar demands made by producer interests, usually well heeded by government. These include protection against foreign competition, price supports, marketing controls, and outright subsidies.

There are interventions on behalf of political constituencies other than producers, such as price controls, employment regulations, labor-market intermediation, and other actions reducing work incentives and productivity.

In the United States, regulation on behalf of the consumer has greatlly increased in recent years. Much of it pursues worthy objectives. It is the spirit of much of this regulation that is alarming, because it amounts to a denial of the market system. It rejects the view that competition produces the best result for producers and consumers, that there is an invisible hand that guides private self-seeking toward public benefits. The producer is depicted as the consumer's enemy, who seeks to deceive him, exploit him, overcharge him, and engage in all those practices that, in a competitive market with alert buyers, should be eliminated by the operation of the market itself.

Consumer legislation, like the antitrust policy of the U.S. government, starts with the presumption, undoubtedly justified, that markets and competition are not perfect. The invisible hand often fumbles. There is a need, consequently, for enforcement of competition and for protection of the consumer. At issue is how far these policies should go. Antitrust policy that breaks up efficient firms simply because they are large, consumer protection that makes the consumer pay more for the protection than he finds worthwhile, go beyond their legitimate objective.

Environmental legislation also has opened a new source of intervention in the market. Principally it has done so by imposing high costs on producers to attain arbitrary standards. The result has been misuse of productive resources for unproductive purposes, a reduction of productive investment, and a general slackening in productivity gains.

The consequences of this increasing market intervention are reflected in lagging productivity. In the United States, productivity gains in recent years have been disappointing in the extreme. For the last five years, productivity has grown at only 0.75 percent annually, contrasted with 1.66 percent during the preceding five years and over 3 percent during the early 1960s. If growth of GNP in the American economy has been quite satisfactory nevertheless, exceeding substantially the growth experienced in Europe since the recession of 1973–1974, it has been mostly because of the rapid increase in the labor force and in employment, including an increase of 21 percent of working-age women.

The poor productivity performance of the United States, to be sure, cannot be blamed exclusively on recent government intervention in the market. Higher energy prices, declining research and development expenditures, and mounting inflation have all contributed. However, some of these seemingly exogenous events also are consequences of government actions that could be listed under the heading of market interference.

Freeing the Markets

Not all that is happening in the United States goes against the free market, however. There have been some notable moves in the opposite direction. Dissatisfaction with big government has been demonstrated, for instance, by the passage of "Proposition 13" in California. That proposition placed a ceiling on property taxes, confronting local authorities with the need to adjust the level of public services to the reduced level of revenues. Deregulation of airlines by the federal government has broken a long trend in that field toward more regulation, and the success of the measure is leading to pressure for similar action in other regulated fields, including railroads, trucking, and radio. A strong movement is afoot to amend the Federal Constitution to require a balanced budget. President Carter has set as an objective the reduction of federal spending from its present level of 21.5 percent of GNP to 20 percent by 1982.

Much more needs to be done, of course, to reverse the trend toward mounting government intervention in the United States. The great difficulty is that by now the passage of new interventionist legislation has become institutionalized. Large numbers of able and conscientious people see their function in life as passing and administering such intervention. They have strong political support from organized groups. Nevertheless, I believe that the trend can be turned as popular discontent with the state of affairs mounts. A better understanding of the way in which the free market works would contribute to that end.

Monetary Policy

In the restoration and preservation of a free-market economy, monetary policy has an important role to play. Traditionally, monetary policy has been regarded as congenial to a market economy. Its purpose is to maintain stability in the broadest sense. By helping to promote price stability and avoid recession, it contributes to a framework within which the market can operate with greater confidence. The same has been true with regard to the international sphere. There, monetary policy, historically, has aimed at maintaining stable exchange rates, which have contributed to the framework of stability within which the market is expected to operate. Failure to achieve this objective is not the sole fault of monetary policy, although monetary policy carries its share of responsibility.

There are some forms of monetary policy, however, that are interventionist. In the United States, they are referred to as credit controls and credit allocation. They take the form of restricting or favoring particular forms of credit and particular purposes. The Federal Reserve has always taken the position that these policies are not appropriate for a central bank except under emergency conditions. I might add, however, that reserve requirements to be held by banks against deposits are not regarded in the United States as anything but a means of carrying out a general monetary policy compatible with a free market, since the effect of such measures on the supply of credit has no significant selective or allocative impact.

In the international field, the counterpart of selective credit control is foreign-exchange control. It, too, reaches deeply into market processes, interfering with trade or capital movements. The United States has experimented with controls over capital movements in various forms, such as through the Interest Equalization Tax which was in force from mid-1963 to early 1974 and the Voluntary Foreign Credit Restraint Program imposed on banks and other financial institutions from early 1965 to early 1974. In my judgment, the experience with these measures demonstrates that, as far as controlling capital flows is concerned, they were not successful enough to do much damage. They did, however, succeed in driving much of the international lending business abroad, so that today many large American banks do an important share of their business offshore and are urging the creation of an international banking facility in the United States that would allow them to operate as they would abroad.

Exchange Rates

As mentioned earlier, I regard the maintenance of stable exchange rates as one of the traditional functions of monetary policy, in support of well-functioning international markets. The view has sometimes been expressed that floating rates, such as we have now between the dollar and other major currencies, are more consonant with free-market principles. A fixed exchange rate is regarded by some as a form of price fixing inimical to the working of the market like any other form of price control. Others have welcomed floating exchange rates because they supposedly allowed governments to pursue independent monetary and fiscal policies, without regard to the state of the balance of payments. In their view, the floating exchange rate was to be placed in the service of more forceful government action rather than of a well-functioning market.

Whatever the theoretical merits of this debate, the experience of recent years has shown that floating exchange rates involve considerable problems.

We have seen wide swings in rates that soon were reversed. We have seen currencies polarized into strong and weak. We have seen the mounting threat of protectionism. Floating rates are superior to a system of exchange controls, and to a system involving frequent and violent foreign-exchange crises. They do give expression to the market-oriented principle that exchange rates should reflect fundamental market forces, such as prices, interest rates, payments balances, and incomes. But to the extent that these fundamentals permit, stable rates clearly are to be preferred. Fixed rates imposed by government action, such as in the European Monetary System (EMS), will have a wholesome effect to the extent that they bring these fundamentals into better alignment among nations at low rates of inflation and adequate levels of employment and to the extent that they do not lead to distortion of exchange rates for third currencies such as the dollar.

Recent U.S. Monetary Policy

Monetary policy in the United States now confronts a particularly critical period. Consumer-price inflation during early 1979 has accelerated to a 13 percent annual rate. At the same time, there is a general expectation of either a substantial slowdown or an actual recession ahead. At this critical juncture, the road signs that monetary policymakers in the United States normally use have ceased to point reliably. Interest rates have long ceased to be a good guide to policy, because inflation distorts their meaning. In nominal terms, and by historical comparison, interest rates in the United States today are very high. In real terms, that is, after allowance is made for expected inflation, they may well be negative. Certainly after applicable taxes they are negative to most taxable debtors and creditors.

Lacking clear guidance from interest rates, U.S. monetary policy for a number of years has been oriented principally by the growth of the money supply. By that standard, which has been periodically published and communicated to the Congress, policy probably was too easy during the first half of 1978, since the announced targets were continually exceeded. Since the fall of 1978, however, the narrowly defined money supply virtually ceased to expand for six months. This phenomenon could have been interpreted as an extreme tightening of monetary policy, although that certainly was not the intention of the Federal Reserve. It could have been interpreted as evidence that a recession was immediately ahead, causing a reduction in the demand for money. It could be interpreted as a shift out of money, particularly demand deposits, into other assets offering better returns, to escape the drastic losses inflicted by inflation on non-interest-bearing balances. Meanwhile, bank credit continued to expand rapidly, which the banks were able to finance from sources other than deposits, including from the Eurodollar market.

The Federal Reserve's reaction, in the face of these perplexities, was largely to ignore its monetary guideposts. Continued adherence to these guideposts would have required a reduction in interest rates to induce the money supply to resume its projected rate of growth. In fact, interest rates were raised on November 1 to strengthen the dollar. Thereafter, the federal-funds rate, that is, the interbank rate that the Federal Reserve directly influences, rose somewhat further while most other short-term rates have shown little net change. Meanwhile, the inflation accelerated to a rate of 13 percent, thus reducing real interest rates.

Since money supply as well as nominal interest rates has ceased to be a reliable guide to monetary policy, some other standard clearly is needed. It is needed at least until such time as the monetary aggregates reestablish some stable relation with the economy or until inflation is brought down so that nominal interest rates once more become meaningful. A standard that seems plausible to me is that real interest rates should be positive. This is a calculation that can readily be made for short-term rates, although for long-term rates it is necessary to derive some measure of expected inflation by one of the techniques employed by econometricians. To be meaningful, real rates should be positive by a good margin to overcome the effect of taxes. That effect differs among different groups of lenders and borrowers according to their income-tax bracket.

As I have noted, short-term interest rates in the United States have been negative in real terms of late. I believe that this has implied an insufficiently restrictive monetary policy, as indicated by my votes in published records of the Federal Open Market Committee (FOMC).

Most recently, conflicting and confusing signals have continued in the American economy. The money supply has once more resumed its expansion. Signs from the real sector of the economy, on balance, have pointed toward a slowdown. The dollar has been strong. Inflation has advanced to a very high rate. Accelerating inflation itself constitutes the major threat to continued stable expansion of the economy. It also, unless brought down visibly and convincingly, poses the principal existing threat that we confront to the free-market system.

Under these conditions, good counsel is to be found in a view that has been gaining ground in recent years and that is particularly consistent with what I believe to be the proper role of government in the economy. It is a policy of steadiness, of avoiding brusque changes in monetary as well as other macro policies, and of avoiding what has come to be called "fine tuning." The belief that we can steer the economy with precision reflects a belief in the virtues of big government. Experience has not born out this belief. Efforts to steer the economy closely probably have exacerbated cyclical functuations. They have also pulled the government more and more deeply into interventionist activities.

A policy of steadiness, not reacting sharply to every cyclical move in the economy, seems to be the best way not only to reduce these fluctuations in the long run but also to limit the role of the government and assure the survival of a free market.

7 A Committee Member Looks at the Outlook

The Outlook

At this juncture, I believe the economy is close to the full-employment zone. Although inflation threatens to accelerate as we come close to the 5–6 percent range of unemployment, I would not regard that fact as indicating that this rate of unemployment is below the "constant-inflation" rate of unemployment. The acceleration that we observe is the result of special although very troublesome circumstances, including government actions on minimum-wage and farm-price legislation, strikes and dollar devaluation. A determined anti-inflationary policy should be able to overcome the effects of circumstances of this sort. The fact that inflation seems to be accelerating, nevertheless, may be a warning that the constant-inflation rate of unemployment is higher than many of us would have liked to think.

Although the unemployment data may be exposed to crosscurrents, there can be little doubt that we have done very well on unemployment. The administration's year-end objective of 6.2 percent was passed in January of 1978. The recent experience suggests that because employment is more uniquely related to the rate of growth, it is a more meaningful variable than unemployment. Unemployment is a function, principally, of both growth and labor-force developments. One must question the feasibility, therefore, of setting simultaneous targets for growth and for unemployment. In any event, overall unemployment is no longer the top priority, although sectoral unemployment, especially that of teenagers, continues to be a major social problem.

In restraining inflation, on the other hand, we have done poorly. There is a clear threat that inflation is accelerating and a great deal of evidence that expectations of future inflation are accelerating.

A simply policy rule should follow from the combination of facts. The rule is that at any time the least-attained policy goal should have priority. Today that goal is the restraint of inflation. The validity of the proposed rule is supported by the growing concern over inflation and the increasingly expressed view that inflation is indeed our number-one problem.

Still another policy proposition follows from the circumstances described. It is that we must now get ready for a soft landing. We have had a long and fairly vigorous expansion. We have a good chance of extending this expansion

---

This chapter was originally presented on April 26, 1978, before the National Association of Business Economists' Seminar on Money Markets, St. Louis, Missouri.

provided we are now prepared to allow it to taper off gradually. This would still be consistent with further reductions in unemployment. But as time goes on, these reductions should be increasingly the result of structural measures and less that of expanding aggregate demand. That would be the way to phase gradually into the long-term rate of growth of perhaps 3.5 percent. Since the economy has not yet accumulated irremediable imbalances that could block stable growth, we have a chance now of attaining that admittedly rare condition. An essential proviso is that the redressable imbalances that exist, especially the large federal deficit, the current-account deficit, and, above all, of course, inflation, are brought under better control.

Federal-Reserve Forecasting

After these general remarks on the outlook, I would like to examine in detail how the Federal Reserve goes about formulating its view of the outlook and its policy targets. This subject is of particular relevance because, under the Federal Reserve Reform Act of 1977, the Federal Reserve in its quarterly presentations to Congress is now required to take account of "past and prospective developments in production, employment, and prices." The Board already is under congressional pressure to make explicit numerical projections in this regard, although the legislative history of the Act indicates this is not required. Under the House-passed version of the Humphrey-Hawkins Bill, moreover, the Federal Reserve would be required once a year to present its intended policies for the year ahead and their relationship to (1) the short-term goals set forth in the *Economic Report of the President* and (2) medium-term trends in employment, production, and prices for the three calendar years beyond the period considered in the *Economic Report*. I have doubts that the Federal Reserve can do this in any meaningful way. This is partly because of the inherent uncertainties of economics, which make projections and targeting, as we have just observed in the case of unemployment, a high-risk occupation—all the more so when undertaken for five-year periods. More particularly, however, it is the structure of the Federal Reserve System and the Federal Open Market Committee (FOMC) that militates against a meaningful exercise of forecasting and target setting. The committee print that is now before the Senate Human Resources Committee wisely does not require five-year projections.

The Federal Reserve System has a staff of economists, at the Board and in the Reserve Banks, that is probably second to none in the world. This staff engages in careful and detailed forecasting exercises every month. The results, of course, are fully available to the FOMC. However, a staff forecast is not that of the FOMC. Moreover, it would be very unwise to present the staff forecast to the Congress, even as a staff exercise. That would tend to politicize the process, would militate against firm analytic positions being taken, and would make it psychologically difficult for the staff to modify its forecast quickly in the light of changing circumstances.

Policymakers' Forecasts

For the individual member of the FOMC, it is quite impossible to take the staff forecast literally. Precise numerical forecasts are the product of computers and, in the U.S.-government context, of the need to have hard GNP forecasts for budget making and revenue estimating. Experienced users of such data will tend to think in terms of ranges, of probability distributions, perhaps skewed, and quite likely even of altogether different scenarios.

As policymakers, the members of the FOMC will tend to factor into their own assessment of the future the chance that they have, if the economy develops differently from what they expect or desire, to take action that might help bring the economy back on track. This may lead to rather different evaluations of risks and probabilities than those a passive observer might arrive at.

Given this wide range of possible outcomes, it is most unlikely that all the members of the FOMC would arrive at a uniform forecast. It would not be meaningful for the FOMC, moreover, to vote on the outlook as such. Truth, or even probability, cannot be determined by majority decision. In the nature of things, there can be no fully agreed FOMC forecast, although means, medians, broad consensuses, and the like could be developed. Any such overall consensus would undoubtedly conceal a large number of differences on specifics.

Policymakers' Targets

Where the setting of targets is concerned, such as for growth, unemployment, and inflation, the case is different. Targets calling for action can be established by majority decision. Very likely, however, the sets of such targets chosen by individual FOMC members would vary greatly. They would reflect different value judgments, different tradeoffs, different degrees of time preference, and differences of views concerning the effectiveness and the lags of the instruments to be employed in pursuit of these targets. Conceivably no single set of three objectives might command a majority. Only broad ranges, or even qualitative descriptions of targets, might attract a consensus.

Furthermore, one must question the very meaning of any setting of targets for the real sector of the economy by policymakers that have only quite limited powers. An FOMC member may believe that certain levels of growth, unemployment, and inflation are achievable if all the powers at the disposal of government were brought to bear. But the Federal Reserve wields only a fraction, in my opinion a very modest one, of these powers. If the much larger powers outside the grasp of the FOMC are not brought to bear, or are brought to bear in ways not conducive to the attainment of these targets, what is the meaning of the FOMC saying that it has such and such targets? This very practical consideration is buttressed, at a more theoretical level, by the familiar proposition that the number of instruments must be at least equal to the number of targets. The Federal Reserve in effect has only one instrument—monetary policy. Discount rate, open-market operations, and reserve-requirement changes are only variants of the same tool, permitting only insignificant goal differentiation. It is not possible to achieve independent levels of growth, unemployment, inflation with this single instrument. These factors—the difficulty of reaching a highly specific consensus and the limitations of control—are the underlying reasons for why the FOMC has been wise not to try to set highly specific targets.

Targets and Proxies

What the FOMC typically has done is to specify some financial variable or variables, as a proxy for real-sector targets. In recent years, the monetary aggregates have served this function. Naturally one takes for granted that FOMC members' ultimate concern is with real-sector variables and not with some financial magnitudes. But agreement on a proxy is often feasible where agreement on a set of real-sector targets would be difficult.

This presupposes, of course, that there is a reasonably close link between the financial proxy, say the money supply, and the real sector. Most people believe, rightly in my opinion, that this is true only to an approximation. In addition, focusing on a proxy variable such as the money supply also can be justified by a belief that the real sector responds to monetary-policy action only after a long lag.

The use of a proxy variable greatly facilitates the decision process. There are several reasons for this. First, only one variable needs to be determined, instead of a whole set. Each FOMC member chooses the value of the proxy variable he believes most likely to achieve his real-sector preferences, possibly including variables other than the familiar targets of growth, unemployment, and inflation, and including also diverse trade-offs among all these. Second, the proxy variable, if it is well chosen, will be subject to the control of the FOMC. This is clearly the case of the money supply, although only to a much lesser degree than that of interest rates. Finally, a proxy variable that is within the purview of the FOMC encourages arrival at a consensus or at least at some immediate decision, precisely because action on it is needed and can be made immediately effective. Futile debate over matters that the Federal Reserve cannot control thus is replaced by purposeful discussion of something it can control.

In the FOMC's discussion of the desirable setting of the proxy variable or variables, the expected real-sector effects, possibly quite different in the anticipations of different members of the Committee, will play a large role. The Committee is unlikely to mistake an instrumental variable for an ultimate one. But the decision process is greatly aided by focusing on the instrument. At a time when the need to bring down inflation imparts a clear preference for moving a money-supply target in a downward direction, this advantage is particularly pronounced.

Congressional Presentation

The nature of a group decision, as described, makes it difficult to formulate targets for the real sector for presentation to the Congress, as has sometimes been proposed. The FOMC does not formulate such goals internally for its own purposes. It probably is wise not to engage in an overly formalistic exercise of that sort, so long as the consensus, to the extent that there is one, can be expressed through a proxy. Such an attempt could polarize, perhaps paralyze, a group otherwise capable of action.

There is a second reason why explicit formulation of detailed real-sector targets would be undesirable. In all probability, the exercise would generate pressures on the Federal Reserve, emanating from the public, the administration, and the Congress, for more credit creation and monetary expansion. But, as noted, consistency among real-sector targets, and consensus on them, is difficult to achieve even in a small and quite professional group such as the FOMC. The chances that targets urged by outside groups should turn out to be consistent and feasible must be evaluated with even greater skepticism.

Adequate coordination between monetary policy, fiscal policy, and other government policies must, of course, be achieved. The present procedure for coordination is simple, albeit largely implicit. The Congress, the administration, and the Federal Reserve all develop their forecasts of the economy and their views of appropriate policies in the light of information about the forecasts, targets, and operating plans of the others.

The most explicit and continuous communication concerning expectations and policy intentions probably is provided by the Federal Reserve. As already mentioned, the Fed must report to the Congress quarterly on its one-year money-supply targets, taking account of past and prospective developments in production, employment, and prices. Given the ability of the monetary authorities to implement their money-supply targets, therefore, Congress and the administration are enabled to form reasonably dependable expectations of future growth of the money supply. The ability of Congress and the administration to generate reliable expectations in the fiscal and other areas may be subject to greater uncertainty, although the Budget Control Act of 1974 has helped in this regard. But an appropriate fiscal-monetary mix can be made to emerge from actions based on these sets of expectations.

This form of fiscal-monetary coordination, to be sure, is somewhat looser than those who believe in centralization of macro decision making might like to see. It should be noted, however, that coordination of expectations is the best that can be attempted, since full control of monetary and fiscal variables, in the nature of a market economy, is not possible. Moreover, there is no single focus of policy even for fiscal-policy decisions and other government policies. In varying degree, these policies are determined by interaction between the Congress, the political forces in the Executive Branch, and the bureaucracy.

Congressional and Executive-Branch Moves to Influence Federal Reserve Policy

The Federal Reserve communication with Congress and with the administration should of course be forthcoming and meaningful. It should not, however, change the role of the Federal Reserve.

There are grounds for concern that there have been so many legislative proposals in recent years that have sought to reduce the degree of independence the Federal Reserve has historically enjoyed. In the case of the Federal Reserve Reform Act the legislation was substantially modified before passage, and the modifications in the Humphrey-Hawkins bill have not yet been completed. Yet both these projects of law explicitly require that we set targets and provide for congressional review of our performance. This could accord the Congress a growing influence over Federal Reserve policies in the years ahead. I believe that members of the Congressional Budget Committees would give ample testimony to the congressional bias toward enacting programs—the sum total of which is inflationary. It is my expectation that a similar bias may develop in congressional recommendations concerning monetary policy.

This worrisome trend is reinforced, since legislation subjecting the Federal Reserve to a General Accounting Office (GAO) audit—and the GAO is the investigatory arm of the U.S. Congress—is well advanced in the Congress.

The Federal Reserve fought this legislation for many years, because it feared that GAO audit would go beyond a financial audit and become a performance audit of our monetary policy. Fortunately, under the evolving bill, monetary policy is still exempt from the GAO's sway, but no one can tell for how long. If our monetary-policy decisions ever are audited, it will not be difficult, with the benefit of hindsight, to demonstrate that Federal Reserve policies have fallen far short of perfection. The more numerous and more specific the targets that we are required to announce because of legislation, the more glaring will be the inability to attain all or perhaps even any of them. Once such "failure" is documented by an official audit, what could be more reasonable than for Congress itself to take over direct control of monetary policy to remedy this "mismanagement," and what would be the predictable consequences?

There are many arguments for and against central-bank independence. They turn on the degree to which monetary policy follows the democratic process, the degree of coordination with fiscal and other policies, the need for the executive—or the Congress—to have adequate control of all policy instruments. But fundamentally there is only one issue. It is inflation. The founding fathers of the Federal Reserve System knew very well that for politicians the power to print money represents a temptation difficult to resist. It was clear to them that more executive or congressional control over the printing press would mean more inflation. Independence of the central bank would mean less inflation. That was the basis on which the legislators who designed the Federal Reserve Act made their choice. It remains to be seen whether their successors will abide by that choice.

The Business Cycle and the Federal Reserve

The current business expansion has proceeded in an environment characterized by a fair degree of consensus on matters of economic policy that during past expansions have been subjects of controversy. First, there seems to be widespread, although not complete, consensus that the alleged trade-off between unemployment and inflation is not an appropriate basis for policy. There may be such a trade-off for a few months or even quarters. There is none in the longer run. Over the years, in fact, inflation and unemployment have moved up together so that one could speak of a positively sloping Phillips Curve. That is how we eventually reached a condition of double-digit inflation and nearly double-digit unemployment. We have moved down some distance from those levels, but both unemployment and inflation are still unacceptably high. There is a degree of consensus, however, to the effect that we cannot fight one evil while ignoring the other. Both unemployment and inflation must be brought down simultaneously.

I believe that there is a degree of consensus also with respect to the appropriate rate at which the economic expansion ought to proceed. It should be a moderate rate of expansion—I do not call it "growth" because that to me denotes a growth of capacity, not higher utilization of existing capacity. That, indeed, seems to be widely expected for the period ahead and seemed to be widely regarded as appropriate.

On former occasions the argument frequently was made that the presence of substantial excess capacity justified and indeed called for a rapid rate of expansion, in the 6–8 percent range. According to that prescription, such a sprint was to be followed by quick fiscal and monetary restraint as the capacity ceiling was approached to slow the economy down to its long-run potential-growth rate. Such attempts to accelerate the economy even after it was well into a cyclical expansion had caused the economy to slam hard into the capacity ceiling, generating inflation and subsequent recession. Today it seems to be widely recognized that fine-tuning is beyond our powers. In the present expansion, the need for moderation is underscored by the still very high level of inflation.

There is a high degree of consensus also, I believe, on the need to bring down inflation and not to accept the present high level. Inflation today is widely recognized as causing severe damage, to investment, to consumption, therefore

This chapter was originally presented on October 11, 1977, at the 1977 Annual Meeting of the National Association of Business Economists, Philadelphia, Pennsylvania.

to employment, and to our social and financial institutions generally. I hear much less frequently the view that a stable rate of inflation such as we have had for the last two years, with some ups and downs, can be regarded as the equivalent of price stability. I would be greatly concerned if such a view took hold, because once it were believed that 6 percent is as good as zero, it would only be a matter of time before we would be told that 1 percent over 6 was nothing, that 2 percent over 6 were quite acceptable, and so forth.

I might become guilty of occupational bias if I were to claim that there seems to be a greater consensus also on monetary policy. Certainly, there is greater agreement today that the monetary aggregates must be the major guide to policy. That is, in the main, the consequence of inflation, which makes the money supply a more compelling guide than interest rates. But outside the Federal Reserve there are, of course, those who argue that of late the aggregates have moved faster than consistent with bringing down inflation, matched by others who argue that they have not moved fast enough to prevent a rise in short-term interest rates. The Federal Reserve is in the middle, and I would merely point out that so far at least the course of the aggregates has been consistent with a stability of long-term interest rates remarkable for this stage of the cycle. I would add that if we interpret long-term interest rates in real terms, and make allowance for the fact that to most private debtors interest payments are tax deductible, real long-term rates are indeed very low and for many borrowers probably negative.

The continuation of the expansion at an adequate rate depends on a balanced advance of the major components of aggregate demand. The expansion is now well into its third year and, therefore, no spring chicken among its kind. But I do not believe that expansions typically die from old age. Historically they have died from imbalances. Something—inventory accumulation, business investment, housing, durables consumption—has gone off the rails, usually first on the upside and then on the downside.

The present expansion has not produced any major upside imbalances. It is experiencing two significant downside imbalances: the trade deficit and the slow advance of business fixed investment. As for the trade deficit of about $30 billion for the first eight months at an annual rate, this is reflected in the national accounts in negative net goods and services exports of "only" about $8 billion, because net military transactions and services that enter the GNP accounts bring in some $21–23 billion. Historically, net exports have been a positive factor in the GNP accounts, and their current shortfall must currently be compensated by other elements that are strong.

That consideration adds further importance to the role of business capital spending. The rise in this sector from the economy's cyclical trough has been only about half what it has been on past occasions. Possible explanations of this performance follow.

Does Business Have the Money?

Are business cash flow and liquidity sufficient for a higher rate of capital spending? On the whole, yes. Business cash flow is substantial, equaling $129 billion or 7 percent of GNP for domestic nonfinancial corporations in the second quarter of this year. Based on past cyclical experience, a cash flow of this magnitude would be consistent with about $20 billion more in business fixed investment than that which actually occurred in the present recovery. The liquidity position of business likewise has improved, with less short-term debt relative to long-term debt, at least until quite recently, and less debt of all kinds relative to equity. These liquidity gains, to be sure, to some extent reflect a deliberate preference for liquid assets over plant and equipment.

Nevertheless, it is worth noting that some of our largest enterprises have experienced a fundamental change in their financial structure. From a condition of low-bonded indebtedness and almost pure equity financing, some enterprises during the 1960s moved to a higher debt-equity ratio, because at the time that appeared to promise higher profits. The consequence, however, is that firms like these cannot engage in a great amount of additional debt financing without also increasing their equity.

A second reason for low investment could be that business may feel no great need for new investment. The rate of capacity utilization in manufacturing currently stands at about 83 percent. Pressures on capacity, with attendant bottlenecks and shortages, typically have been felt at around 88 percent. Thus there is not a great deal of excess capacity available. If we put 4 percent additional capacity in place over the next year and simultaneously were to experience a rise in industrial production of about 9 percent, which would reflect an expansion in GNP of about 6 percent, somewhat stronger than seems likely, we would a year from now be operating at nearly 87 percent of capacity. One good year's growth, in other words, would pretty much chew up the present excess capacity, unless new capacity comes on stream at a quickened pace.

Our present rate of growth is not quite that rapid, and absorption of spare capacity accordingly may take longer. But neither are we putting in place all that much additional capacity. The projected growth of plant and equipment spending for 1977 of 13.3 percent amounts to perhaps a 6–7 percent increase in real terms. It implies an increment to the economy's productive capacity in manufacturing of quite possibly somewhat less than 4 percent, although probably it is more than 3 percent. Thus, some capacity pressures might be felt in particular sectors sometime within the next year and a half.

The present level of 83 percent capacity utilization has indeed historically been close to the trigger point for accelerated capital spending. It seems to be indicative of the level at which many businesses begin to feel the need for additional capacity, given the lead time it takes to bring it on stream. There has been one instance, the 1959–1960 recovery, in which capital spending did not take off after reaching 83 percent of manufacturing capacity. But that recovery was unusually weak by historical standards, as capital spending lagged somewhat from the start.

In every particular situation, both with respect to a single business and with respect to an entire economy, there are, of course, special factors to be considered. One special factor right now is the large amount of investment that will be needed—not to expand capacity but to meet the requirements of the environment and of health and safety. Such expenditures accounted for about 5 percent of private industry's outlays for plant and equipment in 1976. Some part of our existing capacity, moreover, may have been made obsolescent by the sharp rise in the price of energy. Both factors suggest that the amount of investment required may be larger and that the time at which it should be initiated should be earlier than in the past.

On the other hand, there is a great deal of excess capacity in basic industries in other countries around the world. Domestic bottlenecks could conceivably be met by larger imports, at a cost of course, to our balance of payments and to our share in markets. World excess capacity could be considered as a factor working toward postponement of business capital spending.

The Level of Profits

Corporate book profits as stated in the national income accounts have made a good recovery, reaching $174 billion or 9.3 percent of GNP in the second quarter of 1977. This is only half a percent away from the average of the 1960s, which spans the historically low profit-GNP ratios of the early 1960s and the high ratios of the mid-1960s. I might add parenthetically that this corporate-profit figure includes some $6.2 billion of profits of the Federal Reserve System, in addition, of course, to profits of other financial corportions and profits transferred from abroad.

This profit figure does not take into account, however, adjustments to be made for inventory valuation and capital consumption as also recorded by the Department of Commerce and implied by notes in 10-K statements required by the Securities and Exchange Commission (SEC). Such adjustments bring profits for the same quarter down by about 20 percent or to 7.5 percent of GNP. These massive overstatements of operating profits are the result, of course, of inflation. Taxes are paid largely on unadjusted profits.

Further adjustments could be made by applying the principles of general-price-level accounting (GPLA) or current-value accounting (CVA). GPLA adjusts profits for, among other things, the gain or loss from inflation on the net-monetary-asset position, that is, for the gain of a debtor from the reduction through inflation in the real value of his net debt. CVA adjusts additionally for changes in the market value of assets and in particular the decline in market value of bonds issued at interest rates lower than the high rates typically prevailing during inflation.

Using 1975 domestic profits of U.S. nonfinancial corporations, the $102.3 billion of conventional profits before tax are reduced by GPLA to $68 billion, of which operating profits are only $43.9 billion and gains on net monetary position $24.1 billion. CVA produces, for 1975, total profits of approximately $146 billion, of which only $73 billion are operating profits. The impression that CVA is not a particularly good guide to what happens to corporate profits during inflation is strengthened by the fact that for 1974 this method of adjustment raised conventional profits before taxes from $102.9 billion to $193.1 billion, of which $55.7 billion were operating profits.[1] The stock market seemed to think otherwise.

These bookkeeping profits from depreciation of debt in terms of purchasing power or in the market unfortunately produce no cash flow for business. If they were meaningful, one would expect the stock of many highly leveraged corporations, especially those with large amounts of low-interest debt, to sell at a premium in the market. This is not the case. In fact, the stock market, by putting relatively low price-earnings ratios on many stocks, seems to be telling us that the earnings of these corporations are not worth as much as they seem.

Some further insight into the profit picture can be obtained by looking at the share of profits in GNP and at the return on corporate capital. That the share of profits in GNP has fallen does not by itself prove that the return on corporate capital as a whole has also fallen. Today, a much larger part of business investment than formerly is financed with debt. Consequently, the part of the return to capital that goes to equity holders would be smaller even if the share of total capital income in the GNP had remained unchanged.

The experts are not agreed as to whether the share of capital as a whole has indeed fallen, nor on whether or not the rate of return on this capital has fallen, in any permanent sense, if capital is measured by book value. There can be no doubt, however, that the rate of return has fallen if corporate capital or net worth is measured on a replacement-cost basis. That, it seems to me, is a more realistic approach. On a replacement-cost basis (not making allowance for gains from net-monetary-asset position), the rate of return today stands far below the 1960s.[2]

One can look at this drop in the return on capital in two ways. One interpretation says that the drop reflects a fundamental trend in the economy. Capital, according to this view, has become less productive, which has reduced the demand for it, and thus has lowered the price paid for its services. The other way is to note that this analysis conflicts with the presumption that maintenance of our historic rate of growth requires a higher rather than lower rate of investment. According to that view, a faster rather than a more slowly rising stock of capital is needed, if not immediately, then probably in the near future. This needed investment is unlikely to be undertaken unless it yields an adequate return. That suggests that the underlying demand for new investment is there but that businessmen have not been able to convert it into projects that adequately cover their capital costs.

From the fact that the return on existing capital, measured as the average product of capital, is low today, it does not follow that the return on new investment, that is, on capital measured at the margin, must also be low. To be sure high energy and environmental costs may have impaired the marginal product of capital. But if those are right who believe that continuation of our historic rate of growth requires a higher rate of investment than in the past, technological and price adjustments may be ahead that would raise the marginal product of new capital relative to that of the old capital.

Whether the return on new investment today is historically low or not, the significance of this rate of return cannot be fully evaluated without looking at the cost of capital. The cost of capital, today, presents a peculiar and complex picture. For most firms, the cost of capital consists of a combination of the cost of debt and the cost of equity, in the proportions in which the firm finances through borrowing, new equity issues, and retentions. At present rates of inflation, which, of course, need not be expected to persist into the indefinite future, the inflation premium in a 9 percent bond is of the order of perhaps 5 percent, allowing perhaps 1 percent for risk and perhaps 3 percent for the real-interest component. Since the entire interest is tax deductible to a corporate borrower, the cost of debt capital taken by itself may well be negative today.

The cost of equity capital—for purposes of capital budgeting this must be applied to investment from retentions as well as from new issues—is high today. That is the message conveyed by the prevailing low price-earnings (P-E) ratios on corporate stock. This message needs to be qualified, however. The market may be setting present P-E ratios on the basis of expected future earnings materially different from today. Furthermore, the market probably adjusts present earnings for inflation. Inflation-corrected P-E ratios may conceivably be higher and the inflation-corrected cost of capital lower, therefore, then would appear from the stock-market page.

A rough judgment of the adequacy of profits in the light of capital costs is provided by a juxtaposition of the net worth of U.S. corporations computed on the basis of the replacement cost of their assets with the valuation of assets implicit in the bond and stock market. Today, this financial-market valuation of enterprise falls well short of the replacement cost of its assets.[3]

Under these conditions, the firm can acquire additional assets and capacity more cheaply by purchasing an already existing firm than by building a new plant. Mergers, takeovers, and even repurchase of the firm's own stock become a more rational use of money than new capital spending. The ratio of replacement cost to stock-market valuation of assets historically has been negatively correlated with the level of business fixed investment. Today, that relationship actually considerably underpredicts the existing level of capital spending. The valuation of assets in the market, based on expected earnings and on risks, apparently is so adverse that it does not even appear to justify the present sluggish rate of investment.

I have devoted considerable space to an examination of the determinants of business fixed investment because it occupies so central a position in the business outlook. The influences surveyed point to three possible scenarios. If low rates of return and high cost of capital were to dominate the situation, investment would remain sluggish and would fail to give needed support to the expansion. Second, if the prospects of pressures on capacity that are now emerging were to lead to moderately accelerated capital spending, that would carry the expansion forward while other sectors possibly subside. Such a development would make for a long-lived expansion. Third, if response to capacity pressures is delayed until bottlenecks and shortages are actually on us, we might eventually find ourselves in a scramble for capital goods. A sudden bunching of orders and expenditures for capital goods would add to inflationary pressures, lead to uneconomic investments, and might bring the expansion to a halt as imbalances of that sort have done in the past. Developments in the area of capital spending, especially the rise in appropriations, support the expectation that the second scenario—a long expansion carried forward by investment spending—will materialize. But it will take good sense on the part of business, and willingness on the part of government to encourage business capital spending, to stay on that track.

Notes

1. See Richard Kopcke, "Current Accounting Practices and Proposals For Reform," *New England Economic Review,* September/October 1976, pp. 3–29, for method of calculation. Differences between Kopcke's figures and those shown here reflect subsequent revisions in Department of Commerce estimates of conventional profits.

2. George Terborgh, *Corporate Earning Power in the Seventies: A Disaster,* Machinery and Allied Products Institute, August 1977, pp. 1–11.

3. J. Tobin and W. Brainard, "Asset Markets and the Cost of Capital," *Economic Progress, Private Values and Public Policy,* ed. B. Balassa and R. Nelson (Amsterdam: North Holland, 1977), pp. 235–262.

Some Technical Aspects of Monetary Policy

Most recoveries follow a typical pattern, but many of them also have their special features. In the monetary area, one of the special features of the present expansion has been the very modest increases in the money supply with which it has been financed. Since the first quarter of 1975, which is the first year of the expansion, M_1 (currency and demand deposits) has risen by about 5 percent, M_2 [M_1 plus savings and time deposits in banks excluding large Certificates of Deposit (CDs)] by about 9.5 percent, and M_3 (M_2 plus time and savings deposits in thrift institutions) by 12 percent.[1] Since GNP in nominal terms rose at an average rate of 12.7 percent during the four quarters ending March 1976, the seeming disproportion between the behavior of money demand and of GNP is notable. Yet this result has been achieved not, as one might suppose, in a context of rapidly rising interest rates. On the contrary, interest rates now are lower than at the beginning of the expansion in April 1975. Nor has the moderation in the growth of the money supply been accomplished at the cost of sluggishness in the real sector. The average rate of real gain is broadly in line with the average of past expansions.

The rate of M_1 growth, indeed, has been far below what standard models would have predicted. A standard money-demand function shows an overprediction of M_1, compared to what was actually realized, of $19 billion over the last seven quarters. It was in the light of such hypothetical money-supply requirements that many observers called for a more rapid growth of the aggregates during the initial phase of the expansion. Their argument was often buttressed by reference to the large excess capacity then prevailing in the economy. Some observers also called for massive "front-loading" of the money supply, in the form of a rapid increase in the aggregates during a short period, to be followed by more moderate growth rates thereafter.

A variety of explanations have been adduced for the surprisingly moderate demand for M_1, given the vigorous expansion of nominal GNP and the moderate decline of interest rates. One has been a historical tendency of the velocity of M_1 to accelerate pronouncedly during the early phases of an expansion. The average relationship between M_1 on one side and income and interest rates on the other, as derived by econometric methods, averages away some of the differences in behavior during early and late phases of expansion. Past experience of very high interest rates may have awakened balance holders to the gains

---

This chapter was originally presented on May 6, 1976, before the Sixth Annual Washington Roundtable of the Institutional Investor Institute, Washington, D.C.

obtainable from more economical balance management, and these new methods seem to have been carried over into periods of lower rates. Various regulatory actions facilitating the use of savings deposits for money payments, such as telephone transfers between demand and savings accounts and authorization for businesses to carry savings deposits of up to $150,000, have reduced the demand for M_1. The demand for M_2 and M_3 has been less affected.

The Federal Reserve's long-run and short-run growth ranges for the monetary aggregates have been set with these factors in mind. The long-run growth range for M_1, originally 5 to 7 ½ and now standing at 4 ½ to 7 percent, as well as the M_2 range of originally 8 ½ to 10 ½ and now 7 ½ to 10 percent, and the M_3 range of originally 10 to 12 and now 9 to 12 percent, have taken into account the need to bring down the rate of money growth from the high levels associated with double-digit inflation (if in the future inflation is to be brought down further from what I regard as an unacceptable level). These ranges have also taken into account the tendency of velocity to accelerate strongly during early phases of an expansion.

Over the period during which long-term ranges have been announced in accordance with Concurrent Resolution 133 (five times), these ranges have changed only very moderately, in a downward direction. The succession of ranges nevertheless has reflected more variability in money growth than appears at first glance. The base from which one-year rates of growth have been projected has shifted from quarter to quarter by the amount of the realized growth in the quarterly average each quarter. In other words, these successive ranges have been computed, not from the previous base, or from the previous base adjusted forward along the midpoint growth path of the previous range, but from the level of the quarterly averages attained in the previous quarter. A "base drift" has occurred to the extent that actual quarterly average growth has differed from growth along that midpoint growth path. For example, in the case of a 5 to 7 ½ percent range, the midpoint growth path would have meant 6 ¼ percent growth per year, or about 1.53 percent compounded quarterly. If money were to show no growth in any one quarter, a downward base drift of about 1.51 percent would have occurred for the ranges of the following quarter.

Tables 9–1 through 9–3 provide data on the long-term growth ranges and their interrelations with the growth actually experienced.

Various critics have argued that this base drift for the calculation of growth rates causes the actual rates of growth over several quarters to differ from the specified range, even if the range were maintained unchanged from quarter to quarter. The procedure, it has been charged, makes the actual movement of the aggregates a random walk.

In the light of the historical record, this criticism lacks substance. Base drift over successive quarters in the last year has been relatively small. Moreover, such quarterly moves largely have been mutually offsetting. From the first to the second quarter and from the second to the third quarter of 1975,

Table 9–1
Federal Reserve Growth-Range Targets for M_1 Money Stock and Results to 1976: $Q1$

Announcement date	May 1, 1975		July 24, 1975		Nov. 1, 1975		Feb. 2, 1976		May 3, 1976		Actual M_1 stock
Growth-rate ranges (annual rates)	5 to 7.5%		5 to 7.5%		5 to 7.5%		4.5 to 7.5%		4.5 to 7%		(Quarterly average, s.a.)
Base date	March 1975		1975: $Q2$		1975: $Q3$		1975: $Q4$		1976: $Q1$		
1975											
$Q1$	284.1[a]										282.6
$Q2$	286.4	287.5	287.8								287.8
$Q3$	290.0	292.8	291.2	293.1	292.9						292.9
$Q4$	293.6	298.1	294.8	298.2	296.5	298.2	294.7				294.7
1976											
$Q1$	297.2 (298.4)[b]	303.6	298.4	303.8	300.2	303.7	298.0	300.1	296.8		296.8
$Q2$	300.8	309.1	302.1	309.4	303.8	309.2	301.2	305.6	300.1	301.9	
$Q3$	304.6	314.8	305.8	315.0	307.6	314.9	304.6	311.1	303.4	307.0	
$Q4$	308.3	320.5	309.6	320.8	311.4	320.6	307.9	316.8	306.7	312.3	
1977											
$Q1$	312.1	326.4	313.4	326.6	315.2	326.5	311.3	322.6	310.1	317.6	

[a]March 1975 data
[b]March 1976 data (preliminary)

Table 9–2

Federal Reserve Growth-Range Targets for M_2 Money Stock and Results to 1976: *Q*1

Announcement date	May 1, 1975		July 24, 1975		Nov. 1, 1975		Feb. 2, 1976		May 3, 1976		Actual M_2 stock
Growth-rate ranges (annual rates)	8.5 to 10.5%		8.5 to 10.5%		7.5 to 10.5%		7.5 to 10.5%		7.5 to 10%		(Quarterly average, s.a.)
Base date	March 1975		1975: *Q*2		1975: *Q*3		1975: *Q*4		1976: *Q*1		
1975											
*Q*1	623.0[a]										618.6
*Q*2	631.5	633.4	634.3								634.3
*Q*3	644.5	649.4	647.4	650.3	650.3						650.3
*Q*4	657.8	665.9	660.7	666.8	662.2	666.8	660.2				660.2
1976											
*Q*1	671.4	682.7 (681.7)[b]	674.3	683.7	674.3	683.6	672.2	676.9	675.9		675.9
*Q*2	685.2	699.9	688.2	700.9	686.6	700.9	684.5	694.0	688.2	692.2	
*Q*3	699.3	717.6	702.4	718.7	699.1	718.7	697.0	711.6	700.8	708.9	
*Q*4	713.7	735.7	716.9	736.8	711.8	736.8	709.7	729.6	713.6	726.0	
1977											
*Q*1	728.4	754.3	731.7	755.5	724.8	755.5	722.7	748.1	726.6	743.5	

[a]March 1975 data

[b]March 1976 data (preliminary)

Table 9–3

Federal Reserve Growth-Range Targets for M_3 Money Stock and Results to 1976: $Q1$

Announcement date	May 1, 1975		July 24, 1975		Nov. 1, 1975		Feb. 2, 1976		May 3, 1976		Actual M_3 stock
Growth-rate ranges (annual rates)	10 to 12%		10 to 12%		9 to 12%		9 to 12%		9 to 12%		(Quarterly average, s.a.)
Base date	March 1975		1975: $Q2$		1975: $Q3$		1975: $Q4$		1976: $Q1$		
1975											
$Q1$	1003.7[a]										994.8
$Q2$	1019.8	1022.8	1026.1								1026.1
$Q3$	1044.3	1052.2	1050.8	1055.6	1060.1						1060.1
$Q4$	1069.5	1082.5	1076.2	1085.9	1083.2	1090.6	1084.5				1084.5
1976											
$Q1$	1095.3 (1125.4)[b]	1113.6	1102.1	1117.1	1106.8	1121.9	1108.1	1115.7	1114.5		
$Q2$	1121.7	1145.6	1128.6	1149.2	1131.0	1154.2	1132.3	1147.7	1138.8	1146.5	
$Q3$	1148.7	1178.5	1155.8	1182.3	1155.6	1187.3	1157.0	1180.7	1163.6	1179.5	
$Q4$	1176.4	1212.4	1183.7	1216.3	1180.8	1221.4	1182.2	1214.7	1189.0	1213.4	
1977											
$Q1$	1204.8	1247.2	1212.2	1251.2	1206.5	1256.6	1208.0	1249.6	1214.9	1248.3	

[a]March 1975 data

[b]March 1976 data (preliminary)

Each of the five sets of growth ranges so far announced by the Federal Reserve for M_1–M_3 has presented such ranges for a one-year horizon measured from successive base dates. To provide a common terminal point, tables 7–1 through 7–3 extend the ''cones'' represented by each set of growth rates to 1977-$Q1$. The dashed lines in each column of the tables show the horizon to which the ranges given in those columns originally related.

The first set of growth ranges for M_1–M_3 announced by the Federal Reserve on May 1, 1975, was stated in terms of a March 1975 base and growth to March 1976. The four subsequent sets of ranges were stated in terms of a quarterly average base. For visual comparability, the cones implied by the first set of ranges have been restated to quarterly average terms.

To obtain a consistent historical series, the ''actual'' money stock for each base period (last column of each table) is given according to recent seasonally adjusted data. The base level shown for each period may therefore differ slightly from the preliminary base available at the time each set of ranges was announced.

growth rates were on the high side, and the ranges set in those two quarters accordingly represent upward shifts of the long-run paths. But in the fourth quarter of last year, growth rates were on the low side, and the ranges set in that quarter represent a downward shift in the growth paths of the three aggregates. The bases for the ranges set for the year beginning with the first quarter 1976 have returned approximately to those implied by the midpoints of the ranges specified a year ago. The latest ranges were announced by Chairman Burns before the Senate Committee on Banking, Housing and Urban Affairs on May 3. As a practical matter, therefore, base drift has not materially affected the movement of the aggregates. Over the last four quarters, M_1 grew at the low end of its original growth range, M_2 at the midpoint of its original range, and M_3 at the top end of its range.

If deviations from the ranges were to become large, some cognizance of that fact would, of course, have to be taken in the setting of new ranges. The FOMC does, of course, set new ranges in the light of the recent growth of the aggregates in addition to changes in the economy and the outlook that have occurred meanwhile.

Techniques could be visualized that would compensate for base drift above or below the midpoints of earlier ranges. Growth ranges could be modified in such a manner as to get back on the original track at some specified time, assuming that this track had remained appropriate in the light of the economic outlook. Alternatively, in addition to stating the new ranges of growth on the new base, those same ranges could be recomputed in terms of the old base. Either method, however, would tend to be confusing to many members of the public and would add little to deliberations of the FOMC, which in any event has access to these and other calculations.

Moderate base drift in any event has little meaning, given the looseness of the relation of the monetary aggregates to the ultimate objectives—GNP, employment, and price stability. It is these ultimate objectives, of course, which primarily concern the monetary policymaker in the setting of long-run growth ranges.

A problem that concerns me more has been raised by the wider-than-expected spread between the actual growth rates of M_1 on one side and M_2 and M_3 on the other. The growth ranges allow, of course, for substantially different growth paths for each of the aggregates. M_1 may come in low, as it did over the last year, and M_3 may come in high as it did, and yet all three aggregates may be within or close to their respective ranges. But the midpoints of the ranges suggest that there is some expected difference in the three growth rates that under neutral conditions would remain reasonably constant over some period of time. Conditions evidently have been far from neutral. In particular this has meant increasing uncertainty about the reliability of M_1 as a target. Special factors affecting M_1 evidently have been operative on the downside. Meanwhile, M_2 and M_3 have been subject to factors operating on the upside, especially a tendency toward reintermediation at a time of low interest rates for money-market instruments.

The Federal Open Market Committee (FOMC) has responded to mounting instability in the behavior of the aggregates in several ways. In a recent directive, it decided to place about equal weight on M_1 and M_2, whereas previously greater weight frequently had been attached to M_1. Furthermore, the FOMC has responded by widening the two-months ranges for all the aggregates, but particularly for M_1. In the record of policy actions for the February 18 FOMC meeting, for instance, the M_1 tolerance range for the February–March period was specified at an annual rate of 5–9 percent, or 4 percentage points, contrasted with an average range of 3 percentage points found in past FOMC actions. For M_2 the range was 9–13 percent, the 4 percentage point spread here contrasting with a frequently employed spread of 3 percent. Also, the FOMC has at times couched its directive to the Federal Reserve Bank of New York in money-market rather than aggregates terms, making maintenance of "prevailing bank reserve and money market conditions over the period immediately ahead" the primary instruction to the manager while relegating the aggregates to a proviso clause that subjects the stated objective to the condition "provided that monetary aggregates appear to be growing at about the rates currently expected." Such a money market directive was issued at the February 18 FOMC meeting.

A well-known rule of thumb of monetary policy says that when there are disturbances on the side of the real sector, monetary policy should focus on the aggregates and allow interest rates to move up or down to counter the disturbance. Conversely, when there are disturbances on the monetary side, monetary policy should focus on interest rates to avoid transmitting these disturbances to the real sector. What we have seen of late clearly has been a distrubance on the monetary side—the less predictable demand for M_1. To keep M_1 on a fixed growth path under these conditions would mean wide variations in interest rates, in a downward direction in case of an unexpected shortfall in the demand for M_1. The FOMC has taken account of this by giving somewhat greater emphasis to M_2 or money-market conditions and by widening the two-months ranges, especially that for M_1. The effect of the latter move is to reduce the change in the federal-funds rate to be sought by the Open Market Desk in response to a given deviation of M_1 from the midpoint of the specified range. Still another technique would be a narrowing of the funds-rate range within which the Desk is to operate.

Turning once more to the longer run, I would like to draw attention to the small but significant lowering of the one-year ranges for M_1 and M_2. There is, of course, a long way to go until noninflationary rates of money growth are attained. But a beginning must be made. Inflation will not come down for long if the Federal Reserve allows growth rates of the aggregates to move in a procyclical direction. Lower rates of inflation, we have learned from experience, offer the only hope for a lasting reduction in unemployment and the achievement of stable prosperity.

Note

1. All data for the monetary aggregates—M_1, M_2, and M_3—are as of April 30, 1976, March 1976 being the last month for which complete data are available.

10 Innovations in Monetary Policy

Central banks in numerous countries today have established money-supply growth targets. The Reserve Bank of Australia, the Bank of Canada, the Bank of England, the Federal Reserve, the German Bundesbank, and the Swiss National Bank have adopted this approach in one form or another. While I believe that such targets can make valuable contributions under present inflationary conditions, I do not view them as wholly exogenous improvements in central bank technique. They are the consequence, rather, of high rates of inflation.

Historically, central banks have relied primarily on interest rates as their principal guide. In a severe inflation, however, interest rates cease to be a good guide. Nominal rates may rise very high, but they do not convey an accurate measure of the degree of restraint of stimulation implied. To the noneconomist, high nominal rates probably convey an impression of excessive restraint and so may generate political pressure against the anti-inflationary use of monetary policy. To the economist, nominal rates of inflation present the puzzle of translation into real rates. Short-term rates, which must be measured against actual more than expected inflation, often become negative. Long-term real rates must be derived from expectations of inflation, which may differ among lenders as well as borrowers. Since the inflation premium is taxable to the lender and deductible to the borrower, after-tax real rates become largely indeterminate. For a wide range of taxable lenders and borrowers they probably have at times been negative in the United States.

The money supply and its rate of growth, on the other hand, are variables that intuitively relate to inflation. It is easy to see—and perhaps, therefore, more readily possible to convince the public and the legislature—that a 10-percent rate of growth of the money supply over considerable periods will tend to raise prices. Real balances can be computed on the basis of observed rather than expected inflation. But, in any event, real balances play a less important role than real interest rates, in an analysis that consists principally in relating the nominal money supply to nominal GNP and its price and volume components. Thus inflation gives a monetarist—or near-monetarist—tinge to nearly all monetary policymaking. This is particularly so when, as has been the almost

This chapter was originally a paper delivered at the meeting of the Southern Economic Association, Atlanta, Georgia, November 18, 1976. Reprinted by permission of the author. I am greatly indebted to David Lindsey and Ray Lombra for numerous valuable suggestions and to Wayne Ayers for general assistance with the paper. Responsibility for errors, of course, remains my own. The views presented are my own, and do not necessarily represent those of my colleagues on the Federal Reserve Board.

universal experience so far, inflation rates are highly variable and, therefore, hard to predict.

Sticking to a money-supply target does not mean that the policymaker has necessarily changed his view of the transmission mechanism of monetary policy. In particular, it does not mean that he now subscribes to some sort of "direct" effect of money on the real sector. A money-supply target is perfectly consistent with the belief that money works through interest rates and rates of return in a broad sense. For this very reason, under conditions of price stability, the policymaker may have thought it appropriate to work on interest rates directly instead of via the money supply. During inflation, however, he finds that the interest rates his policies produce will have a more predictable effect if he calibrates his action by the money supply and allows interest rates to take on such values as interaction between the money supply and the rest of the economy may determine. To recognize this principle, however, is only to posit a number of questions, both theoretical and statistical, that must be resolved for its application. Today I want to speak about some of these problems as they seem to have presented themselves in American experience.

Definitional Problems

Debates about the proper definition of the monetary aggregates are as old as the effort to quantify these aggregates. I need merely list some currently important issues. M_1 is beset by problems such as the appropriate inclusion or exclusion of government deposits, of foreign deposits, and transit items. In addition, the demand for M_1 has recently been affected by institutional changes that have increased the moneyness of time and savings deposits, such as telephone transfers, NOW accounts, and savings deposits for business. These institutional changes as well as others may jointly have accounted for a reduction in the growth rate of M_1 of as much as 2 percentage points over the past year. Partly for this reason, the relationship of M_1 to income seems to have changed sufficiently to cause ordinary money-demand equations to currently overpredict, in a simulation beginning in mid-1974, by something like \$25 billion.

M_2, which has had a good record of stability in relation to income over the last ten years nevertheless suffers from a variety of frailties. Savings deposits are increasingly serving as transactional balances. Thanks to Regulation Q, changes in market rates of interest lead to disintermediation and reintermediation. Furthermore, while large negotiable certificates of deposit are excluded for weekly reporting banks, they are not excluded for nonweekly reporters. Nonnegotiable large CDs are included for all banks, although banks freely switch one type to the other at the holder's request. Some \$20–25 billion of large CDs, along with an increasing volume of consumer CDs with maturities of up to six years, now are included in M_2. Thus M_2 is spreading in two directions—becoming more monetary at one end and less so at the other.

Given the uncertainties attaching to both M_1 and M_2 and likewise to the higher Ms, a possible remedy would be to give some weight to both instead of making a choice, and over time perhaps to vary these weights, as the Federal Reserve has done. It must be remembered, however, that such weighting systems in effect count M_1 twice, since it is contained in M_2.

Looking beyond M_1 and M_2, it becomes clear that some liabilities of nonbanks included in M_3 and even of nonfinancial institutions are sufficiently similar to some components of M_2 to make the drawing of a strict dividing line implausible. If one wishes to attribute a special quality to bank liabilities, one must consider also the advisability of paying special attention to bank credit as against nonbank credit. This would compel one to consider the asset side of bank balance sheets. It would raise the question, for instance, whether the fact that in the present expansion a large part of money creation has been against government securities rather than against business loans significantly reduces the expansionary power of the money supply thus created.

Finally, all aggregates are subject to the difficulties of seasonal adjustment. Monthly data would be difficult to interpret without adjustment. But different adjustment procedures, even though individually plausible, may give significantly different results in the short run. A study of thirty alternative M_1 adjustments, even after eliminating extremes, showed an average range for monthly adjustments of 4 percentage points in terms of annual growth rates. Annualized monthly rates of growth of the aggregates, therefore, must be treated with considerable reserve.[1]

So much for a small sampling of the conceptual, definitional, and statistical difficulties in establishing a money-supply target. A few comments may be in order also with respect to the level at which the policymaker may want to set his target or targets, although this is more a question of objectives than of techniques.

Strategy of Target Setting

The money-supply growth targets of all central banks today are far higher than is consistent with long-run price stability. In the absence of a trend in velocity, the growth of money over time would thus have to equal that of real GNP in order to maintain stable prices. Given a moderate upward trend in M_1 velocity, the noninflationary annual increase might be of an order not much above zero. It is perfectly obvious, then, that rates of money growth must be brought down over time if ending inflation is a goal of policy. The question is whether this should be done by a unidirectional reduction of the money-supply targets, albeit perhaps a very slow one, or whether anticyclical considerations should be allowed, at times, to cause a reversal of this downward tendency. A steady downward path poses the risk of undesirable cyclical effects, such as a slowing of money growth in the face of a cyclical contraction. The alternative of upward and downward adjustments runs the risk that the intended long-term downward trend will, in fact, never materialize. It also reduces the credibility of the exercise and creates proinflationary expectations. During a cyclical expansion, when an anticyclical stance requires restraint, this potential conflict, however, may lose relevance.

Specification of One-Year Targets

Once basic decisions have been made about rates of money growth, problems arise concerning the manner of specifying the targets. There is the choice between a single number and a range. A single number virtually guarantees a miss but by virtue of that fact also provides a reasonable excuse for missing. The uncompromising character of a single-number target, however, is also more apt to provoke controversy. A target range is easier to hit but, by the same token, a miss may be more severely criticized. At the same time, a range is likely to be less controversial because it is less specific.

Next, there is the phenomenon of ''base drift'' that is invited by periodic targets set in terms of growth rates as required by Concurrent Resolution 133, rather than absolute levels. Base drift occurs when the level attained after three months is not precisely on the midpoint growth path of the range but must nevertheless be used as the base for the next quarter's annual-target range. Base drift could, of course, be corrected by adjusting the new growth ranges so as to bring the projected path back onto the old track with a lag of some months or quarters. This procedure, however, would lead to targets that change quarterly and might involve odd fractions, possibly confusing the public. Alternatively, the midpoint of the original growth path might be chosen for the location of the base of any new target range. It should be remembered, however, that base drift simply increases the flexibility already injected into the target procedure by the use of a range. It is to some extent an arbitrary decision whether to incorporate that flexibility in a wider range or in a less rigid determination of the base.

The degree of flexibility inherent in a target expressed as a range of growth rates increases with the passage of time as the upper and lower limits increasingly diverge in dollar terms. Thus, in the initial weeks after the setting of a target range the policymaker has less room for maneuver—or for error—than he has later on. This could be remedied by using the distance between the lower end and the upper limit achieved after six months or a year as the standard and allowing the policymaker the same degree of latitude early and late in the target period. Graphically, this would imply representing the target ranges by bands of constant widths instead of by cones. Such a procedure, however, would probably allow excessive latitude during the early period following the setting of the target range. This matter is better dealt with by appropriate handling of the two-month targets that the Federal Reserve also employs. This topic, therefore, will be examined next.

Short-Run Targets

Federal Reserve policy techniques—not, of course, its major objectives—are significantly influenced by the decentralized structure of the system. The Federal Open Market Committee (FOMC) meets monthly. In terms of travel time and competing demands on the members' working time at their home base, this seems not an unreasonable frequency, although other arrangements obviously are possible. One month, therefore, is the natural interval for formulating and executing policy decisions. The Open Market Manager at the Federal Reserve Bank of New York, who is in the market every day, must be given instructions for this period. A centralized monetary authority would not be so constrained. It could conceivably make minor policy decisions from day to day, although it might not find that very convenient.

Given the instability of the aggregates over short periods of time, however, a month would be a very short period over which to confine the aggregates to a narrow range. Efforts to do so, aside from producing large jumps in the federal-funds rate, might well cause the Fed to overreact to preliminary indications of changes in the rate of growth that more complete figures could disavow. The money-supply figures do not come into being fully known and accurate on a certain day. They evolve gradually from fragmentary reports. Reasonably hard data are available—and are published—eight days after the end of the statement week. A first revision appears fifteen days after the statement week and further revisions follow quarterly as data on nonmember banks become available.

There are several options for dealing with the problem of short-run instability of the aggregates. One would be to set a very wide range for a monthly growth rate. A second would be to ignore short-term variations in the growth of the aggregates altogether. A third, which the System has chosen, is to average the growth of two successive months in order to get a little more stability into the growth rate. A further variant of this approach would be to lengthen this averaging period. The resulting greater stability of the averaged data would, of course, be purchased at the cost of reduced sensitivity to new data.

Further options are offered by the possibility to employ not only past but estimated data. The FOMC's present procedure, in fact, relies primarily on estimated data. Of the two-months averages, which are employed for formulating short-term targets, only one week is reasonably firm and has been published. The rest of the two months is estimated, although some fragmentary data are available. It would be possible also to lengthen the averaging period forward by including more distant estimates, as well as backward, again trading stability for sensitivity. The longer the averaging period, the more closely must the aggregates be tied to the one-year targets in order to avoid the need for subsequent drastic readjustments. Here again, a problem of base drift presents itself.

Implicit in the various options cited is the question how quickly and strongly the Fed should react to new incoming data, at the risk that they may represent only "noise." By chasing the data, the Fed runs the risk of making false starts, of having to reverse frequently, of misleading the market and whipsawing it. By ignoring new data, it runs the risk of acting too late, of having to act more forcefully than if action had been timely, and perhaps of being pushed off track altogether. Optimal control theory tells us that all new information, in this case particularly the incoming aggregates, should be considered, but that it should be filtered to eliminate noise as far as possible. One possible way of approximating this principle would be to give a lower weight to newer and more uncertain data. Establishing the weights remains a problem however.

The question whether it is wise for the Fed to watch and follow the data closely is often coupled with the question whether it is wise for the market to watch and follow the Fed. It is obvious that, if Fed operations have an influence on the market, the market is bound to engage in Fed-watching. But the nature of the Fed's influence on the market depends very much on the choice of instrument used by the Fed—the federal-funds rate, as at present, or some reserve aggregate. This consideration leads to the much discussed issue of the funds rate versus a reserve aggregate as the policy instrument.

Federal-Funds Rate Versus Nonborrowed Reserves

The Federal Reserve policy strategy is based in large part on the monetary aggregates, but its short-run tactical instrument is the federal-funds rate. Under the fund-rate approach, the Federal Reserve estimates the level of short-term interest rates, including the funds rate, at which the public, given projections of income, will want to hold the amount of money the Federal Reserve intends to supply. Then reserves are supplied in an amount that will maintain that level of the funds rate, and that will cause the banks to generate the targeted amount of money.

Under a nonborrowed-reserves (NBR) approach, the Federal Reserve might estimate, via a multiplier approach, the amount of required reserves that would be related to the aggregates it intends to supply. In such an approach it would then be necessary to estimate the amount of excess reserves and borrowed reserves that would prevail at the short-term interest rates, including the funds rate, consistent with the targeted money supply. In this way it would thus be possible to arrive at an estimate of the volume of nonborrowed reserves that must be supplied to reach the target.

The principle for choosing between interest rates and aggregates as means of stabilizing income developed by William Poole can be applied also, with appropriate modifications, to the objective of stabilizing money or its rate of growth.[2] Given fully known and stable relationships, the choice of an interest rate or aggregates instrument, of course, becomes immaterial. Either instrument fully determines the other. When there are shocks to one or the other of the variables, a simple criterion applies.

When the objective is to keep the money supply (or its growth rate) constant, the policymaker finds himself dealing with a money-demand and a money-supply function. The selection principle then is:

1. If the shock is to the money-supply function, for instance by an increase in banks' demand for excess reserves, a constant interest rate will keep the money supply constant given a stable money-demand function. An interest-rate target, therefore, would be the appropriate one. The supply of reserves would have to be varied in order to accommodate the demand.

2. Alternatively, if the shock is to the money-demand function, a reserve-aggregates target will minimize the impact on the money supply. Keeping the money-supply function constant by, for instance, keeping nonborrowed reserves constant, would allow interest rates to rise as demand increases. This would dampen, although not entirely prevent, an increase in the money supply in response to the increase in demand.[3]

There is a good deal of empirical evidence to indicate that the precision of the two procedures is broadly the same. For a period of one month, the standard error is about 4.5 percentage points of the annual rate of growth of M_1, and 3 percentage points of the rate of growth of M_2.[4] Over a period of six months, the standard error for both procedures reduces to about one-half of a percentage point for M_1 and one-third of a percentage point for M_2. Thus, if we believe that short-run deviations from the aggregates targets are not important so long as longer-run targets are hit, the issue of which of the two approaches is more precise loses much of its importance. If one believes, to be sure, that deviations even for relatively short periods have an impact on the real sector and thus generate a feedback from the real sector on the demand for money, greater attention to such short-run deviations would be necessary. In any event, however, the proposition that short-run deviations do not greatly matter does not imply that they can be ignored. They must be compensated for over the longer run. If no compensation for an overshoot or shortfall over one or two months is provided in the following months, the longer-run result will be affected and must be expected to have its impact on the real sector.

If all this is understood, it can fairly be said that the choice between the funds rate and the nonborrowed-reserves procedure must rest, not on the degree of precision that can be attained in hitting the target, but on other aspects of these procedures.

The funds-rate procedure offers an opportunity to limit the variability of the funds rate and other interest rates in the short run, since it automatically accommodates purely random and transitory shifts in the money-demand schedule, which should not, in any case, be transmitted to the real sector. For instance, it automatically provides a seasonal adjustment for the money supply. The funds rate procedure allows changes in rates to occur gradually and without frequent reversals. Avoidance of sharp interest-rate instability means avoidance of the cost of such instability. Principally, these costs take the form of weakening the market mechanism by increasing the risks of dealing in and owning securities. Greater stability of interest rates reduces unpredictable flows into or out of thrift institutions triggered by Regulation-Q ceilings. Transmission of these elements of instability to the real sector, to investment and savings decisions, in whatever degree they might occur, likewise is avoided if rates are more stable.

A second significant, albeit double-edged, gain from a more deliberate movement of the funds rate is the greater control that it provides over the entire rate structure. When the market knows that the monetary authorities use the funds rate to control the aggregates, it naturally will watch the aggregates closely for a tip-off on future movements of the funds rate. If, in addition, the market knows that the authorities try to avoid erratic movements in the funds rate, it will attribute policy significance to such movements. It then becomes logical for other short-term rates to move in response to changes in the aggregates that are expected to trigger a funds-rate change. All short-term money-market instruments are to some extent substitutes. Through term structure and expectation effects, longer rates may also be affected. Thus, by making the funds rate an important instrument of policy, the money authorities in effect are linking together the entire rate structure and are providing themselves with a lever to move that structure. The manner in which, in some European money markets of the past, the discount rate was linked by law or custom to other rates provides an analogy.

But this role of the funds rate, as noted, is two-edged. The impact of a funds-rate change on market rates may at times be undesirable to the authorities, even though the funds-rate movement may be necessary to control the aggregates. There is a possibility that the authorities might become reluctant to move the funds rate sufficiently fast and far, and if necessary to reverse earlier movements, when that should become necessary to prevent the aggregates from moving undesirably. Overshoots or shortfalls from the monetary targets could then develop. As an extreme case, the authorities might be tempted to regard the funds rate, not as an instrument to attain the aggregates, but as a policy objective in its own right. In that case, the shift from interest rates to monetary aggregates alluded to at the beginning of this paper would have been reversed.

These potential consequences of a funds-rate approach would largely vanish if the authorities were prepared to move the funds rate frequently and sharply, without concern about reversals, false signals, and purely aiming at the closest possible control of the aggregates. In that event, the linkage between the funds rate and other market rates would weaken. If, for instance, the funds rate were expected to fluctuate randomly around some particular value over the next ninety days, Treasury-bill rates presumably would take their cue from that expected average rather than from the day-to-day or week-to-week levels of the funds rate. This partial "uncoupling" of the rest of the rate structure from the funds rate would reduce its usefulness as a lever over other rates. It would also thereby reduce the sensitivity of the demand for money to funds-rates movements which work via short-term interest rates. But it would make the funds rate more maneuverable for the purpose of hitting the aggregates targets.

Use of the nonborrowed-reserves target would probably have precisely this effect of in some degree uncoupling the funds rate from the rest of the rate structure. Over short periods the funds rate probably would move around in an erratic way. Other rates would take their cue from some expected average of these movements rather than from any particular move or level. To the extent that this happened, the potential usefulness of the funds rate as a lever on other rates would disappear, which in some respects would be a loss. Moreover, since some degree of linkage no doubt would remain, there would be a cost, although much diminished, from this hypothetical instability of the funds rate. But reasonably close control of the aggregates over the longer run would be automatically more assured, and the danger of inadvertently slipping from an aggregates to an interest-rate strategy would disappear. The market might lose its interest in Fed-watching, or at least would have to change its method of watching. An incidental potential benefit of a nonborrowed-reserves target would be realized in case the Federal Reserve should ever decide to publish its policy decisions immediately, since announcement of the intended future behavior of nonborrowed reserves obviously would produce fewer complications than announcement of the intended future behavior of the funds rate.

A lesser potential although minor disadvantage of a nonborrowed-reserves approach is that at times the money supply and interest rates may move in inconsistent directions—money and interest rates both moving up or down together. More serious perhaps, the diminished link between the funds rate and the bill rate may make it more difficult to influence the demand for money, which is guided, other things equal, by the bill rate. Unless the bill rate moves, holders of money balances have no portfolio motives to shift between balances and short-term instruments.

To summarize, there is not much that could be done under one regime that could not be done under the other. The aggregates could be effectively controlled, and the funds rate could be partly uncoupled from the rest of the interest rate structure by appropriate handling of the alternative instruments. It is with respect to the costs of such handling, and the risks involved in trying to avoid these costs, that the approaches differ.

Notes

1. Edward R. Fry, "Seasonal Adjustment of M_1," *Staff Economic Studies,* Board of Governors of the Federal Reserve System, 1976.

2. William Poole, "Optimal Choice of Monetary Policy Instruments in a Simple Stochastic Macro Model," *Quarterly Journal of Economics,* May 1970.

3. A more precise statement of this principle is that the relative stability of the money demand function must be compared with the reduced form money stock equation, relating the equilibrium money stock to a reserve aggregate and to income. The stability of the reduced form equation depends both on the instability of the money demand and the money supply function. Because movements in interest rates partially offset shocks to either of these, the stability of a reduced form equation combining both is greater than the average stability of both, assuming their errors are independent. When both supply and demand functions are equally stable, therefore, a reserves aggregate instrument is still preferable to an interest rate instrument.

4. See James L. Pierce and Thomas D. Thompson, "Some Issues in Controlling the Stock of Money," *Controlling Monetary Aggregates II: The Implementation,* Federal Reserve Bank of Boston Conference Series, no. 9, September 1972; Richard J. Davis and Frederick C. Schadrack, "Forecasting the Monetary Aggregates with Reduced-Form Equations," *Monetary Aggregates and Monetary Policy,* Federal Reserve Bank of New York, 1974. Somewhat larger monthly errors over the more recent years 1974 and 1975 under either a Federal funds rate or reserve aggregate procedure have been estimated by William R. McDonough, "Effectiveness of Alternative Approaches to Monetary Control," Federal Reserve Bank of Dallas *Business Review,* August 1976.

11 The Limits of Monetary Control

Monetary policy has been in a rapid state of evolution over the last few years. This can be said both of the economic principles that have applied and of the techniques that have been used. That evolution surely has not ended. A milestone appears to have been reached, however, in one regard. We now seem to have a clearer understanding of how far it is desirable to push control of the money supply as the leading principle of monetary policy in times of inflation.

On the basis of what we know today, it appears that available techniques for controlling the money supply are adequate, and probably more than adequate, to achieve the desirable degree of control. It is certainly possible to develop techniques that could fine-tune the money supply even more precisely than those presently in use. Quite likely some of these techniques will be developed. Nevertheless, there are rapidly diminishing returns and rapidly rising costs to a tighter control of the aggregates. It may thus become advisable to use the instruments that exist or that could be developed with less than their full power. The degree to which their use should be pushed is a very difficult question. It is by no means a foregone conclusion that more control over the money supply invariably is better than less.

The Federal Reserve's Review of the New Monetary-Control Procedure

These conclusions follow in important part from the results of a review of the Federal Reserve's new operating techniques conducted by the staff of the Federal Reserve Board and the Federal Reserve Banks. My interpretation of these extensive and very technical studies, which are available on request from the Federal Reserve Board, is the following.

1. The relationship between money and the real sector has become substantially looser in the 1970s, in the sense that widely used money-demand equations that previously were quite reliable have severely overpredicted money, given GNP and interest rates. A new equation has been developed by Fed staff that seems to take into account the main cause of this downward shift in money demand by incorporating the impact of very high expected interest rates on cash-management practices. But, the somewhat ad hoc character of a

---

This chapter was originally presented on April 3, 1981, before the Midwest Economics and Finance Association, Louisville, Kentucky.

new equation of this sort prevents one from placing full reliance on it. A similar change in the relationship between money supply and nominal GNP—although in the other direction—seems to have occurred also in the United Kingdom, mainly with respect to sterling M_3. Such shifts do not imply that a money-supply target is not useful. So long as there is severe inflation, the basic meaning of a money-supply target always is that less money growth is better than more. In the long run, that will help bring down inflation. But the notion that GNP can be steered directly by controlling the money supply is severely questioned by this experience.

2. The Federal Reserve's review shows that there is a high degree of randomness in any money-supply series, often referred to as "noise," consisting of transitory variations and uncertainty of seasonal adjustment. The estimated standard deviation of the noise factor for monthly changes in *M*1-A and *M*1-B is about $1.5 billion (4½ percent at an annual rate), and about $3.3 billion for weekly changes, based on data for the 1973–1979 period. Such random moves can be expected to be corrected over time as the basic determinants of the money supply assert themselves. A money-control policy seeking to prevent such deviations instead of accommodating them would actually cause them to have an effect on financial markets and perhaps even the real sector. It would in effect shift the irreducible degree of randomness from money growth into interest rates.

3. Because of the random character of some money-supply variations, an effort to control variability encounters diminishing returns in terms of the degree of stability that is achievable. For instance, when the targeted aggregate has moved off its growth path, an attempt to return to that path within a period of less than three months will not add a great deal to the degree of path adherence actually achieved. Any improvement in path adherence, on the other hand, will lead to increasingly higher volatility of interest rates.

4. Short-term deviations of the money supply from path lasting three to six months have only minor real-sector consequences. This generalization, to be sure, needs to be qualified by taking into account the source of the deviation and the degree to which interest rates move as a result of the money-supply deviation from target. It also depends on how large the deviation is and on whether it is fully made up by a compensating deviation on the opposite side of the track or it is merely returned to track.

In any event, there is no basis for the view now sometimes expressed that a deviation of money supply immediately causes a corresponding deviation of GNP. That view seems to be based on experience during 1980, when indeed over- and undershoots of the monetary targets coincided closely with movements in the economy. However, there is no reason to believe in a lagless relationship in which an exogenous money supply affects the economy. Much more plausible is an endogenous money supply dominated by economic activity, which indeed can be expected to follow fluctuations of the real sector contemporaneously rather than leading them.

Tighter control of the money supply by the Federal Reserve would indeed be possible within the limits set by the random influences already mentioned. It would in turn lead to wider fluctuations in interest rates with adverse repercussions on the financial and even real sectors.

I have already observed the costs of wide interest-rate fluctuations, although these fluctuations in 1980 cannot by any means be attributed solely to the Federal Reserve's attempts to control money through reserve targets per se. Such costs include the near-demise of fixed-rate long-term mortgages in many parts of the country, the high-risk premia built into long-term interest rates, the diminishing impact of movements in interest rates on credit availability due to the relaxation of Regulation-Q ceilings and the trend toward floating loan rates, the shift of interest-rate risks from lenders and especially intermediaries to borrowers, the growing volatility of foreign-exchange rates, damage to the housing and automobile industries from wide swings in volume, and the development of a two-tier structure of borrowers with respect to their sensitivity to high nominal-interest rates.

5. This two-tier structure of borrowers deserves an additional comment. A significant number of firms, households, and national economies are not cushioned against the full impact of high interest rates by the tax deductibility of interest, because for them there is no such deductibility. This is the case of business firms that have no profits, and which at best get a loss carryforward from their interest payments. It is true of very small businesses paying a substantial part of their tax at the 20 percent corporate-tax rate for profits between $25,000 and $50,000, which allows them only a minimal deduction. It applies to households taking the standard deduction, although most households with sizable interest-rate payments may be expected to itemize their deductions. Finally, it applies to governmental units, especially developing countries for most of which real interest rates rise dramatically with major upswings in rates.

As a result of this tiering with respect to tax deductibility of interest payments, the upper, that is, the deductible tier is only moderately affected by high nominal-interest rates. For many borrowers in this tier, the real after-tax interest rate may still be negative even with high nominal rates. For them, in fact, debt amortization has in part been made tax deductible, if we regard the inflation premium in the interest rate as the economic equivalent of debt amortization. The cash-flow problem imposed by high interest rates likewise is eased by the reduction in tax payments. For the lower tier, which cannot deduct, real interest rates may be very high. And the cash-flow problem is not mitigated by any tax benefits.

In consequence, a monetary policy that exerts adequate restraint on the upper tier borrowers may impose very severe restraint on the lower tier borrowers, some of whom must be assumed to be already in a weakened position. It may also impose great strains on some financial intermediaries holding part of their portfolios in long-term fixed-rate assets. On the other hand, a monetary policy aiming to take the problems of the lower tier borrowers into account and seeking to spare them high real interest rates would create excessively easy conditions for the upper tier borrowers and would very likely be inflationary. Moreover, negative real interest rates, even though only in after-tax terms, tend to misallocate resources by stimulating less productive investment. The disproportionate expansion of the housing sector in the United States is only one such example. And in many circumstances, negative real interest rates are likely to kindle inflationary expectations.

Implications for Monetary Policy

What I have said so far makes clear that further debate over possible improvements in the control of the money supply is not a primary issue. Very probably, such improvements are possible. The real question is how far precision of money-supply control should be pushed in the face of mounting costs of such fine tuning. In my personal view, there is a good case for incurring some significant costs, in the form of more volatile interest rates, to avoid prolonged overshoots of the monetary aggregates. This is because overshoots become increasingly harder to correct the longer they are allowed to run. If there are forces at work in the economy pulling the aggregates up, the effort to bring them back on track obviously will have to be greater than the effort that would have been required to keep them from overshooting in the first place. Furthermore, historically, our main mistakes have been associated with overshoots rather than undershoots. That is a wind against which one should lean early.

With respect to the prevention or correction of undershoots, I would take a somewhat asymmetrical attitude. I would allow judgment in such cases to be guided in good part by an assessment of interest rates. To prevent or correct an undershoot by generating interest rates that are severely negative in real terms after tax is to invite trouble.

Some weight in assessing the degree of tolerance for overshoots and undershoots must also be given to their impact on the credibility of monetary policy. Prolonged departures from target adversely affect the expectations that guide rational (and irrational) transactors. Unfortunately, there seems to exist a two-tier structure also with respect to expectation formation in response to monetary policy. From the press, from congressional utterances, and from the unsolicited mail that the Federal Reserve receives, there can be little doubt that most transactors evaluate monetary policy and form expectations on the basis of interest rates and not of the money supply.

The year 1980, which produced a bumper crop of such comments, provides telling examples of public responses to money-supply and interest-rate developments. Interest rates rose sharply during the first quarter of 1980 as a strong economy created demands for money and credit. The aggregates were overshooting their targets. At that time, the very predominant interpretation by the public seemed to be that the Fed was tightening rather than easing. On the basis of a money-supply criterion, the overshooting of the aggregates would have had to be interpreted as an easing of Fed policy.

During the second quarter, both interest rates and money supply declined as the economy itself went into a sharp downturn. This time, the predominant interpretation seemed to be that the Fed was easing. Indeed, the credibility of the Fed's anti-inflationary stance was challenged by the seemingly widespread belief that the Fed had switched from fighting inflation to fighting recession. In a strict money-supply approach, this period of undershooting of the monetary targets would have had to be interpreted as one of tightening.

During the third quarter, money supply and interest rates once more moved up sharply, and the economy also turned up. Once more, the majority view seemed to be that the Fed was "tightening" and "aborting the recovery." In a money-supply criterion, the Fed's actions contributed to easing.

The seeming prevalence of an interest-rate rather than a money-supply evaluation of monetary policy does not mean that there were not voices on the other side. But when interest rates and money supply are moving in the same direction, because demand in the economy is pulling them that way, it is difficult to make the case that rising interest rates mean easing and falling interest rates mean tightening. Nevertheless, those who focus on the money supply rather than on interest rates may well form their inflation expectations accordingly. By their standards, expectations of inflation would have mounted during the first quarter and the third quarter and diminished during the second quarter. Moreover, market participants holding this view may well command financial resources that are large relative to their number.

Substantively, it would appear that events bore out the validity of the interest-rate criterion rather than the money-supply criterion. At each turn, movements in interest rates were followed, with a lag of three to four months, by a movement of the economy in the opposite direction. The rise in interest rates during the first quarter was followed by the sharp decline in the economy during the second quarter. The decline in interest rates during the second quarter was followed by an upturn of the economy in the third. To make the case that the money supply, rather than the interest rates, move the economy, one would have to assert that the money supply affected the economy with a zero lag. The overshoots of the first and third quarters would have had to make their impact on the economy instantaneously, and so would the undershoot of the second quarter. Given Friedman's time-honored dictum that the money supply affects the real sector with a long variable lag, this seems hardly plausible. The instantaneous relationship between money and the economy is much more easily explained by postulating that the causation runs from the real sector to money rather than vice-versa, and that indeed, in that case, the economy's effects on the demand for money operate quickly. Furthermore, in 1980, a third factor may have affected both the real sector and money simultaneously. A full picture would have to include the impact of the imposition and subsequent removal of the credit-restraint program on economic activity and the monetary aggregates.

Thus, there exist alternative interpretations of the stance of monetary policy. A majority in the country views interest rates as the principal measure of monetary ease and tightness, a minority, the monetary aggregates. It is probably true that the group stressing the aggregates has a significant following in the money and capital markets, which are capable of setting in motion large amounts of money. They also have a substantial representation among the press. Nevertheless, as I read the press and particularly the never-ending flood of bank, investment-house, and other letters, the interest-rate school by far predominates. For the Federal Reserve, seeking to live up to the standards of one group would only exacerbate the contrary expectations of the other. In the language of the rational expectationalists, there is no agreed structure of the economy. The distribution of rational expectations therefore is extremely wide. I end up by concluding that people are likely to act as they are shown. Announcements about money-supply targets and intended reduction of inflation are all very well. But, what people will believe is what they see, that is, results rather than expectations.

Implications for Improvement of Techniques

In this context, efforts to improve the technique of monetary control certainly should go forward, but with the recognition that they are not an absolutely necessary condition of a successful monetary policy. The existing capability for controlling the aggregates is adequate. The decisive question is how far it should be pushed in the direction of diminishing returns in terms of precision of control and at the cost of increasing instability of interest rates. I believe that some costs of this sort are well worth paying to maintain discipline and strengthen credibility. I, therefore, believe that is is worthwhile to continue to develop improved techniques of control. Even though this may mean creating a capability for monetary overkill, they may improve the trade-off between money-supply variability and interest-rate variability that is one of the principal findings of the Federal Reserve review. Therefore, a brief examination of some of the available techniques follows.

Contemporaneous- versus Lagged-Reserve Accounting

A return to contemporaneous-reserve accounting (CRA) has been urged ever since the Fed abandoned it in favor of lagged-reserve accounting (LRA). Under lagged-reserve accounting, the banks hold reserves this week against reservable liabilities two weeks ago. Not even the Almighty—although statisticians, of course—can change the reservable liabilities of two weeks ago. Conceptually, the banking system could expand enormously this week without feeling any reserve restraint if it believed that it could easily get the reserves needed two weeks later.

Banks like this system because it enables them to know their required reserve while adjusting their money position. The Desk likes it because it offers one more known value in assessing constantly shifting reserve factors. Many economists, including those inside the Federal Reserve, do not like it because it deprives the banking system of the possibility of adjusting by changing its liabilities in addition to changing its reserve holdings. More concretely, under CRA, if reserves were short this week, banks would begin to scramble for them and thereby reduce reservable liabilities during the current week. Under LRA, the scramble for reserves ordinarily would begin two weeks later. Practically, since the Fed knows future reserve liabilities soon after the end of the week in which they are established, the Desk can begin to take them into account at an early moment, in effect reducing the lag by perhaps one week.

The net result of CRA would be to give the banking system two degrees of freedom in adjusting its reserve position instead of only one: given the supply of nonborrowed reserves, it could change its reservable liabilities as well as acquiring or reducing reserves through the discount window. The potential for the first type of adjustment is not large, since every dollar of reserve deficiency or excess would call for a large multiple in terms of a change in reservable liabilities. But the earlier initiation of the process of adjustment represents a modest advantage.

Discount-Window Reforms

Various modifications of discount-window procedure are available. Their relative attraction depends on the reserve regime. The discount window essentially is an escape valve through which the banks can obtain relief from a shortage in the reserves that the Fed provides through open-market operations. Under a regime of lagged-reserve accounting, such a shortage can be absolute—discounting is the sole degree of freedom. Under contemporaneous-reserve accounting, as already noted, there are two degrees of freedom, because selling of securities and calling of loans leaves open a possible, although narrow and painful, avenue of escape from reserve deficiency.

There are various ways of narrowing banks' access to the discount window, most of which imply in some degree a prior move to contemporaneous-reserve accounting. The ultimate restraint would be total closing of the window. This would be equivalent to targeting on total reserves, a procedure under which the Federal Reserve open-market desk would reduce the supply of nonborrowed reserves by the amount of any increase in borrowed reserves, thus holding total reserves constant. Intermediate stages would be a surcharge on the regular discount rates such as prevails at present, a graduated system of several surcharges, a rate tied to a market rate, and, closest to total closing, a penalty rate designed to remain a penalty rate no matter how high market rates went.

The variability of short-term interest rates would increase in proportion to the degree of restriction of access to the window. Closing the window, and placing sole dependence on contemporaneous-reserve accounting and adjustment of reservable liabilities to available reserves would surely generate wide swings in interest rates—provided the Federal Reserve did not moderate these by changing the supply of nonborrowed reserves. Easy access to the discount window, unrestrained by administrative limitations, on the other hand, would make the discount rate the ceiling rate in the short-term market. The issue is made more complex by consideration of bank earnings. A discount rate below the market rate is widely regarded as a subsidy. Lender-of-last-resort operations might be frustrated if a significant penalty rate had to be charged to a weakened borrower. My personal inclination would be in the direction of moderate tightening of access to the window.

The Monetary Base

An old standby for Federal Reserve improvements is the monetary base. Sometimes, it is not made clear by proponents whether the base is to be used as a substitute for an operating target, that is, a reserve aggregate such as nonborrowed reserves or total reserves, or as a substitute for an intermediate target, that is, a monetary aggregate such as M_1 or M_2. As for the base's possible usefulness as an operating target, the Federal Reserve view shows that in the present institutional environment both the base and total reserves would provide less close control of the money supply than would nonborrowed reserves, the present operating target of the Desk. The principal reason is instability in multiplier relationships involving currency and the deposit mix, which injects shocks into the money-supply process.

This seems plausible given the fact that very little is known about currency holdings and the behavior of holders. The volume of currency outstanding amounts to about $500 per capita of the population. Not many holders are likely to reach this "average," and business holdings can hardly be large enough to account for the rest. Various unknown uses, such as possibly the ''underground economy,'' drug traffic, domestic hoarding, the dollar's use and hoarding abroad, and perhaps just plain attrition from loss and destruction, could be hypothesized as possible explanations for the high numbers. Whichever explanation may carry weight, none engenders much confidence in a money-supply control system that assigns a dominant role to currency.

As for the use of the monetary base as an intermediate target, analogous to the monetary aggregates, its principal attractiveness derives from two sources. One is the fact that the Federal Reserve ''can'' control the base with a high degree of precision. The base represents the great bulk of the Fed's liabilities and can, therefore, be closely, although not instantaneously, controlled by adjustment in the Fed's portfolio. Virtually the entire impact of such control, however, would have to fall on the reserve component of the base. Such control would, therefore, impact initially through sharp fluctuations in bank deposits, with only gradual impact on currency circulation.

The consequence for interest rates, liquidity of financial institutions, and all that hangs on them could, therefore, be quite drastic if the Fed were to make unrestrained use of its ''ability'' to control the base.

A second apparent attraction of the base is its close correlation with income, albeit, somewhat weakened of late. In all probability, however, this is a case where the causal relationship runs overwhelmingly from income to the base, rather than from the base to income. I doubt very much that it is possible to control GNP by controlling the volume of currency in circulation. The amount of currency outstanding is determined by the public's demand, which, in turn, is more than anything a function of retail sales. People put currency into their wallets because they intend to go shopping. They do not go shopping because they find currency in their wallets. Currency, therefore, could be controlled only by controlling income. In that sense, using the base as an intermediate target would be a proxy for using nominal GNP as an intermediate target. Money supply as an intermediate target would be eliminated in this framework.

Conclusion

For me, the outcome of this discussion is that it is indeed possible to bring down inflation through money-supply control over time. But, that will not be painless. It will involve what traditional economic theory has always pointed out—the painful process of allowing enough slack in the economy to exert a continuing downward pressure on wages and prices. There is no free lunch to be had by keeping the monetary aggregates precisely on track ''week by week and month by month,'' even if that were practically possible. The Federal Reserve has an important role to play in this process, but it is not omnipotent and not omniresponsible. The budget, regulatory reforms, productivity, and elimination of price-raising government actions all need to contribute.

Part III
International Monetary Problems

12 The Shrinking Economic Base of U.S. Leadership

Everybody agrees that the role of the United States in the world is diminishing and that new centers of dispersed power are developing. In this chapter I shall examine some of the economic background of the process. One of the conclusions will be that erosion of our economic power base has been rather less than recent emphasis on the process of attrition might lead one to believe. Another conclusion will be that the United States has exercised international leadership to some extent despite rather than because of its fundamental economic conditions.

Share of the United States in the World Economy

The shifting share of the U.S. GNP in the world GNP is shown in table 12–1. Data exclude the communist countries throughout. They become less reliable as we go farther back in time, the earliest data given for 1938. The data for GNP are stated in constant prices (1958). They are thus unaffected by national inflations. They do, however, show the effect of currency re- and devaluations.

By the end of the 1960s, U.S. GNP represented approximately 40 percent of the free world's GNP. This is only slightly less than the proportion prevailing in 1938. Int he meantime, it had reached a level of 51.7 percent in 1953, from which it has since declined. With the early 1970s, the U.S. share is approximately back to prewar levels from a largely war-induced peak.

The trade data tell a similar story. In fact, total U.S. trade has gained a little in share relative to prewar. This, however, has been the result of skyrocketing imports, whereas exports, after a postwar peak, are moderately below prewar levels.

To this data, I would have liked to add a set that unfortunately only can be very roughly estimated. It relates to saving. Saving in the American economy has been a very constant fraction of GNP at full employment for many decades. Looking at the major countries in the rest of the world, it appears that their saving ratios in many cases are well above the American, and it seems likely that these countries' saving ratios have risen substantially contrasted with prewar. The share of the United States in free-world saving probably falls some-

This chapter was originally published in *National Strategy in a Decade of Change,* A Symposium, Cosponsored by Stanford Research Institute and the Foreign Policy Research Institute, Airlie House, Warrenton, Virginia, February 17–20, 1972.

Table 12–1
Share of U.S. GNP and Trade in World Totals
(percent)

Year	*U.S. GNP*[a] / *World GDP*	*U.S. Exports*[b] / *World Exports*	*U.S. Imports*[b] / *World Imports*	*U.S. Total Trade*[b] / *World Total Trade*
1938	41.5	14.9	9.7	12.1
1948	51.4	23.8	12.6	18.0
1950	50.8			
1953	51.7			
1955		18.7	13.4	16.0
1958	48.0	16.3	11.7	14.0
1960		15.7	11.2	13.4
1961	46.8			
1963	43.2			
1965	42.2	12.6	16.2	14.5
1969[b]	42.0			
1970		14.0	15.8	14.9

[a]1963 and 1965 percentages are on the basis of U.S. and world GDP at factor cost (in 1958 dollars except where noted).

[b]At current prices

where between it shares, respectively, in GNP and in trade, and it probably has deteriorated somewhat more than the GNP share.

Obviously, GNP, trade, and saving are not the sole or perhaps even the principal determinants of a nation's power base. Even among purely economic factors, they may not be decisive. What is particularly significant about them in the case of the United States, however, is their magnitude relative to each other.

The United States is a country with a very diversified menu of outputs. Industrial raw materials, food stuffs, manufactured products, everything is produced at home. Little is needed from abroad. Large countries naturally tend to import proportionately less than small countries, as a larger fraction of each individual's dealings with the rest of mankind will happen to be with compatriots. Germany and Japan import proportionately less than Holland and Belgium. Germany and Japan, nevertheless, must import many foodstuffs and raw materials, in addition to industrial products, owing to their limited resource endowment. The United States needs remarkably little even when its large population is considered. But the great variety of its output makes for an even higher degree of self-sufficiency.

This variety, however, by and of itself, would tend to encourage a large volume of exports. The United States produces not only copper or machinery, for which world demand is limited. It produces most of the things that everybody needs, to the extent that they are transportable. If there were no equilibrium mechanism tending to equate our exports to our imports, with a small balance perhaps for capital movements, our exports would far exceed our imports. The equilibrium mechanism that prevents this from happening is the tendency toward a high level of prices. The U.S. economy has had to price a large part of its potential exports out of world markets because the world could not pay us for a permanently large export surplus, nor could we endure such a surplus without suffering a rise in prices if the world could finance it. This is the basic explanation of the price disparity between the United States and most other countries. We have become so accustomed to it that we often wonder how, given our prices and wages, the United States manages to export at all. But the basic facts really are the other way about. Our capacity to export, in a physical sense, is much greater than our capacity to import.

At the present time, when the U.S. has long been suffering from a deficiency of exports, this analysis may sound peculiar. It seems to imply a permanent tendency toward a dollar shortage, not a dollar glut. The factors, however, that have produced our payments deficit and the underlying weak trade position are of a less fundamental, although not necessarily transitory, kind. We have superimposed wage and price inflation on top of an initially high wage and price level. American wages and prices were high relative to foreign wages and prices long before the United States began to develop a payments deficit. One condition of getting rid of the deficit undoubtedly has been a reduction in the margin between U.S. and foreign wages and prices. But the reduction does not need to wipe out that margin altogether. Even when many of our goods are not sufficiently competitive to be exported, transportation costs and similar factors will protect them against foreign competition at home, and enough internationally competitive goods will be left over, within our broad spectrum of goods, to provide us with an adequate volume of exports.

Big Inside, Small Outside

So it happens that the United States within the world economy, takes on the characteristics of the ideal automobile: large inside, small outside. We have 40 percent of world GNP, but only 15 percent world trade. Our capacity to save, and therefore our capacity to lend abroad, falls somewhere in between, and probably is much closer to our GNP share than to our trade share. The combination, unfortunately, is not a good one for stabilizing the world's economy or even for exerting economic and political leadership. Compare the United States with nineteenth-century England. There was a country that needed to import heavily to feed and clothe itself, but it was able to back up its lending operations—and the ensuing transfer home of interest and dividends—with a tremendous willingness to buy. The United States likewise is a great potential capital exporter, and only very inappropriate policies have been able to obscure that natural role. But the United States is not predisposed to match its capital exports by a great willingness to import required of a ''mature creditor.'' Given stable prices, the United States would tend to remain a net capital exporter much longer than the United Kingdom did, which early in the game became a mature creditor with a large and reliable deficit on current account financed by investment income from abroad. And when the United States, as a result of inflation at home and vigorous resurgence in the rest of the world today finally does shift toward the role of a mature creditor, a hue and cry goes up from domestic industries that are hurt, and we turn to protectionism. These are serious handicaps for a country that wants to exert international leadership.

There are further difficulties. For a country with a relatively small volume of trade and large foreign investment, a small fluctuation in investment requires a large change in trade if balance of payments are to remain in equilibrium. Foreign countries are sensitive to fluctuations in trade because trade is important to them. Meanwhile, the small role of trade in the American economy makes it unwise and also very difficult to adjust the balance of payments by domestic measures. To deflate or inflate the domestic economy to maintain payments equilibrium would mean to make a very small tail wag a very large dog. Rarely has the United States undertaken deliberately such corrective measures. In consequence, its balance of payments has remained in disequilibrium for long periods. Correcting a disequilibrium by changing the exchange rate was not practicable so long as other countries pegged their currencies to the dollar that had become the world's reserve, intervention, trade, and investment currency.

The capacity to lend and invest abroad constitutes of course an important source of international strength, as does the capacity to import heavily. Nevertheless, foreign lending and investment has many weak spots. Everybody loves a customer. Few love the collector of interest and the reaper of profits. American investment abroad creates frictions. It makes the United States vulnerable, be it to confiscation, lesser mistreatment in the case of direct investment, or to default in the case of loans.

The benefits of foreign investment, too, are not uncontested. Given the world's tax arrangements, enterprises are taxed where they are located. Thus, the tax revenue produced by American investment goes to the host country, when similar investment at home, even if it had been slightly less profitable to the firm, would nevertheless have produced a larger yield to the firm and the Treasury combined. Labor dislikes foreign investment, because it sees it as an export of jobs. Maintenance of full employment would allay this fear. But it would not do away with a more subtle disadvantage suffered by labor. Export of capital means less capital per worker invested in the United States and therefore less productivity and lower wages. The return to capital is kept high by foreign investment, and total GNP increases. But the share of labor in that GNP is adversely affected.

In the host country, the opposite happens, that is, the wages of labor are bid up while the return to capital is depressed relative to its earlier level. Overall, the host country clearly benefits, especially if foreign investment brings along technological improvement, managerial techniques, and intensified competition. But against these advantages must be weighed the less tangible damage to national pride resulting from foreign takeovers. There must be weighed also the quite tangible interference with national sovereignty occasionally resulting from American antitrust and export-control legislation. This sense of grievance mounts if the host country must tell itself that it has indirectly financed American foreign investment by supporting an American balance-of-payments deficit through the acquisition of dollars.

The devaluation of the dollar will not have any great direct effect on American foreign investment. In contrast to American purchases of foreign goods, the purchase of existing foreign firms, or of foreign currencies to use in building new factories abroad, will not be discouraged by the less favorable exchange rate. The reason is that foreign currency earned by the investment now buys more dollars. In other words, the rate of return is unchanged, and what the American investor abroad fundamentally buys is a rate of return. The flow of capital, unlike the flow of commodities, is not affected by the relative price of goods. It is affected by the interest rate. Only to the extent that American devaluation leads to more active business in the United States and less active business abroad, and to a consequent shift in the respective levels of interest rates, will devaluation affect the flow of long-term capital.

One might ask whether the interests of both sides would not be equally well or better served if, instead of American corporations, American individual stockholders were given the opportunity to export capital by purchasing foreign securities on foreign or American stock exchanges. Today, American stockholders are discouraged, if not altogether prevented, from making such investments by the Interest Equalization Tax. This tax is imposed as a general balance-of-payments measure. But in the narrower context of foreign investment one might say that American stockholders are prevented from buying foreign securities so that American corporations, in which they are also stockholders, can export money to make direct investments. A reversal of priorities, giving the individual investor facilities while restraining corporations, would lead to far less friction with the host country. On the other hand, many of the benefits of direct foreign investment on both sides, such as the transfer of technology, management, and competition to the host country, together with the direct participation in retained profits of the American subsidiary, would also disappear.

Since the purpose of this chapter is to discuss the economic base of American international leadership, it would seem natural to discuss the role of American subsidiaries abroad as an element in that leadership. The fact is that hardly anybody ever speaks of this topic, because there is so little to discuss. The suspicion has always existed that the private foreign investment of any country is really a concealed arm of the investing country's government. No doubt the presence of large amounts of American capital and of American-directed managerial personnel does in some sense strengthen the position of the U.S. government abroad. The application of domestic American legislation for foreign subsidiaires is a—quite unnecessary—use of such power. But aside from this, the U.S. government has very little control even over the parent corporations, and the last thing the parent corporations desire is to be used as instruments of American foreign policy. If anything, American foreign investments abroad are hostages given to the rest of the world that can be used by foreign countries to keep the United States on its best behavior.

The argument thus far can be summed up very simply. The United States has a more potent base for international leadership in its ability to invest abroad than in its foreign trade. Investment, unfortunately, is a less viable base for leadership than trade. The circumstance making the United States a bigger investor than trader—the great size and diversity of the American economy—keeps the United States from adjusting its domestic policies according to needs of the rest of the world, which would make these policies a part of its international policies.

United States as a Supplier of Public Goods

The role of the United States in the world enables—or perhaps compels—it to act as a supplier of a wide range of what economists call "public goods." Public goods are those than cannot be charged for by their producer, such as radio programs, a view of a beautiful building, or a depolluted river. Perhaps the principal public good supplied by the United States is military security. In its own interest, the United States must maintain a defense establishment sufficient to assure peace. This assures peace also for the U.S. allies. To the extent that they think that the U.S. effort is adequate, they have little motive to make a contribution of their own to security. This explains the difficulties that the United States has had in persuading its allies to bear their fair share of the burden. The Soviet Union is reported to encounter similar difficulties with its Warsaw Pact allies. Another public good supplied largely by the United States was, until recently, a sound financial climate throughout the free world. Convertible currencies and stable exchange rates were based principally on the stability of the dollar and, in decreasing measure recently, on the willingness of the United States to bail out other nations in financial difficulties.

Another public good has been a climate favorable to free trade. The most-favored-nation clause makes tariff concessions public goods instead of private. A concession that in principle could be restricted to countries making a counterconcession is in fact given free to all other countries.

The United States supplies these public goods fundamentally in its own self-interest. It supplies security because it must protect its own citizens. It supplies a sound financial climate because that benefits its trade and perhaps even more its investments. The same applies with respect to a free-trade climate.

Of course the United States is not eager to be a supplier of public goods. It does its best to internalize the externalities that it creates. In the case of NATO, it presses for burden sharing. In world finance, it works through the International Monetary Fund and other institutions to make other countries contribute. In the trade area, it works through the GATT and through multilateral trade negotiations, trying to maintain discipline and obtain concessions. The nature of the public-goods mechanism makes the objective hard to achieve in most cases. Where the United States is clearly perceived to be acting in its self-interest it is in a weak position to claim that it is acting in the common good and should receive matching support.

How far has the shrinking role of the United States reduced its function as a supplier of public goods? The answer seems to be that the interest of the United States in a sound world financial climate and in a free-trade climate is unchanged but that its ability to deliver this kind of climate has shrunk. The interest of the United States in the world's financial and trade climate must be measured by the exposure of the United States to the balms or rigors of that climate. The share of trade in the American economy has not significantly changed. If ever it was worth the United States' while to pay a price to attain a good climate for its trade, it still is. As far as investment is concerned, the proportion of American assets that lie outside our borders certainly has risen. Hence our exposure and resulting benefits are greater.

The ability of the United States to create a desirable financial and trade climate, on the other hand, to the extent that it is properly measured by the U.S. share in world trade or in world GNP, has declined. We would have to work harder, or pay a bigger price, to attain the same results. We are now in the process of asking ourselves whether that greater effort is still worthwhile.

The ability of the United States to influence the world's financial and trade climate has suffered from still another development—the formation of stronger interests and, in the case of the European countries, of a large unit that is gradually beginning to pull together. A given share of world trade or GNP means different things depending on the pattern prevailing in the rest of the world. A large number of independent countries are more likely to follow American leadership than a smaller number of units moving toward a common policy. Even after the accession of the United Kingdom and three other countries, the share of the European Economic Community (EEC) in the free world's GNP still is well below that of the United States. The share of the EEC in world trade, on the other hand, is already substantially larger. Being able to offer a larger market, the EEC will be able to exert more pulling power than the United States. This is already becoming apparent in the arrangements that various countries are trying to make with the EEC.

The possiblity exists, of course, that the EEC may now begin to be a producer of the same public goods that the United States may be less interested in supplying. As a large unit, it has the power. Where a small country cannot change the climate of world trade or finance sufficiently by its own actions to benefit significantly, a unit of the size of the EEC certainly can, as soon as it has created the means of conducting a unified policy. The question is whether the EEC will see its interest in the same kind of world climate that the United States has desired or whether perhaps it will seek to promote something narrower than that.

Japan

The rapid rise of Japan poses a similar question. Even if its recent 10 percent growth rate should slow down, one would expect the Japanese economy at least to double in size over the next decade. If Japan should turn toward the formation of an economic block of its own, these effects would be enhanced. Past history suggests that propensities in that direction exist in Japan. Moreover, as a country lacking in natural resources, Japan is bound to be a big importer. As such it possesses some of the qualifications for becoming an international economic center that the United States lacks.

In a world of regional blocks or associations, the international economic base of the United States would be further eroded. This would be the result not only of a further shrinkage of the U.S. share in world GNP, trade, and saving, which is likely to continue in any event so long as other countries on average grow more rapidly than the U.S. The ability of the United States to exert leadership and to influence the world climate will diminish also, as these foreign groups coalesce and gain strength. To achieve a given result will cost the United States a larger economic effort. The United States presumably would increasingly question the justification of such efforts.

A Dollar Bloc?

If none of the large units finds it in its self-interest to provide public goods in the form of a free-trade climate and stable international monetary conditions, they can be provided only as a result of cooperation among these units. In that way, the externalities created could be internalized. This is entirely possible, but the risk of failure is considerable.

In such a world, the United States of course will have to ask itself whether it should not form a bloc of its own. The most obvious grouping would be the Western hemisphere. This would have the advantage of geographical logic. It would not necessarily, however, be an efficient combination. The United States even now is far from popular in the rest of the hemisphere. Latin America, moreover, is an uncertain partner, troubled by slow growth, a population explosion, political instability, and the threat of communism. A grouping including Japan in the West and perhaps reaching as far as Spain and Portugal in the East would be more promising economically, although even more difficult politically. Any kind of grouping would expose American high-cost industry to the competition of the nascent industries of the Latin American countries and to the rapidly expanding low-cost industries of the other potential bloc members. The automobile agreement with Canada has shown what can happen. In consequence, there seems to be a good chance that, even in a world coalescing into blocs, the United States might remain more or less on its own.

U.S. Interest in a New World Monetary System

The world monetary system that may have come to an end on August 15, 1971—we have no means of knowing whether in its essentials it did or not—embodied a kind of asymmetry that at one time was congenial to the United States. Through the dollar exchange standard, the United States received easy—not free—financing for its payments deficit. On the other hand, it surrendered the possibility of adjusting its balance of payments by changing its exchange rate. Since until quite recently the United States never seriously contemplated such a move, giving up the possibility was no great sacrifice.

The rest of the world occupied an opposite position. Countries were free to adjust their balance of payments by changing their exchange rate. They did not have easy financing for their payments deficit and had to finance the U.S. deficit unless they were prepared to appreciate their exchange rate.

The United States did not make wise use of the system. For a country with so large a GNP, the gains from easy financing of a deficit of a few billion dollars were no great advantage. The facility for such financing should have been kept unused and in reserve for the day of a real emergency, be it the need to finance a very large capital outflow, or a foreign aid program, or a major war. Instead we chose, perhaps because we could not help it, to obtain continuous financing of a nagging deficit that was not important in terms of resources but had the effect of making other countries dissatisfied with their role in the arrangement. Eventually, as our inflation progressed, the United States began to feel increasingly the disadvantage of having its hands tied as regards the exchange rate. Import-sensitive domestic industries began to press for protection, and the criticism of our trade partners and allies became increasingly embarrassing.

These conditions finally led to the breakdown of the system. They also seem to have led to a substantial change of heart on the part of the United States as well as major foreign countries as to what it is that they seek from the international monetary system. The United States now seems to want freedom to move its exchange rate. All countries agree that greater flexibility of exchange rates, even while parities remain unchanged, that is, a wider band around these parities, is desirable. The United States also seems to have concluded that the opportunity to obtain easy financing of the payments deficit is nothing particularly to be treasured. Meanwhile, the United States has developed a strong phobia against any obligation to make the dollar convertible into reserve assets, an obligation that under the old system had proved not so much damaging as embarrassing to a country accustomed to meeting its commitments. Furthermore the United States has every reason to conclude from its recent experience with its fiscal and monetary policies, whether oriented at financing or at restraining the economy, that it must preserve freedom to conduct its monetary policy, without excessive constraints from balance-of-payments considerations. Fiscal policy has proved an unreliable instrument for the management of the economy.

There is real danger, however, that the United States as well as foreign countries may have become overimpressed with the lessons of very recent experience. In a period of inflation, it is obvious that stable exchange rates have little chance to survive. Rates of high inflation are unlikely to be the same among different countries. If they happen to be the same, different countries may nevertheless find themselves in different phases of the business cycle, calling for different monetary policies. All this creates a need for exchange-rate flexibility that does not really exist when prices everywhere are reasonably stable.

The usefulness of a system in which the dollar in effect is legal tender among central banks around the world may have become obscured at a time when the United States was misusing this facility. By the same token, the aversion to the dollar standard that other countries have developed may reflect more this misuse than a basic defect of the system. The fact that in 1971 the United States succeeded in getting agreement to lower the exchange value of the dollar may have made us too optimistic about our chances for repeating the action under different circumstances. Exchange rates are two-sided. No country of any importance is altogether free to change its rate. On another occasion, even after the dollar had ceased to serve as a reserve or intervention currency, the United States might find that foreign countries, instead of accepting a substantial change in the rate of the dollar, would threaten to retaliate by changing their own rate and retaining their parity with the dollar.

For the sake of a viable international system, one must hope devoutly that fiscal policy will not remain in its present inflexible and ineffectual state but will develop into a flexible and effective tool of policy. In that case, there would be more scope for international coordination of monetary policies, reducing the danger of large flows of short-term funds and hence the need for exchange-rate flexibility to ward them off.

Given the lack of perspective from which we suffer in contemplating our recent experience, it will undoubtedly be well to move slowly in international monetary reform. Considerable agreement already exists concerning the need for a greater range of fluctuations of rates around parities, for easier and perhaps more frequent changes in parities, and for the need for a systematic method of reserve-asset creation. It seems premature, at this time, to attempt to be very specific as to techniques. It may be helpful, instead, to outline some of the characteristics of a system desirable from the point of view of the United States:

1. Above all the system should be of a kind that does not put the United States at odds with its trade partners and allies. A system unacceptable to them will hurt the United States more, through the tensions created, than any financial advantages it will yield. Such a system in any event would be of limited duration.

2. The system should leave a high degree of freedom for domestic monetary policy. In the long run, coordination of monetary policies for the purpose of controlling balances of payments should be envisaged, but in the near future this seems impractical. Even so, countries should reasonably be expected to moderate swings in their monetary policies so as not to exacerbate international flows.

3. Reasonable freedom should be provided for the United States to change its exchange rate. The total lack of control that has characterized the past should be avoided. The United States will nevertheless have to realize that, whatever the legal and institutional arrangments, a change in the value of the dollar creates difficulties for many countries and that there may be limits to the degree of freedom to change the dollar rate no matter what the system.

4. The system should generate adequate pressure on surplus countries to revalue, so as to put an end to the one-sidedness of the old system, which placed most of the pressure on deficit countries. This will be particularly important to the extent that the United States accepts obligations to convert the dollar into reserve assets.

5. The system should reduce the emphasis on gold that was characteristic of the old arrangements.

6. To the extent that other countries choose to use the dollar for private or official transactions, it should be recognized that a special service is rendered by the United States and that the system must contain enough flexiblity of one sort or another to make this role acceptable.

7. Whatever convertibility obligations are accepted by the United States should be meetable without undue constraint on domestic policy. They should not put the United States, which will start out as a reserve-poor country, before a frequent choice between default and depression. Facilities for reducing the exchange value of the dollar may not be immediately helpful in easing such pressures, because devaluation works only with a lag of several years.

8. Unless measures can be devised to endow the United States with ad-

equate reserve assets from the start, the United States will have to increase its reserves by means of payment surpluses. The system must assure that such surpluses lead to the earning of reserve assets by the United States and not simply to the repatriation of dollars previously held abroad.

9. Funding of the present overhang of dollars would be beneficial to the United States, provided it removes the overhang fully and provided the interest rate, and the amortization payments if any, are attractive. It is difficult, however, to envisage a degree of funding so complete that past accumulations of dollars would cease to be a threat to U.S. convertibility or to the ability of the United States to earn reserve assets. Funding of the overhang cannot, therefore, be regarded as a sufficient precondition for convertibility.

10. Convertibility obligations undertaken by the United States should not extend to dollars resulting from short-term capital movements. Nor should the United States be required to guarantee, in effect, the exchange value of such dollars by means of swap arrangements and the like. Decisions by other parties, in short, to use the dollar as a vehicle for capital movements should not lead to special obligations imposed on the United States that others do not share.

11. To the extent that the United States cannot be endowed with an adequate volume of reserve assets, it will be in the interest of the United States to be able to pay for a deficit in dollars. Although the United States should not make use of this under ordinary circumstances, the United States would be well advised to make concessions on other points to preserve this facility for emergencies.

12. The system should allow for freedom of current and capital transactions as fully as is consistent with the foregoing objectives.

The list of objectives here set forth must be compared with similar lists that might be constructed from the point of view of other countries. Considerable areas of agreement are likely to emerge, together with some areas of conflicting interests. The negotiation of an acceptable compromise will take considerable time and should take place in the light of experience gathered meanwhile.

13 Some Thoughts about Balance-of-Payments Discipline

It would be quite wrong, of course, to suppose that growing consciousness of the balance of payments implies that at some point in the past the United States was totally oblivious of this sector of its economy. Benign neglect was never practiced in responsible quarters. President Kennedy's remark to the effect that his two prime concerns were the nuclear bomb and the balance of payments should suffice to lay that story to rest. But the evidence of mounting balance-of-payments consciousness is clearly before us. It comprises the recent actions of the Federal Reserve and the Treasury in the areas of interest rates and other monetary actions, foreign-currency borrowing, and intervention. It encompasses also the nation's realization that economic growth had to slow down, and its mounting concern with inflation, even though domestic considerations are naturally preeminent. Fundamental policies must be in place if bridging actions are to be effective.

Numerous trends have contributed to exposing the United States to greater balance-of-payments discipline: the increasing share of foreign trade in the economy, the increasing openness of U.S. capital markets to foreign borrowers and lenders, the linkage of our capital markets to others through the Eurodollar market, the accumulation of a large volume of dollar balances and other assets in the hands of foreigners, and the evident sensitivity of the dollar to balance-of-payments developments. Each of these factors deserves some comment.

The Rise of the Foreign-Trade Sector

U.S. imports, including invisibles, today represent about 10 percent of GNP. This compares with 3.5 percent in 1938 and 4.6 percent in 1953. In quantitative terms, trade in merchandise and invisibles over these years has about trebled its role in the economy. In qualitative terms, U.S. dependence on foreign supplies has, of course, greatly increased. Oil is only one prominent example.

Since world trade has grown much faster in the postwar period than world GNP, the experience of the United States in becoming more open on current account is shared by many other countries, including leading trading nations like Germany and Japan. But for neither of these has the development been as spectacular as for the United States.

This chapter was originally presented on January 4, 1979, at a meeting of the Balance of Payments Group of the National Foreign Trade Council, Inc., New York City.

The United States has become more open also on capital account. Restrictions on capital movements, such as the interest-equalization tax and the voluntary foreign-credit-restraint program, no longer exist. Many new foreign borrowers have gained access to external capital markets, including those of the United States. The international activity of U.S. banks has greatly increased.

The Eurodollar markets for deposits, loans, and bonds constitute a growing link between the United States and the rest of the world. The amounts lent and borrowed in those markets, to be sure, are funded very predominantly from outside the United States, and interest rates reflect very largely the level of interest rates in the United States. But there is also reciprocal interaction, with effects running in both directions.

Large dollar balances have accumulated in foreign hands, which, in part, are liabilities of the United States and, in part, those of the Euromarket. The magnitude of the Eurobalances is often overstated, owing to the double-counting of interbank deposits. Nevertheless, there is a significant volume of funds in the hands of nonbanks and of central banks that, to a degree, is mobile. There is also a growing stock of Eurobonds denominated in dollars. All these are capable of influencing the demand for and supply of dollar assets and the exchange rate of the dollar. The same applies, of course, although in generally lesser degree, to domestic dollar assets owned by U.S. residents—theoretically they could all be sold for foreign currencies.

Still another international linkage is the apparent sensitivity of the dollar rate to the state of the U.S. balance of payments. This may well be a passing phenomenon. For the time being, however, the weight of the U.S. deficit in determining the exchange rate of the dollar, as compared with other major determinants such as relative rates of inflation and interest rates, seems to be considerable.

In former years—during the interwar period and the early postwar years—the relative absence or low weight of the linkages I have listed served, to a degree, to shield the United States from strong balance-of-payments discipline. The growth of these links, all of which have helped to integrate the United States with the rest of the world, has contributed to a weakening of this shield.

In addition, there are further developments that, without bearing particularly on the linkage between the United States and the rest of the world, have nevertheless served to reduce the relative insulation from balance-of-payments discipline that the United States enjoyed in former years. The principal factors among these are the use made by the United States of the reserve-currency role of the dollar, developments in the area of asset settlement of payments deficits, and recent experience with floating exchange rates.

Effects of Reserve-Currency Role of Dollars

It is in the nature of a reserve currency that it shields the country issuing it in some degree against balance-of-payments discipline. When payments deficits can be met by issuing currency and allowing it to accumulate in the hands of foreign official holders, balance-of-payments discipline, for good or ill, is diminished. There is not the same pressure for balance-of-payments adjustment that is felt by countries that must settle their deficits with reserve assets.

Very different views have been taken of this characteristic of a reserve currency. General de Gaulle complained about the "exorbitant privilege" enjoyed by the United States in paying for its deficits in its own currency. On the other hand, proponents of flexible or at least adjustable exchange rates have pointed out that under fixed rates the reserve country is being deprived of one effective means of balance-of-payments adjustment—a change in the exchange rate. Since other countries peg their currency to the reserve currency, it is they, not the reserve country, that determine the exchange value of the reserve currency. Proponents of strong expansionist policies, finally, have viewed the shield provided by the reserve currency as a fortunate circumstance of which to take full advantage.

In retrospect, it appears to me that the United States made excessive use of the protection against balance-of-payments discipline afforded by the reserve role of the dollar. We became accustomed to payments deficits because they were easy to finance and, up to a point, even desirable to provide the world with liquidity. The evidence is in the increasingly inflationary condition of our economy. It is to be found also in successive devaluations under fixed rates and repeated declines of the dollar under floating rates. The deficits that were financed with dollars went beyond what the rest of the world was willing to accumulate at an unchanging dollar rate. These deficits, and the overexpansion and inflation that lie behind them, probably would have been substantially smaller had the United States been under continuous balance-of-payments discipline.

Reserve-currency status does not, of course, convey complete immunity against balance-of-payments discipline so long as the reserve currency is convertible, that is, is backed by asset settlement. Gold losses associated with payments deficits did exert restraint over U.S. policies, both during the last years of the Eisenhower administration and in the early Kennedy days. But the United States worked hard to minimize the role of asset settlements. Suasion, swap arrangements, the gold pool, and manipulation of the free-market price of gold, all were designed to hold down U.S. gold losses. Eventually the gold window was closed altogether.

Asset settlement, even in the case of a reserve currency, therefore, is an important channel of balance-of-payments discipline. Under floating exchange rates, the analogue to asset settlement is intervention in exchange markets by the country whose currency is being supported, except as that intervention serves the purpose of countering disorder in a narrowly defined sense. The fact that the United States of late has been intervening vigorously and in a coordinated manner, and has mobilized very substantial resources for this purpose, indicates that the United States is not relying on the reserve role of the dollar, unbacked by asset settlement, to shield it from balance-of-payments discipline.

The fact that the United States has been intervening to correct an unjustified exchange-rate situation suggests further that the policy is not to rely on wide swings of floating exchange rates to provide protection against balance-of-payments discipline.

Floating exchange rates, of course, have been long advocated as the ultimate protection against balance-of-payments discipline for all countries. With a floating exchange rate, it was argued, each country could pursue the domestic policies it wanted. Differences in the degree of expansion and inflation would be taken care of by the exchange rate.

Experience with floating rates has not fully confirmed this prescription. Floating rates have had many advantages, as alternatives to controls and as a vehicle for a rising volume of international trade and capital movements. But countries that believed they could escape balance-of-payments discipline by floating soon found out otherwise. Overshooting of exchange rates, accelerated inflation, vicious circles, and continuous narrowing of the room for fiscal and monetary maneuver have been the lot of countries that ignored their balance of payments. These consequences of floating have been more apparent in countries with high degrees of openness. The basic conclusion, however, applies also to the United States. Floating rates provide shelter from balance-of-payments discipline only in moderate degree.

Changing Views of Balance-of-Payments Discipline

I regard balance-of-payments discipline in general, and for the United States in particular, as beneficial. This is the result of the reading of history that I have presented. I am aware that the view is not universally shared in the economic profession. It needs, therefore, some buttressing.

I should add that I am speaking of balance-of-payments discipline principally for deficit countries, and that this discipline primarily involves correction of excessively easy fiscal and monetary policies. It does not involve unlimited exchange-rate depreciation as a means of achieving payments equilibrium. Balance-of-payments discipline for surplus countries is a different matter. They, too, should feel pressure to reach equilibrium, but this should not be accomplished by a degree of relaxation of fiscal and monetary restraints that would encourage inflation.

In a few circles, balance-of-payments discipline has indeed been a dirty word. Criticism of the gold standard has generally culminated in the charge that it imposed excessive balance-of-payments discipline. Historically, there is much to be said for that view. The gold standard is one extreme in a spectrum. The question is how far it is wise to move toward the opposite extreme.

As concerns the United States, it is noteworthy that the Employment Act did not list balance-of-payments equilibrium among U.S. economic objectives, which were broadly defined as high growth, full employment, and price stability. It is perhaps significant that the German counterpart of this Act does list external equilibrium as an objective, in addition to growth, full employment, and price stability. During the early 1960s, when the balance-of-payments problem was much in the foreground, some private groups aiming to specify U.S. economic goals examined the possibility of including payments equilibrium among the nation's economic objectives. Only in 1978, with the passage of the Humphrey-Hawkins (Full Employment and Balanced Growth) Act did an "improved trade balance" become a formal objective of national policy.

The case against balance-of-payments discipline is simple. Whatever a country wants to do is what is best for it. That way it maximizes social welfare. Anything that restrains its freedom of action necessarily means a loss of welfare.

A more jaundiced view of human nature suggests that rejection of balance-of-payments discipline involves an exaggeratedly optimistic view of national policymaking. There is no assurance that every country is managing its affairs optimally or that its policies are designed to maximize its welfare. More likely, they are designed to find the line of least resistance and the lowest common denominator of agreement. The optimistic view seems to see any particular country as managing its affairs competently and achieving its objectives in a stable fashion. Unfortunately, it seems, the rest of the world is unstable and, if balance-of-payments discipline were admitted, would prevent the country from carrying out its wise policies.

On balance, however, a more frequent case may be that a single country feeling balance-of-payments pressure is going off its tracks while other countries remain on theirs. A realistic appreciation of political processes and of the historical reluctance of many countries to live within their means would suggest that balance-of-payments discipline may be appropriate at many times and in many places.

Usually, moreover, policy thinking in a country is not monolithic but runs along a spectrum from more to less conservative policies. Usually, there are defenders of the policies that would be called for by the state of the balance of payments, but frequently they are outvoted. Balance-of-payments discipline would strengthen their hand.

In the United States, this may have been the case at certain times in the past. At present, I believe that a consensus is building along policy lines consistent with the needs of our balance of payments. As I said earlier, these include not only those policies specifically addressed to the value of the dollar but also those with respect to inflation and economic expansion.

Conclusion

If my analysis is correct that the demands of the balance of payments are increasingly heeded in U.S. policymaking, one of the results undoubtedly would be to enhance the attractiveness of the dollar as a reserve asset. Less inflation together with growth moderated to the level of our long-term potential would strengthen the balance of payments and improve the position of our currency.

These policies would also imply a reduction in the degree to which the United States has been relying on the reserve role of the dollar to cope with its balance-of-payments problem. The improvement in the balance of payments, the borrowing of foreign currencies, and the greater role of asset settlement through intervention all point in that direction.

Diminished reliance on the reserve role of the dollar seems appropriate to me. United States experience has shown that, relied on excessively, a reserve currency role can backfire. It has advantages when not used heavily and particularly when kept in reserve for difficult periods. As a steady diet, the resulting lack of balance-of-payments discipline runs a very serious risk of undermining the strength of the currency.

Recognition that the role of a reserve currency is no bed of roses is not, of course, confined to this side of the Atlantic. The countries whose currencies are most frequently nominated as candidates for reserve-currency status, Germany and Switzerland, are making every effort to prevent this from coming about. The nature of their concerns is somewhat different from that of the United States, focusing on fear of disruption of capital markets, overexpansion of money supply, and extreme exchange-rate fluctuations.

The absence of a willing candidate as a successor to the dollar seems to leave matters pretty much where they are at present. But if I am right about the greater acceptance of balance-of-payments discipline in the United States, the status quo has improved: The dollar should be a more attractive reserve asset precisely because that function is likely to be relied on less heavily by the United States.

14 International Monetary Evolution

One piece of wisdom was left to posterity when the attempt to redesign a blueprint for the international monetary system was given up in 1974. The IMF's Committee of Twenty, that had labored for two years on the project, concluded that the international monetary system would continue to evolve. No truer word has been spoken on this seemingly immortal topic. The system certainly has been and is in continuing evolution. Some of its evolution has been along structural lines, changing the nature of its organization. Among present departures in this area are the work on a substitution account, the European Monetary System, and the effort to strengthen IMF surveillance. Drift toward a multicurrency-reserve system could bring a further structural change. The recent upsurge in gold prices has revived suggestions, impractical in my view, for a new fixed price of that commodity.

Policies carried on within the international monetary system as it exists have also been evolving. There have been movements along various spectra of options. One such spectrum runs from fixed to freely floating rates. Here, the initial move toward free floating has been in some degree reversed in the direction of more management. Within a second spectrum, running from preference for appreciation to preference for depreciation, a shift of preferences toward strength rather than weakness of national currencies has been observable. Finally, in the spectrum of options for dealing with payments deficits by adjustment or by financing, a move toward greater emphasis on adjustment may be ahead for many countries in this second round of OPEC-induced payments deficits. I would like to deal briefly with all these elements of monetary evolution.

Substitution Account

The substitution account offers a means of reducing the international role of the dollar and enhancing that of the SDR. Nobody seems quite sure how much of a desire exists in the world for either move. For the United States, the reserve-currency role has become a burden, in a world where the banking systems of foreign countries, as well as foreign branches of our own banks, can freely add to the world's supply of dollars. Some countries are reportedly diversifying

This chapter was originally presented on February 20, 1980, at Columbia University, New York City.

some of their dollar holdings into other currencies. Thus a device like the substitution account, which issues SDR denominated claims against dollars placed in it, could serve several national purposes, provided it can be negotiated.

For the United States, there are alternative options that limit the attractiveness to the United States of a substitution account. One such option is to continue with the existing system, which has advantages as well as burdens. The substitution account, therefore, must be an improvement for all countries, not only for the United States, if it is to be worth establishing.

The big problem in designing the substitution account, numerous technicalities aside, is how to maintain the soundness of an account that has dollar assets and receives dollar interest to back SDR liabilities and pay an SDR rate of interest. These two stocks and flows are inversely related. If the dollar is stronger than the SDR in the exchange markets, interest rates prevailing in the United States are likely to be lower than the SDR interest rate, which is the average of the interest rates prevailing in the major currencies represented in the SDR. If the dollar is weaker than the SDR, dollar interest rates will tend to be higher than nondollar interest rates.

One option is to ignore possible divergences between the assets and liabilities and between receipts and expenditures. That, however, makes the future of the SDR liabilities issued by the account uncertain. It could become a well-backed asset with an adequate interest rate, or it could become the opposite. At the other extreme is the option of complete maintenance of value of the dollar (and perhaps other currency) assets of the account in terms of its SDR liabilities, together with a guarantee of the interest rate in SDR. If such arrangements were made, and their burden were to fall entirely on the United States, the United States might as well forego the account and issue its own SDR obligations. If the entire burden were to fall on the foreign holders of SDRs, they would be no differently situated than if they continued to hold the original dollars contributed to the account. The logical arrangement would be a sharing of the burden, provided this were acceptable to the political authorities of the participating countries. This option would create a very attractive and highly liquid SDR instrument.

Still another possibility would be a maintenance-of-value guarantee for the dollars in the account (and perhaps other currencies as well) in case of dissolution of the account. Additional arrangements would then have to be made to cope with a possible interest-flow gap. It is difficult to assess how attractive potential acquirers of the SDR instruments, other than the original depositors, would find such an arrangement. Another possibility that has been mentioned is to place IMF gold into the substitution account as a means of assuring maintenance of value and possibly of financing deficiencies in the flow in interest. The use of gold would have the advantage of providing a solution, although possibly only a partial one, to the risk of a capital and/or interest gap.

In any event, the account, if negotiated, presumably would start with a moderate amount of assets and liabilities but would be expected to build up over time.

European Monetary System

The European Monetary System (EMS) constitutes another direction of structural evolution, toward creating a zone of exchange-rate stability and incidentally limiting the role of the dollar in intervention by the participating countries. The system now has been in operation for about one year. Neither the hopes nor the fears associated with its creation have been more than partially validated. The system per se does not seem to have produced the greater discipline on its members that would have helped to bring down national rates of inflation. But neither can it be held responsible for the higher inflation now prevailing in countries where inflation was low, before the recent oil-price increases, nor has it led to exaggerated exchange-rate rigidity or payments controls. Some of the smaller members may have felt that their currencies were pulled along excessively by the deutsche mark. Some also may have felt under a constraint to match German interest rates more than they would have wanted to for domestic purposes. That, of course, is what discipline means.

For the United States, the EMS has not had the result that some may have feared—a coordinated European dollar policy aiming at control over the value of the dollar. It has had the anomalous effect of pulling up, relative to the dollar, the currencies of some countries whose rates of inflation were no less than those of the United States, at a time when the U.S. current account was improving. Since the EMS, under the terms of its charter, is to evolve in the direction of tighter cohesion, its effects may change over time.

IMF Surveillance

The IMF has the power, and indeed the obligation, to exercise surveillance over the exchange-rate policies of its members. The Fund has been given the power also to monitor the monetary and fiscal policies of its members, since these are important determinants of exchange rates. Finally, as a third perimeter of surveillance, the Fund can examine members' policies with respect to the financing of their payments deficits. The surveillance process covers countries in surplus, influence over whose policies has always been a weak part of the adjustment mechanism. To implement the surveillance process, the United States had proposed that countries with large imbalances submit to the IMF proposals for dealing with them, that the Fund assess the performance of individual countries in a global context, that the managing director more often take the initiative in arranging consultations with members, and that the IMF examine how payments imbalances have been financed.

The Fund has approached its task of surveillance with a great deal of caution. It is significant, however, that the United States has declared itself willing to accept this degree of IMF influence. Historically, the United States has been resistant to any thought of IMF influence over our freedom of domestic decision making. One may view this evolution of U.S. thinking as evidence that the United States increasingly realizes that its domestic policies may benefit from balance-of-payments discipline, as well as finding greater activity of the IMF in this area in the U.S. interest generally.

Multicurrency-Reserve System

The drift toward a multicurrency-reserve system is not an organized process. It seems to be happening, in some degree, as a result of diversification efforts on the part both of some central banks outside the G-10 group of countries and of some private-sector participants. Such a move is not surprising under a system of floating rates. A diversified portfolio, whether of common stocks or of currencies, has less risk for a given rate of return than investment in only a single company or a single currency. In choosing the desired composition of their currency portfolio, holders presumably will give weight to the distribution of currencies in which they conduct their imports and in which their debts are denominated. That would still leave a very sizable demand for dollar assets. Indeed the share of the dollar in monetary authorities' portfolios of foreign-exchange holdings since 1970 has been fairly constant at about 75 percent.

The world has had experience with multicurrency-reserve systems. Gold and silver, sterling and dollar, gold and dollar, with an admixture of French francs, have all been tried by force of circumstances and have been found to be unstable as holders switched from one asset to the other. A new edition of the old text probably would not turn out very differently. I might note additionally that the countries whose currencies are candidates for reserve-currency status seem to be far from enthusiastic about the prospect. This observation also suggests that the United States on balance has had more burden than benefit from the reserve-currency role of the dollar.

An alternative to a multicurrency-reserve system would be an SDR-based system, which seems far preferable. To be sure, the lack of progress made by that instrument since its creation in 1969 might give one pause. One should think that, if the SDR were a promising financial instrument, the private market would have created and popularized its counterpart, the SDR claim. So far, very few borrowers outside those from the IMF have wanted to borrow in SDR, and few depositors have sought SDR deposits. A demand for such instruments, if it were manifested, could, of course, be accommodated by the private banking system as well as by other financial institutions.

The fact that the interest rate on the SDR has been kept artificially low is not a complete answer. It applies only to the SDR that is issued as a liability of the IMF. The potential role of SDR-denominated claims and liabilities is much wider. Borrowers and lenders could put on such instruments any interest rate commensurate with interest rates in the underlying basket or part thereof or even an independent interest rate.

Nor is it a valid explanation of the failure of the SDR claim to find customers that its rate of return, taking 100 percent of the computed interest and the appreciation or depreciation against particular currencies into account, has been less than the total return on the strongest currencies. Ex post, the same can be said about any successful common stock—it has outperformed total return on an average portfolio. But that does not prevent most investors from preferring diversified to highly concentrated portfolios. In the exchange market, any currency may be expected to position itself so that its total return, interest plus expected appreciation, is equal to that of other currencies, allowing for factors of convenience and political risk. Ex post it will undoubtedly turn out that some currencies appreciated or depreciated in ways not expected, making total returns unequal. An investor gifted with superior foresight could take advantage of this. But the average investor or monetary authority will be better off with the lower risk of a diversified portfolio, of which the SDR claim and, to a lesser extent, the European Currency Unit (ECU) are prime instances.

A means of easing the transition to a multicurrency-reserve system and of avoiding the market effects of sales of dollars for other currencies is sometimes suggested. It consists in an arrangement whereby the monetary authorities of potential reserve-currency countries would make available their currencies to foreign monetary authorities against payment in dollars outside the exchange market. The same avoidance of market disturbance, but with less risk for the buyer and less exposure to reserve-currency status for the seller, could be achieved if a central bank in that situation were to issue SDR liabilities. So long as SDR claims are not widely acceptable among central banks, a central bank issuing such liabilities would probably have to stand ready to convert them back into dollars or into its own currency at the prevailing exchange rate. Eventually, SDR claims might move in official or private-market channels much as bank liabilities denominated in national currencies do today. The risk for the issuing bank, which acquires dollars, would in any event be less if it issues SDR liabilities against these dollars than if it issues its own currency.

No Return to the Gold Standard

The rise in the price of gold has encouraged suggestions that the monetary problems of the world could be solved by putting gold back in the center of the picture, fixing its price (by committing to buy and sell at this price), and starting a new ballgame. The implausibility of these proposals is easily seen if one notes their consequences. Suppose a single country were to fix a price for gold. It is most unlikely that that price would be one at which the market neither wants to sell nor buy gold on balance. If the price is too low, the country will find itself selling out its gold reserves to the market. If the price is too high, the country will find itself acquiring large amounts of gold and pouring out liquidity. The experience of the gold pool of the 1960s, which operated in a world still accustomed to stability, is a faint foretaste of that situation. The experience of the United States during the 1930s is also indicative. Following the rise in the price of gold from $20.67 to $35.00 per ounce, U.S. gold holdings rose from 195 million ounces in January 1934 to 419 million ounces in January 1939, although some of the movement probably reflected war fears.

If several countries were to fix the price of gold, they then effectively would have fixed their exchange rates against each other. We would be back in the Bretton Woods system, but with much higher rates of inflation and greater variation of inflation rates. Exchange rates would quickly get out of line, and the gold pegs would be broken.

Such a result could be avoided only if countries were to subject their domestic policies to a severe discipline designed to keep their domestic price levels and their balance of payments in line with arbitrarily fixed exchange rates. That would mean the full discipline of the gold standard. Some of the proponents of a return to gold seem to desire the imposition of such discipline. Whether that kind of harsh discipline is desirable, or whether it would just make us repeat the experience of 1931–1933, its achievement today seems altogether out of reach. For some countries, moreover, the discipline might work in reverse—forcing them to inflate when they do not want to inflate.

The more likely consequence of the rise in the price of gold is a reduction in discipline, if gold-holding countries were to take advantage of their newfound wealth. Looser fiscal policies and monetary policies, and looser balance-of-payments behavior, could all be financed if present gold profits were mobilized by a write-up of gold assets. It will take some effort to prevent this from happening in particular circumstances.

Between Fixed and Freely Floating Rates

Since generalized floating began in March 1973, the degree of acceptance of free floating has varied from country to country and from time to time. To the extent that there ever was acceptance of perfectly clean floating, there clearly has been a movement away from that position. At the same time, however, there has been some convergence of views internationally that exchange rates cannot be determined by fiat or market intervention but must be left to the determination of fundamental factors such as the rate of inflation, the current account, capital movements, and the rate of interest. It is recognized, of course, that these fundamentals are in good part determined by national policy actions.

The difficulty of controlling exchange-rate movements by intervertion was demonstrated, for instance, in 1977, when foreign central banks bought approximately $35 billion without being able to prevent the decline of the dollar. Japan, over the period January 1979–January 1980, reduced its reserves by about $12 billion without preventing a substantial depreciation of the yen.

Nevertheless, in a minor key, market intervention has been recognized as a means of countering not only day-to-day disorder but also disorder in a broader sense. The history of exchange-rate movements during the period of floating suggests that exchange rates often overshoot on the upside as well as on the downside. Whether this reflects simply speculative bubbles and bandwagon effects or differences in the speed with which asset markets and goods markets clear, a case has been seen to exist for countering excessive market movements. For the United States, this has meant a shift in the preponderance of intervention in the principal exchange-rate relationship, the dollar/deutsche mark rate, from the Bundesbank to the Federal Reserve and Treasury. This has largely relieved the United States of the popular foreign charge of "benign neglect" of its balance of payments and its currency, undeserved as that comment was in the light of U.S. policies outside the exchange markets. Other countries, of course, have intervened in dollars for much larger amounts than the United States. But so long as these interventions are perceived as isolated episodes relating to the particular circumstances of those countries, the action seems to be interpreted as directed toward the country's own currency rather than toward influencing the dollar.

Appreciation versus Depreciation

Much of Bretton Woods thinking about exchange-rate policy derived from a fear of competitive depreciation. If this fear ever prevailed during the period of generalized floating since 1973, it has proved to be superfluous. The much more general tendency among countries has been to aim at a strong currency.

Many factors have contributed to this. Nowadays, a country suffering from unemployment can deal with it by domestic expansion. It needs no recourse to exchange depreciation to promote employment by stimulating exports. A declining exchange rate, on the other hand, has been observed to contribute to inflation and also to reduce the scope for domestic expansionary measures that would create adverse exchange-rate expectations. Vicious cycles of inflation and depreciation have acquired an ominous reputation, and virtuous cycles of appreciation and lower inflation have seemed worthy of emulation.

With regard to the dollar, the case for strength has gained from its reserve-currency role. Weakness of the currency in which the world carries its reserves, in which it trades and invests, is bound to create uncertainty, instability, and a propensity to systemic changes. Not all currencies can rise at the same time, but during a period of worldwide inflation all countries can pursue domestic policies designed to strengthen their currency to their own and the common good.

Financing versus Adjustment

When the first OPEC price increase hit the world and created the prospect of a period of enormous deficits, it was widely recognized that a universal effort to eliminate these deficits by internal contraction or depreciation would be futile and possibly disastrous. Now that OPEC-induced deficits are mounting again, the same issue reappears but with different accents. Countries that relied heavily on financing their deficits instead of adjusting them away during the earlier round will find it preferable to lean the other way this time. Their debt burdens, and the limited capacity of banks to accumulate obligations of particular countries, make this advisable. Thus, within the spectrum that runs from adjustment to financing of deficits for countries already heavily in debt, the accent should shift in the direction of earlier adjustment and less financing. Given that the OPEC-imposed deficits in the aggregate cannot be reduced quickly, this would mean that countries that are able to finance their deficit would have to accept larger deficits.

Conclusion

As we view the evolution of the international monetary system, we have reason to reject the allegation that the system is in the process of disintegration. It is true that fixed rates have come to an end, that we may be moving to a multi-currency system, and that the appearance of shifting trends in lieu of stable rules of international financial behavior may convey the impression of disintegration. But the system has produced on the whole good results. The first oil crisis has been weathered, trade has expanded, international capital flows have been enormous. The ultimate calamity—worldwide trade restrictions and a freezing over of international payments as happened during the 1930s—has been conspicuously avoided. We are now facing a new test, and its outcome will be determined more by avoidance of that ultimate calamity rather than by any particular evolution of the world's monetary system.

15 The International Monetary and Cyclical Situation

Experience with Floating Rates

The floating exchange-rate system has helped us to overcome a period of great difficulties characterized by the oil crisis, a world recession, and high rates of inflation. But there seems to be a widespread sense of uneasiness about the working of this system and where it may take us. There also seems to be a broad-based belief that the exchange-rate fluctuations that have occurred within the floating system have been excessive and that we should act to reduce them. Evidence of these beliefs is the creation of the European Monetary System and the policies initiated in the United States on November 1, 1978.

I would like to examine the sources of this dissatisfaction with the floating-rate system. It is easy enough to point to its defects. But these defects must be evaluated relative to some feasible alternative. There is no doubt that if we could have fixed rates while continuing to enjoy free movement of goods and of capital as we do, that would be preferable. But that is not the option. Worldwide fixed rates could be achieved today, if at all, only by a system of tight trade and exchange controls. That is not an acceptable alternative. We must ask ourselves, therefore, what we do not like about the floating system and how its defects could be remedied.

It is fair to say that the floating system, when it was imposed on the world by force majeure, was oversold and overadvertised. It was thought that the system would allow each country to pursue the domestic policies of its choice, unimpeded by balance-of-payments constraints. It was also thought that the system would insulate national economies against international disturbances. We have seen that this did not happen. Although individual-country experience naturally differs, countries generally found their domestic-policy choices constrained, because efforts, for instance, to stimulate the domestic economy quickly led to depreciating exchange rates and consequent domestic inflation. Efforts to curb inflation created the risk of making a currency too attractive, leading to excessive exchange-rate appreciation or the need for exchange-market intervention that threatened to undermine price stability by excessive increases in the money supply.

The promise of speedy adjustment of payments imbalances through exchange-rate movements has remained unfulfilled, perhaps because the very ease

---

This chapter was originally presented on June 18, 1979, before a meeting sponsored by the Landeszentralbank in Berlin, Berlin, Germany.

with which exchange rates could move has diminished political pressure to adopt appropriate fiscal and monetary policies.

The ups and downs of exchange rates have tended to accelerate world inflation, because prices rose rapidly where currencies declined but remained sticky where currencies appreciated.

Vicious circles seem to have developed in which exchange-rate depreciation feeds inflation and accelerating inflation, in turn, feeds back on the exchange rate. Countries with appreciating currencies have found themselves caught up in virtuous circles, with cheaper imports reducing inflation and reduced inflation further strengthening the currency. These vicious and virtuous circles have threatened to polarize the world into countries with strong and weak currencies, which has come uncomfortably close to splitting the world into strong and weak countries.

It is not surprising, therefore, that the evolution of the world's monetary system has brought us to a phase in which exchange-market considerations have become a major priority. Both in Europe and in the United States, this new orientation has led to new forms or at least a new scale of exchange-market intervention. It is important to be clear, however, what exchange-market intervention can accomplish and what it cannot. Exchange-market intervention can deal with movements that are overly rapid and clearly excessive, of the sort that plainly seem to have occurred. We have lost the earlier faith, if ever we had it, that the market would at all times set exchange rates at the right level. Intervention that counteracts market disorder and helps fundamental factors to assert their influence over exchange rates is promising. Not only does it hold out hope of minimizing the cost of excessive fluctuations, it can also contribute to greater stability of prices, trade, and economic activity generally and thus, again, to greater exchange-rate stability. A precondition of such intervention is recognition of when exchange-rate movements require correction. Nobody can say with any assurance what is the ''right'' exchange rate. But it should not be impossible to recognize market disorder that is producing rates that are clearly wrong.

Intervention in exchange markets will not succeed if it runs counter to fundamental economic developments. That has been proved abundantly by the failure, in 1977 and the first part of 1978, of the efforts of central banks to stem the decline of the dollar. It was only after U.S. policies, in combination with the decline in the dollar, had suceeded in putting the U.S. payments deficit on a clearly declining trend that intervention became promising and was indeed successful. In combination with a high level of interest rates and much improved budgetary picture, intervention was successful in correcting some of the excesses that had occurred in the exchange market.

Lasting stability of exchange rates can come only from stability and international compatibility of the fundamentals—prices, growth, interest rates, and payments balances. National policies, particularly with respect to inflation—

and I regret that I must say this particularly of the United States—have left much to be desired. The growing dissatisfaction with instability of exchange rates provides a further impetus to improve performance in these areas. In other words, if the world wants more stable exchange rates, it must accept a stronger balance-of-payments discipline. Efforts to combate inflation will gain strength from the perceived desirability of reducing exchange-rate fluctuations.

Inflation and exchange rates are related, of course, also in an inverse sense. Not only is exchange-rate stability dependent on control of inflation; the reduction of inflation, in turn, can be aided by an upward movement of the exchange rate. This has become very apparent in the countries that have had rising exchange rates. The contrary—a falling currency causing additional inflation—has been observable in the United States. Exchange-rate policy thus becomes an instrument in the effort to overcome inflation. It should be clear, however, that it is a very limited instrument. Any effort to push exchange rates to unrealistic levels is condemned to failure in the light of the predictable reaction of the markets. Furthermore, such action on the part of any one country could only be at the expense of all the rest. A stronger exchange rate for one country means a weaker rate for others. Less inflation for the first country, therefore, means more inflation for the rest. Only the correction of any prevailing undervaluation of an exchange rate is an appropriate anti-inflation policy.

Furthermore, although each country should seek to achieve an exchange rate that permits appropriate balance in its external accounts, with appropriate allowance for capital movements, it is clear that this should not be done by seeking to coordinate rates of inflation at some common denominator. The world has learned—some countries, indeed, had no need to learn—that inflation is an evil. A prosperous and socially just economic system is not possible without honest money. The objective everywhere must be, therefore, not to coordinate rates of inflation but to reduce them. The proper function of exchange rates in this process is to move so as to maintain payments equilibrium. When all major countries have achieved reasonable price stability, should that day ever come, the need for exchange-rate movements will have been minimized.

Reserve Currencies

A more active intervention policy, relative to market conditions, requires consideration of the currency or currencies in which intervention is to be conducted and reserves are to be held. In the past, the dollar was the world's principal, and for most countries sole, reserve and intervention currency. The United States, meanwhile, relied principally on swap arrangements with foreign central banks to obtain the means of intervention. In execution of the policies initiated on November 1, 1978, the United States has become a country holding foreign-currency reserves of some magnitude, through actions such as borrowings by the Treasury in deutsche marks and Swiss francs, sales of Special Drawing Rights (SDRs), and drawings on the International Monentary fund. As a result, the United States now holds reserves in deutsche marks, Swiss francs, and Japanese yen. This allows somewhat greater freedom of action than sole reliance on swap facilities.

Numerous other countries meanwhile have also added deutsche marks, Swiss francs, yen, and other currencies to their reserves. This is a change from past practice, when the dollar was regarded as the obvious intervention medium because of its wide international usability, the ease with which investments of reserves balances could be made and liquidated in the U.S. money market, and the economies-in-transactions costs that resulted from these circumstances. Recently, some holders of international balances have taken a portfolio approach to the investment of their reserves, seeking to reduce risk and stabilize return by diversification. These activities probably have contributed in some degree to exchange-market instability, although they have not impeded the recovery of the dollar from the low levels of October 1978.

In this way, the deutsche mark, the Swiss franc, and the yen have moved further along the road to being reserve currencies, and only sterling has dropped out. The world as a whole has moved a step further along the road to a multireserve-currency system. The brief experience of the United States in holding foreign currencies for intervention has revealed some relatively minor technical problems that nevertheless deserve to be examined among the pros and cons of a multireserve-currency system. Investments in the currencies acquired cannot be made with the same ease with which investments can be made in dollar assets. This is partly the result of controls on capital inflows of some of the incipient reserve-currency countries. More broadly, however, it reflects the relative narrowness of their financial markets and the fact that large-scale operations in these currencies, both for investment and for intervention, have consequences for the monetary, foreign exchange, and capital-market policies of these countries. Countries holding dollars as reserves have rarely found it necessary to engage in negotiation or even consultation with the United States when they needed to invest or mobilize funds or intervene in exchange markets to buy or sell dollars. The natural breadth of U.S. financial markets has been assisted in achieving this result by special investment facilities offered by the U.S. Treasury through nonmarketable issues of U.S.-government obligations. This has resulted in a very flexible use of the U.S. dollar by foreign monetary authorities. Given the different structure of the financial markets of the incipient reserve-currency countries, the question arises whether it is possible or advisable for them to offer the same kind of facilities.

The German and Swiss authorities have made it clear that they do not welcome the advancement of their currencies to reserve-currency status. The Japanese authorities appear to be taking a neutral attitude, neither favoring nor inhibiting the development of the yen as a reserve currency. The German and Swiss authorities seem to be concerned about both the exchange-rate and the financial-market implications of large international flows in their currencies. Past experience indicates that these movements can indeed cause serious disturbances for monetary and foreign-exchange-rate policies.

From an American point of view, I believe, these concerns are entirely understandable. They throw a new light on the often-made claim that the United States has taken unfair advantage of the dollar's role as a reserve currency. It is true that at times the United States has received easy financing of its international deficit thanks to that role of the dollar. On the other hand, that role has often been a severe burden. It has caused exchange-rate movements that were unrelated to the U.S. balance of payments. It has at times constrained the ability of the dollar to reflect fundamentals of the exchange market, by forcing the United States into the familiar role of the "*n*th currency," that is, the role of a country that must be passive with respect to its exchange rate because that rate is determined by the exchange-market intervention decisions or policies of the "$n - 1$" other countries. The reserve role of the dollar has not interfered with U.S. monetary management, perhaps not so much because of the sheer size of the U.S. short-term financial market as owing to the presence in that market of nonbank investors, including business firms and individuals, which allows the Federal Reserve to control more effectively bank reserves and money supply. This facility is largely lacking in the incipient reserve-currency countries.

But perhaps the principal burden of being a reserve-currency country comes from the softening of balance-of-payments discipline that such a country experiences. It may be helpful from time to time not to have to take unpalatable fiscal or monetary policy measures to restore balance-of-payments equilibrium. But that is a benefit often dearly bought at the price of trouble later. The countries that today are candidates for reserve-currency status do not need and would not benefit from the balance-of-payments support that this role can bring. Neither did the United States in the days after World War II when the dollar became the world's reserve currency. It seems to be the nature of the process by which the market elevates particular currencies to reserve-currency status that the market first singles out currencies precisely because they are strong and that performance of the reserve role subsequently weakens discipline and weakens the currencies. Being placed in the passive role of an *n*th currency whose exchange rate is determined by the exchange rate decision of the $n - 1$ contributes to this weakening. Weakening of discipline and the passive role of an *n*th currency have been the experience of first Britain and then, the United States. It is difficult not to have sympathy for the reluctance of some countries to take the risk of moving along that road.

From the point of view of the world economy, a multicurrency-reserve system has still another risk. This is the risk that, during the latter phases of the Bretton Woods system, was known as the problem of confidence and that focuses on the uneasy symbiosis of dollar, gold, and the SDR. Today, the problem could take the form of how to deal with shifts by the private market and central banks among reserve currencies as they observe changes in the relative attractiveness of these assets. As noted earlier, this has already given rise to reserve diversification on the part of some central banks. No doubt it has given rise also to diversification of corporate-liquidity balances on the part of some large multinational firms. One is bound to wonder whether extension of this system will not give rise to mounting problems of international instability as profit-oriented investment managers take hold increasingly of the management of international balances.

Yet such efforts to benefit from currency fluctuations in the end are likely to be self-defeating for the participants while causing damage to all. Perhaps I may be permitted to draw a parallel with the experience of U.S. stock-market investors. In the late 1960s, "performance" became the rage in the stock market. So-called performance or "go-go" mutual investment funds began to dominate the scene. Gradually it became apparent, however, that in the nature of the market there is no reliable way of doing better than the market. All available information is instantly incorporated into stock prices; there are never any clearly over- or undervalued stocks, and the market is what mathematicians call a "random walk." The subsequent experience of the stock market was that it became dominated by professional operators, became very jumpy, uncomfortable for most participants, and eventually altogether lost the favor of investors. Today all the smart security analysts are buying bonds. I hope that no analogous experience is ahead for the foreign-exchange market.

The stock-market experience produced a very interesting development within the market itself. It was recognized that to minimize risk, at a given rate of return, required maximum diversification. Thus, the best policy for an investor might be to distribute his holdings in accordance with a broad-based stock-market index and to forego the questionable benefits of expensive analysis of individual securities. In this way, "index funds" were born and have had a modest vogue. One could visualize a similar development in the exchange market. Instead of trying to shift from one currency into another in hope of catching those that appreciate, the manager of an exchange portfolio might simply diversify using a principle similar to that of an index fund. In the foreign-exchange field, two well-known index funds already exist—their names are SDR and European Currency Unit (ECU). These "baskets," to return to the language of the foreign-exchange market, provide built-in diversification according to fixed ratios. They eliminate the problems, for the world community, of shifts among reserve currencies. The experience of the stock market suggests that, after initial attempts to do better than the market, an investor may sensibly arrive at a fairly stable distribution of his portfolio. We might find ourselves moving in the same direction in the exchange market, perhaps after extensive and painful experience in vainly trying to do better by shifting around. Might it not be better to move to an index-based system more expeditiously than by moving there via a multireserve-currency system?

I raise the question without feeling at all sure of the answer. Nor, equally importantly, would I know how the world could shift to an SDR or ECU system instead of continuing its present drift toward a multicurrency system. I shall pursue the question in terms of the SDR, since that provides broader diversification and since the ECU is already anchored in the reserves of the countries participating in the European Monetary System. I suspect that an SDR system is preferable to a multicurrency system, provided the SDR is sufficiently attractive and inspires sufficient confidence. To date, we have had relatively little experience with it. Would countries commit substantial proportions of their reserves to an abstraction such as this unit? Or would they prefer the concreteness of individual currencies? Only experience can tell, and I hope it will not be a painful experience.

It should be noted that an SDR-based system can function without large-scale SDR issues by the International Monetary Fund. It could function, for instance, on the basis of SDR-denominated liabilities issued by the central banks of those countries whose currencies today are candidates for reserve-currency status and who prefer this distinction. Such SDR-denominated liabilities would have to be redeemable on demand against a national currency, although not against reserve assets, if the monetary authority owning the SDR claim wanted to use that national currency for intervention. In that way, such a national currency would not be a reserve currency, even though it served as an intervention currency. The monetary authorities owning the SDR claim would have an SDR risk instead of a risk in the foreign currency. The central bank issuing the SDR claim would have an SDR risk too, but, the SDR being a basket of national currencies, the likely range of fluctuations would always be less than that of any single national currency. The necessary legal powers, of course, would have to be established, and interest rates and other features would have to be market oriented and competitive.

A more immediately viable means of moving the SDR closer to the center of the international monetary system—where it belongs by common understanding expressed in the Articles of Agreement of the International Monetary Fund—would be a substitution account in the International Monetary Fund. A substitution account is more than a solution in search of a problem, as has sometimes been alleged. The problem is how to promote the role of the SDR. A substitution account provides such an opportunity. It deserves careful study, therefore, which it is receiving in the IMF. From what I have said it should be clear that the establishment of a substitution account in the IMF, that would receive dollars and issue SDR claims on the account backed by those dollars, must be conceived as a means of long-run improvement of the international monetary system. In that sense, a gradual substitution of SDRs for dollars may meet the purposes of the participating countries, including those of the United States. It should not be conceived or designed as a means for dealing with the immediate international condition of the dollar.

The Euromarkets

No talk about the international monetary scene today would be complete without some reference to the Euromarkets. Of late, I believe, there has been an improved understanding of the role of these markets, especially the Eurodollar market. We are not dealing here with magnitudes in the many hundreds of billions of dollars. Those statistics are the result of adding up interbank deposits, both within and outside the area of the market. Monetary liabilities of the market after excluding all interbank deposits and excluding also all those deposits that are already counted as part of some national money supply, such as the German money supply, are of the order of a little over $100 billion.

Nor are the Euromarkets "out of control," as has sometimes been alleged. They are controlled, in a monetary sense, by the interest rate prevailing in the Euromarket for each currency, the level of which may encourage or discourage borrowing. That interest rate, in turn, is tied to the interest rate in the home country, through arbitrage, provided that there is freedom of capital movements between the Euromarket and the home market. In the Eurodollar market, for instance, the interest rate has closely matched the corresponding certificate-of-deposit rate in the United States ever since controls over the outflow of bank funds were eliminated in 1974 and the aftermath of the Herstatt failure had been overcome. Where, as in the case of the Federal Republic of Germany and Switzerland as well as many other countries, there are controls over flows from or to the respective Euromarket, this interest-rate link will be weaker. On the other hand, it is wrong to say that the Euromarkets do not "create" money and credit but merely intermediate flows that otherwise would take place in equal magnitude through national channels. For the dollar, the proof of that pudding is very simple. If we consolidate the balance sheet of the Eurodollar market with the balance sheet of the domestic U.S. banking system, by adding together the respective deposits and assets, the combined deposit volume and credit volume would, of course, be considerably larger than that existing today in the United States. In particular, the volume of deposits would be larger than could be sustained by existing reserves supplied to the market by the Federal Reserve. That volume of reserves, therefore, could not have come into existence given the policies that the Federal Reserve has pursued with respect to money and credit. To make possible the creation of a volume of deposits equal to the combined deposits of the Euromarket and the domestic U.S. banking system, the Federal Reserve would have had to pursue a considerably more expansionary reserve policy than it actually has. The Euromarket has, therefore, in some measure, "created" money and credit outside the control of the Federal Reserve and has thereby increased the total volume of dollar assets and liabilities in the world, although not by an exorbitant amount.

Much the same situation, broadly speaking, exists for the Federal Republic with respect to the Euromarket, which for the deutsche mark is in good part located in Luxembourg. There is some expansion of deutsche mark money and credit outside the immediate control of the Bundesbank. The reserves that the Bundesbank has supplied to sustain the deposits of the German banking system would not be sufficient if the deutsche mark liabilities of the Luxembourg banking system were added to those of the German banking system.

Both the United States and the Federal Republic have open to them the same opportunity of controlling the creation of money and credit in their currency. They can slow the expansion of money and credit in the domestic market, over which they have control. This will raise interest rates in the domestic market and, given a well-functioning link to the Euromarket, interest rates there, too. Then the combined expansion of the two markets can proceed at whatever the monetary authorities regard as the appropriate rate.

The trouble with this solution is that it compels the monetary authorities to slow down disproportionately the growth of credit in the domestic market. The Euromarket component, although it also will be slowed by higher interest rates, will still be expanding faster than the total market. This is hard on the domestic economy, and particularly on domestic borrowers who have no access to the Euromarket. On the other hand, if the monetary authorities focus only on the domestic market, as they have done so far, ignoring the expansion in their currency going on in the Euromarket, they would be facilitating more expansionary and perhaps inflationary conditions than they intended or are even aware of. Over time, as the Euromarket component of the total market for any currency expands, controls over the aggregate volume of money and credit may altogether slip from their hands under these circumstances.

Several remedies are available. One would be to equalize competitive conditons between the Euro and the domestic sections of the market. This could be done, to an approximation, by removing the competititve advantage bestowed on the Euromarket by the absence of reserve requirements. Reserve requirements could be established on Eurocurrencies. Alternatively, they could be removed on comparable deposit liabilities of U.S. banks, that is, large time deposits of all maturities. A second approach would be to impose special restraints on the expansion of the Euromarket, by subjecting deposits or loans to some relation to capital. The restraint would have to apply to the Euromarket and not the domestic market, since an overall ratio would allow each bank to continue expanding in the Euromarket at the expense of its domestic business. Liquidity ratios, limiting liabilities to some ratio of liquid assets, could also be considered as a means of controlling this market.

It is by no means certain that even adequate controls over Eurobanking will be able to prevent overexpansion in other sectors of the Euromarkets. Financiers have proved inventive in designing new instruments that could escape the reach of existing controls. A market for loans outside the banks, perhaps with bank cooperation, could develop in short-term assets such as commercial paper, as it already exists in Eurobonds. The monetary authorities could always control aggregate credit expansion by raising the interest rate, which would affect all markets. But the dilemma posed by differential rates of expansion in the domestic and the Euromarkets might remain. Ultimately, this might then lead to controls over the movements of capital to cope with such developments.

The world, and in particular the Federal Republic of Germany and the United States, has a great interest in the maintaining of free international capital markets. It is important, therefore, to develop techniques that will keep the expansion of the Euromarkets manageable, without placing domestic markets at a disadvantage and without recourse to controls.

16 Evolution of the International Monetary System

The world business cycle is passing through a phase of great significance for the world economy and the functioning of the international monetary system. The growth rates of the U.S. economy on one side and most industrial countries on the other have been converging. Until early 1978, the United States was expanding at a rate above its long-run potential, while most other countries were expanding well below their potential. According to many projections, we are entering a phase in which the rate of growth of other industrial countries will, on average, exceed that of the United States.

What we are witnessing is a dissynchronized world business cycle, a condition, in other words, where national cycles are out of phase with each other. Much of the turmoil that we are observing in the world today can be traced to this dissynchronization.

Before examining what a dissynchronized business cycle has done to the world, however, we should remember the experience we had with the previous cycle, culminating in 1973–1974, which was almost perfectly synchronized. All major countries, at that time, were moving in step and were then operating at peak capacity. Widespread shortages prevailed. There was no way in which excess demand in one economy could be compensated for by excess supplies in another. Consequently, competing buyers drove up prices mercilessly all over the world. When the bubble burst, inventories were excessive, orders vanished, and, with the additional burden of a quadrupled price of oil, a severe recession became inevitable. It was then that the thought took hold that if the world economy were to continue to be cyclical, as it has been for 150 years or more, somewhat less sunchronization would be helpful. Peaks and valleys would be smoothed out, shortages in one country could be overcome by excess supplies elsewhere, the danger of a severe recession greatly reduced.

Effects of Dissynchronization

That wish has been granted. Five years later, we find ourselves in a dissynchronized expansion. Are the results what we expected them to be? Let me begin with the good features, which do not seem to have attracted a great deal

This chapter was published in *Challenge*, January–February 1979, pp. 13–17, and was based on a paper delivered at the Conference of the "Zeitschrift für das Gesamte Kreditwesen," Frankfurt, Germany, November 10, 1978.

of attention. The United States, and most other industrial countries, are now almost four years beyond the trough of the recession as it was recorded in the United States in early 1975. Continued expansion is expected in the United States at about its long-run potential rate of roughly 3 percent. Other economies, after some slow starts and a few relapses, are now growing at somewhat faster rates. Since the length of cyclical expansion, at least in the United States, has historically been from two to three years, the longevity of the present expansion is a distinct achievement, probably attributable in no small measure to the dissynchronized pattern of the present cycle.

The dissynchronized pattern, however, has not been particularly favorable to the functioning of the international monetary system. The reason is that dissynchronized behavior produced imbalances of trade, which affected exchange rates. These, in turn, affected rates of inflation, which reacted back on exchange rates. Moreover, as the cycle advanced, the approach to full employment generated inflationary pressures in some countries, while excess capacity still was pushing down inflation elsewhere.

During the present cycle, it was the United States that was leading in cyclical phase. The United States, therefore, found its imports rising rapidly, while its exports were lagging, and a large current-account deficit developed. Japan and Germany, expanding slowly, had the opposite experience. Some countries fell in between.

The ensuing divergent pattern of deficits and surpluses set in motion exchange-rate movements which in turn began to influence price developments. The declining exchange rate contributed to inflation in the United States. Rising exchange rates in Germany, Japan, and Switzerland helped to reduce inflation there. The inflation differential further weakened the dollar while the currencies of countries in strong surplus strengthened.

Meanwhile, as the U.S. economy began to approach the full-employment zone, renewed price pressures began to make themselves felt. Previously, the United States had succeeded in bringing inflation down from a peak of around 12 percent in 1974 to the 5 percent zone shortly following the 1974–1975 recession. More rapid expansion, however, and policies supporting this expansion, as well as the institutional pecularities of U.S. collective bargaining, kept the rate of inflation from falling further. A declining dollar and mounting economic activity caused the U.S. inflation rate to reaccelerate from the 5 to 6 percent range after a period of perhaps two years during which it had remained relatively constant.

In the countries whose economies were lagging, an opposite pattern occurred. Maintenance of substantial slack helped to bring down inflation. Policies designed to accomplish this objective were supported, in the case of Germany, Japan, and Switzerland, by a rise in exchange rates. The latter, in turn, responded both to a movement toward current-account surplus and to diminishing inflation. In this way, the leading industrial countries developed sharply contrasting patterns. Some countries, including the United Kingdom and Italy, fell in between, suffering both high inflation and slow growth. These eventually found themselves compelled to restrain their economies in order to remove current-account deficits which threatened further exchange-rate depreciation and inflation.

Rates of Inflation, Interest, and Exchange

It is noteworthy that during this period of contrasting movements, some features of the separate economies involved came into good alignment, while others did not. In the major countries, interest rates came roughly into alignment with rates of inflation. Low-inflation countries had low interest rates, countries with higher inflation had higher rates. Particularly in the United States, Germany, Switzerland, and to some extent Japan, differences among rates of inflation were roughly equal to differences among interest rates. Real interest rates, that is, nominal interest rates adjusted for current inflation rates, were not very different among these countries. Where nominal interest rates were high, they nevertheless were, if not negative, at most barely positive in real terms.

Exchange rates, on the other hand, behaved very differently. For the most part, their movement failed to reflect nominal interest-rate differentials, frequently exceeding these differentials very substantially. Likewise, exchange-rage changes were greater than needed to reflect the change in purchasing power. Over prolonged periods, exchange rates, especially for the dollar, the yen, and the Swiss franc, but only to a lesser degree for the DMark, considerably under- and overshot exchange ralations based on relative price movements.

For the behavior of exchange rates, and the associated behavior of current-account deficits and surpluses, a variety of factors may be held responsibile. One of them is the well-known J-curve phenomenon. An exchange-rate movement that, over two or three years, may be expected to bring about greater balance in the current account, may in the short run produce the opposite effect, or perhaps a delayed effect. The volume of exports and imports does not respond instantaneously to changing prices and/or exchange rates. It takes some time before the more favorable exchange rate—for the depreciating country—and the less favorable rate—for the appreciating country—can have their full effect.

A similar J-curve phenomenon may occur in capital markets, although it has been less clearly demonstrated in that context. A rise in interest rates may be expected to attract capital to the country where it occurs. A rise in interest rates, or the expectation thereof, has an adverse effect on long-term financial and real assets. Bonds, the stock market, and perhaps other assets tend to decline as interest rates rise. The capital losses that investors could sustain from such moves can far exceed any gains that would accrue to others from investing at the new rates. While asset markets seek to establish a new base, therefore, the effect of rising interest rates is not necessarily to attract capital to the countries where the rise occurs. If investors move abroad during this period, the exchange rate may suffer. Once an adjustment has taken place, of course, the widened interest differential may well produce a much enlarged inflow of capital with attendant consequences for the exchange rate.

Pressures on the International Monetary System

All this demonstrates that in a dissynchronized expansion, considerable pressures are likely to converge on the international monetary system. Exchange rates may undergo movements that do not necessarily correspond to their values in any long-run equilibrium. For that reason, it is perhaps not exclusively of historical interest to inquire how a dissynchronized business cycle would have fitted into the precepts of the old Bretton Woods system. That system was exposed to dissynchronized cycles only rarely and in moderate degree, such as in 1958–1959 and the latter half of the 1960s. The prevailing view in those days was that ''when the United States catches cold, the rest of the world catches pneumonia.'' This implied a cycle led by, and synchronized with, the U.S. cycle. Nevertheless, the Bretton Woods system had one clear standard that could have been applied to a dissynchronized cycle: under the Bretton Woods code, only fundamental disequilibrium could justify and require an alteration in exchange rates. A cyclical disequilibrium, with other sources of imbalance absent, was to be ridden out. The ensuring current-acccount deficit was to be financed and dealt with by other adjustment measures, but not by exchange-rate depreciation.

In recent years, market forces have told us that the Bretton Woods prescription would probably not have been adhered to had it still been in effect today. They have told us this by moving exchange rates around rather sharply. The world has fared better under floating rates because in all probability it has been spared a series of exchange-rate crises that could have provoked counterproductive controls on capital movements. But the Bretton Woods precepts are not without their lesson. They remind us that there is a difference between a cyclical and a fundamental disequilibrium. That difference, of course, was never clearcut. No one would argue that the disequilibrium experienced by the world today is purely cyclical. For the United States, it is overlaid by the problem of oil imports. For Germany and Japan, it is overlaid by a variety of structural changes, including a slowing of long-term growth and reorientation toward lesser dependence on exports. Something similar could be said for numerous other countries.

But the cyclical component is important, and the Bretton Woods precept that cyclical movements should not give rise to permanent exchange-rate changes ought not to be altogether forgotten. Nor does today's floating-rate system, to which there appears to be no practical alternative, relieve us of the need to take adjustment action. ''Adjustment'' was one of the key words of the Bretton Woods system. Its successful implementation frequently eluded us, and the Bretton Woods system came to an end. But the need for adjustment has remained under the system of floating exchange rates.

Contrary to the views frequently expressed before floating began, floating exchange rates do not allow a country to adopt any kinds of domestic policies it chooses. A country that were to ignore the effect of its policies on inflation and on its exchange rate would quickly discover, from the behavior of both, the limits of its freedom of action.

Value of the Dollar

The United States has been very conscious that the value of the dollar depends on its domestic policies, and that the value of the dollar is enormously important both for its domestic well-being and for its internatinal economic and political relations. A number of actions attest to this.

First, the United States has brought its cyclical expansion to a soft landing at a rate of growth consistent with its long-term growth potential. This was accomplished by a reduction in the budget deficit which in 1976 stood at $66 billion. Early in 1978, the budget deficit for fiscal year 1979, which began October 1, 1978, was still projected at $60 billion. Now the deficit for fiscal year 1979 is expected to be less than $40 billion. It is recognized that such a deficit is still too large for a fully employed economy, and a reduction to $30 billion is expected for 1980.

Second, the Federal Reserve has tightened monetary policy, by seeking to limit the growth of the monetary aggregates. While the target for M_1 (currency and demand deposits) of 4 to 6.5 percent has been overshot by approximately 1.5 percentage points, it should be recognized that the M_1 target was extremely modest, considering that nominal GNP was expected to rise at a rate of 11 percent. The Federal Reserve is aware of the need for adequate monetary restraint. Recent increases in the discount rate, the latest by a full percentage point to an unprecedented level of 9.5 percent, as well as in the federal-funds rate, which is the principal focus of impact of Federal Reserve policy, attest to this. So does the increase in reserve requirements on large time deposits by almost $3 billion: the successful achievement of our targets for M_2 (M_1 plus bank time and savings deposits other than large negotiable certificates of deposit) and M_3 (M_2 plus deposits in thrift institutions) also is evidence of a policy of restraint.

Third, the United States has instituted a program of wage and price restraint. While the program is voluntary, it does not lack means of enforcement, through the procurement mechanism and through the action of regulatory agencies that set prices for certain regulated industries. The use of the tax system to encourage wage restraint, through a real-wage insurance, is also being proposed by President Carter.

Fourth, the United States has finally enacted energy legislation. A great effort to intensify conservation of energy and develop substitute sources for oil and gas is still ahead of us. Nevertheless, it should be noted that increases in the price of energy have been proportionately no smaller than in most other industrial countries. They have gone less far only because they started from a generally much lower level. The response of U.S. consumers and particularly of U.S. industry to higher energy costs has been about the same as abroad.

Fifth, the United States has also instituted an export-promotion program. The United States is a relative latecomer to this practice, which has been followed far more energetically for a long time by a number of its competitor countries, including Japan, Germany, France, and the United Kingdom. Some of these countries today are concerned about their own large surpluses and about the U.S. deficit. These concerns could be eased if more effective agreements could be arrived at to restrain competition in export promotion. The United States has been trying to facilitate such agreements.

Finally, to support its policies, especially the president's wage and price program, the United States also has strengthened its capacity for intervention in the exchange markets by putting in place a package of $30 billion of foreign-exchange resources, including sale of Special Drawing Rights (SDRs), drawings on the International Monetary Fund, sale of foreign-currency obligations by the Treasury, and enlargement of swap facilities on the part of the Federal Reserve. An increase in gold sales beginning in December 1978 was also announced. The United States expressed its determination to intervene, in cooperation with the governments and central banks of Germany and Japan and the Swiss National Bank, in a forceful and coordinated manner in the amounts required to correct the situation in the exchange markets.

Under the impact of these policies and developments, the U.S. current-account deficit today gives promise of substantial reduction over time. Econometricians have estimated that the full effect of the cyclical gap between the United States and the rest of the world accounts for something like $10 to $20 billion. That is to say, if the entire world were to move to full employment, the U.S. current account, which amounted to about $20 billion over the last twelve months, would be reduced by that order of magnitude. It has also been estimated that every percentage point of depreciation of the dollar, after adjustment for inflation, that is, in real terms, should reduce the deficit by $750 million to $1 billion over a period of two years. The dollar has depreciated, in real terms, about 12 to 15 percent over the last eighteen months, which again would imply a substantial reduction in the deficit. An improvement of 30 to 40 percent is a reasonable expectation.

Moves toward Stability

These developments should help the international monetary system regain a much greater measure of stability than it has recently shown, It is universally recognized that the stability of the system can only be attained by greater domestic price stability resting on appropriate fiscal and monetary policies. Actions in that direction are now under way in all countries.

In addition, evolution is progressing along two lines. Within Europe, action is afoot to create an area of monetary stability among countries willing to achieve a sufficient convergence of their policies to be able to sustain among themselves a system of fixed though adjustable exchange rates. Within the membership of the International Monetary Fund, arrangements have been put in place for surveillance of members' policies with respect to exchange rates and with respect to domestic policies affecting the exchange-rate system. The European effort, if designed properly, can make an important contribution, not only toward stability among the countries concerned, but also toward the strengthening and stability of the international monetary system and to the central role of the IMF within that system.

These developments characterize the present state of evolution of the international monetary system. The system cannot be static, and gradual change must be expected. The system must be capable of dealing with both synchronized and dissynchronized cyclical developments. It will best be able to accomplish this task, the advantages and difficulties of which I have tried to set forth here, if evolution proceeds in an enviroment of international cooperation and freedom of movement for goods and capital.

17 What Makes Exchange Rates Move?

Since the collapse in 1973 of the old system of fixed exchange rates, the world's major currencies have been floating. More accurately, some have been sinking, while others have been drifting up. The dollar, after an initial decline, now stands about 9 percent above the level at which it began its float. The U.S. Congress has voted to continue the system by approving an amendment to the statutes of the International Monetary Fund. How well has the four-year-old system worked to date? How workable does it promise to be hereafter?

Two Bretton Woods Constraints

Different countries have recorded very different experiences. The United States has been distinctly comfortable with floating. American policymakers have been freed of a pair of albatrosses that the old Bretton Woods system had hung around their necks.

One of these birds was gold convertibility. Under the Bretton Woods rules, as they had evolved in practice, the United States was the only country that was obligated to convert its currency into gold. Foreign central banks acquiring dollars could present their holdings and demand gold in exchange. This put U.S. policy in an acute predicament.

Since the United States is a very large country, its major fiscal and monetary policies have had to be guided mainly by domestic considerations, principally full employment, price stability, and economic growth. Policies with respect to the budget and interest rates could respond only marginally to the need to forestall a balance-of-payments deficit and to avoid thereby an accumulation of dollars in foreign hands. But the ensuing vulnerability to gold withdrawals posed a continuing threat not only to the United States, but to the stability of the world monetary system itself.

As U.S. payments deficits and foreign dollar holdings mounted, the United States found itself driven to increasingly embarrassing expedients to avoid gold losses. We tried to control the outflow of capital, thereby damaging American corporations, American banks and investors, and incidentally making London once more the world's banking capital. We found ourselves under pressure to pull back troops from Germany and elsewhere, or at least bring home their dependents. Ludicrous extremes, such as flying a jeep from Heidelberg to

---

This chapter was originally published in *Challenge*, July–August 1977, pp. 34–40.

Detroit to save repair costs in DMarks, became notorious. Valuable international bargaining power had to be invested in persuading foreign authorities not to withdraw gold and to help us window-dress our balance of payments to minimize the visible deficit.

With the suspension of gold convertibility, the long agony of the dollar came to an end. Foreign countries could continue to acquire dollars and hold them. But they could no longer put us under pressure by draining away our limited stock of gold. As a matter of self-interest as well as of international cooperation, the United States naturally would try to keep the dollar an attractive asset for foreign central banks to hold in their reserves. A degree of balance-of-payments discipline therefore remained. But the temptation to reach for uneconomic devices and to interfere with the free flow of capital and goods was much reduced.

The second constraint to which floating put an end was the control that other countries were able to wield over the exchange rate of the U.S. dollar. Under the Bretton Woods system, while the United States stabilized its currency in terms of gold, others stabilized theirs in terms of the dollar. By buying and selling dollars at a fixed rate against their own currency, other countries in the aggregate in fact fixed U.S. foreign exchange rates. They could devalue or revalue if their exchange rate no longer suited them. The United States could not.

Technically, the United States could change the dollar price of gold. But if foreign countries then maintained their peg to the dollar and moved their gold price in step with the United States, as was highly probable, changing the price of gold would not change a single exchange rate. The United States was condemned to passivity in its exchange-rate policy. It was denied this simple, albeit drastic, method of balance-of-payments adjustment. In the light of these handicaps, the much criticized benefit that the United States obtained under the Bretton Woods system—the financing of its payments deficits by countries willing to accumulate dollars—was a poor consolation.

Floating for the Strong and the Weak

Under the floating system, it is the forces of the market and not foreign countries that determine the exchange rate of the dollar. The control, to be sure, that the United States now has over the dollar rate is not very much greater than it was under the old system. For reasons to be discussed later on, intervention in the exchange market generally is not a feasible way for the United States to influence its exchange rate significantly. But while the market-determined dollar rate may not always be what we would like it to be, the market usually will price the dollar more advantageously to us than would other countries pursuing their self-interest. The danger of over- or undervaluation as a result of foreign decisions has been defused.

The United States is not the only country that feels comfortable under floating. Germany, whose DMark is the second most important currency in the world today, also likes the system. It does so mainly, however, for quite different reasons. Floating has freed German monetary policy and liberated Germany from the need to import inflation, which the old system imposed. To keep the DMark pegged to the dollar, Germany, under the Bretton Woods system, had to buy all the dollars that were offered. The German Bundesbank had to create large amounts of DMarks to purchase these dollars. Thus the inflow of dollars expanded money and credit in Germany and inflated the German economy. The restraining power of German monetary policy was undermined, if not totally paralyzed. If the Bundesbank raised interest rates, then dollars flowed in from abroad, the money supply expanded, and the restraint was nullified. The floating system has restored the effectiveness of monetary policy. An inflow of dollars, instead of expanding the reserves of the Bundesbank and the German money supply, now simply drives up the DMark. The Bundesbank has regained its freedom of action.

In addition, a rise in the DMark helps Germany fight inflation by lowering the price of imports. Cheaper imports mean less wage and price pressure. The improved German price outlook in turn tends to strengthen the DMark, which further cheapens imports. In this mamer a "virtuous circle" has got under way, with a rising DMark reducing inflation and reduced inflation encouraging a further rise in the DMark. A rising exchange rate, to be sure, presents a threat for exports such as small German automobiles. But, within limits, Germany appears willing to pay that price for better monetary control and less inflation. Countries with "strong" currencies, such as Switzerland, in general have had a similar experience with floating.

Disadvantages of Floating for Weak-Currency Countries

Countries with weak currencies have fared very differently. Under the old system, a country like Britain or Italy might rely on its fixed rate to help offset domestic inflation. If prices at home rose faster than they did abroad, the slower advance of import prices became a restraining factor. Once the pound or lira was floating, this benefit was no longer available. Domestic inflation was quickly translated into depreciation of the exchange rate. Import prices then went up, giving a further push to inflation, and so on. Even worse, the exchange rate, reacting to expectations of future inflation, might overshoot, lifting import prices even faster than domestic prices. A vicious circle could be triggered in this fashion, with inflation driving the exchange rate and the exchange rate driving inflation. Of course this circle could be broken by adopting strong fiscal and monetary policies that would give the market confidence in the currency. But such policies are harder to make stick when domestic inflation is accelerating than when it is slowing.

This sensitivity of the exchange rate to policies the market interprets as ''soft'' has a further cost: it limits the scope of antirecessionary action. Caught with both high inflation and high unemployment, countries like Britain and Italy have been unable to resort effectively to the usual stimulative policies. The immediate effect is to aggravate inflation and exchange-rate depreciation. The damage inflation does to investment and eventually employment exceeds any immediate gains from stimulating the economy.

Countries in this condition—and there are many more ''weak'' than ''strong'' countries—are condemned by the weakness of their currencies to wait for an ''export-led recovery.'' Quite contrary to the notion that a floating exchange rate would allow greater freedom to stimulate domestically, unhampered by worries about any ensuing payments deficit, floating has narrowed these countries' scope for stimulative action.

In this manner, floating has helped to polarize countries. The strong have become stronger, the weak weaker. For some of the latter, the economic, social, and political pressures associated with inflation and unemployment have reached alarming levels. Questions of ultimate stability and viability of societies loom. This puts the United States on notice that our floating comforts may carry too high a price tag in terms of our enlightened self-interest in the stability of our trade partners and allies. We must not allow ourselves to be trapped into the condition characterized by a medical bulletin reading ''operation successful, patient dead.''

It would be quite wrong, however, to conclude that the solution to this dilemma lies in the direction of a prompt return to fixed exchange rates. Under present disturbed conditions, that road is definitely closed, and it might remain impassable even if the countries with weak currencies managed to lift themselves up to a higher degree of stability. The means simply do not exist today, short of resorting to tight controls over trade as well as capital flows, to stabilize the exchange rate of a strongly inflating currency for any length of time. Nor would the countries with strong currencies, who are doing well under the floating system, want to become entrapped again in the pitfalls of fixed rates.

There is no answer for weak-currency countries, short of mending their policies and achieving a better degree of domestic price stability. This, for the reasons indicated, has become more difficult thanks to floating. They can be helped, on their uphill road, by financial support from the rest of the world. That support has indeed been forthcoming on a large scale. Much of it has taken the form of private lending, some of it intergovernmental or from international institutions. A floating system, with some assistance for the disadvantaged until they can reach firmer ground, seems to be the best that is within reach at present.

If today's weak-currency countries should conclude that floating taxes their strength excessively, one method of achieving at least partial exchange-rate stability would be to attach themselves to a group of countries maintaining stable rates among themselves. The European "Snake" is the prime example. The members of the Snake maintain their currencies stable with respect to other members of the group. They do this because they regard stability vis-à-vis a few major trade partners as worth the loss of some of the policy independence promised by free floating. So far, of course, weak-currency countries have moved in the opposite direction. Italy and France have left the Snake. The United Kingdom has not been a member since the advent of general floating. The costs of policy coordination and discipline appeared excessive to these countries. Sufficient disenchantment with floating might eventually cause them to change their minds, but the road back would be a long and tough one.

Effects of the Floating-Rate System

From the viewpoint of the world economy as a whole, finally, the floating-rate system so far must be seen as predominantly successful. It has done what the international monetary system is supposed to do: facilitate expanding trade and capital movements. Fears that floating might stifle their growth have been quite unnecessary so far. Since the dollar began to float in March 1973, the volume of world trade has increased by roughly 15 percent, despite the recession. International capital markets have never been more active. Banks in major financial centers tripled their foreign loans since 1972, which reached a level of $300 million in September 1976. Between 1973 and 1976, international bond issues nearly quadrupled, reaching almost $30 billion in 1976. Countries that had not been perceived as potential international borrowers have found access to credit. Fears of widespread trade and capital controls have not been realized so far. In fact, by alleviating concerns about payments imbalances, floating rates catalyzed the dismantling of capital-outflow controls in the United States and of capital-inflow controls in Germany. Nor have we witnessed competitive depreciation, trade wars, or any of the other calamities that one might have expected. All this has been achieved in the very difficult environment created by a quintupling of oil prices and an ensuing deep world recession.

Perfection, naturally, has eluded us, and the end of the day is not yet. The impact of floating has been very different for different countries. Polarization is an undeniable fact. The degree of instability, even among currencies of roughly comparable strength, has been a particular surprise. Many developing countries, too, have not been satisfied with the float, in which most of them have had to participate indirectly through a peg to some leading currency or currency "basket." While their criticism is based on an unrealistic comparison with some unattainable fixed-rate system, their desire for greater stability is understandable. Moreover, the worldwide threat of manipulation, competitive depreciation, and controls continues. As countries increasingly reach the limits of their international borrowing capacity, these risks increase. Much therefore will depend on how the system is managed and how it evolves.

Obviously the system is in a state of evolution. Nothing definitive can be said about the experience of four years, particularly in contrasting it with a system that, in essence, had served the world and served it well, generally, since the Napoleonic Wars. Monetary evolution proceeds largely by codifying and formalizing what has come into being spontaneously. Since no country today can be forced to give up any advantage it holds, negotiation of a system differing radically from what exists is not possible.

The New Rules of Jamaica

A set of rules reflecting the status quo was laid down in Jamaica early last year, through amendments of the Articles of Agreement of the International Monetary Fund. The United States has ratified them, and enough countries are expected to follow during 1977 to allow entry into force late in the year. The new rules differ from the old Bretton Woods rules principally in the treatment of changes in exchange rates. Under Bretton Woods, rates were fixed and cound be changed only in the case of fundamental disequilibrium. Under the Jamaica dispensation, rates are to float and to reflect underlying economic and financial factors. Thus, under the old system imbalances in trade and capital movements were to be financed, rates remaining stable in the face of seasonal, cyclical, and other fluctuations short of "fundamental disequilibrium." Under the new rules, they are to be allowed to move from day to day as seasonal, cyclical, and other factors shape the market's judgment. Countries are enjoined not to manipulate the system or to seek an unfair competitive advantage. The International Monetary Fund is to exert firm surveillance over countries' exchange-rate policies and to establish principles to guide these policies. The new system also permits a shift, by agreement, to another system, including a return to fixed exchange rates, the United States retaining an effective veto over any change.

Even though these rules are not yet in force there is widespread awareness of and, it is fair to say, adherence to them. All major countries are aware of the need to avoid actions that could be viewed as manipulation or "beggar-thy-neighbor" policies. Suspicions and accusations there have been, but by and large nothing serious.

The United States and "Clean Float"

Different countries have different interests in the interpretation of the rules, as they have in the international monetary system as a whole. The United States has a strong interest in keeping the float as clean as possible. Part of the attraction of the new system, as pointed out above, is that it puts an end to the control that other countries have wielded over the exchange rate of the dollar. That advantage is realized only, however, if other countries float cleanly.

U.S. interest in a clean float is enhanced by the fact that there is not much that the United States can do, by way of intervention, to affect the exchange rate of the dollar. The stock of dollar denominated assets in the world is enormous. In the view of most economists it is stocks of assets, not flows of transactions, which ultimately determine the exchange rate. To change the stock of dollar assets estimated roughly at $5 trillion in a significant way would require huge intervention purchases and sales. The exchange-market interventions of the Federal Reserve, however, ordinarily are small even compared with the interventions of the central banks of other countries—like dipping into the ocean with a thimble.

The United States has only extremely limited liquid international reserves—mainly $2.4 billion of Special Drawing Rights (SDRs) issued by the International Monetary Fund, and a reserve position in the Fund of about $4.4 billion. Our gold stock is illiquid and is not intended for use as an international monetary reserve. The United States has virtually no reserves of foreign currencies, in contrast to foreign countries that hold their reserves largely in dollars.

Since the dollar is the world's principal reserve currency, other countries can do most of their intervention in dollars. The United States would have to borrow foreign currencies in order to intervene in support of the dollar. It would also have to face the prospect that such intervention would distort the exchange rates of those currencies used with respect to others. The best we can aim to do is to let the dollar float cleanly, rather than try to influence the dollar rate. Of course, this does not preclude intervention to maintain order in exchange markets if there should be technical disturbances. Nor does it preclude action in case the dollar should be driven by market failure or foreign manipulation to clearly unrealistic high or low levels.

Other Countries Can Influence Their Rates

Other countries have a better opportunity to influence their rates, should they want to do so. The stock of assets denominated in most foreign currencies is typically small. Many countries do have sizable reserves. Many countries also have exchange controls which limit the role of the market in influencing their rate.

Fortunately, most of the industrial countries do not seem to have been strongly tempted so far to manipulate their exchange rates. The principal concern has always been that a country might seek to undervalue its rate in order to push its exports and stimulate its economy. But in contrast to the 1930s, countries today know that short of severe inflation they can stimulate domestically by running budget deficits. Stimulation by way of competitive-exchange depreciation worsens a country's terms of trade and, through higher import prices, contributes to inflation.

Overvaluation has shown itself to be a more frequent temptation in the last few years. In an effort to limit inflation and to soften the impact of the higher cost of oil, many countries have borrowed heavily abroad to finance payments deficits. Since deficits somewhere in the world cannot be avoided so long as OPEC has a surplus, some financing of deficits is unavoidable. There is a danger, however, that spending of borrowed money to intervene in exchange markets may become a substitute for adequate adjustment of payments balances, through better fiscal and monetary policies and lower exchange rates. In order to assure proper valuation of the dollar, the United States has an interest in seeing foreign countries avoid intervention aiming at either undervaluation or overvaluation.

There are methods other than exchange market intervention, of course, to influence an exchange rate. Interest rate policy will do it, or changes in the rate of growth of the money supply, as well as changes in controls over capital movements. When such measures are taken, it is often a delicate question whether the objective is to influence the internal economy or the foreign exchange rate. The IMF, in exercising "firm surveillance" over exchange rate policies will have to make this subtle but crucial distinction. Obviously few countries would be willing to give the IMF more control over their domestic policies than they have to give. In the case of the United States, in view of the natural priority assigned to domestic over international concerns, a domestic orientation of policy measures may normally be presumed. This does not apply necessarily to countries differently structured.

Should the IMF Set Targets?

There has been much debate about whether the IMF should establish targets, or target zones, for exchange rates. So long as there are differential rates of inflation, these "targets" might in fact have to be, not rates, but trends in rates, reflecting the changing competitiveness of individual currencies. Or they might be zones around these trends. These would serve to guide and evaluate countries' foreign exchange-rate policies. They should be equilibrium rates toward which market rates would tend anyway if left to themselves, although in the short run there might be substantial deviations reflecting seasonal, cyclical, and random factors. Trying to move or hold rates near such targets or zones would not necessarily interfere with the basic objectives of floating. It might remove some of the anomalies we have experienced, such as the reciprocal ups and downs of the DMark and the dollar. Historically, these movements have tended to be reversed after some time, reflecting the similarity of inflation rates in Germany and the United States. Movements of this kind nevertheless cause disturbances, particularly when new corporate-accounting rules compel their results to be reflected in corporate-earnings statements.

The Difficulties of Forecasting

The trouble with the target approach, quite aside from political problems, is the great uncertainty that shrouds the notion of equilibrium rates. There appears to be no convincing way of figuring out what they should be. This is demonstrated very concretely by the inability of market participants and economists to forecast market rates. Since successful forecasting would be very rewarding, much time and money is undoubtedly being spent on such efforts. None of the standard techniques employed seem to have paid off. Theoretically, purchasing-power parity should be a guide to future exchange rates. This principal says that exchange rates can be expected to move in proportion to differences in rates of inflation. If German inflation is 4 percent and U.S. inflation 6 percent, the DMark should appreciate at a rate of 2 percent per year against the dollar. But we have seen the DMark and the dollar fluctuate by as much as 15 percent against each other, reversing positions within a year or two. This quite fails to reflect the relative rates of inflation that have actually prevailed.

By another theory, interest-rate differentials should be a guide to rate movements. If the interest rate is 5 percent in Germany and 6 percent in the United States, investors will be equally well off in either DMark or dollar-denominated securities if the lower German rate is compensated by a 1 percent annual rise in the DMark against the dollar. But we have seen small changes in the interest-rate differential, which in any event could not be expected to last very long, seemingly trigger off much larger movements in the DMark-dollar rate.

By a third theory, the balance of payments could be regarded as a forecaster of exchange rates, although there is a question whether it tells us anything we do not already know from observing differentials in inflation rates. Experience shows that there are factors that may make the balance of payments very misleading as a forecaster of exchange rates.

Finally, the forward exchange rate could serve as a predictor of the future spot rates. The rate at which market participants are willing to negotiate today for foreign exchange to be delivered ninety days or one year or three years later should be based on the best possible guess that can be made as to what the spot rate will be at those points of time. So long as the forward rate prevailing today differs from the spot rate that the market expects to prevail at these future dates, there is money to be made by buying or selling forward contracts.

Indeed, since the market makes its judgments with the benefit of all available information, it seems difficult to build an econometric model, no matter how ambitious, that could predict better. This latter proposition has not so far been controverted by econometric experience. But the inability of the forward rate to predict the future spot rate correctly has badly disappointed believers in this technique.

Since the market has so often defeated governments and central banks when the authorities tried to hold a rate that the market did not believe in, one is tempted to assume that the market has firm opinions about the "right rate." The market certainly knows a wrong rate when it sees one. As for the "right rate," there seems to be a rather wide range within which views are quite loosely held. This is evidenced, for instance, by the way in which spot and distant forward rates often move together, although the facts affecting the spot rate today might seem to be irrelevant to the spot rate in a distant future. There seems to be little of the stabilizing speculation that theoreticians have relied on to push rates back to equilibrium after they have been knocked off balance.

If we cannot predict exchange rates, we also cannot set targets or ranges for them with much conviction. This reduces the prospect that efforts along those lines will be successful. The United States has less to gain from such a modification of a free float than other countries. Control over the dollar rate would once more pass into the hands of others. Even the problem of convertibility might then reappear.

Nevertheless, floating has not been a panacea for any country and has proved a threat to some. One must anticipate that, if and when countries regain domestic stability, efforts will be made also to return to external stability. Floating abroad, after all, is largely the mirror image of the disorder created by inflation at home. In 1879, Secretary of the Treasury John Sherman put the dollar back on a fixed-rate basis, after it had been floating during and after the Civil War. This was then referred to as a resumption of specie payments. After long hesitation and debate about how to go about it, Sherman declared, "the way to resume is to resume," and did it. Some day another Secretary of the Treasury may undertake the twentieth-century analogue of that operation. But if and when he does, one must hope that, like Sherman, he will have waited until market rates have long been stable and that he will first have accumulated plenty of reserves.

18 Longer-Run Aspects of International Monetary Reform

In the immediate future, the prinicpal consequences of the work done by the Committee of Twenty (CXX) will be measures to which the Committee, in its final report, refers to as "Immediate Steps." These relate to guidelines for floating, strenghtening of the IMF through establishment of a high-level council, a pledge against trade restrictions, and a method to value the SDR (Special Drawing Rights), along with others.[1]

The longer-run future of the international monetary system, however, may well be shaped, in important respects, by what the Committee refers to as the "Reformed System."[2] This long-run plan was left as a torso, agreed in part but with important matters unresolved. It is generally understood that evolution, rather than negotiation and explicit decision and agreement, will have to be relied on for longer-term reform. But the understanding gained in working out the general principles of the "Reformed System," in clarifying the issues and in appreciating more precisely the interests and intentions of the participants, will play an important role in the evolutionary process. The future shape of the system remains uncertain. But the major alternatives will almost certainly be found to have been implicit if not precisely spelled out in the agreed and the unagreed portions of the "Reformed System."

It would be wrong to regard failure to reach an agreement on long-run reform as revealing major conflicts among national interests. The existing disagreements are deep but narrow. Nobody is debating basic issues of the kind posed during the 1930s, such as bilateralism versus multilateralism, autarchy versus trade liberalization, tight control over payments against full exchange market convertibility. The disagreements that separated the members of the CXX can be overcome by an effort of political will. The world has lived so well on the capital generated by past efforts of this kind made following World War II that it seems to have become too complacent to repeat them. It is not a hopeful sign for the future if calamity rather than comfort must be looked to as the mainspring of action. But evolution may very well lead us where cooperation failed to take us. On that trip the "Reformed System" may be a useful guide.

This chapter was originally published in *Aussenwirtschaft* 3 (September 1974):337–346. The views expressed are the personal interpretation of the author and do not necessarily reflect views held in the U.S. Government, or in the Committee of Twenty, nor those of the two principal architects of the American plan, former Under Secretary of the Treasury Paul A. Volcker and former Secretary of the Treasury George P. Shultz.

Antecedents

When the Bretton Woods system finally broke down in the summer of 1971, many observers looked to the United States to come forward with some plan of action for repair and reconstruction. The United States was hesitant. It was widely felt on the American side that the U.S. role in the world had diminished, and that the United States could no longer afford nor effectively assert the kind of leadership that helped to create the Bretton Woods institutions, the Marshall Plan, and the GATT. It took time before the United States was prepared, beginning with the IMF meeting of September 1972, to put forward some components of a plan.

The American approach to international monetary reform, as well as the response on the part of other countries, reflected the experience of the final years of the Bretton Woods system. Everybody understood that exchange rates, in conditions of mounting inflation and differential rates of real growth, could no longer be as stable as they had been during the 1950s and early 1960s. It was clear also that the world wanted a more symmetrical system than that into which the Bretton Woods blueprint had evolved. The original design of that blueprint had been almost entirely symmetrical. The same rules, rights, and obligations applied to Paraguay and to the United States. But because reality was asymmetrical, the system evolved to a dollar-gold exchange standard and eventually, when the dollar had become convertible only in a very limited sense, into something close to a pure dollar standard.

In its early stages, that system suited both the United States and most other countries. The United States received easy financing for its perennial payments deficits. Other countries thereby acquired dollar reserves. The United States was unable, in a system where all currencies were pegged to the dollar, to modify its own exchange rate, but for many years it felt no desire to do so. Other countries could change their rate and could thereby regulate the degree to which the system required them to finance American deficits.

As time went on, both sides increasingly found the benefits of the system less attractive while its costs seemed to become more onerous. The world became tired of financing American deficits and inflating national currencies and price levels in the process. The United States became increasingly troubled by its inability to devalue as the overvaluation of the dollar became more and more evident.

From this experience there developed a universal desire for a more symmetrical system. In such a system, the United States felt, it would have the same ability as others to modify its exchange rate. The United States, so other countries seemed to feel, should be required to make the dollar convertible and settle its deficits in reserve assets like every other country. The role of the dollar would be greatly reduced.

Convertibility

In the fall of 1972 it seemed apparent—which is no longer obvious today—that the decision makers of the world wanted to return to a fixed-exchange-rate system. Academics might prefer flexible rates, but finance ministers, central bankers, the private financial sector, and internationally oriented businessmen saw fixed rates as the rule and floating rates as a temporary makeshift. Yet a system of rates fixed by a peg to the dollar, in which every currency would be convertible into reserve assets except the dollar, was not negotiable. Thus the American reform plan, as it evolved and was gradually presented, had as its keystone the promise of dollar convertibility.

It was clear that convertibility raised severe problems for the United States. But it also held one advantage. A dollar convertible into exchange assets would give the United States an effective opportunity to control the dollar's exchange rate. There might have been ways other than by making the dollar convertible to accomplish this major American objective. Convertibility, moreover, was not a foolproof means of assuring control over the dollar rate. Under the Bretton Woods system, even during the years when the dollar remained convertible into gold de facto as well as de jure, other countries could and very probably largely would have frustrated an American change in the gold value of the dollar by changing their own gold price accordingly while retaining their dollar peg. But convertibility into reserve assets probably was the cleanest way of regaining control over the dollar rate.

Under convertibility, the United States could shift from one fixed exchange rate to another while continuing to convert. Alternatively, by ceasing to convert and allowing the dollar to float, the United States could achieve a rate change in accordance with market forces to the extent that other countries did not intervene in exchange markets to prevent this.

Convertibility at a fixed rate, nevertheless, raises severe problems for the United States. A large economy with a small foreign sector finds balance-of-payments adjustment at such a rate more difficult than one structured inversely. The number of dollars by which GNP must be reduced in order to eliminate one dollar's worth of trade deficit is greater in a nearly closed economy than in an open one. Payments adjustment via the income mechanism is costly. Adjustment via the price mechanism, to be sure, is easier for the nearly closed than for the open economy, becuse the range of possible substitutions of domestic production for imports and the elasticity of supply of exports both are greater in the nearly closed economy. But to activate the price mechanism, given the usual rigidity of prices, would require freedom to alter the exchange rate.

The greater difficulty experienced by a nearly closed economy, such as the American, in adjusting its balance of payments at a fixed exchange rate is not universally accepted. The American economy, moreover, is not all that closed.

Since the 1950s, its average propensity to import has about doubled—from about 3 to 6 percent. But there can be very little doubt that a large country with a small foreign sector has less of an incentive to subject its domestic economy to discipline in order to achieve a balance-of-payments objective than has an economy where the foreign sector is of major importance. The United States is close to being an optimum currency area, that is, one that finds it preferable to adjust its balance of payments by exchange-rate movements rather than by deflating or inflating the domestic economy.

Convertibility is difficult for the United States also because its currency is used so widely in official and private international balances and transactions. Capital movements running into many billions of dollars, in response to interest-rate differentials or speculative incentives, would require very large reserves. The fact that the Eurodollar market can create dollars adds to potential demands on the United States for conversion of dollars, even though the dollars presented for conversion necessarily must be dollars in the United States rather than Eurodollars. Dollar flows among third countries also can give rise to conversion demands if the country losing dollars is in the habit of holding dollar balances while the country gaining dollars is in the habit of demanding conversion.

Finally, planning for convertibility raised problems in the light of the low level of American reserves and the large holdings of dollars by foreign monetary authorities. Resistance to U.S. devaluation in 1971 had shown that it would not be easy for the United States to achieve current-account surpluses sufficient to permit accumulation of substantial reserves. So long as dollars were used in international settlements, moreover, the current-account surplus might merely cause the United States to earn back its dollars and reduce liabilities, instead of acquiring assets. Arrangements would clearly have to be made for dealing with these problems, but they were not spelled out in much detail in the early stages of the CXX discussions. The subsequent unsettlement of all balances of payments resulting from the rise in the price of oil has for the time being materially altered this aspect of the monetary-reform problem, as it has so many others.

Given these difficulties, the American plan might have opted for some qualified form of convertibility. For instance, the United States might have offered to pay in reserve assets for the amount of its trade deficit, or current-account deficit, or some part thereof. This would have avoided the need to convert dollar balances that foreign monetary authorities acquired as a result of capital movements, as well as the need to convert the existing official balances. A serious difficulty, under such a scheme, would have been the allocation of these reserve assets to countries which might have acquired dollars through trade surpluses both with the United States and with other countries as well as through capital movements. Conceivably the IMF could have acted to allocate reserve assets made available by the United States in accordance with some key, such as members' total current-account surpluses, or surpluses with the

United States, or in accordance with quotas. Problems of computation as well as of equity would have been serious but perhaps not impossible to overcome. This, however, was not the road chosen in the American plan.

The Defense of Dollar Convertibility

Instead, the American plan sought to make convertibility livable for the American economy principally by two devices. One was a semiautomatic or presumptive system of balance-of-payments adjustment activated by a reserve trigger. The other was an option to float when exchange losses—or possibly gains—became unmanageable. Particular stress was placed on the need for symmetry—surplus countries were presumptively expected to adjust in response to the same reserve indicators. The method of adjustment was not specified. It might take the form of domestic contraction or expansion at a fixed exchange rate, or, more likely perhaps, adjustment of the exchange rate itself.

Foreign countries who viewed themselves as potential surplus countries saw many objections. One objection related to the postulated symmetry in adjustment. Why, it was asked, should the countries that had succeeded in getting into surplus positions and therefore supposedly were doing things right be required to adjust along with those who had deficits and therefore must have been following bad policies? Why try to cure the quick as well as the sick? This had been an issue that Keynes confronted in designing his Clearing Union, and at that time the United States had taken a dim view of his proposition that surplus countries as well as deficit countries should adjust. Now the situation was reversed. The United States had to overcome considerable resistance before it became generally accepted in the CXX that adjustment should be symmetrical.

A leaning toward automaticity or, as the United States preferred to call it, presumption in a country's response to the indicator or trigger and the choice of a reserve indicator for triggering this response were harder to defend. The United States made clear that no absolute automaticity was intended. Triggering of the indicator was to create a presumption of need for adjustment only. But more than a mere signal that it was time for possibly inconclusive consultation and assessment clearly was needed if reserve movements under convertibility were not to become excessive.

In continuing informal discussions of monetary arrangements during former years, it had become evident that few governments were willing to surrender power over their exchange rate to an automatic mechanism. The automatic version of the "crawling peg," for instance, had been widely rejected in the ongoing dialogue between government officials and academics.[3] For politicians, exchange rates are too important a part of the economy to be left to economists and their contrivances.

The reserve indicator had been evaluated during the public debate over the crawlng peg. There seemed to be a good deal of support for the view that, in terms of the likelihood that the signals thrown off would be the correct ones, reserves would perform as effectively as would spot or forward exchange rates or the current or basic balance of payments. But in a plan that sought to make the dollar convertible, a reserve indicator rather than something else was needed for a reason other than the timeliness of its signals. This simple reason was that, when U.S. reserves ran low while those of other countries ran high, the United States was in imminent danger of having to suspend convertibility. There could be no better signal for urgently needed action.

Fundamentally, the reserve indicator was a replica of the textbook version of the pre–World War I gold standard. The rules of that legendary game—which even in 1914 was not what it used to be, and perhaps never was—told central banks to contract when gold reserves were low and to expand when they were high. The mechanism of adjustment was the discount rate, rather than the exchange rate. The problem with the gold standard, as with the U.S. plan, had been that central banks were more ready to act when reserves were low than when they were high. Reserve indicators, however, involved several additional difficulties.

One problem relates to the nature of these reserves. There is agreement in the CXX that the SDR should become the principal reserve asset and that the role of gold and of reserve currencies should be reduced. In the U.S. view, however, immediate and total elimination of the dollar as a reserve asset would deprive the system of flexibility and would also be inconvenient for those numerous countries, especially among the developing countries that prefer to hold their reserves in reserve currencies. Total elimination of the dollar from reserves, except perhaps working balances, would also, of course, increase the difficulties that the United States might at times experience under convertibility and increase the frequency with which adjustment action may have to be taken by the United States.

Another not fully resolved question concerning reserves is whether they should be interpreted gross or net. For a reserve-currency country, liabilities to official holders are an important determinant of its net-reserve position. If holding of official dollar balances were permitted, a net-reserve indicator might be activated by the ups and downs of liabilities even though the gross-reserve assets of the reserve-currency country remained unchanged.

Still another reserve problem relates to the relative advantages of using, respectively, reserve-stock or reserve-flow indicators. Situations could be visualized in which rapid loss of reserves, even when their absolute level is still high, would require adjustment action. The same could be true, vice versa, for reserves increasing rapidly from a low level. On the other hand, the absolute level of resrerves obviously cannot be ignored and in many cases may be the more relevant concern, especially in a system of convertibility.

The choice of a reserve norm, departures from which up and down to certain levels would constitute warning or action signals, presents another set of problems. Countries presumably would enter the plan with the reserves they happened to have at the time. Gradual movement up or down to the country's norm, which then would be on a rising trend over time, seems appropriate. Norms in the aggregate should add up to a desirable, that is, noninflationary and nondeflationary, level of world liquidity. But countries' views of their appropriate shares in world reserves and of the appropriate rates of growth of these reserves may lead to results inconsistent with existing or desirable aggregate international liquidity.

Even a detailed working out of the foregoing problems would not necessarily guarantee symmetrical functioning of the adjustment mechanism under all conditions. An American deficit or surplus, for instance, might have as its counterpart the surpluses or deficits of a large number of countries. This diffusion would mean that no single country, other than the United States, would necessarily experience a reserve movement sufficient to carry it to a trigger point. Only the United States would be required to adjust in that case. Alternatively, some smaller country or group of countries might have a large surplus or deficit mainly with the United States while the United States was in balance except for these particular relationships. Such imbalance might be sufficient to trigger off the smaller participants but would probably not do so for the United States, nor of course for any third country, with asymmetry in adjustment against the result.

These are highly technical problems that nevertheless contain very marked elements of national interests. The question is not only which solution may be technically superior, but also how these interests can best be balanced.

The second major device by which the United States sought to make dollar convertibility livable, in addition to the reserve-indicator structure, was the option to float. Thus the question whether and in what circumstances the International Monetary Fund might be authorized to allow or disallow a float acquired major significance. This, too, remains on the agenda for the future. In addition, the right to float and its limitations involve the question whether a reserve-currency country, when it wants to float, could request other countries not to peg their currencies to that of the reserve-currency country. If they peg, they would, of course, be impeding the free float of the reserve currency. On the other hand, if the reserve-currency country can deprive others of the right to intervene by the use of its currency—pegging is an extreme case of intervention—difficulties may arise for these other countries in managing their exchange rates.

Evaluation

Some observers suspected the American plan to have been a thinly disguised prescription for a floating-rate system. In suport of this interpretation it was argued that the plan made no provision for dealing with the so-called "dollar overhang," did not concern itself with how the United States was to acquire additional reserves, and ignored the problem of making discrete changes in fixed rates, especially when these were signalled ahead to the market by an approaching trigger point. It was argued that the plan thus failed to provide the conditions that would be prerequisite for a serious effort to achieve and maintain convertibility. Such criticism can be rejected. The plan was presented piecemeal, as it was evolved by a small group working within the U.S. government. Its gestation period, and the attendant staff work, was far more limited than the White Plan and possibly the Keynes Plan had enjoyed in pre–Bretton Woods days. In contrast to those discussions of thirty years ago, the American plan and the work of the CXX as a whole had had a large input of ideas from the academic community and from continuing discussions of international monetary problems within various groups bringing together officials, academics, and often businessmen. The intellectual basis of the effort therefore was as broad and as solid as the world's idea-generating processes could have made it. But the final molding of these diverse and often conflicting inputs into a tightly organized plan of notable internal consistency necessarily had to be the work of a few people.

In the discussion of the CXX, the American plan has been modified and combined with many other elements. In the areas in which the plan was most specific, however—the reserve-indicator structure and the exchange-rate regime—it has set a distinct stamp on the "Reformed System" to the extent it was agreed by the CXX. The way in which the resulting system would work, assuming its unsettled portions to be sensibly compromised, would depend very much on the behavior of national economies. It could be a system of very stable rates, if inflation were avoided, real-growth rates were not too dissimilar, and structural factors in national economies did not change too much. Such an outcome undoubtedly would be pleasing all around.

The system could also, however, turn out to be one approximating floating rates. To at least some of the participants, this would probably be a disappointment. The system is the result of an effort to satisfy a widespread demand for dollar convertibility without yielding to the desire, possibly implicit in this demand, of subjecting the American economy to the "discipline of the balance of payments." The need to protect the American economy against deflation, one that, with respect to the British economy, Keynes had stressed very strongly at Bretton Woods, has given rise to a blueprint with a much higher degree of potential exchange-rate flexibility than many of the participants probably intended when the negotiations began. Meanwhile the world has moved to an improvised system of total flexibility. To date it has not fared too badly with that system. If this experience should continue into the future, a shift to something like the long-term blueprint of the CXX should not constitute as much of a change as might have been the case had it been completed and adopted in 1974.

Notes

1. ''Outline of Reform'' *IMF Survey* June 17, 1974, Supplement, part II, p. 197. I have discussed these ''Immediate Steps'' in *Finance* Magazine, September 1974, and *Challenge* Magazine, September/October 1974.

2. *Ibid,* Part I, p. 193.

3. A proposal popular in academic circles during the late 1960s, involving frequent small exchange rate changes in response to some indicator which would provide flexibility while making speculation on future moves relatively expensive.

19 Why Fixed Rates?

On December 18, 1971, the world's chief trading nations, assembled in the pseudo-Gothic hall at the Smithsonian Museum in Washington, decided to end a period of exchange-rate flexibility of some months' duration and to return to fixed rates. Some of these countries, which had inveighed against the economic evils and political indignities of the dollar standard even while the dollar was still formally convertible, now accepted as their standard a dollar that was inconvertible de jure as well as de facto. Governments and central banks did so despite widespread demands for a continuation of the currency float emanating from academic economists who, on theoretical grounds, believed flexible rates to be the optimal currency arrangement.

Little more than a year later, the rate structure hastily contrived broke down once more. Again a number of currencies began to float. But it became quickly obvious that only the countries whose rates tended to float downwards had a stomach for the exercise. Those who were candidates for appreciation either opted for a new fixed peg to the dollar or so hedged their upward floats as to nullify the true impact of market forces.

Why do governments behave in this way? The apparent advantages claimed for flexible exchange rates are many-fold. They do not relate only to the avoidance of financial crisis, which has been much stressed recently. A country experiencing longer-term balance-of-payment difficulties can also resolve them by floating its currency. Countries suffering from "imported inflation" can cut loose from foreign price levels and inflows of foreign money, and so keep their price levels stable. A country experiencing some kind of difficulty in its exports, be it due to crop failures, or shifting foreign demand, can mitigate the damage to the balance of payments and to employment by allowing its currency to decline flexibly.

The trouble is that these agreeable consequences of flexible rates are not the only ones. If they were, it is hard to see why not only entire nations, but also subdivisions of nations suffering from inflation, "export difficulties," or unemployment, should not have recourse to flexible exchange rates. My home state of Connecticut has been suffering from all three of these difficulties in recent years. Nevertheless, among the many remedies proposed, nobody has mentioned flexible rates. Everybody recognizes that the cost of cutting Con-

---

This chapter was published in *Social Science Quarterly*, 54, no. 1 (June 1973):146–151.

necticut loose from the United States, as would be implicit in endowing the state with an independent currency, would be far too expensive in terms of the benefits that integration brings.

These benefits are numerous and most of them obvious. At a somewhat rarified theoretical level, however, one can define them as an improvement in the allocation of resources. By being part of the United States, Connecticut achieves greater mobility of capital and of labor and can firmly and risklessly rely on the availability of the huge American market with the economies of scale that it offers. Evidently there is some level of integration of a small area with a larger one at which the benefits from better allocation of resources outweigh the sacrifice of the gains that could come from flexible exchange rates. The latter, inasmuch as they are largely concerned with the avoidance of unemployment, we may summarize under the heading of "full utilization of resources."

The question therefore is at what point the benefits from better allocation cease to outweigh possible gains from fuller utilization. The proponents of flexible exchange rates imply that the critical level is at the level of the nation state. Within the area of a nation rates should be fixed in perpetuity. Between nations, they say, there should be flexible rates.

This position lacks general plausibility. It is true that, if Connecticut suffers a depression which cannot, in the nature of things, be cured by devaluation of the Connecticut dollar, labor and capital can emigrate from Connecticut. The federal government can help through contract placements and regional-development assistance. Nevertheless, the dividing line which separates countries does not logically and necessarily separate the economic policies appropriate to the national and the international economy. Small countries that depend heavily on international trade tend to find that exchange-rate changes are profoundly disturbing to their price systems. They have often found it advantageous to keep their currency in a fixed relation to that of large neighbors. In Europe, the tendency of Holland and Austria to move with the DMark provides an example. In the Western Hemisphere, the small countries of the Carribean area and Central America have tended to maintain their dollar parity. Developing countries in general, while their currencies frequently have undergone depreciation, exhibit little interest in rate flexibility. This is so even though one might suppose that for a country that exports, say, coffee, the price of which might double or be cut in half over a relatively short period of time, exchange-rate flexibility would be an important stabilizing factor. They seem to prefer to peg firmly to some major currency.

Meanwhile, the countries of the European community are turning away from exchange-rate flexibility among themselves. They seem to believe that they can reach a level of economic integration at which fixed rates will become preferable, and that fixed rates are indeed a condition of reaching this level. Their efforts have not so far been very successful. But their implied judgment of the relative advantages of fixed and flexible rates is significant.

The result is that, at the present time, the issue of flexible rates is posed for relations among a limited number of countries or groups of countries. In what is probably the very predominant majority of intercountry relationships, fixed rates are preferred. The question is whether the countries that entered into the Smithsonian Agreement, with respect to some part of their international relationships, should consider flexible rates.

It is within this limited set, of course, that most rate changes of importance have taken place in recent years. By itself, this does not necessarily argue for flexibility. Flexible rates not only solve problems, they also present costs. Uncertainty about future rates increases risk. This risk needs to be covered, and whether or not it can be covered through forward contracts or by a risk premium added to normal profit margins, in one way or another trade and investment will suffer. Rate changes also require adjustments in the structure of international trade and of domestic production, neither of which are costless. Thus, even in those international relationships, where in principle rate flexibility may offer an advantage, this advantage must be weighed against the cost. Frequently, it may be preferable to deal with a payments imbalance by means other than rate flexibility, including acceptance of some temporary unemployment. It is unrealistic to say that international stability must always take a back seat to the national government's desire to maintain a free hand for domestic full-employment policy. International instability may also cause unemployment.

It is unrealistic also to compare fixed and flexible rates on the assumption that the movement of domestic prices and incomes will be the same under either system. If that were the case, the choice indeed would be only between a continuous adjustment of rates and temporary rate stability punctured by major re- or devaluations, leading to the same exchange rates over longer periods. In fact, commitment to a fixed exchange rate does influence the rate of inflation. In countries experiencing a payments deficit, the reluctance to devalue strengthens anti-inflationary forces. It is no accident that, over the last few years, as resistance to rate changes has diminished, concern over inflation and the will to resist it have likewise diminished. Inflation under flexible rates would be aggravated also by a ratchet effect. A temporary depreciation of the local currency would raise living costs and hence wages. A subsequent recovery in the balance of payments and in the value of the local currency could not undo that increase. In a country tending toward a weak balance of payments, domestic inflation would be further intensified under flexible rates because equilibration of payments through currency depreciation tends to bottle up inflation within the country. With fixed rates, a payments deficit would be financed out of exchange reserves and would tend to be contained by mounting supplies from abroad.

For surplus countries, the relation between inflation and exchange rates is reversed in some respects. Fixed rates mean ''imported inflation.'' They limit the country's ability to conduct an anti-inflationary monetary policy. This difference between surplus and deficit countries, under the alternatives of fixed and flexible rates, extends to a range of considerations that goes far beyond the ability to fight inflation. In good part, surely, the vogue that flexible rates today enjoy in the United States stems from the fact that the United States has become a deficit country. Deficit countries can afford to view floating rates with equanimity, because for them floating means sinking. Exports improve, import competition diminishes, real wages decline, employment and profits tend to rise. The reverse is true of surplus countries. The United States was deeply concerned about ''competitive depreciation'' during the period of the dollar shortage, that is, from the American devaluation of 1933–1934 to the mid-fifties. It is probably only realistic to concede that our changed condition compels us to take a different view also of the relative merits of fixed and flexible rates.

But to be fully realistic, we must take into account also the response of the surplus countries with whom we want to arrive at a new monetary agreement. These countries see flexible rates, which to them mean appreciation of their currencies, as a threat. To them, flexible rates mean import competition, loss of foreign markets, unemployment, the need to impose controls. That, of course, is the reason why these countries returned to the dollar standard via the Smithsonian Agreement. That is why, in that Agreement, they refused to allow the dollar a measure of depreciation that would have been clearly adequate to resolve the American payments problem. That is why, finally, in the crisis of February 1973, the surplus countries either accepted a new fixed-dollar peg or, like Japan, sought to minimize the damage by hedging an upward float by means of intervention. Flexible rates are unlikely to be acceptable to surplus countries. If imposed by the failure of other arrangements, they are likely to be followed by concealed intervention in exchange markets, controls, and ultimately perhaps by return to fixed rates.

Policymakers in surplus countries are likely to find themselves at odds with flexible-rate theorists because their objectives are different. Flexible-rate theorists think of rate movements as a means of equilibrating the overall balance of payments. Policymakers are primarily concerned with the trade balance, or with the current account, or at best with the basic balance of payments, that is, current account plus long-term capital movements. Short-term capital movements may cause the overall balance to move in a direction contrary to that of any of the three other balances. If the United States adopts an easy-money policy for anticyclical reasons, short-term capital would be driven out. Given flexible rates, the dollar may be driven down. An unjustified and painful adjustment of the trade balance and of the underlying structure of production in the United States and abroad would ensue, which would have to be reversed when money flows back, unless speculation succeeds in keeping the dollar from depreciating. While a theoretical model can be built in which speculation accomplishes this result, policymakers cannot rely on speculators exhibiting a degree of foresight denied to themselves and everybody else. Other theoretical models, moreover, show that speculation may very well be destabilizing.

These considerations lead one to a rather negative view of the usefulness of exchange-rate movements, either under flexible rates or under an adjustable-peg system, as a means of dealing with international imbalances. As far as the current account is concerned, a rate change is known to work with a considerable lag. A flexible rate, or a discretionary rate change, sufficient to balance the current account quickly, would badly overshoot for the long run. Speculation is supposed to prevent this. How speculators can be expected to make good guesses on equilibrium rates two or three years into the future, given all the uncertainties of policy, is unclear.

As regards capital movements, exchange-rate changes of any sort are even less reliable a cure. Flows of long-term capital are little influenced by exchange-rate changes, since the investor in effect buys a rate of return. The attractiveness of a particular foreign asset is not affected by rate differentials. Short-term capital movements of the speculative variety will indeed be squelched by the consummation of the rate change which the speculator anticipated. Arbitrage flows, on the other hand, motivated by interest-rate differentials, call for interest-rate changes rather than exchange-rate changes to stop them. The interaction of spot and forward rates, to be sure, limits the amount of covered arbitrage flows. But it does not reduce these flows to zero, and there are many interest-oriented short-term flows, including through leads and lags, that are not covered. All this is ignored by those who simply focus on the overall balance of payments and believe that, by equilibrating it through flexible exchange rates, the problem of international adjustment can be solved.

All this adds up to a powerful case against flexible rates. It does not constitute an unqualified case for permanently fixed rates, especially under present conditions of inflation. With inflation in the major countries ranging up to 10 percent, permanently fixed rates obviously are out of the question. This environment of inflation is another explanation of the vogue enjoyed by flexible rates.

One could argue, to be sure, that high rates of inflation present an opportunity for as well as a threat to fixed rates. If the deficit countries could restrain their prices, while the surplus countries continued to inflate, currency values would come into balance. On this, however, there is only limited hope. One reason why deficit countries are in deficit usually is their failure to control inflation.

Thus, the inadvisability of flexible rates confronts the infeasibility of permanently fixed rates. This has given rise to precarious consensus on so-called "limited flexibility." The technical problems of limited flexibility have not been fully solved. It is thought that wide bands around parities are part of the answer. Gliding parities encounter widespread skepticism. A plausible method of smaller and more frequent discrete parity changes, reasonably proof against speculation, remains to be devised. I have suggested elsewhere a procedure under which countries would stipulate certain limits within which they would be prepared to see the IMF adjust their effective exchange rates and if necessary their parities, reserving to themselves decisions concerning major changes.[1] In the disturbed climate of present-day exchange markets, that seems the best that we can do.

It is important to note that the "chaos" which allegedly has reigned in the exchange markets has not significantly affected the core of international economic relations—foreign trade and long-term investment. The world, in fact, is becoming increasingly integrated. Trade of the noncommunist world, as a percentage of its GNP, rose by approximately one-seventh during the 1960s. For the United States alone, while our exports stagnated, imports as a percentage of U.S. GNP rose by approximately one-third. In this fundamental sense, the conditions calling for fixed rates are gaining ground relative to flexible-rate considerations. The case for the latter rests principally on prevailing high rates of inflation. If this problem can be solved, we shall probably find ourselves returning to a high degree of de facto if not de jure stability in international currency relationships.

Note

1. Henry C. Wallich, "Monetary Crisis of 1971—The Lessons to Be Learned" (Washington, D.C.: The Per Jacobbson Foundation, Sept. 24, 1972).

Part IV
International Banking and Finance

20 Central Banks as Regulators and Lenders of Last Resort in an International Context: A View from the United States

The term "lender of last resort" implies a degree of specificity that goes beyond what that function can legitimately claim. I have never seen, in visits to central banks, a door marked "lender-of-last-resort department," nor met a vice-president in charge of such an activity.

It is true that there are situations in which the function of a central bank is properly described as lender of last resort. It is true also that a market looks to a lender of last resort, functions better when it knows that there is one, and will try to push some existing institution into that role if none has been appointed by higher authority.

At the same time, markets as well as central bankers know that it is unwise to hoist crisis signals before the condition becomes obvious. Neither market stability nor the credit standing of particular institutions have much to gain from the widespread advertising of a lender-of-last-resort operation. But since concealment also is not an acceptable policy, the part of wisdom often has been not to draw a finer line than circumstances require between what is last resort and what is not. The discussion of last resort matters will deal for the most part with Federal Reserve activities and powers.

Federal Reserve Powers

To meet its lender-of-last-resort responsibilities, the Federal Reserve has a variety of powers that reflect, at least in some measure, the variety of cases that may call these responsibilities into action. For a generalized lack of liquidity, open-market powers and the ordinary facilities of the discount window are appropriate. A generalized lack of liquidity has been the characteristic feature of some historic crises that were met by central banks and, in line with Bagehot's rule, were dealt with by lending freely at a high rate. These crises sometimes focused on the failure or near failure of some major firm, whereas in others there was no obvious single focus. The common denominator, however,

This chapter was originally presented on October 6, 1977, before the Bald Peak Conference on Key Issues in International Banking Sponsored by the Federal Reserve Bank of Boston, Melvin Village, New Hampshire.

was that firms perfectly solvent and under ordinary circumstances liquid, both banks and nonbanks, were unable to obtain short-term credit at almost any price. The famous British crises of 1867—Overend Gurney—and 1890—Baring Brothers—as well as the U.S. panic of 1907 were of that character. The last-named experience finally led to the creation of the Federal Reserve.

A potential crisis of this same type that was successfully forestalled by lender-of-last-resort action was the Penn Central failure in 1970. At that time it appeared that this failure might interfere with the rollover of commercial paper by certain finance companies.

The Federal Reserve assisted a shift of finance-company debt to the banks—both by granting liberalized discount-window credit to the particular banks involved (under the emergency provisions of Regulation A) and by suspending the Regulation Q ceiling on thirty- to eighty-nine-day Certificates of Deposit (CDs), enabling such banks to raise funds through the market.[1] These System initiatives provided needed reassurance to the financial community and helped to halt the general scramble of commercial-paper investors for higher-quality assets. At the height of the crisis, special System advances to facilitate transfers out of commercial paper rose to about $500 million, but by early fall these had been largely repaid.

The specialized emergency-lending powers of the Federal Reserve are appropriate particularly for the case where illiquidity focuses on a particular institution without spreading to the rest of the market. Here the Federal Reserve can supply credit to member banks for maturities of not more than four months and where the credit is secured to the Reserve Bank's satisfaction, at a rate at least one-half percent above the discount rate if the collateral offered is not eligible for discounting at the regular rate. For others (that is, individuals, partnerships, and corporations that are not member banks) the Federal Reserve can, in unusual and exigent circumstances, by the affirmative vote of not less than five members of the Federal Reserve Board, provide emergency credit. Rates on such credit would be set by the Board of Governors at the time credit was granted. To qualify for such credit, the party in liquidity straits must be unable to secure adequate credit from other banking institutions.

The foregoing provisions provide broad powers to deal with liquidity problems of particular institutions. It should be noted, however, that all types of discounts and advances must be secured by assets and in the manner specified in the Act and the regulations or "to the satisfaction of the Federal Reserve Bank," that is, to the satisfaction of the directors of the Federal Reserve Bank making the loan. The requirement that Federal Reserve credit must be secured has meant, in terms of the Board's policies to date, that Federal Reserve lending to any bank can continue only so long as that bank is solvent; the reason for the Board's view has been that collateral obtained from a bank in a state of insolvency might be exposed to legal challenge. Reasonable questions can be asked as to whether insistence on solvency, a criterion which at critical times may be very difficult to apply, really best serves the public interest. Nevertheless the following discussion rests on the policies that are in effect with regard to the solvency issue.

Illiquidity versus Insolvency

Power to deal with insolvency situations is in the hands of the Federal Deposit Insurance Corporation (FDIC). The FDIC, as insurer, can accept a loss. Frequently the FDIC finds it less costly to deal with an insolvency by subsidizing a merger or arranging the transfer of the deposits and the sound part of the assets to another bank through a "purchase-and-assumption" operation, rather than to pay off the insured depositors and liquidate the closed bank. Considerations relating to the welfare of the local community also apply in decisions as to whether a bank should be saved or wound up.

This dualism of functions and powers between the Federal Reserve and the FDIC is neater, to be sure, than the real world, in which illiquidity and insolvency may in some cases be separable and in other cases may merge. A bank or any other firm may be illiquid but not insolvent. Nevertheless, if illiquidity leads to a run and to the liquidation of assets at distress prices, insolvency may follow. Likewise, an institution may be insolvent but not illiquid. However, as soon as this situation is diagnosed, the bank is likely to be closed by the regulatory authorities to protect the creditors.

An institutional division of different types of rescue functions, such as exists in the United States, prevails only in a limited number of countries. Elsewhere, the central bank as lender of last resort may find it necessary to deal with the distinction between illiquidity and insolvency in a more ad-hoc manner.

Interaction of illiquidity and insolvency as presently interpreted is well illustrated by the case of Franklin National Bank. While the Comptroller of the Currency had declared Franklin to be solvent, the Federal Reserve loaned Franklin, on a secured basis, up to about $1.7 billion. When solvency could no longer be assured, Franklin, under the auspices of the FDIC, was taken over by the bank that had put in the highest bid, and the FDIC took over the Federal Reserve loan and that part of the assets not going to the merging bank.

The question is sometimes raised whether banks should be allowed to fail. That is not a meaningful issue. Even the most intensive supervision cannot make sure that no bank will ever suffer losses large enough to wipe out its capital. As far as the stockholders and management are concerned, the bank then has failed. The real question is whether the depositors and other creditors, and in a broader sense the monetary system and borrowers dependent on their banking connection, should be allowed to suffer the consequences. The answer may well have to depend on such circumstances as the availability of alternative sources of credit in particular regions or local communities. Giving too much advance assurance to management, stockholders, and depositors risks losing some of the discipline of the market on which regulators rely to some extent to keep banks "in line." Proponents of 100-percent liability insurance must keep this in mind. So must lenders of last resort. In this imperfect world, perfect safety is not an ideal condition. Regulators, central bankers, and insurers would soon find the odds they had created being exploited against them. In response, they might find themselves driven to regulate and supervise bank operations to a degree inconsistent with the free flow of credit.

International Aspects

The growing internationalization of banking adds new dimensions to regulatory and lender-of-last-resort responsibilities. National legislations, regulations, and supervisory practices differ widely among countries. Nobody would dream of trying to coordinate laws and practices internationally, but increasing regulatory cooperation is possible, and considerable progress has been made. Regulators meet regularly, under the auspices of the Bank for International Settlements (BIS) and otherwise. The result has been a better understanding of one another's problems and interests, as well as cooperative policies with respect to particular issues.

The matrix of international banking relationships has been expanded as a result not only of the growth of old established national markets but also through the appearance of new banking centers, frequently referred to as off-shore centers. As regards regulation, practices among these centers range widely from technically competent and tight regulation and supervision to virtual nonexistence of such efforts. As far as lender-of-last-resort facilities are concerned, it is, of course, very difficult and often impossible for small political entities to exert such a function.

Accordingly, bank regulators and lenders of last resort will find themselves involved in different degree in the activities of their banks abroad. In the case of the United States, the foreign activities of banks and bank holding companies are closely supervised. Bank holding companies and banks need the approval of the Federal Reserve for foreign acquisitions and branches and with regard to the nature of the activities conducted overseas. Foreign branches are examined by the Comptroller of the Currency and the Federal Reserve, except in a limited number of countries where national laws bar such access. Where regulatory and supervisory laws and institutions exist, as is the case in all countries with significant domestic banking activity, it is, of course, the national authority that is the primary regulator and supervisor within its borders. Because of the special characteristic of American bank examination, which focuses on appraising the quality of assets in a way few other supervisory systems do, reliance on local banking authorities for the direct supervision of foreign branches and subsidiaries has not yet occurred.

International banking also raises the question of lender-of-last-resort responsibility. Today, that responsibility is exercised in a framework of floating exchange rates. This eliminates one of the problems that has beset lending of last resort and that has led to probably the most spectacular failures to live up to that responsibility. I would count among those failures the unwillingness of the Reichsbank to go to the aid of its banking system in 1931 and the failure of the Federal Reserve to deal with the mass failures of American banks during the depression of the 1930s. In both cases, the constraints of the gold standard impeded, by the lights of those days, action that might have forestalled the respective crises. I would not, today, belittle the very real concerns of those who had to make traumatic decisions in those days. The Reichsbank feared that Germany's international credit would be destroyed if it violated its 40-percent gold-cover requirement. The Federal Reserve had no means of knowing that the Supreme Court would some day invalidate the gold clause and in that way avoid the consequences, for many borrowers, of a departure from gold. Nor would I argue that all the superior wisdom is on the side of our days. We have not done well enough in managing paper money to be able to claim that. In any event, today we do not operate under the constraints that, forty-five years ago, helped to produce major financial failures.

The multiplicity of possibilities and national circumstances makes it obvious that no general rule can be established for a particular course of action in case of a banking crisis that was not of purely local character. The problem, if it were to arise, could be marketwide or focused on a single institution. It could be a problem of liquidity, of solvency, or of both. It could occur in a market with a strong central bank and regulatory system or in a center where neither exists. It could focus on the home currency or on the dollar and other currencies.

The need for concerted action in such a case nevertheless was recognized by the central bankers who meet monthly at the BIS in Basel. After careful examination of the issues, the central bankers arrived at the same conclusion that I have just indicated: that detailed rules and procedures could not be laid down in advance. But since considerable concern existed at that time about the state of the Eurocurrency markets, the following statement was issued: "The Governors . . . had an exchange of views on the problem of the lender of last resort in the Euro-markets. They recognized that it would not be practical to lay down in advance detailed rules and procedures for the provision of temporary liquidity. But they were satisfied that means are available for that purpose and will be used if and when necessary."

This approach reflects the experience also that the Federal Reserve has had in handling its own lender-of-last-resort responsibility. There are dangers in defining and publicizing specific rules for emergency assistance to troubled banks, notably the possibility of causing undue reliance on such facilities and possible relaxation of needed caution on the part of all market participants. The Federal Reserve has always avoided comprehensive statements of conditions for its assistance to member banks. Emergency assistance is inherently a process of negotiation and judgment, with a range of possible actions varying with certain circumstances and need. Therefore, a predetermined set of conditions for emergency lending would be inappropriate.

In the international field, extensive discussions of the role of host and home-country central banks for extensions of emergency assistance to subsidiary and multinational financial institutions have produced a common understanding of the problem. Cooperation among central banks is clearly necessary. No central bank can avoid some degree of responsibility for events in its market. No central bank can disinterest itself in the international activities of the banks for which it is responsible at home.

An important aspect of the close cooperation among central bankers and other regulators is being implemented through central bankers' meetings at Basel and through a regulators' committee that meets periodically at other times. There can be no question, of course, of making national legislation homogeneous. The differences are too deeply rooted for that. What is possible is to develop a close understanding of the expectations, intentions, and modi operandi of different countries and to make them mesh. Institutions like those under the aegis of the BIS are making this happen.

Cooperation

Cooperation is particularly important where the supervisory and lender-of-last-resort responsibilities are different. Countries meet in one market increasingly frequently owing to the internationalization of banking. As far as regulation is concerned, the role of the local regulator, in most cases the central bank, under present conditions is bound to be major. The local regulator charters and supervises foreign subsidiaries and joint ventures, and, where local legislation so provides, examines them. Foreign supervisors and regulators have different degrees of access to local offices of branches, subsidiaries, and joint ventures of banks and bank holding companies of their own countries, depending on local legislation.

Under these circumstances, the local regulatory authority inevitably has a concern with any problems of liquidity and solvency of banks under its jurisdiction. The financial resolution of both types of problems, of course, is in the first instance a concern of the parent organization. For branches this goes without saying, since they are an integral part of a banking organization. For wholly owned subsidiaries, parents have historically demonstrated a strong sense of responsibility. Banks do not cast their foreign operations in the form of subsidiaries rather than branches to take advantage of limited liability. Nor would such subsidiaries be able to operate on a large scale if the market suspected that in case of trouble the parent would walk away from them. These foreign operations are cast in the form of subsidiaries rather than of branches principally because in that form they enjoy broader powers, better tax status, and greater operating flexibility.

Parents, therefore, expect to back their subsidiaries, even though ultimately that must be a business decision and, where the regulatory framework so provides, a decision of the regulatory authorities of the parent as well as, of course, of the host-country regulator. This is one of the reasons for the Federal Reserve's requirements that adequate financial data for both branches and subsidiaries abroad be kept and made available to examiners in the United States.

As far as American banks are concerned, the great bulk of foreign operations, in dollar terms, is carried out through branches. Subsidiaries typically are small relative to the size of their parents, and usually well capitalized (except in the special case of shell organizations). Minority participants, accompanied by a management interest, so-called joint ventures, are usually those of large banks, which historically have shown readiness to back their offspring, although they may want to limit their support to their own share in the venture. The Federal Reserve, in an interpretation issued in 1976, has made clear that for American banks, which by law must obtain Board approval for this as any other type of acquisition, the Board would take into account the ability of the applicant to support more than its own share in a joint venture. The Board also said that it would give great weight to the potential risks in cases where the joint venture was closely identified with its American parent by name or through managerial relationships.

Evolving Role of the IMF

Since this chapter has been burdened by much technical detail, I would like to conclude by taking a broader and more evolutionary look at the lender-of-last-resort problem. It has often been pointed out that the function of the International Monetary Fund in helping countries in balance-of-payments difficulties has some of the characteristics of a lender-of-last-resort operation. In time, this role of the IMF may expand. It is important to note where the similarities and the differences are likely to manifest themselves.

Central-bank lending to money markets for particular banks in crisis conditions, and IMF lending to national governments, have in common that the objective is mainly to protect the monetary system rather than to help individual banks. Neither should engage in bail-out operations for banks.

The Fund's ability to help countries with balance-of-payments problems, however, depends on the willingness of the borrowing country to meet the

Fund's policy conditions. It is not an unconditional form of assistance. For that reason, banks that have lent to a country cannot take for granted that the Fund will come to that country's rescue.

An important difference between central-bank and IMF lending is that the IMF, unlike central banks, need not and should not wait for a crisis to develop. In fact, the earlier a country applies for assistance to the IMF in the upper tranches of its quota, the sooner a set of policies will be in place that should help the country overcome its difficulties. In that sense, the IMF need not be a lender of last resort.

The IMF role in imposing conditionality and guiding the policies of the borrowing country finds a counterpart in the regulatory activities of central banks. Good national policies, like sound banking policies, should reduce greatly, if not altogether eliminate, the need for lender-of-last-resort activity.

Still another difference between the lending of the IMF and the classical lender-of-last-resort operation may be noted: the Fund's normal technique is not to lend freely at a high rate, but to pay out limited funds on a phased basis after a showing that performance criteria are being met.

These differences reflect, of course, the inherent distinction between a country borrower and a money market or single bank. A country is inherently a stronger debtor, not because it controls a printing press but because adequate policies will make it possible to pay except perhaps temporarily in the direst of circumstances. A country cannot go out of business in the manner of a bank or other business enterprise. Solvency is represented by the existence of the political will to deal with economic difficulties.

Given the great potentialities of the IMF's role, its further strengthening is obviously desirable. This is currently underway through the proposed Witteveen facility, and through quota increases already decided and still to be decided. More adequate resources will enable the Fund not only to meet better such needs as may arise but also to be more effective in influencing the policies of borrowing countries and in that manner enhance the willingness to lend of the private market. In that sense, too, the activities of the Fund could come to constitute a parallel to those of national lenders of last resort: to create conditions of confidence in which the private market can again function adequately.

Note

1. Under section 201.2(e) of Regulation A: "Federal Reserve credit is available to assist member banks in unusual and exigent circumstances such as may result from national, regional, or local difficulties, or from exceptional circumstances involving only a particular member bank."

21 Why the Euromarket Needs Restraint

Anything in the financial field that grows at more than 20 percent per year bears watching, and the Eurocurrency market is no exception. Although it is not large as yet, at its present rate it tends to double in three to four years. That growth rate will no doubt taper off as the market gets larger. But by then it will have become an important driving force behind the money supply in any one currency, considering home and Euromarkets together. Today the mass is still relatively small, but the speed is high. Mass times speed, as the physicists say, equals momentum.

The Size of the Euromarkets

The present size of the market is not easy to determine. But in any event, it bears little resemblance to the gross or net magnitudes sometimes bandied about. Approximately 85 percent of the so-called gross size is accounted for by interbank liabilities. These simply double count the monetary liabilities, which are liabilities to nonbanks. Even the so-called net size, at least in the case of Bank for International Settlements (BIS) estimates, net out only interbank liabilities to banks within the reporting area. BIS estimates still include interbank liabilities to the banks and central banks outside the reporting area, amounting to 2.8 times the ultimate monetary liabilities to nonbanks of about $160–170 billion.

Of these monetary liabilities, some part is already accounted for in national monetary-system data and markets. Precisely what amount this is depends on whether we regard Eurodeposits as most closely resembling M_1 or M_4.[1] Since Eurodeposits are not transactions balances, they cannot be classed as M_1. But their maturity can be as short as one day, in which case they are available for overnight use if converted into immediately available funds. Part of Eurodeposits, therefore, are more mobile than the large CDs included in M_4 because the latter have a thirty-day minimum maturity. Incomplete data suggest that about 45–50 percent of Eurodeposits have a maturity of thirty days or less. Hardly any Eurodeposits have the maximum eight-year maturity of U.S. time deposits. Thus, Eurodeposits totaling about $160–170 billion probably fall somewhere between M_1 and M_4. Classified as M_4, some $55 billion of Eurodeposits are included in the monetary statistics of countries that count such

This chapter was originally published in *Columbia Journal of World Business* 14 (Fall 1979):17–24.

balances as part of their domestic money supply. This leaves $100–120 billion unaccounted for in national monetary statistics, and in that sense these balances are "stateless" money.

To evaluate the monetary effect of this $100–120 billion, it must be allocated to the domestic money supplies of particular countries, either on the basis of nationality of ownership, location, or currency. We shall attempt to do this here only with respect to Eurodollars. The amount of Eurodollars not included in any national, broadly defined money stock amounted to about $85 billion at the end of 1978. They are, of course, not included in the U.S. money supply, however defined. Making some very rough estimates, one might guess that some $52 billion in Eurodollars could reasonably have been allocated to the U.S. money supply.[2] This sum represents 14.5 percent of M_1 but only 5.5 percent of M_4. Nevertheless, with an estimated growth rate of about 40 percent during 1978, this sum, if allocated to M_1, would have raised the growth rate of that aggregate from 6.6 to 10.1 percent that year. Allocated to M_4, it would have raised its growth rate from 10.1 to 11.4 percent in 1978.

Partial data indicate that as much as 20 percent of Eurodollar liabilities to nonbanks may be of less than eight-day maturity and therefore very close to M_1. To some extent, to be sure, this may reflect short maturities of interbank deposits rather than liabilities to nonbanks. If we ignore this possibility, we can very tentatively allocate a part of Eurodollar liabilities to nonbanks to M_1. Of the above-mentioned $52 billion, as much as $10.5 billion would be like M_1. The growth rate of M_1 in 1978 would have been about three-quarters of one percent higher had these very short-term Eurodollar deposits been included.

Money and Credit "Creation" by the Euromarkets

To say that the Euromarket has monetary liabilities does not imply that the market "created" these liabilities. Nor do we assert that "creation" of money and credit by the market is equal to the $100–120 billion of monetary liabilities here indicated. It is sometimes argued that the Euromarket does not create money and credit but merely intermediates flows that, in its absence, would move through the channels of domestic banking and capital markets. Alternatively, it could be argued that the amounts of money and credit created by the Euromarkets are larger than the $100–120 billion above because they exclude certain amounts, estimated at about $55 billion, that are recorded in national money-supply statistics as part of the domestic money supply.

A test of the assertion that the market merely intermediates can be made by consolidating the assets and liabilities of the Euromarket and the U.S. banking system. This consolidated balance sheet of the two markets shows, of course, higher assets and liabilities than the domestic U.S. market taken by itself. Nevertheless, the reserves are unchanged, because the reserves of the Euromarket, if there are any, would in all probability be liabilities of the U.S. banking system and would vanish in consolidation. In other words, there would be insufficient reserves to support the consolidated volume of deposits. Of course, there is no way of knowing whether the Federal Reserve would have accommodated this added demand for credit that, in the absence of the Euromarket, would have presented itself in the U.S. market. Had the Fed not done so, the pressure of unsatisfied demands probably would have produced higher interest rates as the demands shifted to nonbank markets. But if the Fed were accommodating, the growth of the monetary aggregates would have been much more rapid. Thus, determining whether the Eurodollar market creates money and credit over and above what the U.S. domestic market would create depends very much on Federal Reserve policy. In particular, it would depend on whether the Fed were to follow a quantity target aimed at a certain volume of money and credit (in which case the added demand probably would be ignored), or an interest-rate target that would allow the volume of money and credit to adapt flexibly (in which case a large part of the demand would be satisfied).

The expansive power of the Euromarkets, in addition to being measured by their monetary liabilities, can also be measured in terms of the volume of credit to nonbanks. At the end of 1978, this stood at about $240 billion. The difference between this figure and the smaller amounts for Eurodollar liabilities to nonbanks is largely explained by the fact that, while about 10 percent of the Euromarket's deposits come from central banks, this sector is not a significant borrower from the market.

Reformulations and recomputations of the money and credit aggregates that take into account the Euromarkets can be helpful for monetary policy. A better picture of the expansion in any given currency can thus be obtained. But remember that the amounts in any particular currency, especially dollars, are not necessarily allocable to the country of that currency. Dollars borrowed or held in the Euromarket may be destined for expenditure anywhere in the world, not just the United States. It is the world supply of money and credit that is affected. Its national impact may be unpredictable.

Nevertheless, these Euroaggregates must be taken into account to some degree in formulating national monetary policy. That they cannot readily be integrated with the standard aggregates is a characteristic they share with other quasimonies, such as RPs (repurchase agreements) and money-market mutual funds. But Eurodollars, RPs, and money-market mutual funds can be accounted for by allowing a more rapid growth of velocity (V_1, V_2, and so on) and by setting the money-supply target ranges correspondingly lower, as the Federal Reserve has attempted to do. There is, nevertheless, a danger of not fully taking these expansionary elements into account. Moreover, in the case of the Euromarkets at least, there is no obvious limit to the future growth in their share of the combined U.S. and Euromarkets.

The Demand-Determined Market

What drives the Euromarket? That the market is not "out of control" is evidenced by the fact that the interest rate for Eurodollars moves closely with that for U.S. dollars. An increase in U.S. interest rates also raises the Eurorate, usually with a small margin reflecting the cost of reserve requirements and the FDIC assessment. Restrictions on capital movements, such as existed for the dollar until early 1974 and are still operative for some other currencies, can of course weaken this nexus. A lack of demand for loans in the Euromarket at a time of rising interest rates at home may cause the Eurorate to fall to a level where it becomes profitable to move money back to the United States. Below that level, the rate is unlikely to fall as long as this arbitrage demand persists. By the same token, the Eurorate cannot rise with respect to the U.S. rate beyond the level at which it becomes profitable to move funds from the United States to the Euromarket. The Eurodeposit rate, therefore, tends to fluctuate around a point equaling the U.S. rate plus a small margin, the most comparable U.S. rate being that on equal-maturity certificates of deposit.

Thanks to this arbitrage mechanism, the supply of funds in the Eurodollar market has a very high interest elasticity when the flow is from the United States to the Euromarket. The demand in the market has a very high interest elasticity when the flow is back to the United States. Since most of the time the market is expanding, it is the supply elasticity that tends to be the most relevant. The amount lent out is limited, however, by a loan demand that is likely to be relatively inelastic.

It is often argued that the market draws its supply of funds from the U.S. payments deficit, the OPEC surplus, or from similar sources. From this it is sometimes concluded that the market is supply-determined. Absent these special sources of supply, it seems to be implied, the market would find it difficult to grow. This interpretation ignores the arbitrage character of an important part of the supply. It is perfectly true that OPEC funds or funds originating in the U.S. payments deficit have at times flowed into the Eurodollar market. But the market is not dependent on such special sources. A slightly rising interest rate resulting from strong demand for funds will draw virtually unlimited amounts from national markets into the Euromarket.

Evidence that the market does not require such special sources as a payments deficit in the home country is provided by the Euromark market. This market, based principally in Luxembourg, has expanded rapidly. It has been able to draw on a highly elastic supply of funds from Germany, a country that has not had a significant payments deficit for many years.

Given the high elasticity of supply of funds to the Euromarket, the volume of lending must be determined by the demand for loans. This demand, under most circumstances, is likely to be quite interest inelastic. Within fairly wide margins, borrowers are probably always willing to pay the going LIBOR rate plus the spread, particularly since they are paying a floating short-term rate rather than a fixed long-term rate. Only the spread over LIBOR is permanent, which gives it a relatively high weight in borrowing decisions even though it is absolutely small compared with most LIBOR rates.

The spread charged by lenders over the cost of LIBOR probably must be regarded as itself being a function of LIBOR. Its purpose is to pay for the cost of the bank's own equity capital that is needed to support a Euroloan. This equity capital depends on a bank's overall capital-to-asset ratio. For large American banks, the ratio is typically in the 4–5 percent range. When the cost of equity capital is high relative to interest rates, a larger spread is needed to earn the income that, in turn, is required to support this capital. As interest rates rise while the cost of equity capital remains constant, less income is needed by the bank to meet the cost of supporting the incremental capital. This is a partial explanation of the tendency of spreads on syndicated Euroloans to narrow as interst rates rise. Nevertheless, competition and other factors no doubt contribute to the narrowness of these spreads that, as frequently noted, are often inadequate to cover the cost of capital and a reasonable risk premium.

Eurodollars and the Money Supply

In assessing the interaction between the domestic and the Eurodollar markets, it is important to remember that a shift of funds from the United States to the Eurodollar market does not change the U.S. money supply. A demand deposit (in a U.S. bank) that previously had been owned by a U.S. resident is now owned by a foreign resident but continues to be counted as part of the U.S. money supply under present definitions. Exceptions to this general rule arise if the new Eurodeposit is in the foreign branch of an American bank that holds the corresponding asset in the form of a claim on its head office. Deposit liabilities of U.S. banks to their foreign branches, unlike other deposit liabilities to nonresident banks or nonbanks, are not counted as part of the U.S. money supply. The foreign branch of the U.S. bank, however, presumably will not keep the funds on deposit with its parent indefinitely but will redeposit them with a foreign bank or lend them to a foreign nonbank. In either case, the corresponding liabilities of the U.S. parent, or of whatever other U.S. bank the deposit liability may have shifted to, will once more be counted as part of the U.S. money supply. On the other hand, the volume of credit in the U.S.

economy will be affected if a U.S. bank places funds in the Euromarket, whether with its own branch, with another bank, or in the form of a loan to a nonbank lender. The volume of its assets does not change, but a claim of some sort on the U.S. economy is replaced by a claim on a nonresident bank or nonbank.

The relative reduction in the volume of bank credit to the U.S. economy could produce an increase in U.S. interest rates, which in turn would raise Eurodollar rates. In this sense, increasing demand for funds in the Euromarket, if it leads to shifts of funds to that market by banks rather than by nonbanks, may give the supply curve of Eurodollars a very slight upward tilt.

Control of the Euromarkets

We now turn to the need for controlling the Euromarket and a method for accomplishing this task. The Euromarket, as stressed earlier, is not "out of control"; rather, it is controlled by the interest rate, which, in turn, is determined by the interest rate prevailing in the home market, with a reasonably stable margin. An increase in the interest rate in the domestic market, in resupponse to tightening Federal Reserve policy, raises the virtually horizontal supply curve in the Eurodollar market. It thus squeezes out that part of the loan demand which is not prepared to pay the new higher rate. To be sure, if the demand is relatively inelastic, it will take a substantial rate increase to slow down the creation of money and credit in that market. Since the rate on which syndicated loans are based fluctuates with LIBOR and is, therefore, a short-term rate, it may take substantial variations in the rate to achieve a given restraining effect in the granting of medium-term credit. A higher lending rate must, of course, prevail in the domestic market as well, given the normal rate relationships, in order to make possible the new higher rate in the Euromarket.

The manner in which this interest-rate constraint works in the Euromarket discriminates against the home market. The Euromarket expands at a faster rate than the home market at a given rate of interest in the two markets, allowing for the differential. That is the result of the interest advantage for depositors and borrowers, who get a higher yield on the deposits and pay a lower cost on the loan, respectively, in the Euromarket. The rate of expansion of the combined home and Euromarket in a given currency is the weighted average of the growth rates of the two, with the Euromarket having a higher growth rate but, so far, still a substantially lower weight. In order to achieve a desirable growth rate for the combined markets, the central bank, for example, the Federal Reserve, must slow down the expansion of the home market by means of a higher interest rate to compensate for the disproportionate growth of the Euromarket. For U.S. borrowers who do not have access to the Euromarket, the cost of credit is therefore higher. For U.S. banks that do not have such access, the rate of expansion of assets and liabilities will be lower. This is the result of the unequal conditions under which the domestic and the Euromarkets compete. It applies not only to the dollar market but equally to other currencies that have a Euromarket that is not equally accessible to all domestic borrowers and lenders.

Competitive Relations between the Euro- and Domestic Markets

The frequently heard argument that reserve requirements or other special controls over the Euromarket are not needed because the market is controlled by the domestic interest rate of each currency misses the point. It is quite true that, to avoid excessive expansion of the combined domestic and Euromarkets, the central bank need "only" raise interest rates. The point is that these rates will be higher for the domestic than for the Euro component of the combined market. The rate of expansion of the domestic market will be slower. The burden of restraint, therefore, is inequitably distributed. That is the principal reason why reserve requirements should be imposed on the Euromarket. Reserve requirements function as a tax. Their existence in the United States is the principal reason why the Eurodollar market can pay more and charge less for money than the U.S. market. Imposition of reserve requirements would go far toward redressing this inequality of competition.

Alternative Methods of Control

Reserve requirements can be used to equalize costs between the U.S. and the Euromarket. But they can also be used to control the rate of expansion of money and credit. If the central bank limits the supply of reserves, the assets and liabilities that the banks can support with a given volume of reserves will likewise be limited. Many people seem to believe that this is how the Federal Reserve controls money and bank credit. The fact is that before October 6, 1979, it did not. Prior to that time, the Federal Reserve used an interest rate technique of limiting money and bank-credit expansion. It did so by estimating the interest rate at which the aggregates would grow at the desired target rate, given the level and growth of income and other variables. Under that interest-rate strategy, reserves were supplied in whatever amounts were needed to achieve the desired interest rate, with primary focus on the federal-funds rate.

A good case has always existed for the alternative strategy of controlling the monetary aggregates through control of reserves.[3] In that case, the funds rate and other short-term rates would simply find their own level. This alternative strategy was in fact adopted by the Federal Reserve on October 6, as part of the package of measures including also marginal-reserve requirements and an increase in the discount rate. Under this alternative strategy one must expect, to be sure, that the federal-funds rate would prove rather bouncy. Random changes in the demand for money, and possibly random variations in the money multiplier linking reserves and the aggregates, would cause the funds rate to fluctuate considerably in the face of a fixed-supply pattern of reserves. But the excessive emphasis on short-term interest rates that had tended to develop under the funds-rate strategy and that had created political and other difficulties for monetary management could be expected to be muted by this reserves-based strategy.

The reserve strategy naturally necessitates reserve requirements. Calculation of a money multiplier must be based on known reserve needs of member banks. Calculation of the money multiplier would be made easier, and the multiplier itself would gain in stability, if reserve requirements were more uniform among banks and also less divergent among types of deposits. The legislation concerning Federal Reserve membership and associated reserve requirements now pending in the U.S. Congress may open the door to greater uniformity. Any set of reserve requirements covering a broad spectrum of monetary liabilities would eliminate, to be sure, one obvious route to establishing greater competitive equality between the Euro and the domestic markets: to set at zero the reserve requirements on nonpersonal time deposits in the United States. However, the thrust of present legislative proposals in this area is to take into account the possibility of negotiating reserve requirements in the Euromarket.

Prudential Controls

Reserve requirements are not the only means of improving competitive equality between the domestic and the Euromarkets. Prudential restraints of various sorts present at least a conceptual alternative. These might take the form of maximum capital-to-assets or capital-to-deposits ratios, liquidity ratios, or even credit ceilings. The suitability of any of these devices depends on whether, in addition to limiting overall expansion of the combined market in any currency, approximate competitive equality between the domestic and Euro components is also established. If capital controls, liquidity ratios, or credit ceilings simply limit the total expansion of the combined market but leave the domestic market in a condition of competitive disadvantage, then their purpose is not adequately met.

In addition, nonmarket restraints of the type mentioned tend to create market distortions. Capital ratios, for instance, by holding the volume of assets below what the market would want them to be, are likely to widen bank profit margins. The effect is analogous to that of a quota on imports. Depositors will receive less and borrowers will pay more interest than if banks were able to expand as much as they would in the absence of such controls.

Features of a System of Eurocurrency-Reserve Requirements

Some features of a reserve-requirement system may be sketched briefly. The requirements would have to be imposed by each participating country on its banks and their foreign branches and subsidiaries, wherever located. This would ensure that large banks cannot avoid the requirements by shifting their despoits to branches in nonparticipating countries. Banks in these countries, to be sure, would escape. However, the chance that banks of small or financially less advanced countries would be able to attract a significant volume of the world's deposits is small.

Reserve requirements would have to be the same in all currencies, although they could differ by maturity. An attempt to set different requirements for different currencies could easily be defeated, because banks would find it profitable to denominate their deposits and the reserves required against them in the "cheapest" currency in terms of reserve ratios, while making a forward contract with the depositor that would give him the currency he desires to hold. Even with equal requirements in all currencies, a tendency may develop to carry reserves in the currency with the lowest interest rates in order to minimize cost, again using a forward contract to provide the customer with the currency he desires to hold. However, if reserve requirements are modest, that is, in the range of perhaps 2–5 percent, and if interest-rate differentials among currencies are not extreme, these roundabout cost-minimizing transactions are unlikely to develop to any great extent.

Reserve requirements would not be placed on deposits owed to banks in participating countries. Deposits owed to private nonbanks, central banks, other official institutions, and banks of nonparticipating countries would be subject to reserve requirements. These arrangements would make sure that there was no pyramiding of requirements but that deposits of nonbanks in nonparticipating countries reaching the Euromarket through a nonparticipating intermediary would be subject to reserves.

Required reserves would be held in the currency of the deposit. They could be located, however, either in the central bank of the currency in question, in the central bank of the location of the deposit or in the central bank of the head office of the Eurobank or branch carrying the deposit. The last technique would give the home central bank a more immediate relationship with its own commercial bank, allowing it to monitor expansion more effectively. The location of the required reserves is important, of course, for the earnings of the respective central banks. None of the alternative arrangements would require a country to alter its practices with regard to the imposition or nonimposition of reserve requirements on residents. In countries that do not use reserve requirements, only nonresidents would be subject to them. In countries imposing reserve requirements on residents, the level of these requirements would not be limited by the level of the international ones.

Reserve requirements on Eurodollars are, of course, much more easily established by countries already familiar with the technique than by others using different monetary-policy tools. To reach beyond national borders to the branches and, particularly, subsidiaries of domestic banks nevertheless will probably require new legislation, even for some of the countries already possessing reserve-requirement powers. At best, therefore, the process of establishing requirements would be a slow one. Compromises are conceivable under which some countries might restrain the Eurocurrency component of their market by reserve requirements while others do it by capital ratios or other prudential methods. An essential condition of such a compromise would be that restraint exerted through different methods is approximately equal, so that none of the participating banking systems is given an advantage. Nonparticipating countries, of course, would continue to have such an advantage.

The Mounting Pressure for Restraint

As their more rapid expansion causes the Eurocurrency components of national currency markets to gain weight relative to the home components, the desire to put a restraining mechanism in place is likely to increase. At present, Euromarkets are expanding at two to three times the growth rate of most of the domestic markets in major countries. Given a doubling of the Eurocurrency component every three to four years, which would reflect recent growth rates, it would still take well over a decade before the Eurodollar market came within reach of exceeding the domestic market. But it is difficult to contemplate even an approach to such conditions without concern. The discriminatory pressure on domestic financial markets would mount as central banks sought to offset the expansion by restraining primarily these domestic markets. The potential for inflation stemming from continued rapid growth of an increasingly large volume of Euromoney and credit likewise would be alarming. Control of this inflationary potential could not be achieved, to be sure, by placing restraints on the Euromarket alone. Reserve requirements or other restraints could be expected to drive some of the financial activity into other markets, such as those for bonds and commercial paper, where costs would be lower. In the last analysis, overexpansion in all markets can be restrained only by a sufficiently high level of interst rates. But this overall restraint should occur within the context of greater competitive equality between the Euro and the domestic markets.

Notes

1. According to the U.S. definition, M_1 includes currency plus demand deposits at domestic commercial banks. M_4 includes M_1 plus savings and time deposits at domestic commercial banks.

2.

Eurodollar liabilities to nonbank U.S. residents	$25 billion
Negotiable CDs issued abroad and sold to U.S. residents about	$16 billion
¼ share of remaining $44 billion (roughly) allocated to nonbank U.S. residents	$11 billion
Total	$52 billion

See my article, "Euromarkets and U.S. Monetary Growth," *Journal of Commerce,* May 1 and 2, 1979, p. 4.

3. See Henry C. Wallich, "Innovations in Monetary Policy," paper delivered at meeting of Southern Economic Association, Atlanta, Georgia, November 18, 1976, reprinted in Ronald L. Teigen, ed., *Readings in Money, National Income, and Stabilization Policy,* Richard D. Irwin, Inc., Fourth Edition, 1978, and as chapter 10 in this volume.

22 International Lending and the Euromarkets

The Euromarkets are one of the success stories of our day, which needs a few successes. In difficult times, they have helped to keep trade flowing, they have financed investment and development, they have enabled countries to deal with their balance-of-payments problems. The Euromarkets serve as a reminder of what a market system can achieve when it is allowed to operate freely.

But the Euromarkets also have been a cause for concern from time to time. Supervisors, commercial bankers, central bankers, and perhaps even the public have worried periodically about the soundness of the Eurobanks, the soundness of the Euroborrowers, and the possible inflationary implications of the market. Perhaps this worrying has helped to forestall the problems. In a well-functioning market, crises anticipated usually do not occur. I do not mean to imply that grounds for worry have been altogether eliminated; however, the subject to worry about today in the syndicated loan market is spreads.

Euromarket Spreads

The dramatic decline in spreads between lending rates and the cost of money is not altogeher unprecedented. In 1972–1973, spreads also were severely squeezed. For a spectrum of fifteen major borrowing countries, they reached an approximate low, on a weighted-average basis, of 1.11 percent in the fourth quarter of 1973. That was a time of dangerous euphoria, when international indebtedness was much lower than it is today, the expansive forces of the international economy were much stronger, and when one could not anticipate the financing problems that were to follow the rise in the price of oil.

In 1974, spreads expanded once again as the realization of risk in Euromarkets, following the Herstatt and Franklin failures, pushed risk premia to more realistic levels. By the fourth quarter of 1975, they reached a level of 1.63 percent and remained approximately on that plateau through the middle of 1977. More recently, however, spreads once more have been cut to the bone by lessened balance-of-payments financing needs, by the pressure of strong competition among banks (resulting from slack loan demand in home markets), and by a large inflow of funds.

For particular groups of countries, the time pattern varied somewhat, with

---

This chapter was originally presented on May 9, 1978, at the 1978 Euromarkets Conference sponsored by the Financial Times, London, England.

those for non-OPEC less developed countries (LDCs) rising through 1976 and those for small OECD countries declining appreciably after 1975.

Naturally, there are always special circumstances that could explain low spreads on particular loans. At the short end, a one-shot deal at a very low spread, in the hope of being able to employ the funds more productively later, may be preferable to locking them in for a longer period at a not much better return.

At the longer end, there may be considerations of collateral business, ongoing relationships with the borrowing country, hopes of regulatory preferment in winning approval for branches, and the like that may explain, although not justify, extraordinarily low margins. There are fees, especially for lead banks, there may sometimes be balances, and sometimes banks can fund a quarter or even a half percent below the London Interbank Offering Rate (LIBOR), especially if they are prepared to do a little mismatching of maturities. On the other hand, I would not accept a bank's explanation of an unjustifiably low spread on the grounds that the bank had to maintain its share of the market. The implication that, because some banks overlend all others ought to do the same, obviously points to trouble.

Composition of the Spread

What is the anatomy of a spread? The spread must cover at least three elements: (1) the risk premium to cover losses, (2) the contribution to the bank's cost of capital related to the loan, and (3) the out-of-pocket and overhead operating costs.

The risk premium must be evaluated for each individual loan in the light of the circumstances of the borrower. An overall indication of loss prospects in international lending, which, of course, does not apply to any individual loan, can be derived from the loan losses that banks have already experienced. For a small group of American banks, the average loss during the years 1976–1977 on foreign loans has been about one third percent, as against a domestic loan-loss ratio of over three-quarters percent. The range of individual-bank experience, of course, is a good deal wider, especially on foreign loans.

The past, moveover, is not necessarily a guide to the future. Differences in individual-bank experience as well as differences in the credit standing of particular borrowers indicate that it would not be appropriate to impute to the spread some fixed-risk component. But the order of magnitude, to date, of loss experience on international loans, when compared with syndicated-loan spreads, nevertheless provides a useful benchmark.

Further, the spread must contain a contribution toward the cost of the bank's capital. It is a function of the bank's capital to support the holding of risk assets. Of course, if the bank believes itself to be acquiring a risk-free asset—a short-term interbank placement might come close to this—the acquisition would not raise the bank's ratio of risk assets to capital. The return on such an asset might not be requried to make much of a contribution toward covering the cost of capital. But assuming a not unusual capital–total-assets ratio of 5 percent, the spread on a loan of average risk must cover the required income before tax on capital equal to 5 percent of the loan. Given further a not untypical return on capital after tax of 10 percent, and a marginal tax rate of about 50 percent, the loan must earn 20 percent of 5 percent of capital, or 1 percent. These assumptions concerning capital surely are quite modest. Strictly speaking, it might be more appropriate to base this calculation on the ratio of risk assets to capital, which would call for a higher return. For some banks, however, particularly non-U.S. banks, capital ratios may be even lower than the 5 percent illustratively assumed. To the extent that banks and their supervisors regard such ratios as adequate, the cost-of-capital component of the spread is reduced.

Concerning the operating costs of putting on a loan, I have no information, although I have heard compaints about the high level of rents, the high price of lunches, and the costs inflicted by recent U.S. tax changes affecting American citizens abroad.

Putting these data together, it would appear that a spread of 1 percent, which once was considered a minimum, hardly gives a well-capitalized bank an adequate return on capital and a reasonable risk premium, with nothing left over for operating costs. A spread of 0.75 percent does not cover the cost of capital of even a very modestly capitalized bank plus a reasonable risk premium. Banks that are putting on loans at such a spread, or even less, must have substantial funding advantages, or income and other benefits from the loan, aside from the spread, or they are diluting their earnings.

I do not find at all convincing an effort to justify low premia by a misguided appeal to the principle of marginal-cost pricing—that is, that any income above out-of-pocket costs is so much money to the good. There are risks to be taken into account, and there is the bank's balance sheet, with its capital ratios and corresponding cost of capital, to be considered. A measure of cost that ignores these legitimate components of marginal cost undermines the application of a sound economic concept.

While spreads have been declining, maturities have been advancing. In terms of risk, this implies an added cost that is not covered by the movement of spreads. Longer maturities convey an indirect benefit in reducing the prospective bunching of rollovers and in reducing somewhat the disparity between the length of loans and the pay-out period of the investments that, however indirectly and remotely, are financed by them. But the lender must bear in mind that loans of long maturity are almost certain to be tested by a variety of adverse circumstances.

Comparison of Euromarket and U.S.-Bond-Market Spreads

It is interesting to compare changes in the dispersion of spreads among high- and low-risk borrowers in the Euromarket with similar changes among borrowers in the American bond market. In the Eurocurrency market, the rise in spreads was accompanied by a narrowing of the dispersion.Spreads rose most for what had originally been the low-spread borrowers. In the U.S. bond market, spreads widened as interest rates rose during 1973 and 1974. The lower-quality risks had to pay substantially more relative to the higher grades.

In terms of credit risk, it would seem that the American market rationally evaluated changing risks, allowing for a greater increase in the danger of failure among the borrowers where risk was perceived as high to begin with. The Euromarket, to the contrary, appeared to wipe out differences among borrowers and to assign to all of them a similar higher-risk rating. Conceivably, this may reflect the difference between credit risk and sovereign or country risk. The circumstances of 1974 may have been of a sort to exacerbate primarily the element of country risk.

A second and more casual observation may follow from an inspection of quality spreads in the Eurocurrency market and the U.S. bond market. In the Eurocurrency market, the spread, even for relatively weak risks, rarely has gone much above 2 percent, representing a differential over prime risks of perhaps 1.5 percent at most. In the U.S. bond market, the differential between *A*-rated utilities, by no means a weak risk, and U.S. government bonds in 1975 went above 2 percent. Given the absence of country risk in the U.S. bond market, it is hard to avoid the impression that the latter evaluates risks more sensitively and conservatively than the market for syndicated Eurocurrency loans. Whether front-end fees and the like provide reason to modify significantly this assessment cannot be said with any assurance.

Recent Decline in Spreads

Why are spreads declining so sharply in the Euromarkets? Are risks clearly diminishing? Or have banks come under such pressure to lend that the market has become clearly a borrower's market?

To both questions, the answer is yes. The condition of many borrowers has improved. But unfortunately it is also true that the pressure on banks to lend has increased. To that extent, the decline in spreads must be viewed as a very uncomfortable development. Among the pressures converging on the bank are the following:

1. Liquidity is high. Rising assets and liabilities in the Euromarket do not absorb limited supplies of reserves, as they would in national money markets. Monetary authorities, in pursuing their monetary targets, in some cases have overshot, in part because of exchange market intervention. Monetary authorities must bear in mind that money creation in the Euromarket, although historically quite limited, nevertheless occurs, and they must factor it into their overall assessment of liquidity needs.

2. Domestic loan demands in many countries other than the United States have been weak. In the United States, the large money-market banks have experienced weaker demand than the rest of the banking system. They, of course, are the principal U.S. lenders in the Eurocurrency markets.

3. There is pressure to maintain earnings growth, on penalty of being downgraded by security analysts. If their stock fails to advance, their prospects of raising new capital diminish. Yet they need to raise new capital if they want to continue to lend.

4. Banks have built up large establishments and have built in high costs that require continued activity. It would be costly to disassemble and perhaps later reassemble these.

5. Borrowing countries today are exerting powerful pressures, reminding banks of the need to maintain a continuing relationship and meanwhile taking advantage of their ability to repay and refund earlier loans at lower spreads.

6. Finally, all banks look at their peer group. So long as all do the same, no single bank needs to feel that it is making an obvious mistake, That, in some circles, is known as the lemming theory of banking.

Obviously, however compelling these considerations may appear to the individual bank, they do not justify a lowering of credit standards. Banks in the Euromarkets enjoy a degree of freedom from control that is unusual in domestic banking systems, although they, and particularly U.S. banks, are by no means unsupervised and unregulated. U.S. banks, in particular, are subject to the regular examinations and other supervisory activities of the U.S. banking agencies, no matter where their branches and subsidiaries are located. But it is true that the volume of lending in Euromarkets is less directly controlled by central-bank action than is the volume of domestic lending. Hence, banks should be disciplined all the more by high credit standards as they expand in these markets.

The Euromarkets have given evidence of what a market system can achieve when it is allowed to operate freely subject only to prudential supervision. The continuance of this freedom will depend on the responsibility with which it is used.

23 Developments in International Banking

The world of private banking has two sides. One is the substance of the business, the gathering together of money and the allocation of these resources through loans and investments. The other represents the framework, the endless ramifications of laws and regulations that determine what banks can and, more often, cannot do. For the central banker, there is a similar division between his responsibility for monetary and economic stability and his regulatory and supervisory chores that are a necessary counterpart. Both private and central bankers today are compelled to spend too large a part of their time and energy struggling with the framework. This leaves not enough time and energy to deal with what should be the substance. In line with this unfortunate trend, the following discussion will be concerned very predominantly with the framework and with the legislative and regulatory changes that are occurring in it.

National Treatment

In 1978, after extended discussions, the U.S. Congress passed the International Banking Act (IBA). The law reflected the undeniable fact that foreign banks were expanding rapidly in the United States, that these activities were to some extent free from the regulations that confine American banks, and that as a result foreign banks enjoyed a competitive advantage. Accordingly, the basic theme of the IBA has been "national treatment." Foreign banks in their numerous manifestations, as branches, subsidiaries, agencies, are to be treated like American banks to provide equality of opportunity. The alternative to national treatment which is "reciprocity," was discarded as inconsistent with our competitive philosophy as well as impractical. Given the wide disparities of legal treatment to which American banks are exposed in the foreign countries in which they operate, reciprocity would lead to a crazy quilt of divergent rules. Banks from a country with liberal banking legislation would receive correspondingly liberal treatment in the United States. Banks from a country with more confining legislation would be treated correspondingly severely. Both treatments very likely would differ also from the treatment given to U.S. banks in the United States and create competitive inequities.

National treatment, to be sure, is not always easy to define in a country

---

This chapter was originally presented on June 15, 1979, before the Association of Foreign Banks in Switzerland, Bern, Switzerland.

with such diverse banking laws and rules as the United States, which includes national banks, state member banks, state nonmember banks, insured banks, and in the various state jurisdictions. I believe that the IBA has solved these problems fairly. It has placed large foreign banks in the same framework, with respect to reserve requirements and other monetary policy tools, as well as insurance and supervision which large American banks find themselves. The "grandfathering" of existing multistate offices of foreign banks preserves a competitive advantage over American banks and takes care of what would have been legitimate complaints if foreign banks had been required to close existing offices. The outlook of the Act is toward the future, seeking to provide a framework of competitive equality.

Bankers and their supervisors must recognize nevertheless that perfect equality is unlikely to be achieved by law. In the United States, there is no law or regulation, for instance, determining the minimum amount of capital with regard to total assets, or risk assets, or deposits that banks should have. There are certain concepts of capital adequacy employed in bank examinations and in bank holding-company acquisitions. Typically these are based on the capital ratios of some peer group of the bank in question. Where appropriate, we look at these capital ratios on a consolidated basis. This is especially important in the case of banks owned by a bank holding company where the holding company has leveraged the consolidated capital further by issuing holding-company debt.

Because of different international practices with respect to requirements for consolidation, as well as differences in bank accounting in general, it is difficult to compare internationally the capital ratios of large banks. It is clear, nevertheless, that banks of some countries have substantially lower capital-asset ratios on average than do American banks. This leads to a very significant competitive advantage in the pricing of loans.

For every loan that a bank adds to its portfolio, the bank must earn an income sufficient to sustain the added capital needed to support that loan. In other words, the bank must have earnings from the loan to pay dividends and provide for retained earnings sufficient to keep the capital-asset ratio unchanged. If assets rise by 10 percent, so must capital and income after tax. How much of a spread is required to pay for the added capital depends on the cost of capital, the earnings return before taxes, and on the interest earned on the loan. Today, the interest earned on loans is high, of the order of 10 percent or more. But the cost of capital for American banks is also high, owing to the low price-earnings ratios at which their stocks are selling. After tax, a price-earnings ratio of 5 means a cost of capital of 20 percent. Before taxes on incremental income, the cost of capital could be twice that. As interest rates rise in relation to the cost of capital, that part of the cost of capital not covered by the interest on the loan diminishes. Accordingly, the spread that the bank has to charge over the cost of borrowed money to defray the cost of capital also diminshes. That may be one explanation for banks' willingness to accept lower spreads as interest rates have been rising. But at a cost of borrowed money of 10 percent and a pretax cost of capital of 40 percent, a bank with a capital ratio of 5 percent still needs a spread of 1.5 percent on the loan merely to cover its cost of capital, without any allowance for incremental risk or overhead. If interest rates were to return to more normal levels without a change in the cost of capital, the spread, to be adequate, would have to widen proportionately. For banks with capital ratios lower than 5 percent, which is the case of many foreign banks, the cost of maintaining their capital would be less, and they would have a corresponding competitive advantage.

The problem of maintaining adequate capital ratios in American banks transcends, of course, the problem of foreign competition and the advantage that foreign banks with lower capital ratios have over American banks. Capital ratios of large American banks, on average, improved during the years 1975–1976 thanks to relatively slow growth of bank assets. However, during the following two years, they tended to worsen again, as the economy, inflation, and bank lending all accelerated. Over the years, total U.S. bank assets have tended to grow at a rate slightly higher than nominal GNP, which accelerates with inflation.

To prevent a continuing shrinkage of capital ratios during high inflation, banks would have to aim at maintaining a constant rate of return on assets rather than on capital. A constant rate of return on assets will eventually lead to a capital-assets ratio that is sustainable from retentions without new stock issues, although that ratio might be inadequate. But the practice of banks seems to have been to allow the return on assets to shrink while the return on capital was increasing only moderately if at all. There is no stable capital-assets ratio at the end of this tunnel into which the banks have maneuvered themselves.

What I have said about capital ratios should suffice to make clear that the ideal of national treatment is not easily attained. Its superiority to the reciprocity principle nevertheless remains unchallenged. Reciprocity enters in only one regard: reciprocity in national treatment. Just as the United States has made an honest effort to provide national treatment for foreign banks, so the United States would like to see American banks receiving national treatment in other countries. And this means equality of treatment not only in law but in practice. Where the laws are so designed or so administered that foreign banks cannot make progress while local banks do, national treatment de facto has not been achieved, whatever the wording of the law. I expect that these issues will be examined in a study of national treatment for U.S. banks abroad mandated by the IBA, in which the Federal Reserve is participating.

Large-Bank Acquisitions by Foreign Banks

In the last few months, the Federal Reserve Board has approved the acquisition of three large American banks by foreign banks. These acquisitions have raised questions among the Congress, the public, and the regulators themselves. How open to foreign ownership should U.S. banking be?

Ours is an economy open to foreign investment. We welcome foreign competition and foreign capital. The principle of national treatment is embodied in the letter and spirit of the IBA. It has been further reaffirmed in a policy statement issued by the Federal Reserve Board on February 23, 1979, concerning foreign-bank holding companies. This statement also makes clear that safety and soundness of the banking system is the principal criterion for entry and operation of foreign banks, and that foreign-bank holding companies acquiring American banks are expected to be a source of strength to their American subsidiary. This emphasis on the foreign bank as a source of strength to the American bank is not inconsistent with the desire of foreign banks acquiring Americn banks to create what is sometimes termed a "dollar base." Participation in the already large U.S. money market will help to broaden and improve that market. But it is clear nevertheless that the resources of the acquired American banks can be drawn on by its foreign-bank holding company only within the limits set by section 23-A of the Federal Reserve Act and other applicable legal provisions. The Federal Reserve has instituted monitoring procedures to keep abreast of flows of funds between the parent and the American subsidiary and between the American subsidiary and customers of the parent. In addition, the Federal Reserve requires adequate information concerning the situation of the foreign-bank holding company.

There are certain specific advantages for the U.S. banking system and U.S. economy associated with the entry of foreign banks into the American market. Competition is enhanced to the benefit of bank customers. Traditional bank pricing and lending techniques may be shaken up by innovative foreign examples. Foreign acquisitions reduce the market supply of bank stocks, and some improvement in the very low valuation given to bank stocks in the market can be hoped for. An inflow of capital also strengthens our balance of payments.

But the United States has created, somewhat inadvertently, legal limits for the absorption of American banks by other American banks that do not necessarily apply to foreign banks that are new entrants to the U.S. market. These legal limits, therefore, provide favored treatment for the latter as far as acquisitions of American banks are concerned. An American bank seeking to acquire another bank can only do so within its home state, if at all, because the McFadden Act and the Bank Holding Company Act restrict interstate branching and interstate acquisitions of banks. At the same time this American bank is limited in the acquisitions it can make in its home state by state law and restrictions of the Clayton Act, which prohibit acquisitions "where in any line of commerce in any section of the country, the effect of such acquisition may be substantially to lessen competition, or to tend to create a monopoly.'' For a large American bank seeking a merger partner or acquirer, therefore, other large American banks either in or out of state are practically ruled out. A foreign bank may be the only possibility. From the point of view of a foreign bank, meanwhile, acquisition of a subsidiary rather than creation of a branch through merger or de novo may appear relatively more desirable than before. This is the consequence of the restrictions placed on the activities of multistate branches of foreign banks, which now can accept deposits only on the same conditions that apply to Edge corporations (edges, are subsidiaries of U.S. banks limited to foreign trade).

Some moves are afoot to improve the competitive situation of the U.S. banks in these regards. One is a proposal by the Federal Reserve Board to broaden the powers of Edge corporations under the IBA. Another is a governmental study of the McFadden Act, which restricts interstate branching. A third is a legislative proposal to permit across-state-line acquisitions of failing banks by out-of-state bank holding companies. The basic thrust of most of these proposals is toward improving the domestic side of the U.S. banking system. But some benefits are possible also in terms of the ability of U.S. banks to compete with foreign banks in the U.S. market.

Those who are concerned about the inroads made on U.S. banking by foreign acquisitions must bear in mind one fundamental cause of recent takeovers—the low value placed by the market on U.S. banks. This low value reflects a multitude of factors: the attrition of bank capital, and hence of bank earnings, by inflation; the regulatory costs visited on U.S. banks in the erroneous belief that true, that is, inflation-adjusted, bank profits are high; and, from the viewpoint of the foreign investor, the low international value of the dollar. The removal of most of these adversities to banking is in our own hands. In some cases, foreign acquisitions can be helpful to that end. Virtually no contribution, so far as I am able to see, would be made by placing restraints on the entry of foreign banks into the United States. Once more, however, I would like to revert to my earlier caveat: the only reciprocity that the United States seeks is in achieving national treatment for American banks abroad.

Capital Ratios, Liquidity, and Consolidation

The problem posed by differential capital ratios in achieving competitive equality among banks has been discussed. Capital ratios also, however, can be viewed as a means of limiting the expansion of bank credit and of the money supply. Liquidity ratios can be employed for the same purpose. An essential condition of doing either in an effective and meaningful way is the worldwide consolidation of every bank's balance sheet with those of its branches, subsidiaries, and joint ventures. The United States has practiced consolidation, for puposes of bank supervision, for at least ten years. The effect of consolidating typically, although not necessarily, is to show less liquidity and lower capital ratios together with higher concentration of loans to particular borrowers. This is the result of the consolidation process, which nets out intracompany liquidity, lengthens balance sheets as the netting out of subsidiaries' assets and liabilities disappears, and typically adds little if anything to the equity of the parent company. Naturally, there are gray areas in the process of consolidation. Precise instructions issued by the supervisors help to keep ambiguities within limits, however. On the whole, the process has proved quite feasible.

Bank-secrecy provisions in some countries have interfered marginally with consolidation. It should be noted that consolidation and its purposes are not intrinsically at odds with the purposes of meaningful and legitimate bank secrecy. Consolidation is concerned with the overall position of the bank and, where it deals with individual customers, with the bank's overall loans to a particular customer. This information is needed for evaluation of risk. Consolidation is not directly concerned with the deposits of individual customers. Typically, it is deposits of, rather than loans to, customers with which bank secrecy is concerned. Therefore, it should be quite possible to reconcile consolidation with a reasonable degree of confidentiality concerning the deposits of particular customers.

The United States has not tried to use consolidated balance sheets for the purpose of restraining bank credit, either by way of capital ratios, liquidity ratios, or overall credit ceilings. Detailed studies that have been made indicate that it would be extremely difficult to arrive at capital ratios for U.S. banks that would be fair in an overall sense, appropriate to the current and often very different positions of individual banks, and effective in achieving the purpose of macro restraint over economic activity. The nature and quality of bank assets differ enormously. A given capital ratio, therefore, would not imply equal protection for depositors and creditors in different banks.

Notwithstanding these considerations, capital adequacy is, of course, a major concern to U.S. bank supervisors. It represents one of the five categories under which banks are rated, the others being quality of assets, quality of management, earnings, and liquidity. But although differential ratings have proved possible and indeed desirable, rigid standards have not.

This does not imply that capital standards could not have usefulness in particular circumstances. Some countries are indeed applying them as part of their prudential regulatory approach. What needs to be examined is whether an adequate degree of consolidation is observed. Capital-adequacy standards for banks with large unconsolidated subsidiaries are not meaningful, nor would be standards for banks with holding companies unless these are consolidated. Properly designed capital standards could also be employed for monetary control purposes, perhaps on an incremental basis to minimize inequities, if other tools of monetary policy do not suffice.

Similar considerations apply to liquidity as a possible constraint on bank lending. The time has long gone when bank liquidity could be evaluated in terms of the volume of short-term liquid assets—so-called secondary and perhaps tertiary liquidity. Today, bank liquidity consists largely of access to borrowed funds and of the maintenance of a degree of solvency and a standing in the market that assures this kind of access. The concepts of liquidity and solvency are converging.

A distinction can be drawn, however, between liquidity in the bank's home currency and liquidity to meet obligations in foreign currency. Liquidity in the bank's home currency derives strength from its intimate relationship with the domestic money market. It derives strength also from the presence of a lender of last resort who can issue the bank's home currency. In the case of American banks, finally, liquidity derives strength from the presence of an insurer who protects deposits up to a limited amount and who can, in appropriate circumstances, deal with a failing bank through the device of purchase and assumption as employed by the Federal Deposit Insurance Corporation (FDIC) in accordance with its statutes and policies. To the extent that a bank operates in foreign currencies, liquidity must be viewed differently. The matching of maturities of foreign-currency assets and liabilities must be more closely observed. Domestic liquidity does not always translate unequivocally into liquidity in foreign currencies. For this reason, it would probably be difficult to arrive at standards of liquidity that would be comparable internationally.

Reserve Requirements on Euromarket Liabilities

In view of the difficulty of achieving some degree of control of international bank lending through capital standards, liquidity standards, and consolidation, the concept of reserve requirements on the Euromarket deserves intensive study. The Euromarkets constitute an important source of credit and monetary claims. They add to the world's liquidity in a manner that is not readily taken into account by the national monetary policies of the countries whose currencies are involved. Given the competitive advantages of the Euromarkets, and the growing awareness of borrowers and depositors of the opportunities offered by these markets, rapid growth of money and credit creation in these markets must be expected. Over time, expansion in these markets might come to equal or exceed domestic creation of money and credit.

It is important, therefore, to make sure that domestic monetary and credit policies are not undermined and circumvented by the expansion of the Euromarkets. These markets are not "out of control" in the sense that is sometimes alleged. The volume of money and credit that they create depends on the level of interest rates, which, in turn, is closely related to interest rates in home markets. But, typically, interest rates for the depositor in Euromarkets are higher and rates charged to the borrower are lower than the corresponding rates in home markets. This reflects cost advantages such as freedom from reserve requirements, absence of deposit-insurance premia, and economies of scale. It would take more severe restriction in domestic markets, therefore, to bring about a given amount of restraint in Euromarkets. Moreover, it must be expected that as more restraint is exerted in domestic markets, some of the domestic demand will shift to the Euromarket and be met there, although at rising interest rates.

In time, therefore, the Euromarkets are likely to pose a mounting threat to domestic monetary policy. To be effective with respect to the total creation of money and credit in a given currency, both at home and in the Euromarket, growth of money and credit must be slowed increasingly in the domestic market, to the detriment of borrowers dependent on this market. Moreover, as the share of the Euromarket in aggregate money and credit creation expands, the inflationary potential mounts unless domestic monetary policy is geared increasingly toward controlling expansion in the Euromarket via stringency imposed at home. This situation is likely to convey a mounting inflationary bias to monetary policies as the Euromarkets gain on domestic markets.

Reserve requirements or other restraints imposed on Eurodeposits would help to stem this development. So would, of course, removal of reserve requirements or other restraints from domestic deposits. Either action would reduce the competitive edge of the Eurobanking markets and place them more nearly in conditions of equality with domestic banking markets. If the expansion of the Euromarkets proceeds at a rate not greater than domestic monetary expansion, much of the inflationary bias will disappear. Removal of reserve requirements in the United States could undermine this advantage, however, by removing one of the bases of the monetary-policy mechanism.

As matters stand now, control over the volume of money and credit in any currency with a Eurocomponent threatens gradually to slip out of the hands of the central banks. This development has begun slowly but is accelerating and can be expected to accelerate further. That is why the concept of reserve requirements on Euromarkets deserves intense study. An idea such as this takes time to mature, and it is, therefore, essential that we begin our preparations now and prepare this instrument for the day when we may need it.

24 The Future Role of the Commercial Banks

Some of the problems in managing country risk today are quite reminiscent of those of mid 1977. Curiously, however, this is in good part not because the problems have persisted but because, after at least in some degree having gone away, they have now come back with a vengeance. By that I mean, of course, that in 1977 we were still concerned with the problems created by the oil-price rises of 1973–1974. One pressing issue was the allocation of OPEC-induced current-account deficits. Should the deficits end up in the less developed countries (LDSs), where the capital inflow might be most needed, or in the industrial countries that could best finance them? In the period following, the surplus of the OPEC nations largely vanished, a massive deficit appeared in the United States and disappeared again, and the developing countries continued to grow, thanks in large part to continued heavy bank borrowing. Now the OPEC surplus is back bigger than ever. One factor, however, has changed significantly: the ability of the banking system to handle the ensuing deficits on the terms and conditions to which the market has become accustomed.

Until very recently, the market was very much a borrower's market. Minimal spreads, a severely compressed differential among spreads for different borrowers, longer maturities, and the large size of loans all document this condition. There are several reasons why this situation is likely to change. They lie both on the side of the borrowers and of the banks. On the side of the borrowing LDCs there is, first, the higher burden of oil imports. This comes on top of an already visible increase in burden of debt relative to the ability to carry it. At the new level of oil prices, the oil-import bill will absorb, on average, one-third of the export receipts of oil-importing LDCs in contrast to an earlier one-sixth. This leaves less available for debt service as well as for payment of other imports. It changes, in other words, the meaning of a given debt-service ratio.

There is, second, the previous rise in the burden of debt. This rise is by no means spectacular, but neither can it continue to be overlooked. Aggregate foreign debts of nonoil LDCs approximately tripled in the five years from 1973 to 1978 and rose perhaps an additional 25 percent in 1979. These rough numbers ignore unrecorded short-term debt, which adds to the burden, as well as the growth of foreign-exchange reserves, which reduces it. But the proportionate increase in the debt would hardly be much altered if these variables, which

This chapter was originally presented on January 24, 1980, at the conference on New Approaches and Techniques for Managing Country Risk, New York City.

probably rose on roughly the same scale during the period, were taken more fully into account. Since oil-importing developing countries experienced substantial inflation in their foreign trade prices—perhaps 70 percent in export-unit values and 80 percent in import-unit values—the increase in debt burden in real terms is a good deal less. What is more, the real interest rate paid by the average borrower was probably negative. The London Inter-Bank Offer Rate (LIBOR) for ninety-day dollar obligations averaged 7.9 percent over the years 1973–1978, as against an average price increase of about 11 percent. Only in 1979, did LIBOR at 12 percent exceed a rise in the price of primary products (excluding oil) of 10.4 percentage points. Of course, the experience of some countries is bound to have differed from these averages. Because of these differences, the real interest rate, defined as the nominal interest rate minus the expected rate of inflation over the life of a loan, in an international context, is less meaningful than in a domestic context.

But despite negative real interest rates, the familiar debt ratios have tended to increase. From 1973 to 1978, the average ratio of gross debt to GNP rose from 17 to 23 percent, that of net debt (after deducting reserves) to GNP from 11 to 17 percent, and debt-service requirements to total exports rose from 14 to 17 percent, for a group of ninety-nine nonoil LDCs. Recognizing the wide variance of these ratios among countries, as well as great differences among countries in their ability to handle debt, and keeping in mind also the limitations of any form of ratio analysis, these data nevertheless signify some deterioration up to the end of 1978.

It is at this point in the story that the rising price of oil threatens to raise the deficit of nonoil LDCs from $25 billion (including official transfers) in 1978 to perhaps $50 billion (including official transfers) in 1980. This suggests a different response to the problem of deficits than was widely adopted in 1973–1974. If at that time the principle was to finance rather than to adjust, today it may need to be reversed. Many developing countries will be well advised to stress balance-of-payments adjustment in preference to additional financing. Some adjustments are already underway, as witness the devaluations in Brazil, Chile, and Korea. Such adjustments should be easier to make in today's environment than in 1974–1975, because world economic activity is better maintained than it was then.

My main concern, however, is with the lenders rather than with the borrowers. How much of the borrowing of the developing countries will the bank be able and willing to handle? Outstanding claims on nonoil LDCs of all banks reporting to the Bank for International Settlements (BIS) rose at an average rate of 23 percent per year from December 1975 through June 1979. Such a rate of growth exceeds, of course, the rate of overall credit expansion that can be sustained by any banking system not in the grip of galloping inflation.

For instance, total bank credit in the United States, over the same period, grew at an average annual rate of 10.9 percent. Shifts in the composition of assets, implying faster growth of some and slower growth of other components are, of course, always going on and are indicative of the flexibility of the banking system; but as particular components, such as LDC loans, come to constitute an increasing share of the total, their growth necessarily must slow down. Thus, the rapid growth of LDC lending had some of the characteristics of the filling of a vacuum. Lenders, borrowers, and regulators all have an interest in seeing that this vacuum is not converted into a compression chamber. That is implicit in the dynamics of any growth pattern. In the case of bank lending to nonoil LDCs, it is the consequence also of particular limitations encountered by banks in terms of their risk exposure with respect to particular borrowers and their overall ratio of capital to assets.

Banks chartered in the United States already have substantially slowed their lending to developing countries. Between December 1975 and June 1979, their share in total international claims on nonoil LDCs of banks reporting to the BIS dropped from 54 percent to 38 percent. Their share in annual net new lending (after repayments) dropped from 46 percent ($13 billion) to 15 percent ($6 billion). The U.S. bank share in claims on oil-exporting countries dropped from 52 percent to 35 percent; their share in net new lending dropped from 58 percent to 5 percent.

The substantial slowing that has taken place in LDC lending by U.S. banks sometimes is overlooked when attention is focused on the geographic location of the lending office instead of on the nationality of its control. For example, U.S. balance-of-payments data on bank claims cover all banking institutions located in the United States, including the U.S. agencies and branches of foreign banks. Thus, although these data are useful for capital-flow analysis, they do not necessarily reflect the office of the bank responsible for the lending decision nor the country of the bank that bears the ultimate exposure to risk on a loan. Control of lending policy, as well as risk exposure, of course, runs to the bank's head office independently of the country in which the lending office happens to be located.

The slowing of LDC lending by U.S. banks no doubt reflects in part their often-voiced concern about the inadequacy of spreads on syndicated Eurocurrency credits. It reflects also the stronger demand for funds in the U.S. domestic market. Finally, it may reflect tightening monetary policy and rising interest rates in the United States as well as greater monetary ease in many foreign countries, although to the extent that foreign banks make dollar loans, the volume of their lending is also influenced by U.S. monetary policies.

Capitol ratios and LDC-risk exposure of U.S. banks also may be assumed to have played a role in their decision to slow LDC lending. The ratio of equity capital to total assets of the nine U.S. banks with the most international business, after improving from a low of 3.7 percent in 1974 to 4.3 percent in 1976, once more deteriorated to 3.9 percent by mid-1979. Bank earnings have been inadequate to keep bank capital growing in line with the inflation-driven volume of bank assets. Assuming a dividend payout of one-third, banks would have had to earn 18 percent on assets to keep up with the approximate 12 percent average growth of bank assets during the years 1976–1978 if they are to rely almost exclusively on retentions. But new stock issues, which could relieve this situation, have been very difficult to make, given the very low price-earnings ratios characteristic of leading U.S. banks. These reflect, in turn, the market's realization that the real value of bank capital and, therefore, bank earnings is reduced by a factor of about ¾ of the going rate of inflation, making allowance for nonmonetary assets equal to only about ¼ of capital that could protect that capital against inflation.

Foreign banks in many instances are less constrained by capital than are American banks and thus can accept lower spreads. In some countries, lower capital ratios than in the United States are characteristic of most banks. In some countries also, foreign banks receive better protection against inflation by a greater ownership of nonmonetary assets such as participations and real estate. Maintenance of capital ratios has been easier for such banks because a better inflation protection of earnings has permitted stock issues. In some countries, finally, banks are owned and backed by their government.

But it is probably in terms of risk exposure with respect to particular borrowing countries that U.S. banks have encountered some of their most obvious limitations. The in-house country limits set by banks, arrived at normally on the basis of careful country-risk analysis, are, of course, fairly flexible. But banks nevertheless have to watch carefully their concentration ratios, which are monitored by means of the country risk evaluation system employed by the Federal Reserve, the Federal Deposit Insurance Corporation (FDIC), and the Comptroller of the Currency. These focus on the percentage of capital exposed to risk in each particular country. For most industrial countries, regulatory considerations are not particularly inhibiting. Exposures over 25 percent of capital funds in any such country are listed in examination reports, but usually no comment on such exposures is made. For most G-10 countries, lending by many U.S. banks exceeds 25 percent of capital.

For many LDCs, however, exposures even to most of the financially stronger borrowers, would be listed if the level exceeded 10 percent of capital funds, and exposures in excess of 15 percent receive special comment in the examination reports. The largest LDC borrowers would be subject to such comment in a number of U.S. banks. Comment does not necessarily imply that there is an inherent credit weakness, but it is made to alert management to exposure levels. Although banks are not prevented in any way from making loans to LDCs in excess of the comment level, a decision to raise exposure significantly is properly one to be taken in full awareness of the facts by senior management. Qualitative differences in exposure, as inherent for instance in the difference between short-term, trade-related credits and long-term, syndicated loans, are important.

If banks with exposures above the comment level wished to avoid an increase in these exposures, their lending could increase only in proportion to the growth of their capital, that is, roughly on the order of 10 percent of present lending levels. For the group of banks having much the largest part of the loans to Brazil and Mexico, for instance, such an internal decision would mean an increase in loans to Brazil of about $1.5 billion over the next year.

Broader participation in LDC lending by larger numbers of banks would help to make more flexible the supply of bank loans for LDCs. The reduction in the share of U.S. banks in this lending, accompanied by strong expansion, at least until recently, by banks of many other countries, represents one such form of diversification. However, within the confines of U.S. banks, there has been no broadening of participation in foreign lending generally. On the contrary, the share of the nine largest money-center banks in loans to foreign banks and nonbanks remained virtually unchanged at 68.2 percent in December 1977 and 68.6 percent in June 1979. The share of these banks in loans to LDCs stood at 63.9 percent and 64.5 percent during the same period. Meanwhile, fifteen regional banks reduced their share in total loans to foreigners from 17.4 percent to 16.5 percent, while that in loans to LDCs remained constant at 18.7 percent. Other banks, accounting for relatively small amounts, reduced their share of lending to LDCs.

So far, the slower LDC lending by U.S. banks seems to have been compensated by more aggressive lending on the part of the banks of other countries. If the slower expansion of LDC lending by U.S. banks had continued since mid-1979, there would nevertheless be room in the portfolios of banks in other countries or the obligations of creditworthy LDCs. Most of the large non-U.S. banks still appear to have a lower ratio of foreign assets to total assets than do large U.S. banks. They should be able therefore to accommodate a relative increase in foreign lending. It seems likely though, that lenders will have to be offered better terms and that borrowers may have to look toward adjustment rather than financing to an increasing degree. In this regard, it might be noted that Japanese banks have recently also curtailed their foreign lending.

For the longer run one must ask whether the world's banking system can meet increasing demands by the LDCs, even if these demands reflect genuine investment financing rather than the financing of consumption-oriented oil imports. The banks have, in a sense, pioneered LDC lending. Their lending practices have many desirable attributes that would make a continued strong role of the banks in LDC financing constructive.

There is no shortage of funds in world financial markets, thanks not only to OPEC surpluses but also to the demonstrated ability of the Euromarkets to draw funds from all over the world by offering attractive interest rates. Nor is there a shortage of high-quality assets in which OPEC and other surplus countries, if there are any, could invest these surpluses. The difficulty resides in recycling these funds toward the deficit countries, where they would be at some risk. It seems incumbent on OPEC to assume some of the risks inherent in the process.

New forms of bank pioneering may be needed. For instance, banks might take on the role of arrangers or brokers of loans. The risk of such loans would fall on the ultimate lender, instead of a bank substituting its own credit for that of the borrower. Such activities would not strain the banks' capital ratios.

The IMF may have to play a larger role. Banks have been partly at fault in creating a situation in which the IMF has been brought into the financing picture only after the banks have vanished from the scene as willing suppliers of a weakening borrower's credit. Banks have appeared to act as if countries were either creditworthy, in which case they got all the money they wanted, or they were not, in which case no further credit was offered. Some form of cooperation with the IMF, which would strengthen the borrower's performance through IMF conditionality, would be preferable to such an all-or-nothing approach. As we look toward the future, LDCs will need more new forms of financing.

Part V
Banking

25 Banks Need More Freedom to Compete

Public regulation of business has a long history of coddling regulated industries to death. The pattern of excessive solicitude began with the ICC and the railroads. Today the Federal Reserve, together with the other bank regulators and Congress, is doing the same to banking. The Fed keeps banks from paying competitive rates on deposits. Old limitations, such as the restrictions on branching, become increasingly anachronistic in today's world of instant communication. The House of Representatives has passed a measure that would keep the banks from going after new types of business. And the Federal Reserve has been flirting with legislation to "improve," that is, probably toughen, the regulatory setup. If the banks cannot break out of this pattern, they are in danger of going the way of the railroads.

Unlike other industries, banks are subject to few technological constraints. There are only so many basic processes for making steel, but the business of raising money and lending it out can be conducted in an infinite variety of ways. While the steel company, moreover, must freeze its assets in some particular technology for many years, most bank assets are liquid, or nearly so. A bank can shift quickly from one form of lending to another. The liabilities through which a bank raises its funds are also subject to rapid change. Essentially, a bank is a system of information—relating to depositors, borrowers, and their accounts—combined with a fund of liquid capital. This means that the payoff to imagination and flexibility can be high—if the regulators do not put up obstructions. It also means, of course, that the banks continually encounter new nonbank competitors in areas of the business they thought they had to themselves.

Fear of the Money Power

In other countries, banks have been allowed to take advantage of their technological freedom to engage in a wide variety of financial activities. By spreading out, functionally and geographically, they have been able to compensate for the constant erosion of their traditional base. In the United States, the constraints that the laws of nature do not impose on the business have been imposed by the laws of man. Banking, with its three federal and fifty state supervisory

---

This chapter was originally published in *Fortune* March 1970, pp. 114–115, 140, 143.

authorities, and bodies of law to match, is the most overregulated industry in the country.

Why, in an economy freer than most, is banking singled out for this excess of governmental solicitude? The United States has some of the best banks in the world, but it surely has the worst banking system of any major nation. This is not the fault of the banker. It is the fault of the legislator. To be sure, the legislator has tried to deal with real problems. The frequent miscarriage of his more or less well meant efforts was not always foreseeable. But this is precisely the usual fate of well-intentioned regulation.

The history of banking in the United States is pockmarked with bank failures. In the nineteenth century, the United States, unlike many of today's underdeveloped countries, sought to maintain a stable parity for the currency. The financial pressures that elsewhere were relieved by inflation and depreciation of the currency thus had to take the form of bankruptcies. Confronted with frequent failures, the legislator has tried to safeguard the depositor. Other countries have done this by allowing banks to branch out and become so large as to be reasonably safe, or at least easy to bail out. In the United States, fear of the "money power" has blocked this route. Instead, the legislator undertook to tell the banks what they could do and not do—tell them in stultifying detail and, of course, differently in each state.

Successive upheavals brought successive waves of legislation and regulation. Bad banking experience before the Civil War (plus the need to finance that war) gave us the national banking system and the Comptroller of the Currency. Various money panics over the following fifty years gave us the Federal Reserve System. Failure of the Fed to prevent the collapse of nearly two-fifths of the banks in the great depression gave us the Federal Deposit Insurance Corporation (FDIC).

The depression brought other changes on the banks, too. Congress ordered them to divest themselves of their securities business and prohibited payment of interest on demand deposits. Congress also gave the Fed power to limit interest on time deposits and to vary member-bank reserve requirements. All these actions, of course, bear directly on bank profits, but their consequences were not realized for some time. Initially, the most important legacy of the depression was the tripartite structure of regulation, the comptroller having primary responsibility for national banks, the Fed for state member banks, and the FDIC for insured nonmember banks.

These three protectors of the public's interest have done their best to fill their difficult assignment. They have tried to keep individual banks sound and to regulate competition. The first has meant sending out an army of bank examiners to conduct periodic examinations. The second has meant controlling entry and exit through control of chartering, branching, and mergers. There was to be enough competition to check monopoly and assuage popular fears of the "money power," but not so much as to risk failures.

A case can be made for superimposing the caution of the regulator on that of bank management, but keeping banks sound by limiting what they can do is an expensive way of protecting our deposits. In a world where risk and return are positively correlated, returns are likely to be higher on high-risk loans, not only for the bank but also for society.

Holding Back the Tide

Where the banks have been stopped most decisively has been in their attempts to expand, whether geographically or into new lines of business. American restrictions on bank branching and mergers are unique in the world. Left to itself, banking apparently tends toward concentration—banking systems all over the world attest to that. The United States alone has played King Canute to this tide, and very successfully. We still have 14,000 banks, about 85 percent of them with deposits under $25 million. Merger is minutely regulated with a view to its impact on competition. Branching, regulated by state law, is tightly restricted. State-chartered banks can at most branch statewide. Some states disallow all and any branching. To make sure that all banks are treated equally badly, the law in its wisdom has subjected national banks to the branching laws of the states in which they operate.

Resistance to concentration must be understood as a political phenomenon. On the economic merits of the case it is difficult to be dogmatic. Banks have formidable powers to help or hurt other enterprises, and concentration of these powers in a few nationwide branch systems would give one pause. In West Germany and Japan the power of banks, derived not only from their lending activity, have attracted concerned attention. It is also true, however, that West Germany and Japan have had not only the most powerful banking systems but also very remarkable records of economic growth. In any event, the recurrent issue in U.S. bank regulation is not whether the Bank of America or the big New York and Chicago banks should be allowed to form nationwide branch systems. The great bulk of regulatory activity in this field focuses on whether the First National Bank of Jonesville should be allowed to merge with the State Bank & Trust of neighboring Smithville. More of the Federal Reserve Board's time is spent on items in this range than on whether the money supply should be increased.

Econometricians believe they have discovered that it does make a difference, with respect to loan rates, deposit rates, or loan size, whether there are one or two banks in town. But for the people in that town it would probably matter more whether there were one or two supermarkets. No regulatory authority watches over that.

Politically, the issue is simple. Small fish do not welcome competition from big fish, and certainly do not want to be eaten. Legislation designed to protect competition ends up protecting competitors. Ostensibly intended to block the money power, it serves primarily to give the local banker a mild form of local monopoly.

The fragmentation of the American banking system, to be sure, has been less damaging than one might have expected. Through the elaborate system of correspondent relationships between "country banks" and banks in money centers, the small banks have created for themselves many of the benefits of branch banking without losing their independence. Before many years, however, the advent of an increasingly automated payment and credit system may change this. As messages imprinted on paper, called currency and checks, are gradually replaced by messages imprinted on computer memories, distance between the bank and its customer will matter less. A man might bank all year without ever setting foot in, or driving a car into, the premises of a bank. When this becomes possible, big banks will be able to deal with small out-of-town customers. In other words, they will increasingly compete with their correspondents.

At that time, technology quite possibly may prevail over regulation, ideology, and political influence. The United States then may find its banking system becoming more highly concentrated, in substance if not in outward appearance. Skeptics may prefer to believe that local interests will succeed in promoting regulation to prevent this outcome. If the logic of computer technology is defeated, the cost that regulation imposes on the U.S. economy will rise.

Like Digging Holes in a Road

Being a product of successive crises, the banking system and its regulatory superstructure are quite lacking in the orderly design that a good planner would create if he were building from scratch, or even rebuilding. One thing, however, can be said on behalf of the existing superstructure: it is inefficient. Observers have pointed out that, since bankers have the power to choose their regulators, the present system generates competition in laxity. In recent years, when Comptroller of the Currency James Saxon and his successor William Camp liberalized the treatment of national banks, state banks began to convert to national charter, including such giants as Chase Manhattan, Wells Fargo, and Wachovia. When the Federal Reserve was bearing down hard on its member banks through reserve requirements and limitation of borrowing privileges, it found small banks backing away from membership in the system. To preserve its constituency, the Fed has proposed liberalized discount facilities, although many economists question the wisdom of thus weakening central-bank control.

Because bankers can count on the desire of competing regulators to preserve—or enlarge—their constituencies, they are usually supporters of the prevailing tripartite division of power. But it is an enormously inefficient method of loosening the stranglehold of regulation. An unhappy regulator recently compared it to digging holes in a road in order to enforce a speed limit. Still, it is preferable to the alternative of a unified supervisory system pursuing a hard line.

Plans for a unified regulator are in the air. A leading proponent of the idea has been James Robertson, the energetic vice-chairman of the Federal Reserve Board. Robertson wants the Fed to get out of the regulatory business and concentrate more fully on monetary policy. This, to be sure, would have certain advantages. The Fed is unquestionably one of the best agencies in the federal government, with high technical competence, and this resource should be reserved for top-drawer issues. But if the single agency Robertson proposes were to materialize, the banks might find themselves moving from a low-flame frying pan into a rather hot fire.

While the unified regulator so far is only a dream (for many bankers a bad one), other regulatory issues have reached the crisis stage. Congress unwittingly planted a time bomb in the 1930s when it told the banks to stop paying interest on demand deposits and empowered the Fed to fix a ceiling for interest on time deposits. That bomb has finally gone off.

What Congress originally had in mind was to protect the depositor by protecting banks even more effectively against having to compete with each other. Paying high interest to attract deposits, it was argued, made the banks take on high-risk loans. If they did not have to compete with each other for money, they would be safer. Theorists, incidentally, have always questioned this reasoning. They maintain that a well-run bank would normally pick the highest-yielding loans after allowing for a risk discount, so its choice of loans would not depend on what it had to pay for money. But bankers do not read theorists, and theorists do not run banks.

The Fed got its power, which it spelled out under Regulation Q, and nobody paid much attention so long as interest rates remained low. Bankers enjoyed their cheap sources of funds. They were pained, to be sure, that their archcompetitors, the savings-and-loan associations, were expanding so much faster. But few bankers seemed to think that their paying little or nothing on deposits had much to do with that.

Blocked from Getting Even

By 1961, however, it had become increasingly obvious that in a world where interest rates were secularly rising, principal reliance on an interest-free source of funds was not a good way of staying in business. So banks began to sell certificates of deposits at competitive rates. Time deposits zoomed. For the first time since the war, banks were able to hold their own against competing financial intermediaries. The whole nature of the business changed. Earlier, a banker had to limit his lending in accordance with the inflow of deposits. Now if a customer unexpectedly asked for a large loan, the banker could go out and buy the money.

Then the banks ran into Regulation Q. As open-market rates rose above the Q ceilings, big holders ran off their CDs and reinvested in other paper. From a mild device to limit bank competition, Regulation Q was promoted to a powerful instrument of credit control. The banking business was once more turned upside down. Far from being able to buy money, the banker saw even the money he had draining away.

The Fed had two reasons for keeping the screws on firmly in 1966 and in 1969. Foremost was the need, a very real one, to counteract the overheating of the economy. In addition, however, the monetary authorities had to worry about the savings-and-loan industry. Because of their sluggishly revolving portfolios of mortages, the S and Ls could not keep up with the fast-rising pace of interest rates. The banks, with their more flexible portfolios, could have out competed them easily, had not the regulators decided to sit on the banks the first time they had a chance to get even with their old competitors. In the end, both the banks and the S and Ls lost funds to the more competitive open market—the much-discussed phenomenon of ''disintermediation.''

Having made firm loan commitments, the banks began to look around for money. The Eurodollar became a major source. So the Fed felt compelled to move in once more. The Fed could not keep the banks from borrowing abroad, but it could, and last October did, make this borrowing more expensive by subjecting it to reserve requirements.

The banks, under enormous pressure, looked for money elsewhere. Some of them, through their holding companies, began to issue commercial paper. The Fed announced that it might subject commercial paper to Regulation-Q ceilings or to reserve requirements, or both. Imposition of Q would make the sale of commercial paper impossible while market rates were above the ceiling. In this game of cat and mouse, no newly found hole seemed safe.

An Outdated Reliance

When the present high-pressure period is over and bankers can add up the experience, it will become clear, above all, that they need stable and reliable sources of funds. Otherwise, the industry can scarcely hold its share of the financial market. To obtain the funds they need, banks will have to pay competitive rates. In an age of high interest rates, reliance on demand deposits is almost as anachronistic as reliance on passenger traffic would be for the railroads.

Banks do, of course, pay an implicit interest rate on demand deposits, in the form of free check-clearing services. Bankers and their big depositors know very well what that is worth. But the higher interest rates go, the more it pays depositors to economize on the holding of cash balances. As more highly automated payment techniques are introduced, factors adversely affecting the demand-deposit side of the banking business will multiply. Check clearing will increasingly come to be seen as an industrial operation rather than a financial one. The involvement of bank officers with the money mechanism, and the resources that can be obtained from it, will diminish. Their concern will focus onto the raising and use of funds from other sources.

To stay in the running, banks increasingly will have to replace demand deposits with time deposits. Even then, time deposits will be a reliable source of funds only if the Fed can be prevailed on to give up the use of Regulation Q as a credit-control instrument. The banks could help to bring the Fed along by making its job of regulating credit less difficult. If banks issue binding credit commitments to their customers and thus insulate them against credit restriction, they invite stiff Fed policies. If some restraint can be put on these commitments, if necessary by subjecting them to reserve requirements, the Fed might unbend. If the Fed does not, it will have to face up to the fact that, in trying to regulate money and credit, it is undermining the industry through which it must operate.

When the present demand for bank credit lets up, banks will discover also that they are competing not only for funds but also for outlets. To be competitive, they must make it attractive to borrow from banks. In the recent period of strenuous demands for funds, of course, banks have hardly been beset with this problem. But for considerable periods earlier, they had to contend with mounting encroachment on their lending by life-insurance companies and pension funds, and lately new breeds of competing lenders have reared up—finance companies, take-over specialists, high-risk lenders ready and eager to accept equity kickers. In times of less intense demand, the banks will have to adjust their lending to changes in competition and markets.

Historically the banks have succeeded in making such adjustments. As demand fell off for shorter commercial loans, banks shifted to term loans, consumer credit, factoring, and other forms of credit that earlier were considered unbankable. By and large, the regulators have not stood in the way of such innovative financial engineering.

This happy state, however, may not survive. Banks now see opening before them new types of financial business that their flexible technology makes feasible. Universal credit cards, data processing, mutual funds, insurance selling, and specialized high-risk financing are part of the financial wave of the future. Banks have tried to enter these fields through subsidiaries, or through one-bank holding companies, but have encountered regulatory resistance. Because many such activities are deemed "bank-related" rather than banking proper, they often do not fit into the regulatory mold.

Cut off from Much of the Action

The one-bank holding company is an ingenious effort, on the part of large banks, to break out of the regulatory mold. By creating a parent company capable of acquiring other subsidiaries for itself, a bank can indirectly engage in activities that regulation makes it inconvenient or impossible to handle directly. But antibank forces headed by Congressman Wright Patman of Texas have succeeded in getting through the House of Representatives a bill that would in effect strait-jacket one-bank holding companies. If this legislation prevails, banks will find themselves cut off from much of the financial action of the future. Combined with shrinking or unreliable sources of funds, this new form of regulation could condemn the banks to ultimate irrelevance in the financial framework. It might point them toward a useful but profitless existence like that of railroads.

On the other hand, if the banks are allowed to follow where innovative financial technology leads them, we may see them ending up quite far from where they stand today. Their concentration on the routine mechanisms of checking accounts will abate. This might happen quite rapidly if, as is not unlikely, the savings-and-loan associations and the mutual savings banks are allowed to accept checking deposits. The banks cannot hope to expand into other fields unless they are prepared to see freer access to their own home grounds accorded to their competitors. With the money business largely out of the way, banks will increasingly be raising funds from nondeposit sources. And they will increasingly be using their funds for purposes other than commercial loans. There will then be no more reason to regulate their activities than there is today to limit and regulate the activities of finance companies. Ordinary antitrust considerations should then be sufficient to control the banking business, as they have been for business in general.

26 Reflections on Glass-Steagall

The Glass-Steagall Act was enacted thirty-five years ago, mainly in order to protect the public against conflicts of interest in banking, to protect the banks against underwriting risks, and to protect the economy against the supposedly destabilizing effects of banks' securities operations. Since that time, the economic scene has experienced numerous changes bearing on the merits of the issue. Let us reexamine Glass-Steagall in the light of these developments and of current conditions.

What Has Happened

During the life of the Glass-Steagall Act, the economy, the banks, and the securities industry all have had their ups and downs. After working out of the Great Depression and going through World War II, the American economy enjoyed a period of almost unprecedented growth and stability. Capital flows, and their distribution among sectors, seemed adequate to more or less maintain the historical rate of growth.

That growth, to be sure, and the capital formation that supported it, did not compare at all favorably with the growth and savings rates of other industrial countries. It is conceivable that the separation of commercial and investment banking had something to do with our slower rate of growth. It has frequently been argued, for instance, that German reliance on a full-service type of banking system contributed to the high rate of growth of that country since the beginning of its industrialization over 100 years ago. That proposition, however, is not uncontested—with evidence for and against.[1] In any event, the changes that Glass-Steagall wrought on the American banking scene probably were modest measured in the perspective of the overall difference between the American and the German banking systems.

During the 1970s, however, evidence of inadequacies in the flow of capital appeared. The cost of capital rose appreciably, given the decline of stock prices relative to earnings. For new ventures and for small firms, access to the capital market became very difficult. These conditions contrasted sharply with those

---

This paper was coauthored by Ellen D. Harvey.

The authors gratefully acknowledge the helpful suggestions made by Galen Burghardt in the preparation of this article. Responsibility for error is their own. This chapter was originally published in *The Bankers Magazine* 161 (March–April 1978):9–13.

prevailing earlier in securities markets. Questions began to be raised about the continued ability of the American economy to expand and provide jobs.

The commercial-banking industry entered upon the same period in a condition of semistagnation. From 1934 to 1960 the share of bank credit in total funds raised by the nonfinancial sectors of the economy remained low. Thereafter, thanks to numerous financial innovations, commercial banking expanded rapidly. Businesses, homeowners, consumers, all benefited from the broadening availability of bank credit.

Then came the recession of 1974, which brought serious losses. At that time, newly established bank holding companies had been extending their operations into new areas of financial activity, such as mortgage banking, consumer finance, and advising and financing real-estate investment trusts. The holding companies' experience in many cases was sufficiently adverse to justify the conclusion that the banks were fortunate not to have been burdened, at the same time, with securities affiliates. In 1974, Glass-Steagall stood the banks in good stead.

Developments in the Securities Industry

The securities industry, following enactment of Glass-Steagall, likewise underwent substantial fluctuations. Following a slow period that lasted well into the 1950s, "Wall Street" began to move again. That movement culminated in a tremendous upsurge of stock salesmanship, stock ownership, and especially of expectations of future growth. Extreme multiples were paid for the growth prospects of unseasoned enterprises. A new breed of money managers had taken over, with less concern about risk than their predecessors. At the same time, institutional investors tended to concentrate their holdings in a limited number of stocks that offered, as was then thought, unquestioned growth prospects. Capital for these select companies became very cheap, while for the great majority capital was more expensive, although readily accessible.

This tendency toward high risk and a very particular allocation of capital was sharply reversed after the market debacle of 1974. A new philosophy, highly risk averse, focusing on bonds and dividend stocks, began to prevail. What remained unchanged was the tendency of investment managers to adopt the same policies at the same time, once again distorting the allocation of capital.

Meanwhile, the securities industry underwent tribulations of its own, not all of them directly related to events in the economy. In the late 1960s and early 1970s, a surge in trading revealed an inadequate capacity to handle a high volume of transactions, with attendant back-office difficulties and losses. Subsequently, the industry had to cope with governmental efforts to enhance competition and to improve the structure of markets. In the course of these efforts, commission rates on stock exchanges became increasingly favorable to large institutional traders but not comparably so for the small individual stockholder. Mergers and liquidations eliminated a large number of firms and moved the industry toward increased concentration. Meanwhile, under the influence of disappointing investment performance and other vicissitudes, individual investors proceeded to leave the market. Estimated stock ownership dropped from over 30 million to 25 million.[2]

The Roles of Commercial Banks and the Securities Industry

If this brief summary has approximately captured the salient points of evolution in financial markets, several conclusions seem to follow concerning the appropriate roles of the commercial banks and the securities industry in meeting the needs of the economy.

Today, the economy urgently needs mechanisms that will promote equity financing. It is not to be expected that additional facilities for equity investment would necessarily increase total savings, desirable though that might be. But there would be merit in arrangements that would compensate for the diminishing capacity of the securities industry to attract customers and for the damage that inflation has done to equity investment. These purposes could be served by a great variety of actions, including those in the tax area. Here we shall be concerned only with measures relating to the Glass-Steagall Act, especially the participation of banks in the securities business.

As far as the banks are concerned, it seems evident that this is not a good time to encourage significantly larger risk taking. The banks still have to work out some of the problems that arose from high-risk taking in the past. Moreover, the experience of bank holding companies in entering new fields indicates that any further broadening of activities should be approached with great caution. This suggests that an enhanced role of banks in the securities field, if any, should be centered on relatively low-risk activities, such as brokerage and other forms of retail distribution.

Regarding the securities industry, it is obvious that its continued health and viability are essential to the economy. In the past, the industry has done a good job of broadening stock ownership and establishing a broad base for the financing of corporate business. Recent reverses, however, and the inefficiencies in the allocation of equity capital already noted, suggest that a broadened participation by commercial banks, particularly at the retail end, might be desirable.

Retailing Securities

A wider role for banking in the retail end of the securities business can build on activities and functions that already are in place. New techniques, however, also deserve to be explored. Banks traditionally have handled custody accounts for their customers, with purchases and sales carried out through brokers or, where appropriate, in the over-the-counter market. This service rendered by banks has been economically more rational in one important respect than the corresponding functions performed by securities firms. Banks charge separately for custody services; brokers typically render these free in the expectation of being compensated through commissions from customers' trading.

The "unbundling" practiced by banks implies better resource allocation. The customer who does not trade does not get a free ride on the customer who does. It also reduces the pressure for turnover, which, if efficient market theory is right, offers no predictable effects for the customer beyond expenses and taxes.

But the typical charges made by banks for custodial services are high. Operating efficiencies, and perhaps specialized forms of stock ownership through common trust funds or mutual funds (currently barred by Supreme Court verdict), might offer more viable alternatives. The present commission structure, which embodies strong economies of scale for large orders, should enable banks to make available to small investors some of these economies. Bank retail services that have done well—such as the dividend-reinvestment plan—as well as others that have not—such as the automatic-investment plan—seem to embody such economies of scale.

The broad customer base that banks derive from their deposit business suggests that they could play an important role in broadening stock ownership. Some of those activities in which banks now engage serve exactly that function of strengthening and broadening the customer base. This wide coverage also implies that banks could help overcome certain deficiencies in the present structure of incentives in the securities industry.

Because retailing securities could never be more than a sideline for banks, there would be less temptation to engage in the excesses to which the securities industry at times has been prone. If large numbers of banks were to engage in brokerage-type activities, the danger that all would focus their attentions on a limited list of securities, such as the "nifty fifties," would very likely diminish. This contrasts with the behavior of the trust departments of a limited number of large banks during the late lamented period of overoptimism. The inability of smaller banks to engage in in-depth securities research should not be a serious obstacle. Such research is readily available in the market; moreover, its superiority to less sophisticated methods of stock selection has not been clearly demonstrated.

Arguments against Bank Participation

On the suggestions made here, there exists a great body of argumentation, some of it objective, some less so, with pros and cons that can and have been spun out at considerable length. We shall list the principal "con" arguments and seek to evaluate them briefly.

Of all the arguments against bank participation in the securities business, the most telling one is the concern expressed about concentration of power in banking. This has been a historic preoccupation of the American people. No modifications of Glass-Steagall are likely that press too hard on that sensitive nerve.

There could be a concern, for example, that a situation might develop like that prevailing in some foreign countries where banks control a large part of the capital available and become a dominant source of credit. In evaluating this risk, it must be borne in mind, however, that U.S. banks are smaller relative to the American economy than many foreign banks are relative to their nations' economies. This is the result of the market structrue of American banking, which limits branching at a maximum to the area of a state. A further factor limiting the potential size of Amercian banks is the existence of open money and capital markets—commercial paper, bond and equities markets, and even secondary market facilities for mortgages offered principally by the federal government. Mutual savings banks, savings and loan associations, and credit unions further limit the potential expansion of commercial banks. The banks, therefore, would have to go a long way to even remotely approximate the role of banks in some foreign countries.

A real issue of concentration of power in banking could only arise, if at all, in connection with underwriting. There is little power in acting as a broker in secondary securities markets. Only if a large group of investment advisers began to imitate one another, all recommending the same stocks and thus validating one another's prophecies, could there be some semblance of power in that activity. Such power, which is inherent in group behavior rather than in individual units, would diminish as the number of units increased. Growth in numbers would reduce the probability that all would act alike.

In an overall sense, concerns about the power of banking today should be diminishing, not increasing. Banks are increasingly competing, not only with one another, but with other intermediaries that are seeking and obtaining broadened powers. United States banks, moreover, increasingly have to compete with foreign banks. At the national level, competition among even the biggest banks is intense. It is at the local level, outside the money-center cities, if anywhere, that restrictions on entry convey market power to individual banks. There is little basis today for pointing to the danger of concentration of power as an obstacle to structural changes that, in purely economic terms, would be beneficial.

Aside from the question of concentration of power, there is the possible issue of unfair competition. It is often alleged that, as financial institutions, banks enjoy special advantages by virtue of having interest-free demand deposits, access to the discount window (if they are Federal Reserve members), and, thanks mainly to ownership of tax-exempt securities, a low effective income-tax rate. Given these advantages, it could be argued that banks would be unduly favored in competition with securities firms and others that do not enjoy like preferences.

It should be noted, on the other hand, that these advantages are not likely to help banks very much in the securities activities in which they might become engaged. Any marginal funds that banks would have to attract in order to enlarge the scope of their business would have to be interest bearing—the only kind of funds that banks today are able to "purchase."

Funds obtained through the discount window are, at best, marginally cheaper than funds obtained in the market. The discount window, moreover, is not a continuous source of funds. The aggregate volume of money obtained through it is minimal, and access is administered in a manner to prevent the use of these funds for an expansion of business. The fact that banks have been leaving the Federal Reserve System indicates, moreover, that they do not regard access to the discount window as a decisive advantage.

The benefits of a low effective tax rate, finally, are offset, at least in part, by lower interest rates on tax-exempt assets. The marginal tax rate that banks would have to pay on earnings from any additional activity would be the same as that paid by other institutions. Furthermore, despite all these special aspects of bank earnings, the rate of return on bank capital has not been significantly higher than the return on the capital of nonfinancial corporations. Indeed, if an adjustment is made to bank earnings for inflation, through the technique of general-price-level accounting, bank earnings during the present inflationary period are seen to have been severely undermined by the loss of purchasing power of banking capital.

On Balance

In assessing the appropriateness of giving commercial banks greater access to the securities business, the dangers of conflicts of interest must also be taken into account. There is the danger that inside information obtained through commercial-banking activities might be misused for purposes of the securities business. There is the reverse possibility that operations in securities might be turned into a means of supporting the commercial-banking activities of the bank. Finally, there could be a risk of illegitimate tie-in operations, with the availability of other banking services becoming conditional on a customer's use of a bank's securities services.

In the absence of appropriate legislation, regulation, and enforcement, these concerns are not without substance. To an extent, the passage of Glass-Steagall in the 1930s reflected a belief that history had shown them to be valid. In good part, however, these concerns apply to bank participation in the underwriting and wholesale distribution of securities, rather than the retail end of the business.

Furthermore, lawmakers and regulators have worked hard to cope with conflict-of-interest problems and to create conditions that defuse them. Use of confidential information is precluded under the Securities Exchange Act of 1934. And use of the bank's resources to support the securities operations of customers is outlawed under section 5136 of the Revised Statutes. A recent study by the Federal Reserve of private-placement practices of banks indicates that even to the limited extent possible, banks generally have not supported private placements arranged by them by taking part of the issue into their trust portfolios. Tie-in deals are, of course, outlawed under the Bank Holding Company Amendments of 1970.

The danger of conflicts of interest, unfortunately, is inherent in many aspects of financial business. The law has been reasonably effective in dealing with them and probably could deal with new ones that might arise. At the retail level of the securities business, at any rate, this can be asserted with some confidence.

Analysis of conflicts of interest, and more broadly of the appropriate role of commercial banking in the securities area, does point up one very troublesome aspect of regulation in this field. Some types of regulation involve protection from competition. They create privileges that become valuable and tend to be contested. Debate in this area, then, is in danger of becoming concerned with who should be allowed to exploit what particular part of the economic territory rather than with how all participants can best serve the community. In evaluating an anticompetitive statute like Glass-Steagall, the danger of creating and reinforcing special preserves for special interests needs always to be kept in mind.

Notes

1. Neuburger & Stokes. "German Banks and German Growth. 1883–1913: An Empirical View," *J. Econ. Hist.* 710–731 (Sept. 1974); Frendling & Tilly, "German Banks, German Growth and Econometric History," *J. Econ. Hist.* 416–427 (June 1976).

2. *New York Stock Exchange Fact Book* 50 (1977).

27 Some Thoughts on Capital Adequacy

The "pause" on bank holding-company expansion instituted by the Federal Reserve Board in June 1974, indicated the Board's concern about both the present level of capitalization of many of our largest banks and also the heavy use of purchased funds. Since that date the markets have not been propitious for issuance of either bank equity or subordinated debt, and the principal effect of the pause has been to slow down bank expansion. Now, however, the markets are entering into a different phase that may make financing more feasible. At the same time, loan demand has softened materially. In this new constellation of circumstances, therefore, the problem of bank capital takes on a new look. Achieving capital adequacy through appropriate internal and external financing is now a realistic prospect.

The behavior of the stock and bond markets suggests that many banks may find opportunities to issue subordinated-debt capital earlier than new equity. This puts debt capital in the foreground of any discussion of bank capital adequacy. As you all know, the comptroller since 1962 has accepted subordinated-debt capital equal to 50 percent of equity capital plus reserves. The Federal Reserve Board so far has not pronounced itself on the matter.

Debt capital has the advantage of being cheaper than equity capital because of the tax deductibility of the interest paid. Debt capital has an added cost advantage when the interest rate is below the amount that must be earned on the equity. In times of inflation, debt capital has still a further advantage in that it reduces the net-creditor position of a bank. As you know, net creditors, other things equal, tend to lose from inflation while net debtors tend to gain. If the accounts of the banking system were restated in terms of the price-level-accounting technique, as recommended by the Financial Accounting Standards Board, this condition as it affects banks would become more clearly apparent.

Debt capital, however, has significant drawbacks from the point of view of the overall safety of the banking system. Thanks to its subordination to deposits it does protect the depositor. But unlike equity capital, it provides no cushion for the absorption of losses. Thus, it leaves unprotected several other parties that have a legitimate interest in the safety of the banking system—the borrower who needs a reliable source of credit, the insurer, the central bank as a potential lender of last resort, and, broadly speaking, the entire community,

---

This chapter was originally presented on February 28, 1975, at the Management Seminar on "Banking in the Years Ahead—Challenges and Issues," Washington, D.C.

which has an interest in a sound banking and monetary system that goes beyond its interest in the solvency of business generally.

Clearly, to rely on subordinated debt in lieu of equity may be appropriate for different banks in different degree. Factors like the equity ratios of the bank, its policies with respect to purchased funds, its ability to displace over time debt capital with equity from retention, the maturity of the debt, the bank's prospective ability to deal with the problem of repayments, and the nature of the covenants associated with the debt all are obviously relevant.

If debt capital is to be limited to some fraction of equity capital, then the appropriate level of total capitalization, debt plus equity, needs to be examined. There are no good answers to this obviously important question. Statisticians have failed to unearth a good relationship between bank capital and bank failure. Apparently, in cases where banks have failed, it has been predominantly for reasons other than inadequate capital. Nor do insurance-type calculations, based on past loss experience and some high multiple coverage of that experience, suggest to me any reliable guide. The nature of banking risks unfortunately is not actuarial. It resembles, rather, the risks inherent in a common stock, which analysts have divided into the "own risk" of the stock and its "systematic" or market risk. The use of the Beta factor familiar to stock-market analysis rests on this distinction. The own risk can be met by diversification. The market risk is something the holder must bear.

Applying this reasoning to banks, one concludes that the own risk is that of particular misfortunes or errors of judgment that may hurt a bank and that quite likely could be guarded against on the basis of actuarial principles. But the market risk that relates to the prosperity, or lack of it, of the entire economy is something that is essentially unpredictable on the basis of past experience. A broader judgment is required.

Today, we do not need to make such a judgement in precise quantitative terms. Unless bank capital in the past was grossly excessive, it is clear that today the degree of protection of many banks provided by capital is less than adequate. Capital ratios of banks have declined. For instance, the ratio of equity (including reserves) to risk assets declined from 11.2 percent to 8.4 percent during the period 1969 through 1973, the ratio of equity to total assets declined from 7.8 percent to 6.3 percent, and the ratio of equity to total liabilities including capital notes and debentures less cash and due from banks declined from 10.3 percent to 8.5 percent. It would be difficult to argue that, while this was going on, the degree of risk in the banking business has tended to move anywhere but up. More protection, therefore, is needed for many banks, although circumstances differ widely among banks. This protection could take the form of more capital, but it also could take, and in fact to a moderate extent already has, the form of fuller deposit insurance.

It has sometimes been said that the need for more bank capital is the result of inflation and that at high rates of inflation it is simply not possible for banks to generate enough capital from earnings. The first of these statements deserves to be questioned, although the second would have a relevant core of truth if inflation were to continue at a high level, which I do not expect. Over the years 1969–1973, demand deposits increased at an average annual rate of 6.1 percent, demand plus time deposits [excluding large certificates of deposit (CDs)] increased by 8.4 percent. A bank earning something better than 10 percent on its equity, as was the case in recent years for many banks, and retaining something like three-fourths of these earnings, would have been able to match that rate of deposit growth with equity growth from internal accumulation.

What caused bank assets, for the system as a whole, to rise at an annual rate of roughly 13 percent during 1969–1973, thus far outstripping any possible growth of equity from normal retentions, was the use of purchased funds, which enabled the banking system to increase its share in the total supply of credit. I am not arguing, of course, that banks ought to be able to finance their capital requirements entirely from internal sources. But since estimates made by various analysts of the amounts of new bank capital to be raised in the market sometimes reach remarkable levels, one must realize that apart from the effect of purchased funds, a large part of capital needs could have been covered from retentions. On the other hand, if the banking industry finds it desirable, from a profit-maximizing point of view, to increase its share of the total credit business, it seems not unreasonable to expect that banks back up this bigger share by externally raising appropriate amounts of capital.

The concern that is sometimes expressed that large-scale equity or debt financing by the banking system would unduly further increase the already very heavy prospective burden on our capital markets is greatly overstated. This applies in particular to debt financing—the amount of equity that can be absorbed by the market is of course more limited than the amount of debt. An increase in bank debt, through flotation of a subordinated bond or note, unlike debt issued by a nonfinancial borrower, produces no net drain of funds form the market. When the banking system issues such securities, it is paid, in effect, with checks on itself—deposits go down, long-term subordinated debt goes up. The decline in deposits produces excess reserves, and, if the central bank pursues a stable money-supply policy, these excess reserves will be used by the bank to acquire additional assets. The increase in the demand for funds, in the form of a bank-debt issue, is matched by an increase in the supply of funds, in the form of additional bank credit. The simultaneous increase in demand and suppy will not, of course, occur in exactly the same sector of the credit markets.

The observation that an increase in bank capital does not absorb credit, and therefore the nation's savings, in the same manner as financing by nonbank businesses is reassuring. It implies that the capital needs of the banking system can be met without a drain on the economy's scarce capital resources. Borrowing to build a plant, or a home, preempts resources from other uses. It has a social cost. Bank capital financing, in that sense, has no such social cost. Bank capital in effect is "created" like money, by the banking system.

This does not mean, however, that bank financing is costless to the private parties involved. Bank equity, and bank debt, must earn a competitive rate of return. The cost of earning this rate of return is borne by the users of bank services, primarily borrowers and depositors. The need to protect the user of bank services against bank failure thus increases the cost of the services to the users. The share of bank credit in total credit, the share of banks' time and savings deposits in total assets, and the share of bank-related payments in total payments is less than it would otherwise be.

There is an obvious inefficiency in allowing these costs and their allocative consequences to occur when, as noted, there is no equivalent social cost involved in the protection of the banking system through bank equity and debt. This is reflected in the familiar difference between the cost of self-insurance and pooled insurance, that is, insurance sold by an insurance company that pools risks. Bank capital is essentially self-insurance; insurance provided by the Federal Deposit Insurance Corporation (FDIC) is pooled insurance. Viewed as an insurance fund, the aggregate of all bank capital necessarily must be many times greater than the insurance fund of the FDIC, if the same degree of protection is to be provided by either route. Without meaning to comment on the relative adequacies of the two funds, I would note that the capital of the banking system exceeds the FDIC fund by more than a factor of ten.

Obviously the conclusion to be drawn from this fundamental analysis is not that we can do without bank capital because it would be cheaper to achieve one of the principal functions of bank capital by substituting deposit insurance. Full insurance of deposits would create new problems that have been discussed at the academic level for many years. I have always been skeptical of these academic proposals, because virtually riskless banking could encourage a kind of performance banking that might be very destabilizing for the economy. The technical problems involved, such as charging each bank an insurance premium proportionate to the risks assumed, and of monitoring these risks, are considerable. An attempt to institute an examination system equal to the demands of that kind of insurance system might imply less rather than more freedom and flexibility in bank operations.

What does emerge from the analysis is that there exists a trade-off of sorts between bank capital and deposit insurance. Congress has just made a moderate move along this trade-off curve by raising the insured level of deposits from $20,000 to $40,000. This has raised the insured portion of total deposits in insured banks by 5 percentage points, from 61 percent to 66 percent. Further increases, to $50,000, and even $100,000, would raise the insured proportion only to 69 percent and 72 percent. In the course of time, this might become a useful direction in which to move. Obviously, over time, such a policy might also call for a new look at the level and structure of FDIC insurance premiums.

The possibility of substituting insurance for capital suggests that a good objective today might be to raise enough capital simply to halt further erosion of equity ratios on average. Of course, this might nevertheless mean increases for particular banks.

Lest someone should say that to protect banks via the capital route rather than the insurance route is doing it the expensive way, I would like to point out that this cost today is proportionately less than it has been in former years. So long as demand deposits were the chief source of funds for the banking system and so long as interest rates on time and savings deposits were low relative to long-term rates, the secondary function of bank capital as a source of funds was not important compared to its primary function of providing protection. Today, when time deposits have become the principal source of funds at often very high rates, this secondary function of bank capital has gained in importance. The net cost of protection is only the excess of the cost of equity or debt capital, as the case may be, over what it would cost a bank to raise the same funds by some other route. This should encourage banks whose capital ratios have been declining to undertake the job of stabilizing and where necessary increasing them.

28 Inflation Is Destroying Bank Earnings and Capital Adequacy

Bank regulation does not occur in a vacuum. It has to move with the changing economic environment. For the last ten years, a very adverse part of that changing environment has been inflation. Much as it is hoped, and intended, that inflation will be overcome, its effects in the present, as well as in the past, cannot be ignored. And those are considerable.

Inflation has severely reduced the true income of commercial banks. Taking the years 1973–1975 together, the banking system paid out more in dividends than its inflation-adjusted earnings. The seemingly large additions to bank capital from retained earnings shown on the books were largely offset by the shrinkage of bank capital due to inflation. This raises fundamental questions about the ability of the banking system to generate sufficient earnings in order to maintain capital ratios or to sell enough new stock to achieve that purpose.

In an inflationary situation, banks are born losers. They are net creditors, or, in the language of the accountants, they have a positive net monetary position. That is to say, their monetary assets, which account for everything except the building and its equipment, exceed their monetary liabilities. Having more assets that lose value through inflation than liabilities, the real (constant-dollar) value of their capital suffers.

Applying General-Price-Level Accounting

One way of analyzing the impact of inflation is to apply the techniques of general-price-level accounting (GPLA).[1] Doing this for the years 1973–1975, it appears that the earnings of all insured commercial banks, instead of the reported $20.9 billion, work out at only $7.3 billion stated in current (not constant) dollars. The dividends that banks paid out during this period amounted to 112 percent of those inflation-adjusted earnings. Applicable federal income taxes during the same period, instead of being the reported 19 percent of earnings, totaled 54 percent of inflation-adjusted earnings. (These data and others are shown in tables 28–1 and 28–2.)

The GPLA adjustment indicates that over the three-year period, inflation-adjusted earnings were less than half of reported earnings. (See table 28–3).

This chapter was originally published in Bankers Magazine 160 (Winter 1977):12–16.
I am indebted to Don Tucker and Ellen Harvey for the computations of inflation-adjusted bank earnings and capital.

Table 28–1
Inflation-Corrected Net Income after Taxes (All Insured Commercial Banks, 1973–1975)
(thousands of dollars)

Year	*Book Net Income, after Taxes*	*Loss on Net Monetary Assets*	*Increase in Depreciation Deductions*	*Adjusted Net Income*[a]	*Adjusted Income as Percent of Book Income*
1973	6,578,831	3,522,183	232,309	2,824,339	42.9
1974	7,090,908	5,537,192	332,060	1,221,656	17.2
1975	7,254,611	3,351,954	617,405	3,285,252	45.3
1973–1975[b]	23,543,443	14,010,357	1,295,425	8,237,661	35.0

[a]Income figures reported in midyear dollars for that year, computed as book net income minus loss on net monetary assets, minus increase in depreciation deductions, assuming loan loss reserves to be nonmonetary item.

[b]The individual yearly figures were converted to 1975 year-end dollars before summing; the 1973–1975 totals are not the sums of the individual yearly figures reported above.

Table 28–2
Inflation-Adjusted Dividend Payout and Effective Tax-Rate Ratios (All Insured Commercial Banks, 1973–1975)

	Dividends		*Tax-Rate Percentage*	
Year	*As Percent of Book Income*	*As Percent of Adjusted Income*	*Based on Book Income*	*Based on Adjusted Income*
1973	36.9	85.9	20.3	47.3
1974	39.0	226.4	19.1	111.1
1975	41.8	92.2	16.9	37.3
1973–1975[a]	39.1	111.9	18.8	53.8

[a]The yearly income, dividend, and federal-tax figures were converted to 1975 year-end dollars before summing to compute these ratios.

To pay out more in dividends than their adjusted earnings under ordinary accounting procedures, banks, in most circumstances, would require the permission of the regulators. And instead of paying a relatively low effective-tax rate, as is commonly believed, banks on an inflation-adjusted basis paid a rate higher than the regular 48 percent corporate rate. The rate of return on capital, instead of being 11 percent as per book, was 3.6 percent on an inflation-adjusted basis. (See table 28–4).

These inflation-adjusted figures also have an implication, of course, for the banks' capital position and for the safety and soundness of the system. After correction for inflation, the substantial increase in bank capital from $55.1 billion in 1972 to $73.3 billion in 1975 largely disappears. Since banks issued some equity capital during this period and had other adjustments to capital and reserves, the excess of dividends over inflation-adjusted income did not cause capital actually to shrink in inflation-adjusted and constant-dollar terms. But

Table 28–3
Inflation-Adjusted Equity Capital and Reserves (All Insured Commercial Banks, 1972–1975)

	Equity Capital and Reserves				
Year	*Book Values ($ thousand) (1)*	*Adjusted Values*[a] *($ thousand) (2)*	*Ratio (2)/(1)*	*Book Values in Constant 1975 Dollars*	*Adjusted Values in Constant 1975 Dollars*
1972	55,145,918	58,887,078	1.068	70,592,290	75,381,349
1973	61,152,228	65,772,769	1.076	72,508,197	77,986,772
1974	67,395,971	73,803,926	1.095	71,614,959	78,424,052
1975	73,318,913	80,453,233	1.097	73,318,913	80,453,233

[a]Adjusted values in year-end dollars of relevant year.

Table 28–4
Rates of Return on Capital and Capital-Risk to Asset Ratios (All Insured Commercial Banks, 1973–1975)

			Capital Ratios	
Year[a]	*Book Net Income as Percent of Book Capital*	*Adjusted Net Income at Percent of Adjusted Capital*[b]	*Book Capital as Percent of Risk Assets*	*Adjusted Capital as Percent of Risk Assets*
1973	11.9	4.4	8.8	9.5
1974	11.6	1.5	8.6	9.4
1975	10.8	3.3	9.3	10.2
1973–1975[c]	11.0	3.6	8.9	9.7

[a]Rates of return are based on capital at end of previous year.
[b]Based on previous year's adjusted capital expressed in mid-year dollars of the current year.
[c]The individual yearly figures for income and capital were converted to 1975 year-end dollars before summing to derive these ratios.

the increase in inflation-adjusted capital stated in 1975 (that is, constant) dollars was small, from $75.4 billion in 1972 to $80.5 billion in 1975. Meanwhile, the ratio of bank-equity capital to total assets rose from 0.071 in 1972 to 0.075 in 1975, stating both capital and total assets in inflation-adjusted terms, since bank assets in real terms rose even less than bank capital.

GPLA, of course, is only one of several ways in which corporate accounts can be adjusted for inflation. It is not necessarily the most logical way for adjusting the accounts of a manufacturing enterprise, for example, because manufacturers have to do with the prices of many individual products that may move differently from a general-price index like the consumer-price index or the gross-national-product deflator. But for a bank, which is only minimally concerned with particular-product prices, use of a general-price index as a measure of depreciation of its assets and liabilities seems particularly appropriate. That is what GPLA does.

It should not be surprising to find that bank capital tends to shrink during inflation. Bank capital is essentially money, and money loses value through inflation. To maintain the real value of their capital during inflation and its normal growth from retentions, banks would have to earn a rate that, after taxes, would cover the rate of inflation, in addition to providing a normal return. If the very roughly 10 percent rate of return that banks have earned over long periods is regarded as the norm, recent rates of inflation would require a rate of return after taxes higher by at least a factor of one-half to maintain capital in real terms and keep it growing through retentions. Neither bankers, nor the public, nor the legislators would regard such a rate of return on bank capital as at all appropriate. The area of bank earnings and capital seems to be one of the last bastions of money illusion.

The stock market, to be sure, seems to have read the numbers correctly. For several years, bank stocks have sold at relatively low price-earnings ratios. Some observers have attributed this to concern over possible loan losses that banks might incur. At least equally plausible an explanation is that the market has become aware of the attrition that inflation wreaks on bank earnings and bank capital.

Impact on Bank Regulators

What are the implications of these findings for the bank regulator? For the most part, the bank regulator probably will say that he deals with bank earnings and capital as they appear on the books, not as they appear after some theoretical adjustment for inflation. This reaction is a sensible one for many practical purposes. It does not allow the regulator and the banks, however, to escape the logic of the analysis.

That logic is that inflation makes it very difficult to maintain an adequate level of bank capital. The inflation adjustment merely bares the bones of a mechanism that is perceivable broadly also in unadjusted terms. To use purely illustrative examples, when bank assets expand at the rate of 5 percent per year, a rate of return of 10 percent on capital allows payment of a dividend of 5 percent, while accumulating enough retained earnings to maintain the capital-assets ratio constant. But it is the nature of inflation that bank assets and liabilities expand at a rapid rate in current dollars, even though they may rise little or even shrink in constant dollars. If, for example, they expand at 10 percent, a 10 percent rate of return on capital will allow no dividends at all to be paid if the capital-assets ratio is to be maintained without new stock issues. Beyond that, there is no way of maintaining that ratio from retentions unless bank earnings and the rate of return on bank capital rise.

The inflation-adjusted analysis makes clear why efforts of the banks, stimulated by regulatory concern, to improve their capital ratios, may have only limited success under those conditions. Bank earnings are not large enough to permit retentions that would keep capital abreast with assets rising rapidly in current-dollar terms. The underlying weakness of earnings, as revealed by this analysis and as observed by the stock market, makes it difficult, meanwhile, to increase capital by new equity issues. Issurance of subordinated debt can help but is no fundamental solution. If the obvious answer to the problem—to stop inflation—is not immediately in sight, maintenance of adequate capital ratios will be difficult.

From an economic point of view, moreover, there is a real question whether it is advisable, even if it were possible, to increase the flow of equity capital into an industry that experiences so low a real rate of return. Low earnings are the market's way of signaling that capital should flow out of, rather than into, an industry.

What Should the Regulators Do?

If the regulators, for reasons of public policy, believe that the verdict of the market should be ignored, they are in need of some conception of how this public policy, based on considerations of soundness and safety of the banking system, is to be accomplished. Are the regulated banks to sell stock at prices that would dilute equity and earnings, thereby further increasing the difficulty of raising additional capital later on? Do they believe that banks should limit the growth of their assets until acceptable capital-assets ratios are achieved? Curbing the growth of bank assets and, therefore, of the money supply is the job of monetary policy that would have the highly desirable result of curbing inflation. But if the economic situation does not allow the monetary authorities to do that in the short run, limiting the growth of bank credit and money supply through more stringent capital requirements for banks would not be appropriate either. In the best of cases, it would cause a larger proportion of the total flow of credit to move outside the banking system.

In other words, if monetary policy is unable, for the time being, to perform the job of halting inflation, regulatory policy restraining monetary expansion through the clumsy device of capital ratios will not do it, either. It actually may, in the process, do damage to the flow of credit and to the economy.

All this does not mean that regulators should give up the objective of advancing bank soundness by improved capital ratios. There will always be phases of the business cycle and individual banks, in particular circumstances not reflecting the average of the banking system, that permit progress in improving capital ratios to be made. But bank regulators will do well to look for alternative means of ensuring the soundness and safety of the banking system that are less at odds with the present signals of the market.

Alternative Approaches

Protection through adequate capital, including, if necessary, subordinated debt, reflects in essense the principle of self-insurance. Each bank provides individually against the risks to which it is exposed. The alternative is the principle of collective or pooled insurance as implemented by the FDIC. Insurance of deposits up to $40,000 has the twofold effect of (1) reducing the probability and potential magnitude of depositor runs, thereby enhancing the safety of the bank; and (2) assuring depositors that up to the insured limit they will get their money back, in case failure does occur. If the principle of self-insurance meets with obstacles during inflation, an extension of pooled insurance can be contemplated.

The principle of pooled insurance obviously has not been pushed very far today. One reason why it is wise to be cautious in moving in that direction is that this form of insurance tends to reduce the discipline that the market imposes on banks. Today, depositors with accounts of over $40,000 have reason to watch their banks. A large bank that has not kept itself in sound condition may find itself confronted with a tiering of CD rates, that is, with having to pay a premium for large CDs. Going to 100 percent deposit insurance would remove this discipline.

Going to 100 percent deposit insurance, moreover, would not protect a bank fully against runs, since there may be other creditors with liquid claims, such as federal funds. Insurance of all creditors might prevent runs, but not insolvency. Stockholder discipline thus would be preserved.

Stockholder discipline alone, of course, is not as effective a form of protection against unsound banking as is the combined discipline of creditors and stockholders. Moreover, stockholder discipline may evaporate in cases of small banks where management and stockholders are identical. Yet it is important to note that even 100 percent insurance does not altogether do away with all forms of market discipline.

Another extension of the insurance principle is action by the insurer to preserve the continuity of an endangered bank in one form or another. The FDIC employs this option either in the form of assisted merger or of purchase and assumption in case of a failing bank. In the first case, the bank survives: in the second, it does not. In either case, however, the ultimate outcome for stockholders will depend on the condition of the failing bank. Even if stockholders were to contemplate an FDIC-arranged merger as the ultimate outcome in case their bank does not prosper, they will have a reason to discipline their management. Stockholder discipline, therefore, will have been preserved.

Various techniques suggest themselves to enhance the discipline of the market under the various foregoing insurance options. Instead of 100 percent insurance, for instance, one could contemplate a form of coinsurance, leaving some degree of risk, perhaps a very small one, with the creditor. Even 99 percent insurance might be sufficient to keep bankers interested in maintaining a good market rating in order to avoid tiering of their liabilities, without causing depositors and other creditors to run at the slightest sign of trouble.

Graduated insurance premiums would be another way of exerting a form of discipline over bank risk taking. A high-risk portfolio would call for higher insurance premiums than a low-risk one. This would, of course, require careful supervision of banks' portfolios and perhaps other risk-related practices. There might be a danger that the supervisors would ultimately end up as controllers, while the purpose of the proposal should be, of course, to give the banker a wider range of risk options, instead of tying his hands. But the trend toward a growing use of quantitative methods and systems analysis in bank supervision might facilitate the employment of graduated premiums for insurance of bank liabilities.

Conclusion

Several routes toward the achievement of safety and soundness for the banking system are available. Adequate capital has been the traditional major safeguard. It remains the first line of defense in protecting bank creditors. But if inflation makes it difficult for banks to maintain adequate capital ratios out of earnings and simultaneously makes it very costly, if not impossible, to raise capital through new issues, there are alternatives. These would require very careful study before anything decisive can be said. However, that study should be undertaken before we either accept a resumption of the trend toward lower capital ratios or seek to maintain these ratios by uneconomic means.

Note

1. Adjustment of earnings for inflation by means of general-price-level accounting is not the same thing as adjustment of earnings for inflation by restatement in constant dollars. Restatement in constant dollars simply means to divide current-dollar earnings by a price index. General-price-level accounting is a complex process involving a distinction between monetary and nonmonetary items on a balance sheet, the nonmonetary alone being adjusted by a general-price index. The resulting change in the relation of assets (partly monetary, partly nonmonetary) and liabilities (almost always monetary) causes a change in net worth, which in turn raises or lowers income. GPLA, unlike current-value accounting, does not take into account changes in asset values that result from changes in interest rates or from debt restructuring.

29 Framework for Financial Resiliency

The American economy, having passed through a long period during which risks were escalating, now seems to be clearly in the process of reducing financial risks. The data that accompanied the escalation phase are familiar. Nonfinancial enterprises increased the ratio of external to total financing from the low levels of the 1950s; within external financing they increased the role of debt relative to equity and, within debt, that of short-term to total debt. Cash and liquid assets declined in relation to short-term liabilities.

For the banking system, an analogous process meant diminishing capital ratios, increasing reliance on purchased funds, increasing "maturity intermediation" (transformation of short-term liabilities into long-term assets), and reducing the proportion of secondary liquid assets.

Most of these trends, in part displayed in tables 29–1 through 29–4, had been continuing with only minor interruptions since the end of World War II, at which time the economy was perhaps overly liquid as a result of financial consolidation in the 1930s and the exigencies of wartime finance. In point of fact, it is difficult to indicate a historical period when the financial structure was "right."

A process of rebuilding liquidity and restructuring balance sheets has been underway for most nonfinancial and financial enterprises for well over a year. We do not know how far it will go. We do know that similar reversals in 1967 and 1970 were no more than interruptions of a longer trend toward higher risks. I believe that the present phase of consolidation is different. The shock waves that emanated from the events of 1973 and 1974 seem to have set in motion a trend toward greater financial caution, which promises to achieve a much more satisfactory degree of financial consolidation than has occurred on previous occasions.

The financial system is not condemned to move toward ever higher degrees of risk with ever greater reliance on government to stave off ultimate calamity. On the contrary, the degree of risk taking in an economy fluctuates in long-term cycles, extending over a series of business cycles, and the elevation of risk exposure on one side of this cycle produces results that induce an extended period of movement toward safer financial configurations. If we think of insolvency as the ultimate brink toward which the escalation of risk leads, the early part of the long-term cycle represents an exploration of approaches to the brink.

This chapter was originally published in E. Altman and A. Sametz, eds., *Financial Crises—Institutions and Markets in a Fragile Environment* (N.Y.: John Wiley & Sons, 1977), pp. 160–172.

Table 29–1
Internal and External Sources of Funds of Nonfinancial Corporations
(billions of dollars)

	Annual Flows[a]					
End of Year or Quarter[b]	*Retained Profits after IVA and CCA*[c]	*Capital-Consumption Allowance*[d]	*Gross Internal Funds*[e]	*Short-Term Debt*[f]	*Long-Term Debt*[g]	*Net Equity Issues*[h]
1946	3.2	4.6	7.8	6.0	3.5	1.0
1947	6.9	5.7	12.6	7.9	5.2	1.1
1948	11.9	6.8	18.7	3.2	5.2	1.0
1949	11.3	7.8	19.1	−3.6	2.9	1.2
1950	9.3	8.6	17.9	18.4	4.0	1.3
1951	9.9	10.0	19.9	8.0	5.8	2.1
1952	9.9	11.2	21.1	−0.2	5.8	2.3
1953	8.2	12.9	21.1	0.3	4.0	1.8
1954	8.7	14.6	23.3	−0.4	4.5	1.6
1955	12.2	17.0	29.2	15.4	6.1	1.7
1956	10.5	18.4	28.9	5.6	7.5	2.3
1957	10.3	20.3	30.6	1.0	8.5	2.4
1958	8.1	21.4	29.5	1.6	8.1	2.0
1959	12.1	22.9	35.0	10.5	7.5	2.1
1960	10.2	24.2	34.4	4.3	7.1	1.4
1961	10.2	25.4	35.6	8.0	8.7	2.1
1962	13.0	28.4	41.4	6.6	10.2	0.4
1963	14.9	29.5	44.4	11.8	10.1	−0.3
1964	19.3	30.7	50.0	11.3	9.8	1.1
1965	23.4	32.6	55.9	21.4	13.4	—[i]
1966	25.0	35.4	60.4	16.7	18.3	1.3
1967	22.2	38.9	61.1	8.9	21.2	2.4
1968	19.5	42.6	62.1	29.9	22.2	−0.2
1969	14.3	47.3	61.6	32.5	21.5	3.4
1970	6.0	52.7	58.7	11.4	27.0	5.7
1971	10.3	57.7	68.0	9.9	31.1	11.4
1972	18.2	62.0	80.2	25.2	33.2	10.9
1973	15.7	68.1	83.8	44.4	39.8	7.4
1974	0.1	77.6	77.7	53.1	44.6	4.1
1975	15.2	88.6	103.8	−3.7	33.9	9.9
1976-I	25.2	94.8	120.0	37.3	24.6	7.2
Averages:						
1946–1950	8.5	6.7	15.2	6.4	4.2	1.1
1951–1955	9.8	13.1	22.9	4.6	5.2	1.9

Table 29–1 continued

	Annual Flows[a]					
End of Year or Quarter[b]	*Retained Profits after IVA and CCA*[c]	*Capital-Consumption Allowance*[d]	*Gross Internal Funds*[e]	*Short-Term Debt*[f]	*Long-Term Debt*[g]	*Net Equity Issues*[h]
1956–1960	10.2	21.4	31.7	4.6	7.7	2.0
1961–1965	16.2	29.3	45.5	11.8	10.4	0.8
1966–1970	17.4	43.4	60.8	19.9	22.0	2.5
1971–1975	11.9	70.8	82.7	25.8	36.5	8.7

Source: Flow of Funds Section, Board of Governors of the Federal Reserve System.

[a]Nonfarm corporations.

[b]Numbers for first quarter 1976 are preliminary and are at seasonally adjusted annual rates.

[c]Retained profits are on the old NIA basis through 1961—reflecting only the inventory-valuation adjustment (IVA)—and are on the new NIA basis after 1961—reflecting the inventory-valuation adjustment plus the capital-consumption adjustment (CCA) for underdepreciation. Retained profits include foreign-branch profits.

[d]The capital-consumption allowance is from the NIA and is primarily tabulated by the IRS from tax returns filed by nonfinancial corporations.

[e]Gross internal funds: retained profits after IVA and (since 1962) CCA plus capital-consumption allowance. Totals may not add because of rounding.

[f]Short-term debt: commercial paper, acceptances, finance-company loans, U.S.-government loans, construction loans, 60 percent of bank loans, not elsewhere classified (N.E.C.), profit-taxes payable, trade debt, and miscellaneous liabilities.

[g]Long-term debt: tax-exempt and corporate bonds, multifamily and commercial mortgages, and 40 percent of bank loans N.E.C.

[h]Net equity issues: new equity issues less equity retirements.

[i]Less than 0.05.

Nobody quite knows where it is. Some bold spirits press forward and, if they are observed not to fall over, others conclude that the terrain is safe and follow. Eventually some do go over, and the rest, having suffered a severe scare, fall back. The scare occasioned by the latest exhibitions of financial brinkmanship has been sufficient to induce a very sizable retreat toward safer ground.

It is this process of approach and retreat that I examine in somewhat more detail here. Underlying the process is a hypothesis that people's expectations of a major calamity are formed, much like other expectations, on the basis of a weighted sum of past experiences. Recent experience under such a hypothesis typically receives high weight and experience far in the past low weight. If a major financial crisis, such as the 1930s, is only a few years behind, heavy weighting of recent past experience will make firms and households cautious. As the experience fades into the past, it receives diminishing weight relative to more recent experience when nothing adverse happened. Thus the restraint of

Table 29–2
External Sources of Funds of Nonfinancial Corporations: Percentage Distribution of Annual Flows

End of Year or Quarter[b]	*Annual Flows*[a]			
	External Sources of Funds (billion $)[c]	*Short-Term Debt/ External Sources*[d]	*Long-Term Debt/ External Sources*[e]	*Net Equity Issues/ External Sources*[f]
1946	10.5	57.1	33.3	9.5
1947	14.2	55.6	36.6	7.7
1948	9.4	34.0	55.3	10.6
1949	0.5	n.m.	n.m.	n.m.
1950	23.7	77.6	16.9	5.5
1951	15.9	50.3	36.5	13.2
1952	7.9	−2.5	73.4	29.1
1953	6.1	4.9	65.6	29.5
1954	5.7	−7.0	78.9	28.1
1955	23.2	66.4	26.3	7.3
1956	15.4	36.4	48.7	14.9
1957	11.9	8.4	71.4	20.2
1958	11.7	13.7	69.2	17.1
1959	20.1	52.2	37.3	10.4
1960	12.8	33.6	55.5	10.9
1961	18.8	42.5	46.3	11.2
1962	17.2	38.4	59.3	2.3
1963	21.6	54.6	46.8	−1.4
1964	22.2	50.9	44.1	5.0
1965	34.8	61.5	38.5	—[a]
1966	36.3	46.0	50.4	3.6
1967	32.5	27.4	65.2	7.4
1968	51.9	57.6	42.8	−0.4
1969	57.4	56.6	37.5	5.9
1970	44.1	25.8	61.2	12.9
1971	52.4	18.9	59.4	21.7
1972	69.3	36.4	47.9	15.7
1973	91.6	48.5	43.4	8.1
1974	101.8	52.2	43.8	4.0
1975	40.1	−9.2	84.5	24.7
1976-I	69.1	54.0	35.6	10.4
Averages				
1946–1950	11.7	56.1	35.5	8.3
1951–1955	11.8	22.4	56.1	21.4
1956–1960	14.4	28.8	56.4	14.7

Table 29–2

End of Year or Quarter[b]	Annual Flows[a]			
	External Sources of Funds (billion $)[c]	*Short-Term Debt/ External Sources*[d]	*Long-Term Debt/ External Sources*[e]	*Net Equity Issues/ External Sources*[f]
1961–1965	22.9	49.6	47.0	4.3
1966–1970	44.4	42.7	51.4	5.9
1971–1975	71.0	29.3	55.8	14.8

Source: Flow of Funds Section, Board of Governors of the Federal Reserve System.

[a]Nonfarm corporations.

[b]Numbers for first quarter 1976 are preliminary and are at seasonally adjusted annual rates.

[c]External source of funds: short-term debt, long-term debt, and net equity issues.

[d]Short-term debt: commercial paper, acceptances, finance-company loans, U.S.-government loans, construction loans, 60 percent of bank loans, not elsewhere classified (N.E.C.), profit-taxes payable, trade debt, and miscellaneous liabilities.

[e]Long-term debt: tax-exempt and corporate bonds, multifamily and commercial mortgages, and 40 percent of bank loans N.E.C.

[f]Net equity issues: new equity issues less equity retirements.

[g]Less than 0.05.

n.m.–not meaningful

experience diminishes over several relatively mild business cycles until the resulting escalation of risk leads to a new crisis and the process begins once more.

Within this framework, I examine some of the mechanisms and elements in the post–World War II environment that propelled business firms and banks in the direction of higher risk as recollections of past calamities faded. Three types of mechanisms were at work: (1) genuine changes in the degree of risk, especially as a result of government action of various sorts, (2) a change in perception, in a downward direction, of the probability of particular events, when the actual probabilities had not declined, and (3) changes in attitudes toward risk, that is, a reduction in risk aversion.

I begin by examining case 1, representing changes in objective reality that imply a reduction in risk. Government has had a reasonable, although far from complete, degree of success in using countercyclical fiscal and monetary policies to reduce business risk from major recessions. Even in 1973–1974 it took the combined interaction of food shortages, the oil crisis, a simultaneous cyclical downturn throughout the industrialized world, and the accumulated maladjustments of previous years, including almost ten years of inflation, to produce the most severe recession of the postwar period. In addition to the risk reduction resulting from macroeconomic stabilization, the government has employed microeconomic measures to limit economic and financial risks for individuals and businesses, among them programs for income maintenance, governmental

Table 29–3
Total Sources of Funds of Nonfinancial (Nonfarm) Corporations: Percentage Distribution of Annual Flows
(percent)

End of Year or Quarter[a]	*Total Sources of Funds (billion $)*[b]	*Gross Internal Funds/Total Sources*[c]	*Memo Ret. Profits/Total Sources*[c]	*Short-Term Debt/ Total Sources*[c]	*Long-Term Debt/ Total Sources*[c]	*Total Debt/Total Sources*[d]	*Net Equity Issues/ Total Sources*[c]
1946	18.3	42.6	17.5	32.8	19.1	51.9	5.5
1947	26.8	47.0	25.7	29.5	19.4	48.9	4.1
1948	28.1	66.6	42.3	11.4	18.5	29.9	3.6
1949	19.6	97.5	57.6	−18.4	14.8	−3.5	6.1
1950	41.6	43.0	22.3	44.2	9.6	53.8	3.1
1951	35.8	55.6	27.6	22.3	16.2	38.5	5.9
1952	29.0	72.8	34.1	−0.7	20.0	−19.3	7.9
1953	27.2	77.6	30.1	1.1	14.7	15.8	6.6
1954	29.0	80.3	30.0	−1.3	15.5	−14.1	5.5
1955	52.4	55.7	23.3	29.4	11.6	41.0	3.2
1956	44.3	65.2	23.7	12.6	16.9	29.6	5.2
1957	42.5	72.0	24.2	2.4	20.0	22.3	5.7
1958	41.2	71.6	19.7	3.9	19.7	23.5	4.9
1959	55.1	63.5	22.0	19.1	13.6	32.7	3.8

1960	47.2	72.9	21.6	9.1	15.0	24.2	3.0
1961	54.4	65.4	18.7	14.7	16.0	30.7	3.9
1962	58.6	70.7	22.2	11.3	17.4	28.7	0.7
1963	66.0	67.3	22.5	17.9	15.3	33.2	-0.5
1964	72.2	69.3	26.7	15.6	13.6	29.2	1.5
1965	90.7	61.6	25.8	23.6	14.8	38.4	—[e]
1966	96.7	62.5	25.9	17.3	18.9	36.2	1.3
1967	93.6	65.3	23.7	9.5	22.5	32.2	2.6
1968	114.0	54.5	17.1	26.2	19.5	45.7	-0.2
1969	119.0	51.8	12.0	27.3	18.1	45.4	2.9
1970	102.8	57.1	5.8	11.1	26.3	37.4	5.5
1971	120.4	56.5	8.6	8.2	25.8	34.1	9.5
1972	149.5	53.7	12.2	16.9	22.2	39.1	7.3
1973	175.4	47.8	9.0	25.3	22.7	48.0	4.2
1974	179.5	43.3	0.1	29.6	24.9	54.4	2.3
1975	143.9	72.1	10.6	2.6	23.6	-21.0	6.9
1976-I	189.1	63.5	13.3	19.7	13.0	32.7	3.8

Source: Flow of Funds Section, Board of Governors of the Federal Reserve System.

[a]Numbers for first quarter 1976 are preliminary and are at seasonally adjusted annual rates.

[b]Total sources of funds: gross internal funds plus external sources of funds. See tables 29-1 and 29-2 for data and definitions.

[c]See table 29-1 for data and definition.

[d]Total debt: short-term debt plus long-term debt. Totals may not add because of rounding. See table 29-1 for data and definitions.

[e]Less than 0.05.

Table 29–4
Selected Outstandings and Ratios of Nonfinancial (Nonfarm) Corporations

	Outstandings (billion $)					*Ratios of Outstandings*			
End of Year or Quarter[a]	*Liquid Assets*[b]	*Short-Term Debt*[c]	*Total Debt*[d]	*Historical-Cost Equity*[e]	*Current-Cost Equity*[f]	*Liquid Assets/Short-Term Debt*	*Short-Term Debt/Total Debt*	*Historical-Cost Equity/Total Capitalization*[g]	*Current-Cost Equity/Total Capitalization*[g]
1946	33.5	41.5	80.5	96.5	113.3	0.807	0.516	0.545	0.585
1947	35.1	49.5	93.7	110.6	133.9	0.709	0.528	0.541	0.588
1948	36.3	52.5	102.2	124.5	148.9	0.691	0.514	0.549	0.593
1949	39.4	49.0	101.5	136.0	155.7	0.804	0.483	0.573	0.605
1950	44.0	67.7	124.1	151.6	173.8	0.650	0.546	0.550	0.583
1951	46.7	75.9	138.1	168.0	192.2	0.615	0.550	0.549	0.582
1952	46.6	75.8	143.8	179.1	202.0	0.615	0.527	0.555	0.584
1953	48.6	76.6	148.5	191.5	214.9	0.634	0.516	0.563	0.591
1954	48.9	76.4	152.9	201.0	222.5	0.640	0.500	0.568	0.593
1955	54.2	92.0	174.5	216.3	245.3	0.589	0.527	0.554	0.584
1956	49.7	97.8	187.8	231.2	269.0	0.508	0.521	0.552	0.589
1957	49.2	98.8	197.4	244.8	286.6	0.498	0.501	0.554	0.592
1958	51.7	100.6	207.4	255.2	297.2	0.514	0.485	0.552	0.589
1959	57.1	111.7	225.9	269.8	313.2	0.511	0.494	0.544	0.581
1960	53.0	116.1	237.6	281.0	320.0	0.457	0.489	0.542	0.574
1961	56.5	123.0	253.2	292.4	329.5	0.459	0.486	0.535	0.565
1962	59.6	129.8	270.2	308.2	343.7	0.459	0.480	0.533	0.560
1963	64.2	141.8	292.3	322.6	359.1	0.453	0.485	0.525	0.551

1964	65.1	153.5	313.7	342.6	380.6	0.424	0.489	0.522	0.548
1965	67.8	175.3	348.9	364.9	405.8	0.387	0.502	0.511	0.538
1966	64.1	192.0	383.9	392.2	439.3	0.334	0.500	0.505	0.534
1967	68.8	201.6	414.6	418.3	473.7	0.341	0.486	0.502	0.533
1968	76.7	231.3	466.6	439.6	508.2	0.332	0.496	0.485	0.521
1969	78.9	263.9	520.7	466.7	553.4	0.299	0.507	0.473	0.515
1970	78.5	275.8	559.6	485.7	595.5	0.285	0.493	0.465	0.516
1971	89.1	285.4	600.4	514.0	643.3	0.312	0.475	0.462	0.517
1972	93.1	310.7	658.6	548.3	701.3	0.300	0.472	0.454	0.516
1973	100.1	356.0	748.8	598.6	780.1	0.281	0.475	0.444	0.512
1974	113.1	412.0	844.3	653.5	922.2	0.275	0.488	0.436	0.522
1975	132.4	408.4	874.7	646.0	1002.1	0.324	0.467	0.425	0.534
1976–I	133.2	412.6	883.2	n.a.	n.a.	0.323	0.467	n.a.	n.a.

Source: Flow of Funds Section, Board of Governors of the Federal Reserve System.

[a]Numbers for first quarter 1976 are preliminary.

[b]Liquid assets: demand deposits, currency, time deposits, U.S.-government securities, state and local obligations, commercial paper, and security R.P.'s.

[c]Short-term debt: commercial paper, acceptances, finance-company loans, U.S.-government loans, construction loans, 60 percent of bank loans N.E.C., profit-taxes payable, trade debt, and miscellaneous liabilities.

[d]Total debt: short-term debt plus long-term debt.

[e]Historical-cost equity represents the capital stock of nonfinancial corporations using historical-cost accounting. Financial assets are valued at par or book value, while fixed assets and inventories are valued at historical cost after deducting depreciation on a straight-line basis, which is the most common accounting method used in published statements of condition. The number for 1975 is preliminary.

[f]Current-cost equity represents the capital stock of nonfinancial corporations using current-cost accounting. Financial assets are valued at par or book value, while fixed assets are valued at current prices after deducting depreciation on a double-declining-balance basis. The number for 1975 is preliminary.

[g]Total capitalization is the sum of total debt plus historical-cost equity when the numerator of the ratio is historical-cost equity. It is the sum of total debt plus current-cost equity when the numerator is current-cost equity.

assistance to small businesses and farmers and even large firms in distress, lender-of-last-resort facilities, deposit insurance, mortgage insurance and guarantees, and stock-market credit regulation.

Bank supervision and regulation should also be added to this list, since measures of this kind cannot achieve total protection. Regulation, by its nature, cannot cover all contingencies. Some avenues toward excessive risk taking are likely to remain open. If the regulated erroneously conclude that everything not marked dangerous is therefore necessarily safe, they may be misled. Likewise, if the regulated are prepared to accept a certain degree of risk in their operations, regulation that limits particular forms of risk will not keep them from achieving their preferred risk exposure. It will merely foreclose for them their preferred forms of risk, leaving open others that are second best. Thus regulation may lead the regulated toward the selection of risks they regard as suboptimal in kind, even if appropriate in degree.

Next I turn to what seems to be a tendency to reevaluate, that is, change the perception of, risks that in an objective sense are really invariant. This arises, first, because asset markets, like other markets, sometimes develop imperfections. Some assets are not always valued correctly, and innovative operators may then be able to take advantage of this. Their success, however, can spawn imitators whose actions may contribute to an overevaluation of assets that originally were not undervalued. There are many obvious examples of this in the history of the stock and real-estate markets.

Second, a tendency to underestimate risk may occur because the ultimate consequences of excessive risk do not materialize immediately. In terms of probability, a high-risk operation may work out well several times or for a considerable period before the failure whose probability was underestimated occurs. In the interim, erroneous assessments of the true risk may proliferate.

Third, excessive risk taking can result from the tendency of portfolio managers to justify their decisions by reference to the decisions of others similarly situated, rather than by use of objective criteria. When a peer group is employed to represent the standard of sound practice, there is no real check on a developing trend toward riskier portfolios.

Fourth, managers of investments, financial and real, probably tend to underestimate covariance within portfolios or assets or projects they manage. For the expert whose job it is to evaluate the risk and return of a particular asset, the specific risk of that asset very easily comes to dominate his or her assessment of general market risk. In the event, as we have often seen, market risk may dominate, as most factors tend to go up and down together, and the result will be excessive risk taking.

Fifth, even when risk is recognized and a risk premium demanded, it may not always give the protection expected. It is one thing to invest in a B bond and receive a risk premium of 1 percent per year for thirty years. It is quite another to receive the same premium on a ninety-day certificate of deposit. There is in effect no reasonable risk premium that could compensate for substantial risk in a short-term asset. A belief to the contrary is likely to lead to excessive risk taking.

From the discussion of changing perception, that is, reevaluation, of objectively unchanging risks, I now turn to the possibility that fundamental attitudes toward risk may change over time, leading to a greater willingness to accept risks that are correctly evaluated as such. It should be borne in mind that risk aversion is not necessarily good and that risk neutrality is not necessarily bad. Much economic theorizing postulates risk neutrality on the part of the firm and risk aversion on the part of individuals as ultimate wealth owners. In the long run, one may assume, a sample of risk-neutral firms will outcompete a sample of risk-averse firms, even though a higher percentage of the risk neutrals may fall by the wayside.

First, a firm's willingness to accept risk may increase over time as older executives who experienced the last big crisis retire.

Furthermore, the attitude of managers toward risk tends to depend on the structure of penalties and rewards. A manager who expects to be penalized for losses but not to be greatly rewarded for gains is very cautious. Another who has a chance to make it big if he wins, and thinks he can always find another job if he misses, leans in the other direction. The increased use of stock options and management bonuses may encourage this attitude. It appears that, in the investment business at least, the structure of rewards and penalties was moving in the second direction before recent calamities struck.

Finally, there may be a tendency to accept greater risk with respect to the investment of money derived from past gains than with respect to the original investment.

These situations, although based only on casual empiricism, seem to provide at least a partial explanation of behavior observed in the not-too-distant past. If my basic hypothesis is right—the highest weight in the formation of expectations attaches to recent, often traumatic, experience—most of the mechanisms pushing for greater risk taking are now operating in reverse. The bright young men have learned a lesson, or perhaps they are gone altogether. Greatly increased risk premiums indicate a heightened awareness among investors as to the risk being assumed. These premiums in turn create an incentive for firms to move to less exposed positions. The location of the brink has been thoroughly explored, and some have fallen over. The question is how far the retreat from the brink will go and how long it will last.

There is no signpost telling us where danger ends and safety begins. There are only more-safe and less-safe positions. A fully informed investing public accurately gauging economic risk makes asset choices that guide firms to positions reflecting public preferences. We should bear in mind that a universal effort to achieve maximum safety may send us on a long and thirsty journey, as each of the travelers tries to improve liquidity or protect solvency by forcing a less advantageous position on the rest.

Improvement in balance-sheet structures, both of nonfinancial and financial corporations, is obviously very much needed. I conclude with a short account of a few measures government has taken, and a few it could take, to shorten and ease the trip, and to reduce artificial incentives to riskier financial structures.

First, the monetary authority has not sought to resolve liquidity and solvency problems by inflating the economy. The rate of growth of the money supply M_1 has been moderate over the last two years, and the Federal Reserve plans to keep it that way. We have learned, moreover, that whatever power inflation might have had in the past to float the economy off any financial shoals has vanished today. Inflation has revealed itself as a threat to liquidity and solvency.

What government has done of late through its fiscal policy is to take on some of the burden of debt that needed to be incurred if savings were to be invested and jobs protected. Over the entire postwar period, however, the federal government has been the one sector that has sharply reduced its debt relative to its income. As a result, all other sectors together have found their debt-income ratios rising. While this may have been an additional factor making for higher risk, I do not accept for a moment the implication that the government should increase its debt in order to spare the private sector the need to increase its own. The private sector can live with higher debt-income ratios than those of the late 1940s and the 1950s. But the substitution of public for private debt capacity during the recent recession has been beneficial for the restructuring process as well as for the maintenance of income levels. I need hardly add that what is beneficial during a recession may become a threat as recovery advances.

I have in the past examined two devices that may reduce the economy's inherent pressure toward escalating risk. One is a change in our tax system designed to eliminate the tax bias toward debt and against equity. We can achieve this by reducing the tax deductibility of interest, thereby increasing the tax base so that the corporate tax on dividends and profit retentions may be simultaneously reduced. If the same tax rate were applied to income going into interest payments, dividend payments, and profit retentions, the tax system would be neutral with regard to the corporate choice between equity and debt. The problems of phasing into such a system—it can only be done gradually—are not inconsiderable but can most likely be solved.

A second reduction in our financial risk exposure applies to the banking system. The present insurance of $40,000 per deposit protects 63 percent of the dollar value of deposits in insured banks, but leaves particularly large banks vulnerable to withdrawal of deposits in excess of $40,000. The historical loss experience, even including the U.S. National Bank of San Diego and the Franklin National Bank of New York, indicates that it would cost little to raise the level of insurance even up to 100 percent. Doing so, in addition to providing insurance, would also help to minimize liquidity problems such as arose in the case of Franklin National, where a rapid runoff of certificates of deposit forced the Federal Reserve to substitute its credit for that of large depositors. However, it may not be wise to go to 100 percent insurance, even if some of the inherent regulatory problems would be dealt with by graduated premiums. Full-deposit insurance may eliminate the discipline now exerted over banks by the marketplace. Nor is insurance a full substitute for a continued effort by banks to improve their capital positions. Nevertheless, enlarged deposit insurance is one of the avenues open to the government to increase the safety of our financial structure.

Part VI
Investments and the Stock Market

30 What Does the Random-Walk Hypothesis Mean to Security Analysts?

The theory has gained ground recently that throwing darts at the stock-market page is just as good a technique of picking securities as are charts or fundamental analysis. This theory is supported by a good deal of evidence. Certainly it is not refuted by showing that some managers have done better than the averages. In a world in which some stocks rise faster than others, half the portfolios will always rise faster than the other half. The difficulty is knowing in advance which half.

How to Measure Performance

What are the facts? To begin with, it is quite wrong to compare simply the return on different investments. Risk is another dimension that must also be considered. The rate of return can be measured by dividend plus capital appreciation. Risk can be measured by the variability of the rate of return. Fifteen percent return per year after year for sure is better than 30 percent one year and zero the next, even if it does average out to 15 percent. That at least seems to be the view of the majority of investors. For when rates of return and their variability are compared, they turn out to be positively correlated—high returns are associated with high variability. Investors demand to be paid for accepting risk—they are predominantly risk averters. The pricing of securities in the market reflects this.

Given these facts, it is meaningless to say that portfolio A has outperformed portfolio B because it has risen faster. Portfolio A is better only if its return is higher without being more variable than the return of portfolio B. Otherwise it is matter of taste whether the investor prefers high return with high risk, or low return with low risk. Most stock-market comparisons overlook this.

Risk the Price of Performance

It follows, next, that if the highest expected rate of return is the investor's objective, regardless of risk, it is quite possible to put together a portfolio that

---

This chapter was originally published in *Financial Analysts Journal*, March–April 1968, pp. 159–170.

is likely to advance more quickly than the averages. The investor need only choose securities with high risk. On average he is likely to do better than with a low-risk portfolio. But, the risk being high, in a good number of cases he will do much worse. If he does well he will think he has been smart. If he does badly others at any rate may say he was foolish. Neither is true. He simply took a higher risk. In one case chance made it pay off, in the other it did not.

One proper function of securities analysis is, therefore, to measure the variability of return on stocks, that is, their risk. This is not difficult to do in terms of past performance. The future is something else again. The proper function of a portfolio manager is so to diversify securities in his portfolio as to achieve the least risk for a given expected return. These are the areas where securities analysis makes a contribution to investment performance.

Where it probably ceases to do so is when the analyst believes he can spot stocks that are substantially undervalued. One might think that, with all the effort being put into it, analysts should be able to discover many such situations. On the other hand, if the analysts are all intelligent, and all have about the same information, and all have done their homework, why should any such bonanzas be left? Stocks then will sell for what competent judgment thinks they are worth. Further research is useless.

Mutual Funds versus Random Performance

This is borne out by an increasing number of studies of mutual-fund performance. Some of these have compared averages of mutual funds with averages of portfolios randomly chosen, by various methods familiar to statisticians, that is, with "dart-throwing" portfolios. Others have employed different techniques. The result is always the same—mutual funds do no better than random. In the most detailed such comparison I have seen, by George Douglas, an average of random portfolios, all containing the same number of securities, beat an average of mutual-fund portfolios by about 3 percentage points for a given amount of risk.[1] If allowance is made for brokerage and other expenses of the funds, which Douglas did not do, this difference may lose significance. *Fortune* magazine recently showed that, while the performance funds had done well over a short period by buying high-risk stocks, most of them would have done even better most of the time had they not traded but simply held the portfolios that they started out with.[2] Others have made similar findings that selection is no better than random choice.[3,4,5]

Random Walk—Narrow Version

All this supports the "random-walk" theory of the stock market. In its narrow version the theory says that the next move of the market or of a stock cannot be predicted from any past behavior. This warning is addressed mainly to chartists, who believe that past patterns can predict the future. A considerable volume of statistical testing has been done by high-powered techniques, which largely confirms the verdict.[6] Naturally there are plenty of efforts, mainly on the side of the industry, to disprove the random walk. Usually it is by someone who claims he has done better previously, and may be able to prove it. But this sort of proof often leaves open the question whether it was skill or luck, and whether the performance can be repeated in the future.[7,8,9] So long as there are averages some people will have above average success. And with large numbers of people in the business, chance will explain some remarkable success stories.

Random Walk—Broad Version

There is a broader version of the random-walk theory. It says that in a well-functioning market, all known information has already been full discounted. The next move of the market will reflect information not yet known. In the face of such perfect pricing, further research into stock fundamentals is clearly useless. When new information comes, stocks adjust instantaneously, so that no one can buy or sell quickly enough to benefit.

This is an idealization of even so good a market as the New York Stock Exchange. News does not travel instantaneously; it is not acted on immediately; some people have inside information. Prophecies can be self-fulfilling—if enough people follow a leader, the leader is running something akin to a pool operation. Moreover, a few rare individuals may genuinely be able to see farther ahead than the rest. Thus the broader version of the random walk probably is only approximately accurate. In a study of the 1965–1966 Value Line contest John Shelton found that the contestants did slightly better than a random walk would suggest.[10] But the margin would scarcely have covered brokerage commissions, and in the 1967 contest, the difference in performance seems to have been less significant.

Great Men and New Techniques

Further, it is quite conceivable that from time to time someone discovers some effect or relationship not previously known to the market, that can profitably be exploited. For a while he will do better than random. But as the technique becomes known, its universal use will so alter stock prices as to make it useless.

One such technique that seems not be effectively expolited is that developed by Harry Markowitz, based on the covariance of stocks, that is, the degree to which different stocks tend to move together.[11] Obviously a portfolio is better diversified if the stocks in it have low or negative covariance. Stocks with higher individual risk can be put into such a portfolio without raising the risk of the entire portfolio beyond the level the investor wants to accept. The reason for thinking that investors have not yet fully exploited the degree of covariance among stocks is that stocks which tend to move independently from others, and should therefore be in demand for purposes of diversification, do not sell at a premium that one would expect to result from such diversification demand. But the ''gimmick'' is becoming known, and once it is being widely exploited, it, too, will cease to have value.

A Good Market Is a Random Market

Trying to explain the random-walk hypothesis to a securities expert is like putting a person through psychoanalysis: the securities analyst, who in this case occupies the place on the couch, resists what he is learning because, like the patient in real analysis, he does not like it. But as the facts begin to fall into place for him, he wonders how he could ever have overlooked them. He also finds that, in many respects, he is a great deal happier with his new understanding.

The random-walk hypothesis says little more than that the stock market is a very good market. A good market is a competitive market. None of the participants possess market power, that is, power to influence prices. Such market power, where it exists, could take the form of significant control over the supply of or the demand for stocks, that is, an element of oligopoly. Or it could take the form of power to issue self-fulfilling prophecies. An investor who can influence the action of others, by what he says or is seen to do, is issuing such prophecies.

A good market also requires wide and rapid spread of information. There must be no inside information.

These two properties of a good market—absence of market power, and information equally available to all—are required also for a random-walk market. To deny the random walk is to question the goodness of the market.

Obviously the stock market is not a perfect market. Thus, as I said earlier, the market is unlikely to be a perfect random walk.

Implications of Nonrandomness

But if it could be demonstrated that the stock market is very far from a random walk, some of the implications would be distinctly embarrassing to Wall Street.

For one thing, as pointed out, it would reflect adversely on the quality of the stock market as a market. Reforms would be in order to reduce market power and improve the flow of information. For another, if professionals could do significantly better in the market than amateurs, a question of social policy would be raised. In boxing, we do not allow professionals to fight amateurs, in order to avoid injury. In the stock market, the amateurs very often are people of modest means, or "widows and orphans." If there were strong reason to believe that professionals are becoming rich by buying stocks cheap from widows and orphans and selling them back dear, something would probably have to be done to stop the slaughter. The random-walk hypothesis protects the professional against demands for inconvenient reforms.

Social Usefulness

Does the random-walk hypothesis imply that securities analysis, aside from measuring risk, performs no socially useful function? I have pointed out earlier what, in my opinion, securities analysis can do and what it cannot do. It is important for the good functioning of the economy that securities be correctly priced. Incorrect pricing can produce serious disturbance. Here is the main social contribution of securities analysis. But approximately correct pricing could probably be obtained with a fraction of the manpower now employed in securities analysis. Once the best available judgment has put prices where they belong, there is no social benefit in duplicating the work. Furthermore, since enough investors will be analyzing securities in their own self-interest, it is hard to see why the marginal investor, and therefore any investor, should pay for securities analysis. Correct pricing of securities, like T.V. and radio, is a public good available free to all even though it costs money to produce. Anybody can get the benefit of the combined best judgment by simply accepting the prices set by the market.

Performance Stocks and Funds

The randon-walk hypothesis is not invalidated by the recent success of performance funds and that of numerous investors investing in performance stocks. Part of this success probably is justified by the high risks that are run. Part of it may be explainable in terms of self-fulfilling prophecies, for which the random walk does not allow. Part of the success may be chance—where hundreds of thousands of people are operating, a certain number are always bound to be right. For instance, the probability of correctly predicting a fall of a coin ten times in a row is approximately one in a thousand. Among the hundreds of thousands of people who are trying to predict major turns in the stock market, there must be hundreds who have been right ten times in a row. If we knew who they were, we would celebrate them as geniuses. Chance accounts for a lot, particularly when the word "performance" is attached to a fund or stock *after* the event. The period, moreover, during which these miracles have been worked is short in many cases and therefore insufficient for statistical evaluation.

Nevertheless, I do not in the least want to deny the possibility that there are some superior minds at work, or that some new techniques have been discovered. But the theory of the random walk says, as I pointed out, that as the new techniques are learned by others, they become valueless. Performance investing, for instance, may drive stocks to such high-risk levels that a performance return becomes no more than adequate to compensate for the high risk.

In summary, the randon-walk hypothesis is neither as implausible nor as damaging as some analysts seem to think. It leaves a useful function for securities analysis, and the analyst can make his peace with the hypothesis if he finds it plausible.

Conclusions

What conclusions are to be drawn from all of this?

1. It is important to repeat that the dart-throwing theory does not say that a portfolio cannot be selected that is likely to outperform the market. But it will have to be a portfolio with a higher risk than the market.

2. Some superior individuals may be able to do consistently better than random. Superior performance for a few years only proves nothing. Somebody has to be holding the stocks that go up fast without being penalized for the risks taken.

3. Switching frequently probably is a useless expense. The investor should choose the degree of risk he wants to run, put together his portfolio accordingly, and hold.

Notes

1. George W. Douglas, *Risk in the Equity Markets: An Empirical Appraisal of Market Efficiency,* Yale Ph.D. Dissertation, 1967.

2. Arthur M. M. Louis, "Those Go-Go Funds May be Going Nowhere," *Fortune,* November 1967.

3. Irwin Friend and Douglas Vickers, "Portfolio Selection and Investment Performance," *Journal of Finance,* September 1965.

4. William F. Sharpe, "Mutual Fund Performance," *Journal of Business,* January 1966, Pt. II.

5. Michael C. Jensen, "The Performance of Mutual Funds in the Period

1945–64,'' Paper presented at the Annual Meetings of the American Finance Association, Washington, D.C., December 30, 1967.

6. Paul H. Cootner, editor, *The Randon Character of Stock Market Prices,* M.I.T. Press, 1964.

7. Robert A. Levy, ''Random Walks: Reality or Myth'' *Financial Analysts Journal,* November–December 1967.

8. Michael C. Jensen, ''Random Walks: Reality or Myth—Comment,'' *Financial Analysts Journal,* November–December 1967.

9. Robert A. Levy, ''Random Walks: Reality or Myth—Reply,'' *Financial Analysts Journal,* January–February 1968.

10. John P. Shelton, ''The Value Line Contest: A Test of the Predictability of Stockmarket Changes,'' *Journal of Business,* July 1967.

11. Harry M. Markowitz, *Portfolio Selection,* Cowles Foundation Monograph 16, John Wiley & Sons, Inc., 1959.

31 Radical Revisions of the Distant Future: Then and Now

The stock-market peaks of 1929 and 1973, and their corresponding troughs in 1932 and 1974, pose the question of rationality in the markets. Both events can be rationally explained only on the grounds that they represented extreme revaluations of the future. Short-term cyclical developments, however severe, could not justify the revaluation in quick order, both up and down, of the present value of future-income streams the larger part of which, at any reasonable interest rate, is many years away. A radical revision of present preception of the distant future is required to justify such movements. In this chapter, I want to review very briefly what seems to me to have been the nature of these revisions and their probable causes.

The rise of the stock market to its 1929 peak plainly seems to have reflected "new-era" thinking. Over a period of about two years the market doubled, from a base that was itself the peak of past experience, into wholly uncharted territory, with very little support from cyclical factors. The move seems to imply an expectation, not of very high growth, as was expected during the pre-1973 years, but simply of a shift to a new level. If an investor is told that a stock has a very high expected growth rate of earnings and therefore dividends, the investor may pay a high multiple for it but probably will discount that growth severely. Otherwise, if the expected growth rate exceeds the discount rate and growth goes on forever, the stock's value becomes infinity, and even in Wall Street no one seems to have been ready to pay this. But if an investor is given absolute assurance that a stock will rise to some level within a given period, he would not be concerned about the growth rate but would push the stock immediately to its full expected value discounted only at the risk-free interest rate. That approximately seems to have been what took hold of investors' minds in 1927–1929.

No doubt there was plausible reasons, as always. There were going to be no more recessions, there were going to be no more cyclical risks, stock earnings would be capitalized at bond yields, and the more you leveraged, the better you would do.

The rationale for performance investing and go-go funds during the late 1960s and early 1970s was not quite so unsophisticated. Nor was the speed with which the market advanced comparable to the pre-1929 episode. I abstract here from various other episodes when the market approximately doubled over a short period of time, such as 1933–1934, 1935–1937, and 1942–1946, be-

This chapter was originally published in *Journal of Portfolio Management*, Fall 1979, pp. 36–38.

cause these were essentially cyclical recoveries, not involving substantial moves into uncharted market territory. The pre-1973 years, however, were characterized by extreme growth expectations for particular stocks, although generally not for the economy as a whole. The fact that high growth involved high risk and had to be supported by high rates of return was recognized.

Growth stocks, therefore, were not stocks that were expected to move almost immediately to a new higher level and then perhaps stay there, while the earnings of the company caught up, but stocks that would have a high but steady rate of growth. There may have been seriously flawed thinking in the assumption that there could be many such stocks in an economy that was widely understood to be growing at only 4 percent or a little better. Also, the underlying analysis of the capital-asset pricing model was sufficiently complex to be really accessible to only a limited number of professionals who, then, were able to attract a considerable following. It contrasted with the simple concepts of the so-called new era, which could readily be mastered by everybody and thus brought on a mass delusion instead of an expert's delusion as in the pre-1973 period.

I now turn to the postpeak periods of the two episodes. The drop in the Dow-Jones average from a peak of about 365 to a low of about 45 in 1932 is only slightly less when corrected for a 20 percent decline of the price level (90 percent unadjusted versus 85 percent adjusted). Once more, this move seems to imply a totally different evaluation of the distant future. No doubt there were other factors contributing to the speed and depth of the drop—margin calls, corporate and personal bankruptcies, distress sales. But even the levels of the early recovery into the middle 1930s reflect a view of the future very different from that of the new era. That new view, of course, soon began to surface in the economic literature of the day in the form of the stagnation hypothesis. The frontier was gone, population was stagnating, investment opportunities were exhausted. The euthanasia of the rentier seemed near.

Nevertheless, a few years later, the Dow-Jones registered its 1937 peak at a level that, price-adjusted for the level of consumer prices, was well above (50 percent) the 1927 level of 155 from which the new-era boom had taken off. In the midst of gloom and doom, and all the New Deal bitterness in Wall Street, the market showed considerable strength, aided probably by the great difficulty of getting a living yield out of bonds. Triple-A corporates were then yielding 3.32 percent and older issues with higher coupons were being called with distressing predictability.

The post-1973 experience has been quite different. The drop was far less steep as was, of course, the recession associated with it. Accordingly, the cyclical recovery carried the market quickly to levels not far distant from pre-1973 levels, at least in nominal terms. Inflation adjusted, however, there has been virtually no recovery to the time of this writing (May 1979). The Dow-Jones average is where it was at the bottom in 1974, and the Standard and

Poor's index is only about 10 percent better. Evidently, short-run experience once more has drastically changed the perception of the distant future, if the market is to be interpreted as rational.

Again, there are plenty of reasons. There is inflation. There is the oil problem. There is the cutback of medium-term growth expectations from about 4 to 3 or 3½ percent. There are the shrinking share of profits, or the declining return on capital, and other articles of faith that do not always stand up to quantitative analysis.

But aside from events in and beliefs about the real world, there are changes in attitudes that need to be examined if we are to see clearly where this latest reevaluation of the distant future has come about and where it is taking us.

First, a very pronounced change in attitudes toward risk seems to have occurred. This is expressed in stock-market multiples that have been cut to less than one-half of their peak levels in 1973. Part of this can be accounted for by reduced growth expectations. But the rest must be risk aversion.

Risk taking as such has by no means disappeared. It has shifted, however, to the single-family housing market, although most participants in that market may not see it that way. Willingness to take risk also seems to be shifting to the option market, where it is doing the economy no particular good.

Second, the valuation of equities today seems to be conducted on somewhat perplexing principles. Total return as an investment concept seems to be out, earnings matter little, dividends are decisive, but the growth of dividends is not. In the pre-1973 days of growth euphoria, when the growth of dividends was expected to come from the growth of companies and their earnings, it was appropriate to put a heavy discount on expected growth, and that good principle was not sufficiently observed. Today, the growth of dividends comes largely from inflation. Should this type of "growth" be discounted equally? I believe not, and this has nothing to do with expectations of inflation. So long as interest rates move with inflation, the future-earnings stream and the rate at which it should be discounted rise equally, implying an unchanging present valuation for the stock at any rate of expected inflation. Discounting inflation and discounting real growth are different matters, and the discount rates to be applied are differently determined.

Expectations of real growth for a company could be sadly disappointing, and yet inflation will increase its sales and, unless profit margins shrink, also its dividends. Expectation of dividend increases in a time of inflation does not seem to be a very high-risk assumption. Yet the market today seems to place about the same discount on inflationary growth of dividends as on real growth.

Equally hard to understand is the seeming faith that risk aversion can be satisfied by bond investment. In a time of unstable inflation, bonds are far from riskless. If inflation were to accelerate, the associated rise in interest rates would depress the market price of outstanding bonds while also reducing their purchasing power. Puzzling also are the belief that bonds provide an acceptable yield when interest rates on new issues have a hard time keeping up with the rate of inflation and the apparent view of trustees that bonds under these conditions are anything but annuities. At a rate of inflation of 10 percent, the half-life of a dollar is about seven years.

Finally, there is something to puzzle about in the conclusion that, because stocks have been a poor inflation hedge in the past, they will also be so in the future. Presumably, as inflation continues to reduce the real value of equities at constant nominal prices and reduces price-earnings ratios, the ability of equities to serve as an inflation hedge should improve. Failure of earnings to rise with inflation would imply far-reaching structural changes in the economy.

What could be the reasons for this massive change in investment attitudes that in turn supports the deflated view of the future in this inflationary environment? One might guess that it has something to do with the professionalization of the securities business. Very likely this tends to homogenize views, increasing the herd instinct among bulls and bears respectively. The rewards-penalties system for professionals works in that direction. It is dangerous to be wrong in support of an unpopular cause. The portfolio manager who loses money on stocks shows poor judgement. If he puts his client into bonds that lose purchasing power from inflation, the client is dying a hero's death. Professionals have made the market efficient, in the narrow sense that there is nothing of predictive value to be learned from the past data of the market. It is far from clear that they have made it rational. There may be something to be learned from the history of mass delusions in the market after all.

32 Does the Volatility of Growth Stocks Demonstrate Irrational Behavior?

The bear-market experience of 1969–1970 has yielded its usual crop of complaints from critics who forgot to speak up while prices were advancing. But the depth and suddenness of the gyrations have also elicited comments of a different order. "I have seen my stocks cut in half in past bear markets," says a businessman investor, "and accepted it as a normal fluctuation. But when they drop 80 percent, what does that mean?" Or from a European banker: "The value of American industry now fluctuates as much as 5 percent in one day. Have you Americans become so hysterical that you no longer have a sense of value?"

The facts are on the record. In the face of an economic decline of—until now—unusually modest proportions, the market has taken its third worse spill since the 1920s. Some stocks have been virtually wiped out; daily movements, both of the averages and of individual stocks, have been exceptionally wide.

Does this demonstrate irrationality?

The point I shall make here is that the recent greater volatility of the stock market is, in part at least, the result of wide swings in interest rates at a time when stock values have increasingly come to be based on growth instead of on dividends. To that extent, this greater volatility is entirely rational. Before supplying the evidence I must guard against one misinterpretation. I am not arguing that growth orientation destabilizes stock prices because growth expectations are less stable than dividend expectations. It happens to be true, apparently, that growth expectations are rather unstable. Let a reputable growth stock miss its usual earnings growth for only one quarter, and the market sometimes acts as if the rest of the decade no longer counted. The price collapses, the stock is downgraded in analysts' reports, and all that was researched and written about it seems to count no longer. But in the absence of really good reasons, such behavior must be regarded as irrational. What this article will be concerned with is rational behavior in the face of novel circumstances.

An Inevitable Adjustment

The point to be made is that even when the growth expectation of a stock is entirely stable, unaffected by recession, a change in interest rates will hurt the

---

This chapter was originally published in *Institutional Investor*, October 1970, pp. 40–42.

growth stock more than the dividend stock. Interest rates have changed more drastically in recent years than in any comparable prior period. Long-term corporate-bond rates have gone altogether outside the range of civilized financial experience. Rates of 9 and 10 percent on good bonds are possible only in a severe inflation, and in one that is expected to continue. The rise of long-term rates in the face of declining business has made this very clear. In all recessions since World War II, long-term rates came down after business had peaked out. Their rise now implies that the market does not expect high rates to be a temporary phenomenon. It expects them to be long-lasting. Under these conditions, stock prices are bound to adjust downward, unless earnings and expected growth rise proportionately to the inflation, which so far does not seem to have happened. With earnings unchanged or even reduced, stocks must adjust to compete with the higher yield level available in the bond market. And it is growth stocks that must make the widest swing to accomplish this adjustment.

Take a stock with a dividend of $6 and little expectation of growth. When the bond rate is 6 percent, this stock might sell at 100. If the bond rate rises to 9 percent and is expected to stay there, the stock will have to make some corresponding adjustment. If the market demands from it a yield of 9 percent, it will fall to 67.

Take, on the other hand, a stock paying no dividend, but with earnings of, say, $3 that are firmly expected to grow at 10 percent per year. In some markets, that stock might also sell at 100. Its dividend return would be zero, but its expected growth return, at a price of 100, would be 10 percent or $10 for the next year. (This pricing can be brought into conformity with the familiar, and unrealistic, valuation formula $P = \frac{D}{r - g}$ by assuming, realistically, that growth does not go on forever and that the growth return must be discounted at a rate containing a substantial risk premium.)

Suppose that, in response to a rise in the bond rate from 6 percent to 9 percent, the market sought to reprice this stock to raise its return by one half, that is, to 15 percent. Suppose the stock drops by as much as the dividend stock to 67. Its earnings are still firmly expected to grow at 10 percent. But unfortunately, at a price of 67, 10 percent growth per year is only $6.70 on the stock. The growth return has not increased at all. The same would be true if the stock fell to 50 or 25 or 10. A growth of 10 percent, converted to dollars on the basis of whatever the price happens to be, can never produce a growth return of more than 10 percent.

Search for Support

What keeps the stock from falling to zero in its effort to attain a higher growth return is, of course, the reduction in its price/earnings multiple. If the earnings hold up and grow as expected, giving hopes of future dividends, at some level the risk becomes very small. At that point the stock will find support.

Most stocks fall between the extremes of pure dividend return and pure growth return. But their overall return, combining dividend plus growth, is variously divided between the two. Some stocks are mostly growth, with little dividend; others are mostly dividend, with little growth. Suppose that, in the above example, the growth stock was actually paying a dividend of $1, giving it a dividend return, at a price of 100, of 1 percent and, with a growth return of 10 percent, an overall return of 11 percent. When that stock declines, the dividend part of the return begins to rise. At a price of 67, it would have risen to only 1.5 percent, for a total return of 11.5 percent. But at 20, the dividend return from the $1 dividend would be 5 percent. Combined with the unchanged 10 percent growth return, this would bring the overall return to 15 percent, which is the level the market demanded. Given the great reduction in the multiple, the market might be satisfied with less, and the stock might find support somewhat before it had dropped to a 15 percent return basis.

In the case of a stock with a combined growth and dividend return—the normal case—the entire burden of achieving a higher overall rate of return is thrown on the dividend component. The growth component never changes—assuming the favorable case that growth expectations do not deteriorate. Consequently, the change in price that is needed in order to arrive at a given higher overall return is larger the greater the share of the growth component is in the overall return.[1]

In the untutored old days, when growth was not much considered, stocks sold on dividends or earnings, and small fluctuations sufficed to achieve a change in the rate of return that the market might require. Today, with growth increasingly in the picture, wider swings are needed. These swings become extreme when interest-rate fluctuations are as wide as they recently have been. None of this implies irrationality, or hysterical revisions of growth expectations. It is simple arithmetic.

Growth versus Dividends

Experts in discounted-cash-flow technique can translate the proportion into their own idiom. A dividend stock yields a larger part of its lifetime dividends over a given nearby period of years than does a pure growth stock. The latter, too, will eventually pay dividends, or nobody would pay more than discounted liquidating value for the privilege of owning it. But less of this stream of dividends comes in the near future and more in the distant future. An increase in the interest rate at which future receipts are discounted hits distant receipts harder than those nearby. Consequently, a rise in market rates of interest will depress growth stocks more than dividend stocks.

One could complicate the analysis further by introducing tax considerations. They happen to work in the same direction as the increasing growth orientation, that is, they tend to aggravate price swings when interest rates change. One of the attractions of a growth stock is the relative tax protection it enjoys. When competitive market factors demand an increase in its overall rate of return, the weight of the dividend component in the overall return increases relative to the growth component. The dividend component does not enjoy a tax shelter. Hence, as the stock drops and thus increasingly becomes a dividend stock, its tax position deteriorates. This may call for further price concessions.

To conclude: There are factors in the market which, everything else equal, make for wider fluctuations. These factors originate in the increasing growth orientation of modern stock-valuation practice. They have nothing to do with irrationality and hysteria, which some critics impute to our markets, even though these markets no doubt are not free from such defects. This conculsion is not controverted by the apparently growing speed of price adjustments in present markets. It has often been noted that, in recent years, bad news concerning a stock has produced an immediate sharp drop in the stock followed by a relatively flat movement. In former years, a more gradual downward movement seems to have been more normal.

These sharp drops no doubt are to some extent the result of institutional trading. Individual investors might be expected to require more time to evaluate the true meaning of a piece of adverse information and to act on it. But sharp and sudden price changes, insofar as they correctly evaluate a new piece of information, must be regarded as an improvement in the performance of the market. The correct market valuation is arrived at almost instantly; nobody has a chance to transact at or near the old price that now no longer reflects the true value of the stock. We have a better market, a more nearly random walk, because this market is harder to beat.

Whatever the ailments of the stock market, this much seems clear: investors are mistaken when they blame their losses on increasing market irrationality and hysteria.

Note

1. Devotees of the special version of the valuation formula which combines dividend return and growth return will see this at once. The formula says

$$\text{Return} = \text{Dividend Rate} + \text{Growth Rate, that is,}$$

$$= \frac{\$\text{Dividend}}{\$\text{Price}} + \text{Growth Rate}$$

On the right-hand side of the second expression, the only term that changes as price goes down is the dividend term. The growth term is invariant with respect to price and contributes nothing to the adjustment of the overall rate of return.

33 Performance and the Bond Market

It is a comforting thought that one can be right about bond prices without being right about everything else. In the mid 1930s, I had a job analyzing bonds in the investment department of a New York bank. We then developed a theory that government bond prices would rise, which turned out to be an excellent and profitable prediction for several years. The underlying reasoning has stood the test of time less well. It was based on the assumption that the public debt would soon be reduced and that government bonds would acquire a scarcity value.

Since that time the bond market has expanded enormously. There are few countries, even making allowance for size, that have a bond market comparable to the American. Our bond market does a tremendous job of financing, year in and year out. It differs in that regard from the stock market, which raises a much smaller net amount for business at much greater cost, the reason being, of course, that one of the principal functions of the stock market is to provide high liquidity to existing assets in addition to doing new financing.

Our bond market has stood up relatively well even under the onslaught of a virtually unprecedented inflation. Although long-term rates have been rising, it is evident that the current very high rates of inflation have not driven up interest rates commensurately. The bond market evidently believes, in my opinion reasonably, that these rates of inflation will not continue. The more moderate inflation premium that current long-term rates seem to reflect nevertheless points to an expectation on the part of the market concerning future inflation that is higher than I would like to see.

We should not take the ability of the bond market to resist even temporary spurts of high inflation for granted. In Germany, the rate of inflation currently is well below ours; it seems to be running a little above 7 percent. But the German long-term bond market, in the context of a vigorous anti-inflation policy, nevertheless has suffered severely. Rates are as high as 11 percent. New issues have had to be confined to intermediate maturities. The German experience is a warning of what inflation can do to a normally well functioning bond market.

One of the things that inflation has already done to the American bond market is to widen price movements. This is not confined to the depressing effects of high market yields on low-coupon bonds. As has often been pointed

This chapter was originally presented on May 16, 1974, at a meeting of the Bond Club of New York, the Bankers Club, New York City.

out, high interest rates make for greater volatility even of high-coupon bonds. Wider swings in prices, in turn, increase the importance of price changes relative to interest yield in the total return on bonds.

The concept of total return has been widely discussed in recent bond-market literature. Total return, over a given period, means adding together the yield to maturity, the net appreciation or depreciation during this time, plus the yield from reinvestment of interest during that period. The concept of total return was borrowed, of course, from the stock market, where it has had a long and somewhat checkered history. In the stock market, the theoretical logic of adding together dividend and capital gains is hard to refute. A company, after all, has the option of paying out its earnings or retaining them, so that dividend yield and appreciation becomes alternative ways of conveying profits to the shareholder. As a practical matter, I have always felt uneasy about treating a bird in the bush as if it were a bird in the hand. The stock market, I suspect, has the same reaction as it contemplates the relative merits of a dollar's worth of dividends and of expected growth. Investors who have tried to rely on total return, moreover, have had some rude awakenings since 1968.

But total return in the stock market is one thing, and in the bond market it is another. In the bond market, total return depends heavily on the time period over which it is measured. Usually this is taken as one year. Over a period of one year, bond prices often have moved by considerably more than the yield to maturity. I should add that I am using the term "capital gains or losses" for only that part of a bond's price changes that is not the reflection of its steady movement toward par at the time of maturity. In some years, total return has been more than double the yield to maturity, in others it has been negative. Going to quarterly periods, the relationship becomes even more extreme. Quarterly price movements have been quite large, quarterly yield to maturity is necessarily small. For short periods, therefore, the price movement tends to dominate the interest return.

This points up a basic weakness of the total return concept in the bond market. If we reduce the period over which the return is computed from a year to a quarter, a month, or a day, and if we then annualize the "return" obtained from the price changes during these miniperiods, we get sky-high rates of total return, positive or negative. If a bond with a 9 percent coupon, selling at par, goes up 100 basis points in one day, the annualized total return is 369 percent, ignoring the minimal matter of reinvestment of interest.

If, on the other hand, we lengthen the period over which total return is computed, and if we happen to choose the period that the bond has to run to maturity, the effect of interim price fluctuations washes out altogether. All that remains is the familiar old yield to maturity, plus reinvestment of interest if we are compounding.

The contrast between total return in the stock market and the bond market is obvious. In the stock market, the price of a common stock at any future time is uncertain. There is no fixed sum to be repaid at a fixed date. Based on history, moreover, the trend of the stock market has been up, although the last few years raise some questions. In the past at least, therefore, total return has meant adding a positive amount of growth to the dividend return.

Total return in the bond market is different. There is at least one point—maturity—when the future value of the bond is certain, assuming a good-quality bond. Price fluctuations are bound to be temporary and bound to wash out. There has been no discernible secular trend in interest rates, moreover, if we go back a couple of hundred years and treat the extremes of the 1940s and 1970s as temporary aberrations attributable to depression and inflation respectively. Under these conditions, the odds for getting a positive capital-gains component in the total return are much smaller than they are in the stock market.

A total bond return higher than the yield to maturity can be derived from various sources. The questions concerning the likelihood of attaining such an extra return do not apply equally to all sources. An effort to anticipate swings in interest rates by switching into and out of the market is one thing. Careful switching among comparable bonds that seem to have got out of line pricewise with one another, or painstaking analysis of the changing quality of particular bonds suggestive of future reevaluation by the market, reflects quite a different kind of approach. I am more sanguine about these day-to-day efforts to make minute portfolio improvements than about the prospect of catching the big swings in the market. I also believe that the opportunities for portfolio improvement are greater in the bond market than in the stock market. Bonds probably are more analyzable than stocks. With bonds, we are concerned with solvency and the quality of credit, in contrast to stock analysis, which focuses on the entire future of an enterprise. Thus it seems promising, in the case of bonds, to take advantage of minor imperfections of the market, which keep value from being recognized instantaneously, to achieve a modest improvement in total return over and beyond a buy-and-hold strategy.

Nevertheless, the stock market carries a lesson for the bond market. Publication requirements for mutual-funds portfolios have made possible very detailed testing of investment performance. These tests seem to show that, with a very few noteworthy exceptions, an active strategy does not on average beat a passive investment strategy or even a random selection. Most people, of course, will never believe this, because they see some stocks rising faster than others and because those who pick the winners naturally allow their customers (and perhaps themselves) to think that they were smart. But superior performance must be repeated over a succession of periods to be regarded as other than fortuitous. Proper allowance must be made for risk, moreover, because on average higher risk leads to higher return. It means nothing to show that the ABC Fund has beaten the XYZ Index, unless an adjustment is made for risk, and unless the Fund has beaten consistently the Index.

In the bond market, it has been difficult for outside observers to perform tests of the same kind, because there is little published information available about bond portfolios. Individual portfolio managers can test their own performance, now that indexes of the bond market are being developed. This technique, however, is still in an early stage, because nobody is quite sure what a good index of the bond market is.

The evidence derived from the stock market suggests, nevertheless, what we are likely to find out about the bond market if tests were possible. There is one good reason for expecting consistent above-average performance to be as elusive in the bond market as it has proved to be in the stock market. If enough intelligent and hardworking people are in the market, overvalued and undervalued securities will be few and far between. Every new piece of information will be analyzed with a sharp pencil and the conclusions will be translated at top speed into bids and offers. That is what economists call an "efficient market," that is, one in which all information is evaluated instantly, and assets therefore at all times are priced as correctly as human ingenuity will allow. Thus, even the possibility of improving portfolio performance by continually seeking out bonds that are slightly out of line may be quite limited. Too many people are searching. Moreover, what to some may look like a movement out of line may eventually turn out to have been a well-founded upgrading or downgrading of a changing situation.

The study of performance in the bond market is still in its early stages. These observations are a deduction from plausible premises, not based on empirical evidence. But regardless of whether performance investing pays off for the portfolio manager or not, some other possible consequences of the striving for performance needs examination. Once more the stock market, where our experience reaches farther back and where the consequences have come into clearer focus, serves as an example.

It is probably not controversial to say that the early promise of performance investment has not been validated in recent years. Individual investors, pension funds, universities, may have demanded high rates of return, and portfolio managers may have promised them. Both have been disappointed. Meanwhile, however, structural changes, most of them in my opinion adverse, have occurred in the market, traceable in part at least to the impact of performance investing. The market now seems to move faster in response to a piece of news than it did in the past. By itself this would be an advantage. But as a result, the steps by which it moves often are bigger. This has increased the risks of being in the market, or at least people's perception of them. Higher risk, in turn, seems to have induced some investors, particularly small ones, to abandon the stock market. Reduced participation and higher risk have tended to depress the level of prices below what it might otherwise have been, to the detriment of investors and seekers of capital alike.

Meanwhile, the investors remaining in the market have become an increasingly homogenous group, predominantly institutional. They are believed by many to have certain well-known behavioral characteristics—such as all holding the same view at the same time. This has further increased volatility and risk in the market. At the same time, it seems to have given rise to the peculiar phenomenon of the two-tier market, which has only begun to unwind. Needless to say, a market that makes the cost of capital very low for a few favored firms, while making it very high for most others, is unlikely to do a good job in allocating capital.

Turn now from the stock market to the bond market. Some of the phenomena that first occurred in the stock market are already visible in the bond market also. I do not mean to say that this observable parallelism is due entirely to performance investing. There may be other reasons why the bond market, too, is becoming more volatile, why it seems to be fraught with higher risk, and why it may be starting to induce the withdrawal, voluntary or otherwise, of some of the participants.

Of late, even something like the two-tier phenomenon seems to be reproducing itself in the bond market. Two rather distinct evaluations appear to be developing for utility bonds and for other corporates. Naturally, there are always plausible reasons for investment policies that bring this about. There was no lack of arguments to support the proposition that a small number of American corportions deserved price-earning ratios of thirty or so while a large number of others were relegated to the five to ten range. In the case of the stock market, the argumentation in many instances has already come unstuck. In the case of the utilities, I would merely point out that on purely arithmetical grounds, the number of times by which net operating income covers interest requirements cannot be as high at an interest rate of 9 percent as we have been accustomed to expect it when interest rates averaged about half of that. A very great increase in the return on equity would result if coverage were to remain unchanged.

In conclusion, three concerns bear repeating. First, I have tried to illustrate some of the difficulties attaching to the very concept of ''performance'' in the bond market. Second, whatever the concept, the achievement of superior performance in some respects is likely to be even more difficult than it has proved to be in the stock market. I should add that this evaluation relates to the portfolio management of publicly traded bonds and not to the special skills that may be employed in setting up private placements. Third, the uninhibited pursuit of performance may cause damage to the bond market as an institution and may have adverse consequences also for those who rely on it as investors, as borrowers, or as dealers.

This process of trying to get the most out of a piece of machinery, such as is the bond market, at the expense of possible damage to the equipment itself, today is not limited to the bond and stock markets. We have done the same to our currency. We have done it to the international monetary sysem. We barely avoided doing it to our price system. The need for a greater concern with the machinery, with the abiding fabric of our economy and our social institutions, even at some cost in immediate results, a greater concern with the long run and less emphasis on the short run, is something to which we should all give serious thought.

34 The Protection of Savings in a Time of Inflation

Inflation has made it almost impossible for savers to achieve financial security. In times past, heads of American families could reasonably believe that, barring acts of God, they could safely provide for their families' and their own future. Today, inflation puts all provision for the future at risk. It is difficult to visualize a more drastic deterioration in the quality of civilized life than this.

Today, only the government can provide a degree of financial security. The Social Security System, whatever its financial vicissitudes, no doubt will always be able to take care, more or less, of its beneficiaries by drawing on one source of funds or another. The result is that, through inflation, a strong bias is created in favor of public and against private provision for the future.

Individual Savers and Inflation

The individual saver can protect himself against inflation, to a limited degree, by demanding an inflation premium over and above the interest rate. This premium, however, reflects at best a very uncertain guess as to the future. The bonds, mortgages, insurance policies, and pension contracts that were written ten to fifteen years ago obviously were based on totally erroneous expectations of future rates of inflation. I hope and believe that the high inflation premia built into today's interest rates and contracts will turn out to be as excessive as their predecessors have proved inadequate. But there is really no way of predicting inflation. The economists' glib phrase "the expected rate of inflation" simply strikes an average across a wide range of ignorance. One should not be compelled to entrust the college education of one's children or the protection of one's widow to assets based on that kind of expectation.

In addition to this fundamental insecurity, inflation confronts the saver with a variety of difficulties that would remain even if the actual rate of inflation did not deviate too drastically, over the average of the years, from the expected rate built into interest rates. The following sections review some of these problems as they affect different types of assets that the saver may acquire.

This chapter was originally presented on April 1, 1976, at the Regional Meeting of the Society of Actuaries, Washington, D.C.

Bonds and Other Fixed Claims

Although bonds generally are not held by households directly, they are indirectly held through households' interest in life-insurance policies, pension funds, and bank deposits.

If we assume, as has sometimes been asserted in the past, that the real, that is, the inflation-free, rate of interest on high-grade corporate bonds is of the order of 3 to 4 percent, the apparent inflation premium typically contained in coupons of newly issued high-grade bonds is of the order of 5 to 6 percent. This corresponds roughly to the rate of inflation that has prevailed over the last year. It falls far short, of course, of the peak rates experienced in 1974. It is well above the average rate of inflation experienced since the period of relative price stability of the early 1960s came to an end. There are various distortions introduced by inclusion of such a premium in the interest rate, even if the level of the premium should turn out to be approximately correct.

First, the true meaning of an inflation premium depends heavily on the tax status of the recipient. To a nontaxable pension fund, the premium means more than for a taxable investor. For example, to an investor in the 50 percent bracket the after-tax return is less than the amount of the supposed inflation premium. The real return, in other words, would appear to be negative. It is conceivable, however, unless virtually all bonds are sold to tax-exempt or low-tax investors, that more highly taxed investors nevertheless regard themselves as receiving a positive real return even after tax. They could take this view if they anticipate a lower rate of inflation. That would imply that the true inflation premium inherent in a 9 percent coupon, for example, is less than appears. If that were the case, and if these expectations were shared by nontaxable investors, the latter would be getting a higher return than they require. Their gain would be analogous, in an inverse sense, to the gain that high-bracket buyers of tax-exempt bonds enjoy when these bonds have to be sold in part to low-bracket investors.

The inflation premium, in an economic sense, is in fact a repayment of capital. The holder, if he accumulates these premia, keeps the purchasing power of his investment intact, assuming his inflation expectations have been correct. The obligor, at the time of maturity of the bond, will owe a debt of greatly reduced purchasing power. But he will in effect have amortized it over the years. By the same token, the government, in treating the full interest it pays as an expenditure instead of as partly constituting debt repayment, is thereby overstating its deficit.

What has been called the "duration" of a bond thus becomes substantially shorter thanks to the high coupon. It implies that many borrowers will be issuing new debt more frequently to replace that which has in effect been amortized. The true meaning of the term structure of interest rates, that is, the yield spread, differs somewhat under these conditions. Finally, there is a distortion in the national-income accounts: true interest paid and received is overstated by the accounts, and corporate profits are understated to the extent that part of interest paid really represents repayment of principal.

How should we expect the saver to behave under these conditions? The long-term bond that he owns, directly or indirectly, in truth comes close to being an annuity. If he consumes the full coupon, he is in fact consuming his principal. For the beneficiary of a pension fund or a life-insurance contract who is not concerned with a positive terminal value this may not be a serious matter. For the outright investor the issue is crucial.

To the owner of savings deposits, similar considerations apply. He should regard as a real return only that part of the interest he receives that, after taxes, exceeds what he considers an appropriate inflation premium. A low-bracket saver holding a long-period savings certificate might find that he still receives a positive rate of return. For the average saver with a passbook account, the current rate permissible under Regulation Q recently has implied a negative real return. This can be said with assurance, because in the case of deposits payable on demand the loss of purchasing power is measured better by the current rate of inflation than by the expected rate, since the loss has already been realized.

Variable-Rate Instruments

The market has to some extent put remedies at the disposal of at least the sophisticated saver. Money market and bond funds allow him to receive rates commensurate with the flexible rates paid and received by large borrowers and lenders. To the extent that such interest rates reflect the rate of inflation, these instruments receive a variable inflation premium, that is, they enjoy a form of indexing. Some bank holding companies have issued medium-term notes tied to short-term rates, with redemption features enhancing their liquidity. Since the return on bank assets is relatively flexible, the issuer can offer such obligations without excessive risk. In the Eurocurrency market, variable interest rates are charged to borrowers based on the prevailing interbank rate. Thus, there is no lack of instruments offering some form of indexation.

The question has often been raised whether it would be advisable for governments to offer an indexed obligation. The British government, caught up in the problems of much higher rates of inflation than those prevailing in most other countries, has issued two types of savings bonds that are protected against loss of purchasing power and are available in limited quantities to individual investors. The interest rate on these securities is minimal. Thus, as a price of protection against loss of principal, the saver is expected to forego a significant return. The response of the public to the bonds so far is reported to have been good.

In the United States, the federal government has never issued an indexed bond. The objections raised to such a security have been numerous—the openendedness of the commitment, possible pressures on private borrowers to offer similar instruments that would be excessively risky for them, and the problem of what to do if prices should trend down have been prominently mentioned. The principal objection has always been, however, that the offer of such a security would be taken as evidence that the government had given up the struggle against inflation. In view of the efforts that have been made and continue to be made to counter inflation, and of the significant degree of success that has been attained, this "throwing-in-the-towel" objection would scarcely be plausible.

When I was a professor at Yale and somewhat inclined toward intellectual innovation, I had come to the conclusion that while it would be a mistake for the government to offer general indexing of its debt, it might be desirable to experiment with a small issue of indexed bonds. This would supply some experience of the terms on which the bond might be sold and could also save some money for the government, assuming that the interest rate required to make it saleable would be very low. It continues to be my purely personal view, not shared, I believe, by other members of the Federal Reserve Board, that experimentation with such a security would be desirable. I would regard it as unwise, however, to put a substantial part of the public debt on such a basis. That might induce other borrowers to do the same, would expose these borrowers to excessive risk, and would create other problems in the capital markets.

Stocks as a Hedge

Scholarly research has shown that the stock market has protected the saver against inflation at best over long periods of time and often only with considerable lags. These two qualifications deserve to be underscored. In the inflation of the last ten years the stock market surely has offered very little protection. Over the decade ending in 1975 the real rate of return on equities as indicated by the Standard and Poor's 500 stock index combining dividends and capital gains, has been negative: about −3 percent. Since 1926, the starting point of the famous study by Lorie and Fisher showing an average annual rate of return of 8.1 percent at year-end 1974 in current dollars, the return in constant dollars has been about 5.9 percent. Over this period, therefore, the stock market has provided a return that covers the pure rate of interest plus a modest premium for risk after taking care of inflation. It has not done a great deal more. As a final sidelight on the stock market and inflation, note that during the interval between the recent return of the market to the neighborhood of the one-thousand level on the Dow-Jones index and its last prior attainment of that level, the consumer price index advanced by about 30 percent.

The main point with respect to the impact of inflation on the savers' equity holdings, however, goes to the relationship between inflation and corporate accounting. Everybody by now is aware of how inventory profits and underdepreciation lead to overstatement of corporate profits. There is far less unanimity as to the kind of accounting system that can fairly and comprehensively portray inflationary effects.

Simply to adjust for these distortions, as the revised national-income accounts of the Department of Commerce do, does not fully meet the situation. Such an adjustment does not take into account that corporations are either net debtors or, less frequently, net creditors, and as such gain or lose from the change in the value of money. As far as the national-income accounts are concerned, such gains or losses are not part of national income and thus very properly are excluded from the accounts. The net worth of corporations, however, is affected by the impact of inflation on their net debtor or creditor positions. This impact therefore needs to be separately accounted.

The adjustments made by the Department of Commerce also do not take into account the fact noted earlier—which is ignored also by the tax law—that the inflation premium contained in the interest rate is a repayment of principal rather than an expense. By treating this premium as an expense, the debtor tends to understate his true profits. He does so all the more because his tax liability is reduced by the full amount of the interest payment including the inflation premium. Of course, corporations also receive interest that in part may represent return of principal. On these receipts, a corresponding inflation adjustment would be appropriate that would reduce profits.

The proposed price-level-accounting principles of the Financial Accounting Standards Board (FASB) would treat the gain or loss from the net debtor/creditor position as ordinary income. Logical though this may seem, it hardly reflects the true nature of this gain or loss. Corporations that are net debtors in some sense gain in a profit and loss sense. But the inflation gain accrues in illiquid form; it cannot be used to pay wages, dividends, or to increase plant, equipment, or inventory, although in some circumstances a firm may be able to borrow against it. It does add to the tax burden. Accordingly, it has been pointed out that a corporation could continue to make good profits by this accounting system up to the day that it goes into bankruptcy.

Other accounting systems, such as current-cost or current-value accounting, seem to have more flexibility in this regard. The new requirement of the Securities and Exchange Commission (SEC) for disclosure of replacement costs of inventory and fixed assets goes in the same direction. The principal criterion for potential usefulness to the investor seems to be whether the noncash inflation gains are taken into income or credited to some reserve or net-worth account. Treatment of these noncash gains as current income, ignoring their lack of liquidity, risks seriously misleading the investor.

Given these complexities, it is not surprising that the stock market reflects and protects against inflation, if at all, only over long periods and with long lags. In addition, the saver must always contemplate the possibility that corporate profits, on which the value of his stocks rests, may be overtaken by one of the most basic propositions of economics: the law of diminishing returns. As the supply of man-made capital increases relative to other factors of production, its return must be expected to diminish.

Inventions and innovations may slow down, or perhaps altogether forestall, that development. At a time when many observers anticipate a shortage of capital, it would not be surprising to see the tendency toward diminishing returns temporarily reversed. Simply put there is a great uncertainty about the return to equity in our economy, and in times of inflation that uncertainty is greatly increased.

Real Estate and Inflation

Real estate differs from man-made capital in that it has the law of diminishing returns working in its favor. Relative to other factors of production, the scarcity of land is increasing. In the United States, the real-estate saver also has on his side the tax law, which allows him to deduct interest and taxes and to roll over some capital gains, in contrast to the owner of equities, who experiences double taxation of dividends.

But the saver whose principal asset is his home nevertheless is hit twofold by inflation. The price of land and structures has been rising, and the interest rate at which these higher priced homes must be financed is higher likewise.

The homeowner, like the corporation, pays an interest rate containing an inflation premium. This means that he is amortizing his debt, in an economic sense, more rapidly than the familiar form given to him by the lender, showing the breakdown of his monthly installments into interest and amortization, would seem to indicate. He is thus saving more than he may recognize, and perhaps more than he can afford and still maintain his desired consumption standards.

If inflation were to continue, the homeowner is likely to find, as the years go by, that the monthly payments become easier to meet because his income tends to rise. He may also find that the value of his home is appreciating. But in the meantime inflation may have made him "house poor" in a painful way. This is the reason for the numerous efforts that are being made to design and make palatable to the borrower and to the Congress novel types of mortgages with variable rates, graduated payments, and similar features that seek to overcome the adverse impact of inflation on saving in the form of homeownership.

Behavior of Savers

For many years, it was said that inflation would depress the propensity to save because people would not find it worthwhile to accumulate financial assets that were losing their purchasing power or because people would rush out and buy things to beat inflation. In recent years, as inflation tended to accelerate all around the world, this prediction has not stood up well.

What we have observed has been a rise in the savings rate in most of the major countries. Since the inflation has coincided, to some extent, with mounting unemployment, it is not easy to disentangle the effects of inflation and recession. Recently, as both inflation and recession have begun to moderate, savings rates show signs of coming down. However, the desire to restore some normal relationship of wealth or liquid assets to income, in addition to the fear of losing a job, should be playing a role in pulling up the savings rate. Hence the prospect for continued high saving should be good. Although there may be temporary spurts to overcome pent-up needs for durable goods, the restoration of savings to the desired relationship to income will probably take longer. People's desire to protect their future seems deeply engrained. Bringing inflation down will make it easier to fulfill that desire and must remain a major national objective until it is achieved.

35 The Future of Futures

The financial-futures markets, since their inception in the mid-1970s, have had a tremendous vogue. In terms of volume, they have been a huge success. The number of contracts outstanding on the four organized exchanges on which financial-instruments futures are dealt in is on the order of 200,000. The average daily volume of contracts traded so far this year is about 20,000, compared to about 7,000 for the same period last year. The peak volume occurred in September, when over 600,000 fiancial-futures contracts were traded during the month.

Achievements of the Financial-Futures Markets

These impressive results are a monument to the power of financial innovation. Forward markets in financial assets have always existed and continue to exist. But organized futures markets, with their homogeneous contracts, reduced credit risk, and low transactions costs have made attractive and accessible to many what previously was of interest to only a few.

Simultaneous with, and in fact somewhat ahead of, the development of the financial-futures markets has been the development of options markets for common stocks. These have had a similar growth experience, to the point where the exchange-traded options volume in 1978 on all exchanges combined had come to equal approximately three-fourths of the volume of the New York Stock Exchange. Many of the considerations applicable to financial futures are applicable also to the options markets.

It is somewhat surprising, nevertheless, that a phenomenon so large and dramatic as the growth of the futures and options markets should have produced so relatively few obvious and visible consequences. The activity in these markets seems to be mostly turnover, with very few net results of any sort. To someone like myself who is more at home in the foreign-exchange market, it is not particularly alarming to observe such phenomena as heavy trading among financial institutions with only a very moderate residual of customer transactions, such as is characteristic of foreign-exchange markets. In the New York foreign-exchange market, the share of customer transactions, according to a

This chapter was originally presented on November 1, 1979, at the Commodities and Financial Futures Conference sponsored by the Federal Bar Association and Commerce Clearing House, Washington, D.C.

survey by the Federal Reserve Bank of New York some time ago, stood at about 5 percent of total transactions, the other 95 percent representing interbank trading. On the other hand, in the forward market for foreign exchange, which is an important part of total foreign-exchange trading, they deliver what they sell.

To underline how strongly some people feel about delivery, let me mention an instance from the Congress. It seems that two administrative assistants (AAs) were talking about their respective congressmen. They were not being particularly complimentary. The first AA said, ''Your man would sell his old mother for a nickel.'' ''So would yours,'' the second AA replied. ''Yes,'' said the first AA, ''but mine would deliver.''

It is true, of course, that the many useful functions that the financial-futures markets can perform do not necessarily depend on taking or making delivery of the underlying assets. A position can be hedged, risk transferred, the benefits of less risky and presumably cheaper and more plentiful credit realized through contracts that are closed out prior to the delivery date. The financial-futures markets perform a kind of unbundling job, such as has been thought desirable in many areas of the economy. They allow the activity of generating assets such as mortages to be separated from the taking of the financial risk inherent in interest-rate fluctuations. They permit the same to lenders, such as banks, who are expert at analyzing default risk but may not want to be exposed to interest-rate risk.

Information on expectations about future developments becomes more widely available as speculators and hedgers express their views of the future through the prices they bid and offer. The fruits of possibly very costly research into the business and financial outlook are thus made available to the public through the prices of financial futures.

Some Questions

These are valuable services. The trouble is that the theories that tell us about their availability in principle cannot tell us very much about how important these services are quantitatively. Inquiries into the views of market practitioners, as contrasted with economic theorists, provide a picture of conflicting opinions about the merits of the futures markets that is firmly held but with probably little basis in factual evidence. The Federal Reserve and Treasury surveyed a number of market participants as part of the study by these agencies of the futures market and discovered one set of opinions that was favorable to the futures markets and another set that was unfavorable. Those who thought well of the markets—generally the majority—claimed that the markets provide important social benefits by enabling hedging and improving the general liquidity of markets. They saw no adverse impact on the price of the underlying securities. Activity in futures was thought to be useful for banks. Potential problems could be monitored and controlled. Moreover, usefulness of the markets was expected to improve over time as more potential hedgers became aware of these possibilities.

The other side seemed to believe more or less the opposite on each of these issues. Most of the activity, it was said, was pure speculation, not hedging. Financial-futures markets were mainly the preserve of wealthy investors and speculators creating unnecessary risks. There was a serious danger of adverse effects on the underlying securities, such as increasing their price volatility and affecting the level of their price thereby complicating Treasury debt management and Federal Reserve open-market policy. The markets also created risks for participating banks.

There seems to be available only a moderate amount of information to resolve these disagreements. We know that the great majority of contracts is closed out prior to their delivery dates. We also know that up until now the number of banks participating is a small fraction of the total banking community. In addition, the market participants interviewed in the Treasury-Federal Reserve study seemed to believe that in the early stages the futures markets were primarily speculative. Nevertheless, all this does not prove, although it might suggest, that the bulk of the activity reflects speculation rather than hedging.

Evidence of impact on the price of the underlying securities is scanty, in large part because of the short lives, thus far, of the financial-futures markets. In the commodity markets, the preponderance of the evidence seems to suggest that futures trading has brought about some beneficial smoothing of seasonal fluctuations. Some observers of the financial-futures markets have suggested that there may be some very temporary impacts of futures trading on the price of the underlying securities, especially at the time when contracts mature. Some market participants believe that the possibility of a squeeze on the price of particular Treasury securities exists because the deliverable supply may not be fully adequate.

Information from Futures Trading

The value of information supplied about the future as a result of financial-futures trading may be questioned on the grounds that the prices in Treasury-futures markets tend to differ from forward prices implicit in the yield structure of spot markets. If the futures market says that the Treasury-bill rate eight or nine months hence will be 10 percent, and the yield curve says that it will be 11.5 percent, who is right? Moreover, given such frequently occurring differences, why is it that arbitrage is insufficient to eliminate them? Transactions costs, minor risk factors, timing difference in the data, or the difficulty of shorting Treasury bills may be responsible. But in any event, the information generated by these competing markets seems to suffer from some fuzziness.

And, granted that there is value in the information provided by the prices resulting from massive trading, one might still ask whether this is an efficient way of supplying information? People who bet on horses are said to believe that their activity encourages racing and thereby improves the breed of horses. People who bet on future prices of securities are presumed to render a valuable service by generating information. One is bound to wonder whether both parties are not trying to do things the hard way. There must be cheaper ways of producing better horses and better information.

The Viewpoint of the Regulator

Whichever way the balance of truth may point, one thing is certain: The futures markets present a challenge to those charged with regulating these markets. They pose some of the basic questions that all regulators must confront. Is it appropriate, in a democracy, to interfere with the free play of market forces even if it could be shown that there is no immediate and obvious social benefit to be observed from the play of these forces? All regulation comes at a cost in terms of freedom of markets and self-determination of human beings. In our present environment, given the prevailing mania to regulate everything and anything, the marginal cost of regulation in these terms is particularly high. Do any potential injuries that futures trading might inflict justify this added cost?

Even if it can be shown that regulation would help to prevent some demonstrable abuses, these may well pertain to a small minority of cases. One might ask whether it is justifiable to limit the freedom and the opportunity for profit of the many to protect the few against the consequences of their folly. This question is being answered in the affirmative in much of our contemporary regulation, particularly in the consumer area. I suspect that protection for the few is being bought at an excessive cost to the many.

Looking at the enormous regulatory burden that today falls on the banks, there certainly is a heavy cost involved in imposing still another regulation on more than 14,000 banks who will have to read and study complicated material until they discover that it pertains to only a small fraction of their number who today are participating in futures markets. The mere presence of this additional regulatory burden may become an obstacle to the entry of more banks into the futures markets.

It is not obvious that it makes sense to try to control, via regulation, a risk in the very limited area of financial futures that is totally pervasive in banking. No bank engages in perfect maturity matching. Every bank, in a sense, is a comprehensive futures contract, with a long position that typically has a longer maturity than the short position. If we do not prevent a bank from buying bonds and mortgages and financing them with demand deposits or ninety-day certificates of deposit (CDs), it is doubtful to me that we should single out the special risks of financial futures for special regulation.

If, however, we accept that some kind of regulation is needed, should it not at least reflect economic reality to the extent possible instead of artificial legal and accounting principles? For instance, does it make sense to allow a bank to engage in futures transactions to "hedge" some particular asset or liability, even if that does not reflect the bank's overall risk exposure to interest-rate changes? A bank may be in a reasonably well hedged position if both its assets and liabilities are tied to floating interest rates. Would it make sense, under such circumstances, for the bank to hedge separately any particular asset or liability, thereby in effect unhedging its overall position? This is one of the questions that the federal regulatory agencies today seem to be facing.

Likewise, would it be appropriate to impose position limits on banks, perhaps in relation to their capital, when the degree of their exposure to risk in futures markets may differ widely, for identical dollar amounts, with the maturity of the futures contract? A bank can be safer with a large volume of very short-term futures, particularly if they fit well into its overall balance-sheet exposure, than with a small volume of longer-term futures not well adapted to the interest-rate risks it faces.

If, as a reluctant regulator, I contemplate questions like these that today confront the federal regulatory agencies, I arrive at the conclusion that less may be more. Rather than try to write tight rules that will keep many of the banks out of the futures markets and may disorient some of those who enter, it may be preferable to first limit regulation to a requirement that banks establish sensible rules and sound internal controls, and then to monitor the existence of and adherence to these rules and controls through bank examination. Such rules will already be adhered to in well-run operations and impose discipline rather than restrictions where needed.

As a regulator, the Federal Reserve today, together with the Treasury, is required also to consider and advise the Commodities Futures Trading Commission (CFTC) on the type of futures contracts to be authorized. It has been the particular virtue of our exchanges trading financial futures to provide a framework in which futures trading can take place with minimum credit risk and minimum cost while limiting the exposure of the trading parties through margin requirements and marking to market. There remain certain risks affecting the issuer of the underlying securities, in particular the U.S. Treasury. However remote, in theory, the danger of a corner or squeeze may appear, under the particular circumstances of ownership of Treasury securities that prevail today, it cannot be discounted altogether. A good share of many Treasury issues today is owned by the Federal Reserve and by foreign monetary authorities, neither of which would be likely to be available to arbitrage special situations. Under these conditions, it is not impossible for a well-financed operator to establish a dominant position in a particular issue. Whether or not such an operator could establish a corner or at least exert a squeeze depends largely on the interest elasticity of the market, namely, the alertness and institutional freedom of action of owners of that issue and adjacent issues. I believe that it is wise to establish precautions against such a contingency, along the lines taken by the Treasury and the Federal Reserve in their advice to the CFTC. Spreading of similar contracts over different months on different exchanges, delivery of securities from a basket rather than restricting delivery to a single security, uniform reporting of positions in new contracts to the CFTC, and making sure that exchanges have equally effective rules for dealing with emergencies seem reasonable precautions.

The ingenuity of the writers of futures contracts is not, of course, exhausted in the devising of Treasury and Government National Mortgage Association (GNMA) securities contracts. I find an intellectually fascinating innovation the concept of a futures contract denominated in terms of some common-stock index. Such a contract, to be sure, gets away altogether from the concept of a deliverable security. But it fits in with the principles of capital-asset valuation and would permit a type of hedging against systemic or industry risk that would offer very interesting opportunities to equity investors. The feasibility of such a contract must remain in doubt until the details have been worked out, but I hope that efforts along those lines will continue.

Misdirection of Risk Taking?

This chapter began with comment on the large volume of transactions in futures and options markets by all market participants today. Where such large values are at stake, usually a number of clear facts emerge. This has not been the case in futures markets. We know little about their effects—good, bad or indifferent. The simple conclusion from this might be that, if we cannot make up our minds about the nature and consequences of what we see, there must be less here than meets the eye.

I believe that this usually plausible conclusion does not follow in the present case. There is, I suspect, a consequence flowing from high activity in futures markets and in stock market options that we have not evaluated sufficiently. It has to do with the effect of such trading on the demand for securities, the underlying securities as well as other. I am not speaking here of volatility or minor price variations when contracts mature. Rather, it is the absorption of speculative and risk-taking activity into what is essentially a better operation that concerns me.

Demand for futures and options is not demand for the underlying securities. The willingness to take risks that is absorbed in futures and options markets is withdrawn from the equities markets, among other areas. The supply of such willingness to take risks is not unlimited. Even though the volume of money absorbed by the futures and options markets is small, that is not a proper measure of their effect on the demand for equities. Someone who buys futures or options obviously is a potential investor in equities. In the futures and options markets, one can get a much bigger ''bang for a buck'' than by buying into the dull old stock market. I do not know what the bettor then does with the rest of his savings. From the Securities and Exchange Commission (SEC) study we do know that only 5 percent of investors questioned in one particular survey said that they were following a strategy of combined options and fixed-income securities. Thus, the option buyer apparently does not put his surplus funds into bonds. But given the high risk he runs in his futures and options, he is unlikely to put the rest into stocks. Perhaps he buys real estate or life insurance. Perhaps he leaves protection of his old age to his pension fund and social security and foregoes significant saving activity in the hope of making a killing on futures and options. It is in this substitution of betting on securities instead of investing in them that the main economic effect of this trading must be sought, to the possibly great damage of our economy, which badly needs equity investment.

I do not see a remedy for this absorption of risk-taking capacity into what is essentially a betting activity coming from any regulation or restriction placed on that activity. That, I believe, would be a futile attempt. Rather, what is needed is to make equity investment more attractive. If we could find a good way of eliminating the double taxation of dividends, and if we could limit the taxation of capital gains to the taxation of real gains rather than of the capital itself, as inevitably happens after a period of severe inflation, equity investment would again become attractive. It might even then be able to compete with futures and options. Our economy, more than individual investors, would be the beneficiary.

36 An Economist Looks at Debt Capacity

Tall oaks from little acorns grow. Suppose that, instead of raising millions for a mammoth corporation, you were negotiating to purchase a corner grocery. You are agreed with the seller as to price—the entire outfit, with annual earnings of $1,500 after owner's salary is to be yours for $10,000. At that moment the seller calls in a financial adviser. ''This enterprise,'' says the adviser, ''is not making adequate use of its debt capacity. It needs to reshape its capital structure. Let the buyer take $4,000 in bonds, at 7 percent. The earnings of $1,220, after interest of $280, at the same multiple of 6.7, will support a stock valuation of $8,200. Total value of the enterprise is now $12,200.''

''Ridiculous,'' you say, ''It's the same old grocery, just packaged differently. If we agreed that it was worth no more than $10,000, why should splitting its capitalization into stocks and bonds make it worth more?'' Why indeed? But that is precisely what the wisdom of corporate financial officers, investment bankers, and last but not least utility-regulating commissions, consists of—packaging a given company in such a way as to maximize its value in the market. If they can do it, why not the seller of the grocery?

Tax considerations could be one answer. Traditional wisdom of Wall Street long antedates, however, the introduction of the corporate income tax. The great financiers of the dim past, no less than the sharp-pencil boys of today, have believed in exploiting debt capacity. It is not illegitimate, therefore, as a first approximation, to examine the case as it would present itself in the absence of the corporate income tax. The classical presentation of this case is that of professors Franco Modigliani, of the Massachusetts Institute of Technology, and Merton Miller, of the University of Chicago.[1] Their assertion, in simplest terms, comes down to this: a company is a company is a company. When its earnings stream is $1,500 (or $1.5 billion, for that matter) a rational market will capitalize this stream at the same value whether the stream takes the form of equity income, or of interest, or both. Splitting the stream, and thus splitting the capitalization, should make no difference.

To this the traditional wisdom of Wall Street replies that there are certain investors who, for reasons of preference or law, buy mainly bonds. An ''all-equity'' capitalization disregards this important segment of the market. By tailoring the corporation's capital structure to the market's preferences, the firm's ''cost of capital'' can be reduced. This is the same as saying that a

---

This chapter was originally published in *Investment Banking and Corporate Financing*, Spring, 1969, pp. 43–70.

higher aggregate value can be obtained for the firm's securities, since the cost of capital is simply the rate at which the market capitalizes the firm's earnings. When both debt and equity are involved, that rate will be a weighted average, of course, of the return on debt and the return on equity.

The traditional wisdom is not oblivious to the fact that debt means risk. A firm that borrows carries financial risk, in addition to the economic risk that it must accept even if it finances purely with equity. But it is assumed that within safe limits indicated by experience, the risk resulting from fixed charges will not affect the value of the equity. That is the meaning of a "safe debt capacity," the amount of debt that can be carried without reducing the price-earnings ratio that the market assigns to the equity.

Modigliani and Miller disagree with this view. They rest their case, however, not on opinion, but on a simple mechanism that they presume to be operative in the market. Suppose Wall Street were right. A leveraged company, that is, one with debt in its capital structure, would then sell for more than an unleveraged one, assuming the two to be identical in all other respects. What would a smart investor owning stock in a leveraged company do? He sells his stock and buys unleveraged stock. He also borrows and buys more unleveraged stock, until the ratio of his personal debt to the value of the stock purchased is equal to the debt-assets ratio of the leveraged company he has just sold. If that company, for instance, finances 40 percent of its assets with debt, the investor would finance 40 percent of his new, unleveraged stock with debt. If the interest he pays is less than the return on the stock, he is obviously ahead.

To be sure, he is now on margin, whereas previously he owned his stock outright. He seems to be carrying more risk. But that is an illusion. The stock he previously held outright was leveraged, that is, the company itself held its assets "on margin." The new stock is unleveraged, and the company accordingly carries less risk. If the debt-assets ratio of the leveraged company and of the investor after he had made his switch are the same, the risk run by the investor should be the same.

What the investor has done is to internalize the risk. With his first holding, he had his risk via the company. With his new holding, he has the risk in his own portfolio. If the degree of risk is the same, but the income is higher, he is clearly ahead.

As far as the market is concerned, the investor's switch will depress the leveraged stock and push up the unleveraged. If enough investors make the switch, the price-earnings ratio of the leveraged stock will fall, that of the unleveraged will rise. Eventually the differential will become so large that the switch no longer pays. At that point, it can easily be shown, the market valuation of the two companies will be the same. Leveraging a company will have ceased to pay.

The following example tells the story in numbers.

	Company A Unleveraged ($)	*Company B* Leveraged ($)
Income	100,000	100,000
Interest (5 percent)	0	25,000
Bonds	0	500,000
Stock value (PER 10)	1,000,000	750,000
Value of capitalization	1,000,000	1,250,000

Owner sells one percent of B stock.	7,500
He borrows an amount equal to one percent of B's debt	5,000
He buys A stock	12,500
Cost to owner of share in B's income	750
interest on personal debt (5 percent)	250
total cost	1,000
Share in A's income	1,250

On this reasoning, if leveraged companies sold for more, the market itself would correct that. The higher valuation of leveraged companies would cause their stocks to be sold until the advantage had disappeared.

What is implied in the model is a certain relationship between leverage and the price-earnings ratio. The model says that any degree of leverage, no matter how small, will have a proportionate adverse affect on the price-earnings ratio. The traditional Wall Street view implies that within the range of safe debt capacity, leverage does not affect the price-earnings ratio. Leverage in excess of that safe amount, on the other hand, will severely reduce the price-earnings ratio.

Likewise implicit in the model is that the cost of capital to the firm does not change with the debt-equity ratio. It is the same for all levels of that ratio—leveraging does not pay. The Wall Street view is, of course, that leveraging reduces the cost of capital within the range of safe debt capacity. Beyond that, the cost of capital rises sharply. Both propositions are illustrated by figure 36–1, with acknowledgments to Modigliani and Miller.

So far, the lesson of Modigliani-Miller for the practitioner of corporate finance seems to be that it accomplishes nothing by injecting leverage into a corporate structure. But we have not yet taken into account corporate taxes. Once that is done, it quickly becomes apparent that the proposition can be made to yield the opposite conclusion.

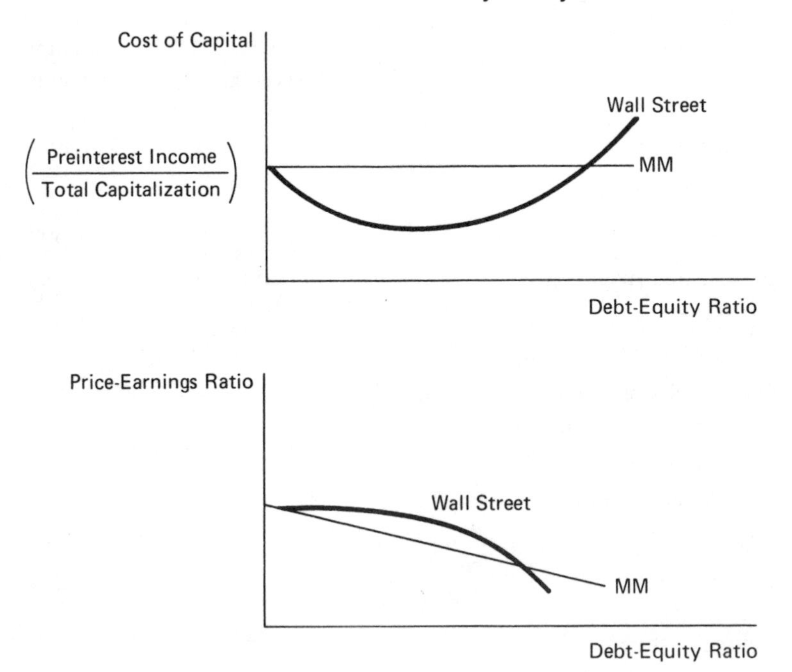

Figure 36–1. Debt/Equity Ratio, Cost of Capital, and Price/Earnings Ratio.

Interest is tax deductible, dividends are not. Of two otherwise identical companies, the more highly leveraged has one clearcut advantage: it pays less tax. In the Wall Street view, this advantage is destroyed if leverage is pushed too far. When debt substantially exceeds the safe capacity limit, the cost of capital becomes so high as to outweigh the tax saving. Debt financing, to be optimal, must stop before that point is reached.

But in the Modigliani-Miller version, the cost of capital is the same for all degrees of leverage—in the absence of taxes. When the tax deductibility of interest is taken into account, therefore, high leverage becomes an obvious advantage. It does not raise the cost of capital. It does save taxes. Ergo—do not be hamstrung by Wall Street's—or public-utility commissions'—notion about safe debt capacity. They are too cautious. Debt will not hurt you. Go ahead and use it.

This side of the argument, again, can be buttressed by observing the market at work. Suppose it were true that the securities, both stocks and bonds, of highly leveraged companies were severely depressed relative to unleveraged stocks and bonds. What does the smart investor do if he were confronted with this inverse of the previous case? He sells his unleveraged stock. With the proceeds he buys both stocks and bonds of the leveraged company. He mixes his equity and bonds in the same proportion in which they appear on the liability side of company's balance sheet. If the company has 40 percent bonds and 60 percent equity, so does he. In other words, he undoes the company's leverage by holding a balanced portfolio. In effect his position is the same as if he held 100 percent stock in an unleveraged company—which is how he started out. A simple calculation, analogous to the earlier one, shows that the switch makes him better off if unleveraged stock sells at a premium.

The switch tends to push down the unleveraged stock and raises the stock and bonds of the leveraged firm. If enough investors do it, the premium on unleveraged and the discount on leveraged securities will disappear. From the viewpoint of the issuer, this means that he can take advantage of the tax advantage of debt financing without fear of depressing his securities beyond their proper worth, that is, without raising his cost of capital.

What are we to think of these propositions? If pushed very far, they run counter to everyday experience. The market (as well probably as the Internal Revenue Service) will not allow a corporation to finance itself 99 percent with debt. It is closer to the margin of what Wall Street considers the safe debt limit that the real question arises. Does the safe limit, beyond which highly leveraged securities become seriously depressed, lie out somewhat further than commonly thought?

The Modigliani-Miller proposition proceeds at a high level of abstraction. In arguing that, without incurring great risk, the investor can create for himself the same leverage that the corporation can, it disregards limited liability, the risk of margin calls, and lenders' rationing of credit to individuals. In arguing that the investor can do the reverse, that is, can undo the company's leverage, other factors are disregarded. For instance, the investor must be prepared to take the company's bankruptcy in his stride, on the assumption that what in reorganization he loses as stockholder, he gains as bondholder. Only then can he regard his mixed portfolio of stocks and bonds as the equivalent of an all-equity portfolio in unleveraged stocks. Any difference between the investor's pro rata claim on the company's income and the actual return—dividend, capital gain, and interest—on the assets held by the investor also becomes invisible from the high vantage point of the analysis.

Research done to verify or refute the theorem has come out on both sides. This is understandable. It is not easy to find companies that are similar in most respects but differ decisively in their financial structure. Nor is it easy to disentangle the effects of the tax from what would happen in the absence of the tax.

What seems plausible, at least to this writer, is that management is paying a high premium to hold down financial risk. Stockholders have at their disposal the means of protecting themselves against the financial risks run by their corporations—by balancing their portfolio between stocks and bonds, and by diversifying among corporations. From the sophisticated stockholder's point of view—not the widow's and orphan's—corporations could profitably have more highly leveraged capital structures than they typically do. Management is differently situated—it cannot balance and diversify to protect its own interests against the possible consequences of high financial risk. But risk-minded management would probably find that the limits of profitable debt financing set by the market, if it were to explore them, are farther out than commonly supposed.

Note

1. Franco Modigliani and Merton H. Miller, "The Cost of Capital, Corporation Finance, and the Theory of Investment," *American Economic Review,* June 1978.

Part VII
Economic Growth

37 Economic Growth in America

Economic growth has been a continuing process since the North American continent began to be settled by immigrants some 350 years ago. Interaction of population growth with a rich supply of natural resources and capital has made the presence of growth clearly visible at all times. The American experience contrasts in this with that of Europe, where before and even after the Industrial Revolution contemporary observers might often have been unaware of the underlying growth tendency. In the United States, it would have been difficult to interpret the process of industrialization as implying a continuing deterioration in the position of labor, as the equivalent British process did in the eyes of Marx.

The evolving American condition was perceived, of course, not as "growth" but as "progress." Progress has many dimensions. It clearly contains the qualitative elements that today are seen to be lacking in growth. By definition, progress is good. Growth recently has come under increasing challenge.

The advent of the growth concept has split progress into its quantitative and qualitative components. For the purpose of economic analysis, this is a step forward. In the dimension measured by output, progress has become quantifiable. The growth component of progress, to be sure, is not completely unambiguous. There can be aggregate growth of output without per-capita growth if population is increasing at the same rate. Growth may have costs in terms of damage to the environment, consumption of irreplaceable resources, disamenities of industrial life, and so on. Growth not only differs from progress, it can differ also from welfare.

An effort to translate growth into welfare recently was undertaken by James Tobin and William Nordhaus.[1] In their study, the authors adjusted the conventional GNP downward for the creation of disamenities, for the using up of irreplaceable natural resources, and for a variety of other costs. They also adjusted it upward, however, for the increase in leisure time that has come with a rising per-capita income. The authors did not attempt to quantify qualitative changes in the content of output. Automobile and airplane travel, radio and television, paperbacks and long-playing records may or may not be progress, but in the Tobin-Nordhaus analysis they do not affect growth other than through their value added to the GNP.

This chapter was originally published in Chester L. Cooper, ed., *Growth in America* (Westport, Conn.: Greenwood Press, 1976), pp. 60–74.

The quantification of progress has been on the agenda of economics for a long time. The difficulties encountered along the way indicate the quality of the intellectual achievement that is represented by the conceptualization and measurement of the GNP. Marx was almost entirely nonquantitative. Schumpeter's process of "economic development" was quantitative in that it sought to analyze the sources and behavior of business cycles. But it was only after the GNP concept had been developed that it became possible to go beyond an "index of production" and to add up the infinite variety of output in a single number.

It was a fortunate coincidence that the development of GNP concepts and data matched so closely the major revolution in economic theory of the times—Keynes' *General Theory of Employment, Income and Money*. The components of GNP isolated by the national-income accountants happen to be precisely those stressed by the new theory. An immediate quantification and testing of the theory thus became possible.

When economists first began to talk about GNP, it was clearly understood that GNP was not coextensive with welfare. In popular discussion, it was customary to add a caveat to that effect, much as newspapers would add a parenthetical definition ("the sum of all goods and services produced") when they used the term for a lay readership. Both economists and the press have meanwhile dropped their respective practices. In the case of the economists, it is difficult to say whether this occurred because the distinction was taken for granted or because it began to be lost from sight.

There can be little doubt that, particularly following the recession of 1957–1958, economists began to go overboard in their glorification of growth. In part this was a political response to the slow growth of the late 1950s, in part a reflection of the impact of Sputnik. The interest of less developed countries in catching up helped to cast growth in the role of an all-absorbing goal at that time. Only a little earlier, "stability" had occupied center stage. The Employment Act of 1946, which still stands as the nation's statement of economic purposes, speaks of "maximum employment, production and purchasing power" and does not even mention the word "growth." It was only through subsequent reinterpretation that "maximum employment" has been identified with growth and "maximum purchasing power" with price stability. Explicit growth consciousness is a product of the 1950s and 1960s.

During this period of exaltation of the growth objective, the question was rarely asked whether the deliberate stimulation of growth, through the tax system, through fiscal and monetary policy, and other devices, represented rational policy. Nevertheless, the question did not remain unexamined insofar as it bears on intergenerational equity. In a growing economy, each generation is richer than its predecessor. Insofar as accelerated growth requires more saving out of present income in order to raise human and physical investment that will pay off only in the future, the present generation is reducing its consumption and welfare for the benefit of the next. So long as saving and investment decisions are made through the market, this process of intergenerational transfers may reflect each generation's notion of its own maximum welfare. Even then there may be factors external to the market process that might obstruct attainment of an optimal position. But when policies are deliberately directed toward accelerating the rate of growth beyond that which the market would produce, matters become far less certain. It is by no means to be taken for granted that very rapid growth maximizes the welfare particularly of the older members of the present generation.

Problems of this kind played an important role in the growth theorizing of the 1960s. Fundamentally, this theorizing involved the translation of the classical stationary state into a stationary model of stable and endless growth. While this brought interesting insights into the nature of the economic system, it unfortunately also distracted the attention of many theorists from more immediate problems. "Golden rules" of growth contributed little to solving the pressing problems of developing countries. The assumption, implicit in most of this theorizing, that all resources, including land, could be increased without diminishing returns so that ultimately growth became identical with population growth, was seriously misleading. Here the new ideas about limits to growth have made a valuable point. But it is not only the environmentalists and Malthusians who have raised questions about eternal growth.

Even though progress was built firmly into the structure of American thought, economists as well as philosophers have always been aware of intellectual difficulties. Doubts whether the good life really consists of the acquisition of more material goods are traditional. In a more gloomy vein, the question has been asked whether the goodness of life can be increased at all in a society where individuals are greatly concerned with their position relative to each other. If satisfaction results not from one's absolute standard of living but from one's position in the income scale, there is no way for society as a whole to improve itself. The rise of any one of its members necessarily implies the descent of another. The American emphasis on keeping up with the Joneses makes this model less implausible than appears at first sight.

Although economists have been fascinated by the growth process, they have not typically seen in it the ultimate stage of economic life. In the past, on the contrary, that ultimate outcome has been the stationary state. In it, all forces of growth have spent themselves. Population growth has come to a halt, by a Malthusian process or otherwise. Capital accumulation has ceased because accumulation of a large stock of capital—or exhaustion of complementary resources—has reduced the return to zero. It took ingenuity and readiness to abstract from the problems of land and resource shortages, to translate this model into permanent equilibrium growth. One must add, however, that stationary-state theorizing also had no good answer to the problem of nonreproducible resources. Those resources could in fact not be substituted, for effectively slowing the rate of growth to zero would only postpone the day when they would run out. One is bound to suspect that somehow economists have never taken the problems of coal, oil, and metals very seriously, although they have worried greatly about food and land.

A more attractive vision of the end of growth, put forward by Keynes some fifty years ago and no doubt shared by many economists, was that some day humanity would get done with the business of providing for the physical needs of subsistence and turn its mind to higher things. This view has much in common with the changing life-styles that developed among the younger generation during the 1960s. Many young people expressed disenchantment with what they considered the extremes of materialism in America. They argued for and found for themselves different sets of goals and different forms of enjoyment. They were less farseeing than Keynes, however, who realized that some generally accepted level of adequacy would have to be achieved before this great transformation in man's outlook could take place.

The great difficulty with achieving such a level is not that there is some limit on total output that prevents mankind from reaching it. At 3 percent growth per capita, income doubles from one generation to the next. If the standard of living of one generation seems inadequate, surely the next, or the next, will achieve adequacy.

The difficulty with any level of adequacy that may be obtained is that it does not remove inequality, given our present arrangements. Those at the top of the income distribution may be quite willing to call a halt to further progress. They would probably have been prepared to do this a hundred years earlier as well. Near the top, it is always difficult to imagine how things could get much better, and it is not difficult to practice moderation. But life looks different at the other end of the income distribution. The inhabitants of the lower brackets are continually exposed to a demonstration effect from above. They know how they would spend their money if they had twice as much of it or four times as much. They would be quite unwilling to accept a ceiling on their progress unless the top brackets were cut down, by taxation or otherwise, to something approaching equality. But the leaders in the income distribution would be altogether unwilling to accept this. It is one thing to level off, it is quite another to come down.

The stationary state is superior in this regard to the unspecific Keynesian vision of putting the satisfaction of material wants behind us. In the stationary state, inequality of incomes is sharply reduced by the disappearance of a return to manmade capital. When the rate of return on capital goes to zero, so does the income share of its owners. Land will still yield a rent. Full equality of incomes could be attained only by redistributing or altogether eliminating ownership of land and by evening up inequalities resulting from unequal human endowment. But since the stationary state probably lies far in the future, if anywhere, its equalizing tendencies are of no great avail.

What applies within an economy applies, of course, across nations as well. It is perhaps conceivable that the United States, having reached a high level of income, might decide to slow up or altogether discontinue its growth to conserve resources and the environment. Its example would hardly be followed, however, by the developing countries. They would probably insist on catching up to the American level before slowing or stopping their growth. But in that case the restraint practiced by the people of the United States would have relatively little effect in holding down world demands on resources and environment.

One redeeming feature of the impasse created by inequality is that it always remains open to single individuals to drop out of the growth race. A person who wants to consume less can do so without others doing the same and without the government compelling him. He can even help others by putting his surplus earnings into the bank where his neighbors, less enlightened than he, can borrow them to consume or invest more. Or else the antigrowth-oriented individual can decide to earn less by working less. In that case, he will make sure that the fruits of his labor do not become a drain on resources and environment. Anyone not satisfied with the prevalent growth scene need not limit himself to protesting. He can do something about it.

The new life-styles that arose during the 1960s as part of the protest against growth lacked conviction in other respects as well. Not only did they ignore the very human desire for some level of adequacy and for equality at that level, their proponents also weakened their cause by adopting antievolutionary attitudes and by taking the achievements of their civilization and in particular of their economy too much for granted.

They were correct in believing that American postindustrial society has risen beyond the stage of social Darwinism. Survival even in a highly competitive society need no longer be survival according to the law of the jungle. But we have hardly yet attained a level of perfection and success at which we can afford to neutralize and even contravene the many processes of natural selection built into society and into the economy. When rewards to success are withheld by the tax system, when educational efforts are devoted mainly to raising the untalented to the level of mediocrity instead of raising the talented as far as possible above it, when the thrust of the law is shifted from safeguarding society to protecting those who are probably guilty, society is undermining some of its principal protective mechanisms. In the end, if all goes well, such a society may well be a more just and humane one. But in a world in which other societies employ more positive processes of selection and survival, the antievolutionary society may not prosper.

Within the narrow confines of the economic mechanism, the error of taking the functioning of this economy too much for granted was perhaps understandable. Many years of prosperity, accompanied by promises of unswerving future growth, led young people to downgrade the dreary tasks of production. Existence seemed assured and not worth making a fuss over. Why worry about where the next meal was coming from? Events of the early 1970s have made painfully clear how very far we still are from that blessed state. Production still matters, and to keep it flowing smoothly still remains a challenge worthy of the ablest minds.

It was not only the recessions of the early 1970s and the dramatic miscarriages in the areas of food and other commodities, petroleum in particular; for the United States, the belief that growth had either proceeded far enough or in any event could be relied on to proceed adequately hereafter was shaken by evidence of the sharply declining role of the United States in the world economy. Once the long overvaluation of the dollar had been ended by repeated devaluations, it became apparent that per-capita income in the United States had ceased to rank significantly above that of other industrial countries. These other countries, moreover, for many years had been growing more rapidly than the United States and seemed likely to leave the United States behind. In all these respects, the 1960s proved to be a poor time to conclude that growth in America had ceased to matter.

This inopportune conclusion, to be sure, was one that was arrived at and to some extent acted on by only a small elite. The educated young and their moneyed elders represented the leadership that naturally gets to the frontiers of existence first. For the same reasons, it was the United States and a few highly industrialized countries that first reached levels of income where the usefulness of continued national growth could be questioned. For these elites and front-runners, the question was perhaps bound to arise whether the individuals who sought new life-styles, as well as the societies that have traveled the road of industrialization and resultant growth, have been on the right track. It is conceivable at least that, like many other pioneers, either or both took the wrong turn and will have to suffer the consequences. It is indeed altogether unlikely that the first roads that provided dramatic breakthroughs into the new future, be it of affluence or of contempt for it, would prove to be the right ones. Experiments and pilot projects often have to be written off. That could apply equally to the Western nations' great experiment in raising their living standards by making heavy demands on resources and environment, and to the efforts of a small elite within these nations to put a stop to that experiment during the 1960s.

There is a lesson, nevertheless, both in the success of Western growth and in recent attempts to halt it, for it has become clear that growth is a powerful process following its own laws and that it is not easy to start or to stop this process.

One need examine only the tremendous technical difficulties, quite aside from social and political ones, that stand in the way of halting economic growth. Suppose there existed a national will to prevent further increases in GNP. To begin with it would become immediately apparent that that is not really what we had in mind so long as population is still growing. To combine a constant GNP with rising population implies a decline in per-capita income. Presumably then, halting GNP growth would have to mean halting GNP per-capita growth.

With no great effort of the imagination one can today visualize population growth being brought to a halt. But if nothing else happens, zero population growth (ZPG) would accelerate rather than retard per-capita growth. The main reason is that new savings would no longer have to be devoted, in part, to equipping the additions to the labor force with new tools. The stock of capital per worker would rise more rapidly than before. Thus, halting per-capita growth would be more demanding under these conditions. It takes a greater effort of the imagination to visualize a prohibition on an increase in the capital stock. People apparently want to save in order to provide for their old age, and the more they do so, the richer they get. This saving is one of the principal sources of growth. One can visualize a fiscal system in which the government absorbs all new savings by borrowing and neutralizes them by expenditure on public consumption. The savers would still have their claims that they could draw down in old age, but the stock of physical capital would not increase. Even this, however, would not kill off all growth. As physical assets employed in production wear out, they must be replaced. If there is technological progress, they will be replaced, at no higher cost, by more efficient equipment. Growth thus could proceed without new saving. If the new technologies are resource saving or environment protecting, it might indeed be difficult to persuade people that this kind of growth should not be allowed to go forward solely in order to enforce a rigorous zero-growth policy. And in the unlikely event that government succeeded in stopping all forms of growth of productive enterprises, it might still be possible for ingenious individuals to engage in private growth-oriented activities on the do-it-yourself system.

Growth is likely to prove a hardy plant. Attempts to stop it will turn out not only misguided but also futile. Departing from the pragmatic expectation that growth is here to stay, a sensible policy should try to guide it in a manner that would neutralize threats that growth supposedly carries. The question before us, in other words, is how to grow safely.

It is unlikely that agreement will be reached about the risks of continued growth. That debate has been going on since Malthus, and there will always be occasions to cry wolf. However persuasive the contrary case, it will never be possible to prove that some particular wolf will not actually arrive and stay.

Economists contend that depletion of low-cost resources will be gradual, that it will manifest itself in price increases, which will stimulate production, substitution, and resource-saving research, and eventually, if necessary, discontinuation of use. Many economists probably believe that this equilibrating process can go on indefinitely, except possibly with regard to population growth and the associated need for reproducible primary products, principally food. It is in fact immaterial whether we visualize this process as occurring within a context of continued growth or of a steady state. Unless the equilibrium mechanism functions, total exhaustion of resources and the environment will occur in a context of stability as well as of growth. The difference is only one of time. The strict logic of those who foresee doomsday requires a shrinkage of economic activity to some minimum that would be sustainable on the basis of recycling after the original supplies of natural resources have been fully used up.

Economists cannot predict what precise course events will take. What they can do is to make sure that the adjustment mechanisms are in good operating order. Prices must be free to give their signals. Markets must be capable of responding to the signals. Where markets do not operate properly—and this may frequently be the case—devices must be introduced to make them operational. With these mechanisms in place, we can allow events to take their course with confidence. If the school that believes continuing growth is possible is right, the mechanisms will channel this growth and shift resource use in directions that insure continuity. If the opposite side is right, the same mechanisms will so increase costs on all sides that continued growth eventually becomes impossible. This would occur, however, not in the form of catastrophe and collapse. Rather, it would be a gradual slowing and eventual phasing out of growth into a stationary state. The question of which side is correct can be left for events to decide. Immediate action should be directed not toward the futile effort to halt growth, but toward improving the mechanisms that will make growth safe, if it does continue.

The functioning of the equilibrium mechanism can be traced in the areas of nonreproducible raw materials, in the closely allied areas of population and food, and in the area of environmental resources. It will become apparent that the mechanism is reasonable although not perfectly effective with respect to nonreproducible natural resources, that with respect to population and food its effectiveness is substantial but not necessarily adequate, and that with regard to the environment its natural functioning is often at present inadequate but capable of great improvement.

In the markets for metals, minerals, and other nonreproducible resources the functioning of the adjustment mechanism can be observed with great clarity. A rise in the demand for or a decline in the supply of any such product tends to raise its price. This sets in motion the familiar combination of a more intensive search for supplies, a reduction in use, and the development of substitutes. The fact that raw material prices have accelerated sharply over the last year is no evidence to the contrary. As pointed out above, it reflects the coincidence of business cycle peaks in a number of leading countries. Over long periods of time, moreover, the price of unexploited reserves of natural resources, such as petroleum underground, ought indeed to rise. This is the market's way of putting a competitive rate of return on such assets. In equilibrium, their yield must be equal to the yield of any other form of capital. In the absence of such a yield, there would be no reason for holding these reserves. There would then be a tendency to use them up more quickly than their long-term scarcity would justify. The price of such resources brought above ground, of course, will reflect the cost of lifting them as well as the value of the underground reserves. If lifting costs dominate, they may obscure the secular increase in the price of the underground reserves.

The proper function of this mechanism requires the market to have correct expectations of future demand. Advancing technology may make underground reserves obsolete, as for a while seemed to have happened with respect to coal. Required also is stability of ownership rights. Fear of future expropriation of oil reserves or concern over the gradual encroachment of recreational and environmental interest on timber reserves puts a discount on these assets.

Government intervention in markets is another threat to the effective functioning of the adjustment mechanism. The U.S. government's attempt to hold down the price of natural gas along the classical lines of public-utility rate regulation is a case in point. Tying the price that a monopolistic seller can charge to the level of his costs makes regulatory sense where the supply is infinitely expansible, as, for instance, in the case of telephone service. The appropriate price of a scarce natural resource, be it natural gas, or oil, or anything else, does not depend principally on cost of production, and it is a mistake to regulate it as if that were the case.

The appropriate price of the natural resource, the supply of which is limited, is a function of its scarcity, not of the cost of bringing it above ground. In this respect, the OPEC countries have shown a better understanding of pricing principles than some of their critics who have pointed to the minimal marginal cost of Arabian oil. The price set by monopolists may of course be—and in the case of petroleum probably is—above the appropriate long-run level, in which case the owners eventually will find themselves holding an unsalable remainder as the resource is made obsolete by advancing technology.

The role of technology in first making certain resources usable and subsequently making them obsolete deserves special comment. It will be recalled that the Reverend Robert Malthus derived his classical dilemma from the interaction of the supposedly arithmetic growth of food and the geometric or exponential growth of population. Experience over more than a century has disavowed Malthus and seems to have given the verdict to Ricardo's marginal analysis. Ricardian scarcity—which regards supply as unlimited provided ever larger resources are invested per unit of output on ever less fertile land and less productive mines—rather than the absolute supply limitations of Malthusian scarcity seems to be the rule. One may attribute this to the behavior of technology, which has made possible the exploitation of increasingly more marginal resources. To maintain an exponentially growing supply, technology must itself grow exponentially, and it has indeed been shown that this is probably a realistic view of the behavior of technology.[2]

With respect to food and population, the functioning of a corrective self-adjusting mechanism is observable also. The adequacy of its functioning, however, is less assured. Food production, too, admits the use of advancing technology and provides opportunity for massive substitutions. If owing to rising meat prices, people increasingly were to turn to a vegetarian diet, far larger numbers could be fed from the produce of the soil than under the inefficient present system, which grows food to feed animals to feed humans. Food supplies, moreover, have price elasticities that are far higher in the long term than in the short.[3] Nevertheless, sufficiently rapid population growth can bring about the Malthusian calamity.

The behavior of population undoubtedly is sensitive to technological (primarily medical) influences. The decline in the death rate demonstrably tends to be followed by a lag, by a decline in the birth rate. Population can be stable or grow at a constant rate both when birth and death rates are high and when they are low. The difference is in the average age of the population. The important questions today with regard to the adequacy of the adjustment mechanism are two: Will the decline in the birth rate follow sufficiently quickly on the decline in the death rate that has already taken place all over the world to bring the present population explosion in the developing countries to a halt? And second, assuming the whole world to have run through the population cycle that leads to low death and birth rates, will the mounting cost of rearing children sufficiently depress the birth rate to achieve stability as per-capita income increases?

Present trends in the United States suggest that the economics of child rearing tend to have this effect. Moreover, if population is to be restrained further, which seems unnecessary in a big empty country like the United States but is indeed necessary in many other countries, there is much scope for internalizing the adverse externalities of child rearing. Much of the cost of every child must be borne outside its immediate family. Internalization, through the familar tax mechanism, would probably reduce the indulgence in the consumer good "children." But this mechanism seems to have its greatest potential strength in a country like the United States where it need not be invoked at present population levels, while it may be ineffective in developing countries where children still are regarded as "producer goods." Population probably is the sector where the world is most seriously vulnerable to unconstrained growth. This is hardly a problem of growth in America, however, which is the theme of this paper.

It can be argued, of course, that even the American population is excessive in those areas that now are badly crowded. Because this crowding is unnecessary, given the supply of space in the United States, it becomes necessary to inquire why the equilibrium mechanism that presumably governs the geographical distribution of people does not lead to a more even spacing. That mechanism takes the form of rising rents and rising disamenities for city dwellers. Apparently the prevailing costs and disamenities are not sufficient to keep people from coming to the city or to induce enough of them to leave.

The economics of urban immigration and emigration require more study than they have so far received. It may turn out that the familiar price mechanism is operating adequately and that this has been obscured in the past by a very long lag. But the conclusion might also be that the mechanism is not operating with sufficient strength. In that case, a tax to internalize the adverse externalities generated by an immigrant into a crowded area, or a subsidy to internalize the positive ones generated by an emigrant from the city, would be appropriate. The immigrant raises rents and crowds the sidewalks not only to his own disadvantage but also to that of all the previous residents. In contrast to the behavior of most other markets, where an increase in price calls forth an increase in supply, immigration into the city does not increase the supply of available space, although it may, because of higher rents, lead to an increase of the supply of shelter. This might make public intervention in the market for urban real estate more appropriate than it would be in markets with a different supply mechanism. Different views are sure to emerge concerning the appropriateness of such policies. What matters for the purposes of the present analysis is that if the equilibrium mechanism that operates in the market for urban space is not considered adequate, the means are at hand to make it adequate without interfering with the free choice of the market participants.

Where environmental resources are concerned, for which at present there is no market, such as clean air and water and attractive views, the principle just enunciated with respect to urban space applies with even greater force. Almost all use of environmental resources generates mainly externalities. The users of these environmental resources, polluters of water, air, and scenery, suffer little from the damage that they do. This is a serious defect of the market system, fundamentally resulting from the fact that these environmental resources are not appropriable. Recent environmental legislation has sought to cope with the problem by regulation and prohibition. We have set standards for automobile emissions and for the emissions into the air and into rivers by utilities and manufacturing installations. This approach is not internalization, and it is highly inefficient. A better procedure would be to levy a tax on emissions and thus deflect the costs of environmental damage on the polluter himself or on the supplier of the defective equipment. By setting the tax at an appropriate level, any desired standard of environmental cleanliness could be achieved. It would be achieved efficiently, however—that is to say, those who could reduce pollution at little cost would do so to a substantial degree while others, for whom the cost was higher, would continue to pollute substantially.

A similar result could be achieved by offering a subsidy to those willing to cut back pollution. Economically, the immediate results of tax and subsidy could be made identical. In the long run, however, a subsidy would probably attract more polluters into the industry or other activity. That, of course, would be counterproductive. An even more efficient device than a tax on pollution would be the auctioning of licenses to pollute. This would make it unnecessary to guess the level of tax by which pollution would be reduced to a tolerable level. That level could be controlled simply by the volume of licenses.

The process of internalizing adverse externalities does not, to be sure, completely replicate the process of a free market. A political process is needed to set the admissible level of pollution, and hence the required tax. Nevertheless it is evident that the threat that growth poses to the environment, through pollution, can be controlled by these means. If pollution should rise very rapidly, the tax will have to be very high. It may have to become so high that an increase in production becomes unprofitable. Further investment then will come to a halt. If this process repeats itself in all lines of economic activity, the marginal return to capital will have been reduced to zero and growth will come to an end to the extent that it is dependent on an increase in the capital stock. This is the stationary state, which economists have long envisioned at the end of a shorter or longer period of growth. Properly handled, this end should be a "soft landing." There is no need for the hard landing of global catastrophe envisioned by the critics of growth.

The environmental conditions that would be brought about through this process would not, to be sure, be those of ideal purity and cleanliness. It is theoretically possible to achieve such standards of perfection, but only at very high cost. The internalizing taxes would have to be very high. Substantial growth otherwise possible would have to be foregone. It is not likely that people would be willing to pay this price unless new technologies could be developed that would reduce it. An ultimate stationary state, therefore, if it is reached by this route, must not be envisioned as one of great environmental perfection. Air and water will still be dirty although short of the level dangerous to health. Not all views would be beautiful, not all cities spacious and uncrowded. In this respect, the future that we are preparing for our children may be poorer than our present. But thanks to higher income it will be a richer one in other respects. That seems to be the likely outcome of growth in America.

Notes

1. James Tobin and William Nordhaus, "Is Growth Obsolete," Cowles Foundation Paper 398 written for *Measurement of Economic and Social Performance,* Milton Moss, editor, Studies in Income and Wealth Series, vol. 38, National Bureau of Economic Research, New York, 1973.

2. Chauncey Starr and Richard Rudman, ''Parameters of Technological Growth,'' *Science Magazine,* 182 (October 26, 1973): 358–364.

3. Luther Tweeten, ''The Demand for U.S. Farm Output,'' Food Research Institute Studies, 1967, vol. 7, pp. 343–369.

38 Is There a Capital Shortage?

Concern about an impending capital shortage has become widespread. A variety of studies of investment requirements over the next five or ten years, as well as of the adequacy of private and public savings and financial arrangements for converting these savings into investment, have already been completed. The generality of this concern attests to the importance of the issue.

There are indeed reasons for posing these questions. The experience of the last few years has confronted us with the limits of our capacity to produce. That same experience has shown us that there are limits to our capacity to finance. Meanwhile, new demands are being made on our economies. Important decisions may lie ahead—to increase our efforts to provide resources or to cut back our aspirations. Failure to make the right decisions may lead to economic imbalance, with the risk of more inflation, insufficient jobs, disappointing living standards.

In examining the requirements for new capital, it becomes immediately apparent that the answer differs from one country to another. The rate of investment and of savings, relative to GNP, varies widely. Investment runs from about 15 percent in the United States to close to 40 percent in Japan. Net savings differ even more dramatically, running from 5 percent in the United States to 25 percent in Japan. A flow of investment and savings that might be perfectly adequate in one country might bring the economy of another to a grinding halt. What matters is not the level of these flows, but their relationship to the structure of individual economies, to the levels maintained in the past, and to the requirements of a future that is bound to be, in large measure, a continuation of that past. For that reason, my comments are addressed principally to the United States. Some of the data appended, however, will also serve to provide a comparison of the United States with other countries (tables 38–1 through 38–3).

Tests of Capital Adequacy

Capital inadequacy can show up in various forms. First, it may manifest itself in bottleneck situations, with some industries having adequate capacity for high-level operation of the economy and others not having enough capacity to supply the needs of consumers and of other industries when all are operating at

---

This chapter was originally published in *Challenge*, September–October 1975, pp. 30–36.

Table 38–1
Gross Savings, 1970–1972 (Annual Average)
(percent)

	GNP	
	Japan	*United States*
Households[a]		
net savings	13.5	5.3
depreciation	3.3	3.2
Corporations		
net savings[b]	5.8	1.5
depreciation	8.6	5.8
Total private		
net savings†	19.3	6.8
depreciation	11.9	8.9
Government[c]		
net savings	7.3	−1.0
depreciation	1.0	—
Statistical discrepancy	−1.2	−0.4
Total gross savings	38.2	14.3
Total net savings	25.4	5.4

Source: Henry C. and Mable I. Wallich, "Money and Banking in Japan," in *Asia's New Giant: How the Japanese Economy Works* (Washington, D.C.: The Brookings Institution, 1975).

[a]Includes households, private unincorporated businesses, and private nonprofit institutions.

[b]Includes inventory-valuation adjustment.

[c]Government and government enterprise.

Table 38–2
Household Savings as Percent of Disposable Income for Selected Industrial Countries, 1960–1972

	1960	*1965*	*1970*	*1971*	*1972*
Japan	19.2[a]	17.5	20.7	20.2	21.0
Germany	15.0	15.9	16.7	15.0	15.1
France	9.7	11.1	12.7	12.3	12.1
United States	4.9	6.0	9.0	9.0	7.2
United Kingdom	4.7	6.1	5.2	4.9	5.0

Note: Definitions differ from those underlying national statistics; therefore, ratios, too, will not be the same as those derived from national sources. Disposable income includes households and private nonprofit institutions serving households.

[a]1961 figure.

a high level. Frequently this is a problem of bottlenecks for raw materials and industrial materials. But more highly finished goods may also be affected. In the United States, there is probably a good deal of this capital inadequacy, as the shortage experienced in 1973 and 1974 indicates.

Table 38–3
Savings and Savings Rates in Selected Industrial Countries

	Savings as percent of GDP				
	Corporate	*Government*	*Household*	*Total*[a]	*GDP*[b]
Germany					
1961	6.0	7.8	5.5	19.3	333.4
1965	4.5	5.0	7.7	17.3	462.0
1969	3.4	6.1	7.9	17.3	605.7
1970	3.7	5.8	8.4	18.0	687.0
1971	2.4	5.5	8.3	16.2	762.5
1972	1.9	4.6	9.1	15.5	834.6
1973	1.2	6.1	8.4	15.7	930.6
France					
1961	3.3	4.0	6.4	13.7	328.2
1965	2.9	4.8	7.6	15.3	489.0
1969	4.6	4.9	6.8	16.3	722.8
1970	3.7	4.9	8.3	16.9	808.2
1971	3.9	4.5	8.2	16.6	898.9
1972	3.8	4.4	8.1	16.3	1001.9
1973	3.7	4.3	8.6	16.7	1146.2
United Kingdom					
1961	4.4	0.9	4.3	9.6	27.14
1965	4.9	2.3	4.2	11.4	35.35
1969	1.9	6.5	3.1	11.5	45.74
1970	0.1	7.8	3.4	11.1	49.96
1971	—	—	3.2	11.9	55.65
1972	1.2	—	3.4	7.4	61.18
1973	—	—	—	—	—
United States					
1961	2.5	0.9	4.0	7.6	525.7
1965	3.6	2.1	4.1	9.8	692.1
1969	2.0	1.9	4.6	8.5	927.9
1970	1.2	−0.6	6.2	6.9	983.2
1971	1.7	−1.2	6.3	6.8	1059.7
1972	2.2	−0.1	5.1	7.2	1161.9
1973	2.2	0.6	6.2	9.1	1297.5

Source: OECD, *National Accounts,* 1961–1972, 1962–1973, vol. 1.
[a]Savings excluding depreciation by OECD definitions.
[b]In billions of local currency.

It should be borne in mind, however, that the pattern of demand may shift and that the past is no exact guide to the bottlenecks of the future. In a worldwide economy, moreover, insufficient supplies in one country can often be met from abroad, unless the unusual synchronization of cyclical peaks experienced in 1973–1974 is repeated.

Second, an overall shortage of capital with respect to the labor force is possible, even if capacity is fairly evenly distributed among industries. There would then not be enough jobs to provide full employment even when industry is operating close to capacity. This condition, too, I believe prevails in the United States as a result of inadequate past investment.

Capital capacity, in other words, seems to fall short of labor-force capacity. This is a serious condition, which labor has as urgent an interest in remedying as does business. The peak of labor-force growth, reaching 2.4 percent during the five-year period 1970–1974, seems to be behind us, but projections for the remainder of the 1970s and the early 1980s still show labor-force growth in the range of 1.6 to 1.8 percent per year.

When capital shortages of the two types described so far are not present, one really cannot speak of a shortage of capital, either in the United States or in any other economy. However, a society can be dissatisfied with its total supply of goods, or with the rate of growth of that supply. Social strains, or inflation, could be evidence of such a condition. Alternatively, a society may be willing to accept a low rate of growth but may find itself falling behind economically and politically. This condition could be remedied by a more ample supply of capital, if the nation so chose. There is some doubt, however, as to how much of an acceleration of growth can be accomplished by increasing the supply of capital when other factors of production grow at an unchanged rate.

Another test of capital adequacy is the rate of return on capital. In the United States, this rate of return has declined severely when properly adjusted for inflation. This would suggest that the demand for capital is low. However, the rate of return measures the average productivity of capital, not its marginal productivity. It is quite possible that average productivity has been depressed by the many adverse factors that have impinged on business—international competition, strength of labor unions, inflation, widespread hostility toward business, government regulation and taxation. But the return on capital at the margin, that is, for new investment, may nevertheless have risen. This would seem to be indicated by the willingness of business to borrow at very high interest rates and sell new equity even on adverse terms.

The Demand for Capital

In the United States, there is no shortage of capital in the short run. There is enough excess capacity materially to increase production. But absorption of this existing excess capacity, important as it is, constitutes a short-run problem. Concern over the adequacy of the stock of capital and its growth through investment pertains to the medium and longer run. In that perspective, it becomes necessary to take into account, in addition to the possible inadequacies already existing, the emerging new demands for capital. Some of the investments for which demand is rising are of a kind that will not add much, if anything, to output. At the same time, there may be other areas of investment where prospective demands promise to abate.

Areas in which demand for capital is clearly rising include: (1) environmental investment, which is largely unproductive; (2) health and safety investment, which contributes to productivity at best indirectly; (3) mass transit, which promises to contribute to overall growth by reducing the need for less efficient modes of transportation; and (4) energy investment, which will in some respects act as a drag on the economy because relatively expensive energy will be substituted for cheap imported oil.

On the side of diminishing demand one may count; (1) investment in housing, as population growth slows down and as housing construction, owing to its very high cost, shifts increasingly from the customary single-family home to apartment-house dwellings and mobile homes; (2) various forms of nonresidential construction such as schools, for which a rapidly declining birthrate is reducing requirements; and (3) inventory investment, the need for which, one may hope, will be held down as better control methods are developed and as inflation abates.

The great bulk of investment in the American economy is private investment, and the largest part of this is investment made by business firms. Gross private domestic investment has remained fairly stable historically in the neighborhood of 15 percent of GNP, with a slight dip during the 1960s and a slight rise in the early 1970s. Within this total, business-fixed investment has averaged close to 10 percent of GNP, with a tendency to rise over the last ten years. This upward trend becomes even clearer when the data are stated in constant instead of in current dollars. Most of the areas of rising investment demand—environment, health and safety, energy—are also in the business sector. Only inventory offers an opportunity here for an easing of demand.

Thus, it is business investment that must be our principal concern. Among the various studies of capital requirements, there is a remarkable degree of agreement that nonresidential investment, as a fraction of GNP, will have to average 11.5 percent contrasted with a historic 10.5 percent. It is principally to take care of this increase that the necessary savings and financing techniques must be found. Taken by itself, this is not a very large amount. The demand side of the saving-investment process seems to generate no insuperable problems. This is not so on the supply side, however.

The Supply of Savings

It is on the supply side of the saving-investment process that adverse changes have occurred and remedies need to be applied. Historically, savings rates in the United States over the past twenty years have fluctuated within a narrow band for both households and businesses. Personal savings have ranged from 3.4 to 5.7 percent of GNP, business savings, including depreciation, between 10 and 12 percent. Typically, there has been some compensatory movement, so that the sum has ranged around 15 to 16 percent of GNP.

Consumer saving has been remarkably insensitive to inflation. Apparently, the frequently predicted tendency of inflation to diminish saving incentives has been approximately compensated by the desire of households to maintain some prudent relationships between wealth and income. In fact, the savings-GNP ratio has been near the top of its twenty-year range for the past three years. There is little reason to expect it to rise further.

Business saving has suffered severely from inflation. Inventory profits have been very high, but these profits are of questionable value to their owners. They generate no cash flow, are not available for investment or dividends, and generate a tax liability. Likewise, an adjustment must be made for depreciation based on original instead of replacement cost. When these two adjustment factors are deducted from corporate profits, a case can be made that domestic nonfinancial corporations did not earn their dividends in 1974. In other words, this dominant component of the American corporate universe, excluding only financial corporations and foreign subsidiaries, can be said to have had negative net savings.

Some qualifications are required in making this case. Inventory profits, after all, are not altogether valueless. Moreover, corporations also have some benefits from accelerated depreciation methods. Finally, since interest is wholly tax deductible, corporations have the advantage, in that the tax on the inflation premium is paid by the bondholder, not by the corporation.

Inflation is not the only cause of declining business savings. The decline in the rate of return, which was mentioned earlier, can hardly be attributed to inflation alone. Hence, there can be no assurance that an ending of or, much less desirably, an adjustment to continued inflation would restore profits to their historic proportion of GNP. Yet a return to this historic proportion is one of the esssential conditions for an adequate flow of savings. The other and, indeed, crucial condition is a better saving performance on the part of government.

Historically, government has sometimes been a net supplier of savings, through debt repayment, and sometimes a net user. The saving or dissaving of the federal government and of state and local governments have sometimes moved in opposite directions, partly compensating each other's effect on the total savings flow. During the last few years, both the federal and the state and local governments have been net borrowers.

In periods of recession, the danger that government borrowing may crowd out a substantial volume of private-sector borrowing is small. The danger mounts, however, as recovery proceeds. Once full employment is reached, obviously any resources that government draws on for itself must lead to a reduction of resources available to the private sector, other things being equal.

The stance of government at full employment, whether as a net supplier or net demander of savings, can be estimated on the basis of the full-employment surplus or deficit. Since the early 1970s, this computational variable has fluctuated around an average of approximately zero. At the present time, it shows a moderate deficit. The projection given in the fiscal 1976 federal budget indicates a rapid rise to a surplus of $61 billion by 1980.

If this projection were probable, the outlook for an adequate flow of savings would be very good. The projection, however, is the result of its assumptions. Continued moderate inflation is expected to push taxpayers into higher tax brackets, and this substantial rise in the effective tax burden is not expected to be counteracted fully by tax cuts. Likewise, the projection assumes only moderate expenditure increases and few new spending initiatives.

History provides ample reason to question both assumptions. The effects of inflation on tax brackets have already been compensated for repeatedly by tax cuts, principally in 1969 and 1975. A slowdown of government expenditures is more desirable than probable. Meanwhile, the trend of state and local affairs, where there is less fiscal flexibility, suggests that deficits in that sector will continue. A federal surplus of some magnitude would therefore be required merely in order to get the public sector as a whole into a zero-deficit position. A substantially larger surplus would be required to offset the shortfall of savings below expected investment in the private sector, once the economy returns to high employment.

Constraints in Financial Markets

The uncertainty about the future overall flow of savings noted in the previous section is compounded by constraints that may appear in the financial markets. For many years now, the capital structure of corporations has moved in the direction of a higher share of debt relative to equity. This appeared to be the way to maximize profits at a time when credit was readily available and borrowers' ratings went unchallenged.

The events of the last few years have changed that picture. Borrowing became less easy, and credit ratings were tested. In good part, the consequence was not a shift toward more equity financing but toward more debt in short-term form as longer-term financing became less easy (table 38–4). Now the need for a stronger equity component in corporate capital structures has become pressing. Yet internal generation of equity has become more difficult, while external financing is suffering from the relatively low level of stock market prices.

Another change may affect the banks, whose role in the financial picture

Table 38–4
Aggregate Capital Structure of Nonfinancial Corporations, 1965–1974
(billions of dollars)

Year	*(1) Short-term Debt*	*(2) Long-term Debt*	*(3) Equity*	*(1)/(2)*	*[(1) + (2)]/(3)*
1965	172	176	404	.975	.864
1966	189	194	437	.978	.878
1967	198	215	471	.921	.879
1968	228	238	506	.956	.921
1969	259	261	551	.991	.944
1970	269	290	594	.927	.942
1971	278	321	645	.865	.932
1972	302	356	706	.847	.934
1973	349	394	765	.887	.971
1974	404	438	876	.922	.963

Source: Board of Governors, Federal Reserve System, *Flow of Funds Accounts,* 1974.

had expanded in recent years. Banks have become increasingly cautious, partly because of past overexpansion and mounting risk, partly because of a generally declining capital position. Thus the role of banks in the financing of investment may become more limited.

The stock market, too, has become a less productive source of funds, owing to diminishing buyer interest. Individuals have been net sellers of equities for many years. Of late, the interest of institutional investors has also shifted to some degree away from equities and toward bonds.

Another financial constraint is the level of the money supply. A rapid expansion of the money supply would run the risk of engendering inflationary expectations that, by themselves, might raise interest rates and choke off financing. A more moderate growth of the money supply consistent with a gradual return to price stability, on the other hand, limits the banks' ability to contribute to the flow of financing.

Studies of Capital Requirements and Availability of Savings

As noted earlier, studies of capital adequacy abound. A few of them are compared in table 38–5. Their selection implies no intention to downgrade others that are not mentioned. Those chosen predominantly arrive at the conclusion that there will be no shortfall of savings; the selection was made because this writer questions that conclusion.

Table 38–5
Comparison of Studies of Capital Requirements
(percentage)

	New York Stock Exchange	*Duesenberry*[a]	*Friedman*	*Data Resources Inc.*	*National Planning Assoc.*
GNP growth	8.6	8.7	10.1	8.5	10.1
Inflation rate	5.0	3.0	6.2	4.3	6.0
Real GNP growth	3.4	5.5	3.7	4.0	3.9
Unemployment rate	—	5.0	5.5	5.0	5.5
Long-term interest rate	—	7.5	—	8.0	—
		Percentage of GNP			
Gross private domestic investment	16.4	15.8	15.8	15.5	16.4
Nonresidential	12.1	11.6	11.5	11.4	12.3
Inventory	0.4	0.9	0.8	0.6	0.6
Residential	3.9	3.3	3.5	3.5	3.5
Total savings	14.2	15.8	15.8	15.5	16.4
Business	10.5	10.2	10.8	10.7	11.7
Personal	3.9	4.7	4.9	4.6	4.9
Government	−0.2		−0.1	0.4	0.1
Federal		1.3			
State		0.3			
Other[b]	—	−0.1	0.2	−0.2	−0.3
Investment gap	2.2[c]	0	0	0	0

[a]Refers to 1980, the end of the projection period.
[b]Statistical discrepancy less net foreign investment.
[c]Represents an average annual gap of over $50 billion for the twelve-year projection 1974–1985.

After removing the multi-billion-dollar tags from the estimates by expressing all amounts in percent of GNP, it appears that the investment requirements projected in the different studies are not very far apart, ranging from 15.5 percent to 16.4 percent of GNP. It is in the projections of savings that larger differences show up; these run from 14.2 to 16.4 percent of GNP.

There is surprisingly little difference among projections of business savings. The principal uncertainty inevitably attaches to projections of government savings. By a slight majority, the projections incline toward a very small government surplus, when federal, and state and local budgets are combined. If the expectation of a state and local deficit is correct, this implies a more sizable federal surplus.

The most extensive examination of investment requirements and savings flows is that by Duesenberry and Bosworth, about to be published by the Brookings Institution and summarized by Professor Duesenberry in his testimony before the Ways and Means Committee of the House of Representatives in January 1975. This study concludes that we can avoid a capital shortage, "but just barely." This conclusion is based on the projection of a substantial federal surplus of 1.3 percent, equal in the terminal year 1980 to $31.7 billion. For the private sector alone, a deficiency of savings of 1 percent of GNP, or $23.7 billion, is calculated. The Duesenberry-Bosworth study goes farthest in making the point that is common to all studies: avoidance of a capital shortage depends crucially on getting the federal budget under control.

Tax Remedies

Several studies of capital requirements feature proposals for tax reform designed to increase the flow of savings. Typically, they involve measures that would affect the distribution of income as well as reduce the Treasury's revenue. In the second respect, at least, such measures might prove counterproductive, since they would increase the Treasury's borrowing needs. A more moderate but perhaps less controversial device may be mentioned here. It focuses on improving the capital structure of corporations.

Even if an improvement in budgetary posture makes overall capital flows adequate, problems of corporate-debt capacity and equity financing remain. The debt problem is in good part the result of the fact that interest is tax deductible while corporate profits retained or paid out in dividends are taxed to the corporation. A tax structure that would place the same burden on all three forms of disposing of net operating income—interest, retentions, and dividends—would avoid this bias and would facilitate and encourage equity financing. The tax rate could be set so as to produce the same revenue as the present tax structure, if a reduction of the tax burden of corporations should prove economically or politically impractical.

Such a tax structure could not be introduced overnight, because it would drastically change the relative position of corporations with high and low indebtedness. But it could be applied to corporate debt and equity created in the future, if the necessary safeguards against loopholes were built in. Alternatively, the revised tax structure could be phased in gradually, giving firms an opportunity to modify their capital structure over time. The result, I believe, would be easier financing and stronger credit.

Capital Imports and Exports

There can be no doubt that there is at least a possibility of a serious capital shortage in the United States. Whether it will materialize depends very largely on whether Congress can avoid deficits in the federal budget and even achieve a surplus. Resolving the capital-shortage problem by means of better budget policy would be by far the preferred solution. Should this solution fail to come about, the United States will have to ask itself to what extent, if at all, it can still perform as a capital exporter. The United States ceased to be a net capital exporter when the current account went into deficit in the late 1960s. The high cost of oil imports probably has prevented the United States from becoming a capital exporter once more, although it should be noted that the U.S. current-accounts deficit is small relative to what might be considered this nation's appropriate share in the aggregate deficit imposed on oil-importing countries by the oil-exporting nations. As the oil problem comes into balance, the United States will have to ask itself very seriously whether it would be advantageous to remain a capital importer.

Summary and Conclusions

1. There is a distinct possibility that a capital shortage may appear in the United States, once the economy moves back to a high level of economic activity.

2. Higher demands for capital are ahead, mainly as a result of prospective increases in environmental, energy, health and safety, and mass-transit investment. These increases probably will be only partly compensated for by relatively modest declines in the share of housing and perhaps of inventory accumulation in total investment.

3. The principal threat of a shortage of investment funds arises not from increases in demand, but from uncertainty about the adequacy of savings. One source of uncertainty is the decline in corporate profits that becomes apparent once realistic accounting methods are employed. Another is the apparent trend of the federal as well as of the state and local budgets toward larger deficits.

4. Studies that conclude there will be no capital shortage appear to rely heavily on the assumption that the federal budget will be in surplus and will be supplying capital to the private sector. Continuation of the federal-financing patterns of recent years would do little to fulfill this hope.

5. In addition to the possibility of an overall capital shortage, business may experience constraints in its financing because of the existing heavy burden of debt, especially short-term debt. In order to strengthen the equity base and facilitate financing, it is suggested that the method of taxing corporations be shifted gradually, without loss of revenue, in the direction of taxing income used to pay interest while reducing the present tax on the portions of income used to pay dividends and retained in the business.

39 From Multiplier to Quantity Theory

Monetarism today stands at the center of the economic scene. Ten years after the ascendancy of the "new economics," a new doctrine is in vogue that is sharply critical of its Keynesian predecessor. Monetarism has established itself as an important part of intellectual discourse, has become influential with the press, and has captured the attention of the public. Central banks all over the world orient and explain their policies in terms of the monetary aggregates. The financial markets take their cue from data which, a few years back, were little observed and in many countries not even published. Even the nomenclature employed all over the world—M_1, M_2—is the handiwork of Milton Friedman, the originator of monetarism.

Increasingly, monetarist prescriptions play a role in political discussions. Policy objectives are being expressed and debated in terms of growth targets of the money stock. The elected representatives of the people have discovered the attraction of monetarist doctrine because it plays down the effects of fiscal policy. Deficits can do no major damage so long as the central bank does its job right, and that is where monetarism places the ultimate responsibility. Central bankers, for the same reason, have tended to preserve a degree of faith in Keynesianism.

The trend of public discussion conceals two important facts. The first is that the present vogue of monetarism is a child of its times just as Keynesianism was. Keynesianism came out of the Depression; it followed and in some measure reflected the disappointment over monetary policy which had been held in high esteem during the 1920s, an earlier monetarist period. Monetarist doctrine—like Keynesian—has had some degree of relevance at all times. But the strong vogue of monetarism is the consequence of inflation, which has undermined many Keynesian precepts and assumptions and has lent strength to monetarist analysis. This historical evolution from unemployment to inflation is reflected in the dominant concern of the two sides, Keynesianism being oriented

---

I am greatly indebted to David E. Lindsey for intensive discussions and numerous suggestions in the preparation of this chapter, and I also gratefully acknowledge the helpful comments received from G.L. Bach, George Clay, Rogert Dugger, Milton Friedman, C. Lowell Harriss, Donald Hester, Thomas Mayer, Walter Salant, Paul Samuelson, Francis Schott, Beryl Sprinkel, Jerome Stein and John Wilson. The views expressed herein are those of the author, and do not necessarily represent the views of the Board of Governors of the Federal Reserve System. This chapter was originally published in: *Economic Progress, Private Values, and Public Policy*, ed. Bela Belassa and Richard Nelson (Amsterdam: North Holland, 1977), pp. 279–295.

toward curing unemployment, monetarism predominantly toward curing inflation.

The second important fact is the narrowing, in recent years, of the analytical gap that has separated monetarists and Keynesians. Much of the debate now is not over how the economy works, but over what we want to get out of it, that is, over values and policies. My principal purpose in this essay is to examine the process by which changes in the economic climate, from the unemployment of the 1930s to the inflation of the 1970s, have progressively strengthened the monetarist case. To begin with, I shall examine the coming together of the two sides in terms of their view of the economy.

The Keynesian Monetarist Synthesis

The long debate between Keynesians and monetarists has reached a substantial measure of agreement. This agreement does not cover matters of policy, which often reflect value judgments. It does imply that a common view is being approached of the analytical framework of the economy. There is a common ground now as to how the economy works, what are the critical relationships. No longer do the two sides seem to speak different languages or to be looking at a different world.

What they say in the newfound common language, to be sure, still distinguishes Keynesians from monetarists. They differ about the shape of relationships that both sides regard as important, and the magnitude of particular effects. But the analytical differences have narrowed down to the point where the difference between a fair representation of the two doctrines has been reduced by one student to the sign of a single coefficient in a large system of equations [Stein (1976)].

The process of integration has followed along two lines. On the one hand, monetarists, in developing their framework, increasingly have found themselves employing concepts and relationships originating in the Keynesian world. No longer is there a simple equation of exchange, $MV = PT$, which everybody must fill with his own analytical ideas to keep it from remaining a tautology. Money, we now clearly perceive, works mainly through interest rates, not through some mysterious black box, even though some echoes of a "direct effect" continue to reverberate. The range of interest rates and rates of return is wide, wider indeed than the original Keynesian conception, some rates being implicit rather than quoted in the market. These rates affect asset values, the wealth of consumers, the relation of market to replacement value of assets, the propensity to spend of households and firms. These effects all find their place in a sufficiently detailed version of the familiar Keynesian *IS–LM* framework of the economy.

On the other hand, monetarists have imposed on the precise nature of these relationships their own particular stamp, which Keynesians have largely had to accept. They say that the relation of money and interest rates is far more complex than the simple Keynesian liquidity-preference doctrine implied. A difference exists between nominal and real values, which the Keynesians had tended to ignore. Under plausible assumptions, monetary policy may be more powerful than fiscal policy. The money supply rather than the interest rate may be the best intermediate target for monetary policy. Inflation may become as serious a threat to welfare as is unemployment. The Phillips Curve, the principal analytical device of the post-Keynesian era, may lose its meaning in the long run. Long lags in response to policy actions may make flexible anticyclical policy destabilizing. These are some of the concrete and very un-Keynesian propositions with which the monetarists have filled the essentially Keynesian analytical framework. The central bank much of the time during recent years has found itself in a crossfire between Keynesians and monetarists. Often the criticism of monetary policy coming from the Keynesian side has been less concerned with techniques than with values, for example, the relative willingness to take risks on the side of inflation. By contrast, most of the criticism coming from the monetarist side has been over techniques, for example, the use of interest-rate versus money-supply targets, and the degree of stability of a money-supply target.

The Federal Reserve itself has come a long way in the course of these discussions. After ridding itself of the sense of powerlessness that beset it during the late 1930s and most of the 1940s, it first moved back to the policy targets of the 1920s, based on the reserve position of banks. By gradual steps it shifted toward increasing emphasis on the monetary aggregates, as demanded by monetarist doctrine. But it has shied away from full endorsement. The monetary aggregates are not all that matters. Interest rates also are important, and so is the international value of the dollar, even under a floating regime. Accordingly, a fixed rate of money-supply growth, regardless of its consequences for interest rates and exchange rates, is not practicable. At best, the monetarist emphasis on a stable—and moderate—rate of money growth can be employed to support a policy of moderation in financing budget deficits and inflation.

It would be quite wrong, however, to interpret the movement toward the present Keynesian-monetarist synthesis as a graduate discovery of immutable verities. The analytical structure, to be sure, has a considerable degree of general validity. It can be employed to explain widely differing states of the economy. But the economy has passed through a variety of states, and particularly of states of expectations, beginning with the expected unemployment of the late 1930s and 1940s going out to the full-employment expectations of the 1950s and early 1960s, and ending with the inflationary expectations of the late 1960s and early 1970s. In each of these phases, in my view, the behavior of the economy has been different, although capable of being represented by the same analytical relationships. The magnitudes of particular effects, the parameters and elasticities, the response to particular policy actions, have been typically different.

These views, I realize, may be at variance with the results obtained by econometric methods. The econometric approach, to be significant, requires and implies stable relationships or at least stable changes therein. To data drawn from long periods, such as from the early 1930s, to the present, researchers usually apply one of the tests available to examine the stability of the structure over time. I am aware also, of course, that contemporary observation may lead to false conclusions. For a long time people believed to observe that the earth was flat.

At the same time, even well-validated econometric results may be misleading. As an example, I might cite the finding that the demand for money has been very stable as a function of income and an interest rate, from which follows the conclusion that monetary policy had approximately the same expansionary power during the 1930s that it had at any other time. The demand function employed in such tests typically is a logarithmic one. If the elasticity of the demand for money with respect to the long-term interest rate then is -0.5, an increase in the money supply by 10 percent will bring down a long-term rate of 6 percent, to 4.91 percent and will bring down a long-term rate of 2.5 percent to 2.05. If the elasticity for the short-term rate (which during the 1930s reached 0.05 percent and during World War II was pegged at 0.375 percent) is -0.3, an increase in the money supply of 10 percent would bring down a short-term rate of 0.75 down to 0.56 percent. I am perfectly willing to accept these results, but I doubt that, under the conditions of the 1930s, they imply a potential for an effective monetary policy.

If the relevance and even the validity of particular propositions changes over time, an examination is called for of the evolution of Keynesian and monetarist propositions. The periods it must cover are the three periods already cited—that of expected high unemployment with prices nevertheless sticky downward, that of expected fluctuations in the neighborhood of full employment with reasonable price stability, and the final period of expected inflation combined with temporary unemployment.

The Demand for Money

The stability of the demand for money is a key proposition of monetarism. It is contrasted, by its sponsors, with the alleged instability of the Keynesian investment multiplier, and has been tested extensively with greater and lesser degrees of sophistication. If the demand for money is a function of both income and an interest rate, there is no reason to expect velocity (the income-money ratio) to be stable. It must be predictable, however, given the interest rate.

Intuitively, one may expect this degree of predictability to have increased since the middle 1930s, for two reasons. At low rates of interest (1) a larger percentage change in the money supply is likely to be required to achieve a given absolute change in rates, and (2) the low cost of carrying idle balances leads to reduced effort in making precise adjustments in cash balances. At the very high interest rates experienced in 1974, smaller percentage changes in the money supply are likely to be associated with a given interest-rate change, while efforts to economize on cash balances would be well rewarded. These observations apply particularly, of course, to M_1, and their validity does not depend on the uptrend in velocity that appears to have occurred over several decades thanks to improved payments technology, or, possibly, owing to increasing wealth.

If these considerations are valid, monetary policy in 1974 would have had more power than during earlier periods, both because a given percentage change in M would produce a wider absolute swing in interest rates and because there was less slack in the relationship. It would mean also that the money supply would have to be attuned more precisely to the desired objectives in terms of real and nominal income growth than earlier. The monetarist claim that monetary policy was not powerless during the Great Depression might have formal validity but would have little significance given the large percentage changes in M that would have been required and the modest absolute changes in interest rates that could have been expected, as noted above. The great present power of monetary policy, under conditions of inflation, reflects no eternal verity.

Money and Interest Rates

The original quantity equation $MV = PT$ did not explicitly allow for the relation of interest rates and money, although it is obvious that so acute an analyst of the interest phenomenon as Irving Fisher was aware of it. Keynes remedied this by introducing "liquidity preference." During a period of expected permanent unemployment (at least in the textbooks), this seemed to be the end of the matter: an increase in money reduces the interest rate and, after allowing for a partial reversal of this effect if the ensuing rise in income is taken into account, the interest rate remains at a lower level than initially with no difference between real and nominal rates. This framework seems to make the interest rate a perfectly proper target of monetary policy.

Full employment, and eventually inflation, compel us to extend the sequence of effects, as Milton Friedman has shown. The initial decline in the interest rate leads to excess demand, which eventually raises income. This increases the demand for money, causing interest rates to go up again. If prices also rise, this reduces real balances, which further raises interest rates. If inflation finally becomes imbedded in expectations, nominal interest rates rise still higher to protect real rates.

In the inflationary conditions of the 1970s, this mechanism has become widely accepted. It can reasonably be argued that the central bank has little power to reduce interest rates except for short periods. Even then, the impact is more on short-term rates, which reflect demand and supply in the money market, than on long-term rates, which reflect expectations of inflation over a much longer horizon. It has even been argued that evidence of more rapidly growing money supply causes long-term rates to go up rather than down. However, the implication that this reflects expectations of higher inflation may be spurious; rates would also rise if the market expected the acceleration of the money supply to be compensated by slower growth in the following period. One thing is clear, however; under the conditions of inflation, the only way in which the central bank can bring down interest rates lastingly is to bring down the rate of inflation. Temporarily, at least, this probably requires a period of higher rates that would slow the growth of nominal and probably real GNP.

The inflationary spurts of the late 1940s and the early and late 1950s raise interesting questions with respect to interest rates. The response of interest rates was in no way sufficient to compensate for the inflation loss. This may be attributed to the failure of expectations of inflation to be formed. However, the decline (or reduced growth) in real balances also should have made itself felt in higher rates. Yet the effect, if any, was clearly far less pronounced than what has been experienced since the late 1960s. Evidently, then, the mechanism to which monetarists rightly have pointed since that time did not fully come into play during the 1940s and 1950s.

Money Supply versus Interest Rates as Monetary-Policy Target

If the relation of money and interest rates is fully known, the choice of one or the other as a target of monetary policy makes no difference. Moreover, if money affects the economy through interest rates, it would seem simpler to work directly through an interest-rate target rather than a money-growth target. Whether for these reasons or others, early Keynesian thinking undoubtedly focused on interest rates as the target and test of monetary policy. Monetarist influence gradually has brought central bankers and others around to a policy oriented toward the monetary aggregates. It is important to examine the reasons and implications.

First, emphasis on money (or its growth rate) does not mean that money affects the economy directly, rather than through interest rates, rates of return, and their impact on costs and asset values. Thus, if in a particular situation it should appear that nothing useful is to be achieved by changing these rates of interest, return, and capitalization, it is clear that, other things equal, nothing good is to be achieved by changing the money stock.

Second, the choice between an interest and a money-supply target can be shown to rest on the relative predictability of the real and financial sector. Random shocks to the real sector are best met with a stable money-supply policy that allows the interest rate to vary so as to soften the shock, while shocks to financial sector can be kept from affecting the real sector by a constant interest-rate policy [Poole (1970)]. The monetarist belief in the stability of the demand for money then lends support to a money-supply policy. However, the belief of at least some monetarists in the stability of the private sector, which after all makes up the great part of the real sector, actually could leave some doubt as to which sector monetarists regard as inherently more stable.

Third, the choice between an interest-rate and a money-supply target makes a great deal of *apparent* difference to the way central-bank policy *looks* during cyclical fluctuations. Since interest rates move procyclically, the endogenous forces of the economy will make the central bank look superficially right, even if it takes no action to change the money supply. Since the money supply also tends to move procyclically, the same endogenous forces under a money-supply target tend to make an inactive central bank look superficially bad.

Actually, it is a mistake to judge the central bank purely on whether it takes specific action or relies on endogenous forces to achieve its objective. A driver seeking to accelerate on a downgrade may take his foot off the gas and still find himself getting up speed. A central bank may find the restraint resulting from cyclically rising interest rates sufficient for its purposes. However, there is danger that the central bank may underestimate the extent of the rise in rates required to keep the money supply from accelerating. It may then be permitting excessive expansion by looking only at rising interest rates and not at the accelerating money supply.

The signals thrown off by interest rate and money growth, respectively, may often appear to be in conflict. Financial-market practitioners and monetarist economists are likely to describe in opposite terms a situation where interest rates rise while money growth accelerates, the first viewing the situation as one of "tightness," the second as one of "ease." Historically, the signals thrown off by the money supply have often been the right ones, as in 1968 and 1972. But in the first half of 1974, when interest rates signalled "tight" while the money supply had turned toward "easy," events half a year later showed that interest rates had prevailed over money supply. During the second half of 1974, when interest rates signalled "easy" and money supply "tight," the foundations actually were being laid for a bottoming out of the recession six to nine months later.

The central bank may lean toward an interest-rate target, or at least toward circumscribing a money-growth target with an interest constraint, because of concern about the side effects of wide rate fluctuations. The real meaning of a pure money-supply target is that it produces extreme variations in interest rates.

It is these extreme variations from which the special stablizing virtues claimed by monetarists for a stable money-supply policy must flow. The central bank may reasonably be skeptical of the effectiveness particularly of very low rates. In the light of the surrounding facts, the prospective gains in home construction, consumer durables purchases, inventory building, and business and plant and equipment spending may be quite moderate. Meanwhile the costs of extremely low—as well as of extremely high—rates may be severe in terms of large flows into and out of thrift institutions, international capital flows and exchange-rate movements, and increases in perceived market risks. These costs may provide good reason for the central bank to back away from a stable money-growth path such as monetarists might recommend. Of course so long as it does this, the monetarist case will never be fully tested, and the central bank can always be held responsible for whatever failures occur.

There is an objective test between an interest-rate target and a money-growth target: what happens if the wrong target is chosen and adhered to? A wrong interest-rate target will lead to expansion or contraction, which eventually will cause price increases or decreases. Whichever happens, the effect of persisting in the target will be cumulative. The gap between the targeted and the equilibrium interest rate will widen, the ultimate effect will be explosive. A wrongly set money-supply target does not carry this risk. It will lead to a reasonably stable rate of inflation or deflation, and will in this sense be superior to an interest-rate target.

Whether any of these features would have been sufficient to gain widespread acceptance for a money-supply target will always remain uncertain. The straw that broke the interest-rate camel's back was inflation. The real meaning of interest rates is distorted more severely by inflation than is that of the monetary aggregates. The real interest rate, at least the long-term rate, is not observable, resting as it does on expectations. Real balances are observable.

Relative Importance of Fiscal and Monetary Policy

The choice between interest rates and monetary aggregates as targets of policy, which determines the meaning of a "constant monetary policy," as discussed above, is decisive for assessing the relative power of monetary and fiscal policy. In the early Keynesian period, an unchanging interest rate was the obvious and unquestioned criterion of an unchanging monetary policy. That meant that fiscal expansion would automatically be financed by monetary expansion. For the ensuring rise in GNP, fiscal policy got all the credit, monetary policy got none.

A switch of the definition of "unchanging monetary policy" to a fixed stock of money changes this drastically. Fiscal expansion now raises interest rates. At some point the resulting restraint on private expenditures offsets the fiscal stimulus. After that, fiscal policy loses its power.

The net effect of fiscal expansion even in this framework is not zero. At higher interest rates, the demand for money diminishes and a larger nominal GNP can be accommodated with a given money supply. If downward flexibility of prices were admitted, a real GNP of any size could, of course, be accommodated with a given money supply. But on that assumption, it would have to be asked why prices had not fallen before fiscal stimulus was introduced, thereby returning the economy to full employment and making fiscal stimulation unnecessary. As in all discussions of stimulative fiscal or monetary policy, there is an implicit assumption that idle resources are available, in early Keynesian doctrine without perceptible limits.

A fixed money stock in a growing economy obviously is too extreme a definition of "constant monetary policy." A growth rate of the money stock equal to the real growth rate of the economy or, if there is a technologically determined uptrend in velocity, of the "effective money stock," seems more plausible. But except for the speed with which a fiscal stimulus would be stymied, this alternative definition would make no difference. Under a money-supply definition of "constant monetary policy," therefore, the allocation of responsibility for economic expansion following a fiscal stimulus remains uncertain. Monetarists are free to claim that, with a given expansion of the money supply, exactly the same economic expansion would occur with or without a fiscal stimulus. This reinterpretation raises questions, for instance, about the real effectiveness of the 1964 tax cut, which was indeed accompanied by accelerated money growth.

The relative strength of fiscal and monetary policy is affected also by the exchange-rate income. The shift to floating exchange rates has strengthened monetary policy relative to fiscal policy. In a fixed-rate setting with full mobility of capital, in fact, monetary policy becomes virtually powerless in a small country and loses part of its power even in a large country like the United States. Any effort to change the money supply and thereby interest rates is frustrated by international capital flows. Fiscal policy, of course, is powerful under these conditions because the interest-rate effects of expansive or contractive fiscal action are compensated by international flows.

In a floating-rate regime, the central bank is free to determine the money supply. Interest-rate movements will still be kept within narrow bounds by international capital flows. But these flows, instead of altering the money supply as under a fixed-rate regime, now alter the exchange rate. Monetary policy then becomes effective, not through the usual transmission mechanism running via rates of interest and return to investment spending, but via changes in the relative prices of domestic and foreign goods to the trade balance. Fiscal policy meanwhile loses effectiveness because its interest-rate effects cause capital and consequent exchange-rate movements whose impact on the trade balance offsets fiscal stimulus and restraint.

The floating regime introduced in 1973 has enhanced the relative power of monetary policy in still other ways. The main accretion of power to monetary policy has not come, indeed, from the ability of monetary policy to affect trade balances. In the normal course of events, this mechanism could become effective only with a substantial lag. But because capital mobility usually has been less than perfect, control over the money supply has meant a considerable degree of control over interest rates for most countries.

Expansion and Contraction

During the Keynesian years, it was generally agreed that monetary policy had some contractive power. Its critics often imputed to it a discontinuity: applied in moderation it would produce no results, because the economy was shielded against monetary pressure by its rich padding of liquidity. Vigorous application was said to threaten depression. Its expansionary powers were deemed to be minimal in an environment of high liquidity. (See the end of the first section above for the reason why this view is not inconsistent with a stable demand for money function if that function is sufficiently nonlinear.)

The historical shift from unemployment with stable prices through expectations of full employment and price stability to expectations of inflation has been accompanied by rising estimates of the powers of monetary policy. On the side of contraction, it now seems to be agreed that the scale of effects need not be discontinous. On both sides, contraction as well as expansion, the power of monetary policy has been enhanced by the effect of inflation. Interest rates in inflation can range over a much wider spectrum than during price stability, since real rates can become negative. Obviously this observation is not intended as an argument for inflation.

The question whether seeking expansion by means of monetary policy can ever be like ''pushing on a string'' is capable of several interpretations and answers. If it implies that very large amounts of money may be required in some conditions to produce small effects on interest rates, this has been true in conditions such as the 1930s but does not altogether deny ultimate effectiveness. The same applies if it is argued that under these conditions the lags may become very long. ''Pushing on a string'' might imply that the effects of monetary policy cannot usefully be pushed beyond the point where the marginal benefits diminish sharply while the marginal costs from capital- and exchange-market disruption mount. In this sense, the comment points to a pragmatic limitation on the useful range of monetary policy. Still another picture emerges, finally, if ''pushing on a string'' is interpreted to mean that the central bank finds it difficult to expand the money supply because banks receiving reserves use these to repay debt to the central bank, because recipients of currency and demand deposits convert these into time deposits, and because the banks, instead of adding to the economy's liquidity by lending to firms and households, monetize existing financial assets such as Treasury bills that are already highly liquid. Obviously the central bank can still increase the money supply even under these conditions. But the side effects from such a policy may soon outweight the benefits.

Real Interest Rates and Real Balances

Realized inflation separates the development of real balances from nominal balances; expected inflation separates real from nominal interest rates. The difference in the degree of observability has already been noted. Neither monetarists nor Keynesians have a monopoly on either concept. But as inflation mounted, monetarists were more successful in capitalizing on the emerging distinctions. Many Keynesians and their models were caught napping.

Keynesian doctrine always has had difficulties clearing itself of the charge of reliance on money illusion, whether the charge was levied in connection with involuntary unemployment or with the use of the Phillips Curve. The conclusion that in the long run the Phillips Curve is vertical, so that there can be no lasting trade-off between unemployment and inflation, is not an exclusive property of monetarists. But Keynesians, who have relied heavily on the Phillips Curve as the most important analytical device of the post-Keynesian era, have had much greater difficulty accepting its limitations. If to the vertical Phillips Curve there is added the tentative finding that the disturbances of high inflation reduce capacity utilization and raise unemployment, the long-run Phillips Curve acquires a tilt to the right and becomes positively sloping.

The choice between interest rates and money supply as standards of monetary policy, as already was noted, has been tilted by inflation in favor of the money supply. Real interest rates are not observable, real balances are; a wrongly set interest rate has explosive effects, a wrongly set nominal money-supply target has not. In these regards, inflation has lent strength to elements of analysis and policy that carry a monetarist tinge.

This does not mean that real balances have become a helpful or readily analyzable variable.

The simple monetarist prescription for a stable growth rate of the effective money supply (which allows for velocity trend) does not translate into a similar prescription for the real money supply. Expectations of inflation reduce the demand for real balances. An effort to maintain real balances may imply an increase in nominal balances at an explosive rate. That plainly has been the lesson of the big inflations of history. The observation frequently heard in the course of 1974 that real balances were falling while prices were accelerating was no proof that the supply of nominal money was falling short of the demand. Interest rates, which at the short-term end barely managed to keep up with the rate of inflation, are a better measure.

Most of the analysis linking money and income, moreover, has been done in terms of nominal income and nominal money supply. Deflating both by the same price index would not leave the correlations undisturbed, and there appears to be no well-established body of findings as to what the results would be.

International Developments

The shift to floating rates, itself a product largely of world inflation, has been another development lending strength to monetarists' views and policies. The preference for floating rates, while historically allied to monetarism through the person of Milton Friedman, has long been shared by many Keynesians. The simple Keynesian export-multiplier mechanism, however, requires fixed exchange rates—as well as unlimited international reserves and an accommodating money supply. Fixed exchange rates, moreover, as already noted, make fiscal policy effective and monetary policy ineffective under conditions of capital mobility, although that particular setting was scarcely envisaged by early Keynesian doctrine. Floating rates reversed that relation in favor of monetary policy. Under floating rates, the power of monetary policy did not come from its influence on interest rates—given capital mobility, there could be none—but through exchange-rate changes and the trade balance. More importantly for central bankers, however, floating rates restored their control over the money supply, which under fixed rates was severely impaired by the need to monetize balance-of-payments surpluses. Given imperfect mobility of capital, this was quite enough to return strength to monetary policy, and of course strength of the familiar kind—through interest rates and investment. But central bankers also have meanwhile discovered, of course, that the promised freedom of monetary policy from the shackles of the balance of payments continues only so long as the central bank is willing to ignore what its domestic policies do to exchange rates.

Inflation

It is inflation that has finally put monetarism in the saddle. Inflation has enhanced the relevance of the doctrine, brought some of its propositions into totally new focus, and discomfited Keynesians. This does not mean, of course, that monetarists are tolerant of inflation. The opposite is the case, for a variety of analytical, historical, and ideological reasons.

The monetarists' rejection of the Phillips Curve trade-off is one such reason. Acceptance of a natural rate of unemployment (which must be brought down by structural rather than demand-oriented policies) does not by itself, to be sure, imply a preference for zero inflation. There is still a cost attached to the achievement of stable prices. When unemployment is at its natural rate, inflation continues at a constant rate—that is the meaning of "natural rate." To bring inflation down, unemployment must rise above its natural rate temporarily, until the rate of wage increases has come down to equal productivity gains, so that prices can be stable. But the social cost of this temporary excess unemployment is less than believers in a negatively sloping Phillips Curve would expect. If a positively sloping long-term Phillips Curve can be validated, positive employment gains could be expected from price stability.

High rates of inflation also are seen to impose social costs comparable to those of unemployment, even though this view is not specifically monetarist, since it stresses the unpredictability of inflation. At high rates of inflation, the variance of the inflation rate increases and so, therefore, does the income uncertainty experienced by households. This is true even when aggregate real income is unchanged, so that the gains from inflation equal losses. With risk as a negative argument in the welfare function, this becomes a demonstrable proposition.[1]

Inflation damages the market system, to which monetarists attach major importance. This is the consequence not only of inadequate anticipation of inflation but of the fact also that even with correctly anticipated inflation the real income of many market participants takes the form, in part, of unrealized appreciation in the value of nonmonetary assets. This income generates no cash flow from which interest rates high enough to correctly reflect inflation can be paid, and therefore threatens these units, both homeowners and business firms, with bankruptcy.

The monetarists' predilection for the market system, in turn, seems to derive in the first place from a reading of the evidence that stresses the allocational deficiencies of the political process. More broadly, it seems to be based on a philosophical skepticism with regard to government which contrasts with the Keynesians' stress on government's role as the fiscal balance wheel of the economy and its function in remedying market imperfections.

Finally, the monetarists' view that inflation is a purely monetary phenomenon helps to explain their anti-inflation orientation. If money is the source of inflation, then inflation is easy to prevent by proper monetary policies and its occurrence therefore is the responsibility largely if not exclusively of the central bank. The responsibility placed on the central bank, to be sure, is of a peculiar sort. It arises, not necessarily from acts of commission, but also from the omission of any act that would have been required to maintain price-level stability in the face of outside impulses. The central bank is responsible for failure to maintain stability in the same sense that government can be responsible for any misfortune occurring anywhere within its domain to the extent that it had the technical means of preventing it. In monetarist doctrine the central bank seems to be held responsible for inflation also if, by allowing increases in the money supply, it merely validates pressures coming from other sources, such as excessive wage demands, or monopolistic pricing at home or abroad. In such instances, the central bank's powers may be a necessary condition of inflation, but not a sufficient one, much as possession of a gun may be the necessary but not sufficient cause of a fatal shooting. It has been very difficult for central banks to find grace in the eyes of monetarists, despite their common preference for stable prices.

The Future of Monetarism

If monetarism has drawn much of its strength from inflation, what will be the future of the doctrine if the advice of its proponents, directed as it is toward ending inflation, is accepted and proves successful?

Monetarism is vulnerable in many respects. For a long time, it has had the advantage of being mainly in opposition, of being a critic [Johnson (1971)]. Strategically, its position remains strong, because it is unlikely that monetarist advice of hewing to a stable rate of money growth month after month and perhaps week after week will ever be literally followed, and so long as it is not the monetarists can decline full responsibility. But such an extreme version of monetarism lacks plausibility. Monetarism will be tested and will have to take responsibility for the consequences, including the adverse side effects that central bankers fear.

Monetarism has obvious analytical weaknesses. The close relation between money and income that it deduces from historical experience is the result of a two-way relationship, the chain of causation running from income to money as well as from money to income. If the central bank breaks the causal chain running from income to money, thereby making money exogenous, will the relationship of the two still remain close? Or might there be, particularly at cyclical turning points, a parting of the ways? In the background there always lurks the concern that excessive reliance on monetarist prescriptions might some day land us in a new depression.

There are doubts also about technical matters, such as the choice among monetary aggregates, the claim that lags are long but variable, the role of nonmonetary influences. The difference between real and nominal money balances is troublesome. These are problems that only further experience and research can resolve.

Problems exist also about value judgments. Monetarism is not strongly concerned about some of the side effects of its prescriptions. It relies heavily on the belief that short-run costs may have to be accepted for the sake of long-run gains.

Finally, monetarism may find some elements of future evolution difficult to take in stride. One such development is the move toward an electronic payments system. If technology makes the holdings of demand deposits largely unnecessary, the usefulness of M_1 certainly will suffer. Past experience may provide little guidance as to the relationship between income and the kind of balances or overdraft facilities that may exist in an electronic payments system. Conceivably, interest rates could regain their importance as a target relative to the money stock.

A second and quite unrelated development might occur in the international sphere, if the world economy becomes more integrated. The present tolerance for wide exchange-rate movements might then diminish, as it already has within the EEC. Coordination of interest-rate policies might become desirable as a means of averting large international flows with their attendant changes in exchange rates. This would interfere with the use of pure money-supply targets.

These are long-run possibilities. It has been part of the strength of monetarism that it has always looked to the long run, believing that if fundamentals are right, the short runs will take care of themselves. This was not the view of Keynes, who argued that in the long run we are all dead. The fact is that the number of people alive in the long run keeps increasing. It is true that the long run is nothing but a succession of short runs. But it is true also that the measures taken to deal with short-run emergencies can accrue severe long-run costs. Monetarism, by stressing this fact, has helped to restore a better balance between short- and long-run objectives.

Note

1. For a sample containing pooled cross section-time series data for forty-three countries covering the period 1956–1965, the variance of inflation was shown to be a significantly positive function of the level of inflation. For a time series of U.S. data, employing the seasonally adjusted consumer price index for the years 1948–1974, the same results were obtained. Likewise, the coefficient of variation was a significantly positive function of the level of variation. I am indebted to my wife for supplying the first result and to Robert Dugger for the second and third.

References

Johnson, H.G., 1971. The Keynesian Revolution and the Monetarist Counter-Revolution, *American Economic Review,* May, pp. 1–14.

Poole, W., 1970. Optimal Choice of Monetary Policy Instruments in a Simple Stochastic Macro Model. *Quarterly Journal of Economics,* May, pp. 197–217.

Stein, J., 1976. Inside the Monetarist Black Box, in: J. Stein, ed., *Monetarism* (North-Holland, Amsterdam).

Part VIII
Political Economy

40 Consumers and Producers in America

In our free-enterprise country, the consumer is king. That is elementary. A business will prosper if it can produce a better mousetrap that the consumer wants. It will have to go out of business if it insists on turning out goods that the consumer does not want, or if it just cannot compete. We do not allow the government to make decisions as to what is to be produced and consumed, give or take a few qualifications. The consumer, by casting dollar votes in a free market, makes those decisions. That is what a free-enterprise, market economy is all about. That is why the United States has achieved such a high standard of living.

Thus far the textbook. How about the reality? The consumer, or at least consumer advocates, today are indeed in the saddle. But the consumer occupies this rightful role not only by virtue of competition for his dollar, but through government mandates laid on producers. These mandates are far-ranging. They run from rules concerning what is to be produced, how it is to be produced, and on what terms and conditions it can be sold, to regulations affecting the supply of essentials, such as energy, and further to the tax system, which determines how much the businessman will have left over to invest and, therefore, how efficiently he will be able to produce. In large part, the thrust of these laws and regulations is to improve the lot of the consumer at greater or lesser expense to the producer. Today, their ultimate consequence is becoming obvious to all: Producers cease to be efficient, their costs go up, the consumer pays more, and our standard of living has almost ceased to rise.

The fundamental truth is, of course, that the consumer cannot live without the producer. In fact, most consumers are also producers, as businessmen, workers, farmers, and in every other endeavor. The notion, therefore, that the consumer should be protected against the producer is prima facie open to logical challenge. The law, and even the language of the law, seems to ignore this obvious fact. In regulatory language today, hundreds of pages of which sometimes come to the Federal Reserve Board for approval in a single week, the word *consumer* is used where in the past one would have said people, or individuals, or Americans, or men and women. The law wants us to be a nation of consumers, in confrontation, it seems, with our enemy the producer.

To document this it is useful first to go over some of the most serious

---

This chapter was originally published in *Tax Review,* August 1979, pp. 25–28. It is the text of a speech made at a meeting sponsored by Westminster College, The Chamber of Commerce, and The Rotary Club in Salt Lake City, Utah, on April 24, 1979.

instances where national policy and legislation pit consumer against producer and then to review some of the consequences, which are already becoming only too apparent.

First, there are the transfer expenditures in the federal budget, which as a percent of GNP have risen from 5 percent through most of the 1960s to almost 10 percent for fiscal year 1978. Not all these transfer payments, to be sure, are pure gifts from producers to nonproducers. To the extent that people paid Social Security taxes, and interest was accumulated thereon, they are merely getting their own money back as they would from a life-insurance company. But, of course, Social Security benefits far exceed these amounts, being essentially financed by taxes on the working population to support the retired population. Unemployment compensation, welfare benefits, and a variety of other intrinsically meritorious but nevertheless expensive programs swell the transfers from producers to nonproducers.

The tax system is set up to favor the consumer at the expense of the producer. At the corporate level, taxes are levied on profits that the Department of Commerce does not classify as true profits. During the past year some 36 percent of reported profits after tax resulted from underdepreciation and from inflationary inventory appreciation. These do not add to a company's ability to pay taxes or dividends, or to make new investments. Because taxes must be paid on such phantom profits, less is left for corporate reinvestment and for dividends out of which new investments might be made by individuals. In addition, the double taxation of dividends—once as income to the corporation, and again as income to the stockholder—cuts down a type of income that has a high probability of being reinvested.

At the level of the individual taxpayer, we have a steeply progressive income tax that is bound to work as a disincentive even for income earners in relatively modest income brackets. On the other hand, we do not tax Social Security income, making it more attractive to retire. At the upper end of the income scale, we distinguish between earned and "unearned" income. On earned income there is a cap of 50 percent, on so-called unearned income the tax reaches as high as 70 percent, not taking into account state, local, and capital-gains taxes as applicable. Unearned income is the income from investments that were taxed once before when the taxpayer saved the money and made it available as capital to the economy by investing it. For a society that would like to raise its productivity, this is the most useful type of income and it gets the worst treatment in our tax system.

The capital-gains tax is another instance of antiproducer taxation. It is aimed directly at the enterprise and risk taking that is needed in an economy where investment decisions are made by individuals and not by the state. Today, when inflation has doubled prices since 1968 and quadrupled them since 1943, much of what the tax collector calls capital gains is simply the result of asset prices keeping up, more or less, with inflation. In the stock market, as we know, prices have kept up with inflation less rather than more. The capital-gains tax, therefore, is in large part simply a tax on capital, not on gains. Either way, of course, it penalizes the successful producer. Capital that is employed essentially in consumption, as in owner-occupied homes, receives preferred treatment through roll-overs and lifetime exemptions.

A third area in which the consumer is favored at the expense of the producer is in the treatment of savings. This discriminatory treatment is effectuated through government regulation and through the tax system, which does not allow adjustments for inflation. It is difficult enough, in a country of rising taxes, rising inflation, and diminishing growth, to make ends meet. It is more difficult, under these conditions, to hold expenditures below income to put aside regular amounts. What is most difficult of all, today, is to preserve the real value of what has been saved.

Unlike practices in some other countries, in the United States the saver gets no special tax advantages. At most, savers who happen to be debtors can look on the deductibility for income-tax purposes of the interest paid as a form of subsidy to saving, since debt repayment is a form of saving. The mechanism of the subsidy, which, of course, is quite unintended by the legislator, works as follows. At today's high rate of inflation, the interest rate contains a sizable inflation premium. In an economic sense, this can be thought of as a form of repayment of capital. The value of the principal of the debt diminishes through inflation, while the debtor compensates the lender by paying him the inflation premium. Tax deductibility of the full nominal interest rate, including the inflation premium, can, therefore, be viewed as a special aid to saving. But in order to get this subsidy to saving, the consumer must first have borrowed. All the forces of inflation and taxation work against those not in debt. Essentially it is consumption on credit, rather than net saving, that is supported in this way. On balance, tax deductibility of interest on housing and consumer credit turns out to be simply one more of many devices favoring the consumer against the saver.

The net saver, on the other hand, is really hurt by the same tax mechanism. The interest that the saver receives usually contains some compensation for inflation, even though inadequate in many instances. This premium is not income in an economic sense, any more than are insurance benefits paid for losses from accidents or fire. The latter, naturally, are not treated as taxable income. The inflation premium, whose function it is to make up for the damage from inflation, is taxable. Money is the only depreciating asset on which even a business user cannot charge depreciation.

Unless the saver is well-to-do or even wealthy, moreover, worse treatment looms. Savings or time deposits are the natural investment medium for a small saver. Interest rates on all such deposits below $100,000 are subject to ceilings under Regulation Q of the Federal Reserve and other federal regulators. Passbook savings at commercial banks are limited to 5 percent; time deposits for various periods are capped at somewhat higher rates. All these rates are below market rates and have been for some time, with the exception of the recently introduced six-month money-market certificates, which have been snapped up by many savers who could put up the minimum of $10,000. The plight of the small saver has come very much to the forefront in recent weeks and is under intensive study by government agencies. It urgently calls for redress.

Another area in which the saver encounters adversity is the stock market. I have already commented on the depressive effects of the capital-gains tax, the double taxation of dividends, and the taxation of phantom profits in times of inflation. These factors combine with high government-mandated costs for health, safety, and environmental purposes in reducing the attractiveness of American equities. Pension-fund regulation makes it difficult for investment managers to buy stock, particularly in small and new businesses, and contributes to the dismal experience the savers who invested in common stocks have had over many years. Financial success, in recent years, has been limited largely to those who purchased homes, usually by incurring debt rather than by using savings.

The adverse treatment and experience of the saver in the American economy must properly be viewed as part of our general tendency to penalize the producer and favor the consumer. Without saving, production is bound to suffer. To grow, the economy needs investment. To invest, there must be savings. The United States has become a low-saving country, compared to other nations. The personal-saving rate in the United States is in the range of 5 percent of disposable personal income. This compares with about 14 percent in Germany and 24 percent in Japan. Accordingly, investment and growth in those countries historically have been on a much larger scale than in our own country. Savers are, in fact, among the most important producers, since they produce capital. Their neglect, to the benefit of the consumer, is part of the syndrome of favoring consumption at the expense of production.

Government regulations of a wide variety have also tilted the balance between consumption and production. These regulations are of many entirely different sorts. It is only their common denominator—less production—that is the same.

Many regulations, needless to say, pursue and sometimes achieve good objectives including monetary savings. Thanks to environmental investments imposed on business, we breathe cleaner air and enjoy cleaner water, and, as a result, may have less illness and lower expenditures for medical care. Workers are safer on the job and drivers are safer in traffic, provided we do not allow the greater safety of seat belts and so on to lure us into more risky driving. But the costs are undeniable. The annual compliance costs of energy and environmental regulation imposed on industry have been estimated at $7.8 billion. For consumer health and safety, the analogous costs have been estimated at $5.1 billion. The additional cost of safety features in automobiles have been estimated at $666 per car. Confronted with such numbers, one is bound to wonder whether the consumers appreciate what they get, and where they bear measurable cost, whether they consider it worthwhile.

Regulation proliferates rapidly in many other areas, including the financial, which I have an opportunity to observe and participate in at close quarters. Its purpose usually is to protect the consumer against the producer, although in many cases it also deals with issues of producer versus producer and among competitors. Sometimes it is the public interest in a broader sense that regulation seeks to protect. Usually it is difficult to quarrel with the objective. The problem is with the unintended side effects.

Sometimes these side effects simply imply higher costs. Sometimes, however, there are unintended anticompetitive effects. It is particularly small businessmen, the small bankers, who are hard hit. They cannot personally keep up with the flood of regulation and often cannot afford in-house legal talent. A large firm or large bank, with a specialized staff, obtains a competitive advantage.

A few days ago, *The Washington Post* ran an editorial entitled ''Regulation, Regulation, Regulation,'' in which they took to task the Congress and the Federal Reserve Board for producing 3,000 pages of interpretations and explanations on one single regulation, dealing with the Truth in Lending legislation. Few regulations had a better purpose, and few have ended up creating so much difficulty for bankers and other lenders. Not long ago a banker told me that he could not spend time with customers any more because he was so busy studying Federal Reserve regulations. Sine he can be sued and penalized for failing to obey them, he is probably making a wise allocation of his time. But it is not clear that the customer gains.

In Washington, there exists a built-in momentum of regulatory activity that is a cause for deep concern. The government, through all its labyrinthine channels, is geared up to produce regulation the way Detroit produces automobiles. Many thousands of people in Washington, dedicated and sincere, have assigned to them the job of turning out more regulations. They cannot go home at night with a sense of a job well done if they have not turned out some more regulation. Many people's careers, in Congress and in the agencies, depend on their success in accomplishing more regulation. Their families' livelihood depends on more regulation being written. This way, the supply of new regulations becomes independent of the need for it.

The final result of antiproducer orientation of the U.S. economy is to be read in the productivity statistics. Historically, productivity, that is, output per work hour, has grown at 2–3 percent, on the average, over many decades. Since the late 1960s, there has been a dramatic slowdown. The Council of Economic Advisers estimates annual productivity gains over the past five years at less than 1 percent, down by one-half if not by more. Consumers' real per-capita income and living standards accordingly have stagnated. Much of this slowdown must be attributed to regulation, although the tax system and other factors also have contributed. The effort to benefit the consumer has turned against itself.

Low productivity has contributed to inflation. Because wage earners have been accustomed to good annual gains in the past, gains which the economy can now no longer provide, they have sought to overcome the slowdown of income gains by escalating their demands. They have only escalated inflation, and inflation, by hurting saving and investment, has further reduced productivity.

The value of our currency has declined in consequence. Compared to D-mark and yen, the dollar is worth roughly one-half of what it used to be. The United States has an enormous trade deficit while Germany and Japan have large surpluses. We are being outproduced and outsold around the world, as our nation of consumers vainly tries to compete with these nations of producers.

What is to be done? To continue along the present path will bring continuing dissatisfaction at home and diminishing strength abroad. As we become poorer in relation to others, our influence and our ability to defend ourselves diminish. We need a new orientation.

1. We need to restore a better balance in the relative role of producer and consumer. We must stop taking production for granted, like rain from heaven that falls alike on the just and the unjust. The consumer cannot flourish when the producer cannot perform.

2. We need to review our tax system. The corporate tax, the capital-gains tax, the treatment of so-called unearned income must reflect the need for greater saving, investment, and productivity. Particularly during a period of inflation, the anti-production effects of these taxes need to be corrected.

3. The saver must be given a better break, especially the small saver. The present imbalance in our regulatory and tax framework, which favors debt and penalizes thrift, must be recognized as part of the antiproduction syndrome.

4. The institutionalized outpouring of regulation needs to be restrained. Whether this overpowering proliferation of government activity is consistent with a free society may be debatable, but it certainly is not consistent with a productive society.

In a free society, it takes time for people to realize that government is encroaching. In a totalitarian society, people naturally are much more conscious of encroachments. I had never believed that I would find myself appealing to the authority of the late Chairman Mao Tse Tung, but his thought ''The struggle against corruption, waste, and bureaucracy should be stressed as much as the struggle to suppress counter-revolutionaries'' has a ring of political wisdom about it. As Jefferson put it many years earlier, ''The natural progress of things is for liberty to yield and government to gain ground.'' Very different points of view lead to the same conclusion on this subject.

Economics and Ideology—A Three-Dimensional View

Some forty years ago, two young professors at Columbia University in New York wrote a book that has proved increasingly instructive as time has gone by. In *The Modern Corporation and Private Property,* A.A. Berle and Gardiner C. Means showed that control of the means of production had become largely separated from ownership. Large corporations, they found, were run in the main by managers who had become independent of the stockholders. Berle and Means thought that they had discovered a fact that raised questions about the validity of U.S. capitalism. What they had, in fact, done was to establish the fruitful principle that ownership and control are two separate economic dimensions, and that the old habit of lumping them both under the generic term "capitalism" produced nothing but confusion.

Today, private ownership is under attack from many quarters. Not only economists, but a wide spectrum of U.S. public opinion would like to see a reduction in the inequality of income which is the result, in part, of property income. Concern with the poor, criticism of income-tax loopholes, and opposition to high interest rates all manifest an antiwealth sentiment. There clearly is a desire to decrease the effects of private property on the distribution of income.

At the same time, there is continuing belief in the merits of the free market as the chief means of organizing and directing economic activity. Economists studying the behavior of the economy find that consumers and enterprises are highly responsive to economic incentives, especially to prices. While, in earlier years, they believed that rather simple cause-and-effect sequences determined events, they now observe more sophisticated reactions. Businessmen do not invest money because they happen to have made a profit, but because a nice comparison of interest costs and rates of return shows that it is profitable. Consumers do not spend some fixed fraction of what they earn; they form a long-range view of their income prospects and base spending and saving on it. Workers do not make wage demands simply in the light of employment conditions, but form expectations concerning the future cost of living and act accordingly. Economic relationships, as economists analyze them and embody them in their econometric models, are seen to be increasingly behavioral instead of mechanical. Such complexities have not diminished, but rather have en-

---

This chapter was coauthored by Mable I. Wallich and was originally published in: *Economic Impact* no. 8 (Washington, D.C.: U.S. Information Agency, 1974): 58–61.

hanced, the role attributed to markets and to the prices that are formed in these markets.

Markets and prices, in this view, are a means of control. The economy is guided not by some central agency or plan but by the decentralized system of markets and prices. By responding to prices, producers and consumers decide what is to be produced and consumed.

This form of control has nothing to do with who owns the factories and stores through which the goods flow. They could be owned by large numbers of shareholders. They could be owned by the government. The owners might control the producing units in varying degree, in the sense of supervising and conducting their operations. But, in a more basic sense, it is the price system—not the owners—which does the controlling. The ultimate decision about what is to be produced, which is the essence of economic life, cannot be made by the owners, whoever they are, so long as an economy operates in a market system.

Economic decisions can also be made, of course, by central planning. This system does not require markets, since it can set prices according to other principles such as cost or social priorities. Central planning can function also, if need be, without the use of explicit prices. It can limit itself to determining the amounts that are to be produced and consumed. Central planning, therefore, is the true opposite pole of a market system. But both are forms of control.

The term "capitalism," then, is seen to be applied, in common usage, to two quite different economic functions: the function of ownership, and the function of decision making. Since various combinations of the two functions are conceivable and do indeed exist, the term is unspecific and ill-designed to describe economic reality. There is no unambiguous system of "capitalism." The word could denote ownership with control, ownership without control, or control without ownership. It could be interpreted even as a system of production employing capital but, since capital is used by every advanced economic system known to man, this use would be even more nebulous.

Adding a Third Dimension

These considerations illustrate two of the great dimensions along which man has organized his socioeconomic existence. The first has to do with decision making. Its extreme poles are complete decentralization through free markets and small-scale government units at one end, and complete centralization of planning and control at the other. The second dimension relates to ownership. It runs the gamut from full private to full public ownership, including not only the means of production, but also durable consumer goods. To these two dimensions must be added a third, relating to political control: democracy and individual freedom at one extreme, and authoritarian government at the other.

The dimensions of socioeconomic organizations interrelate in numerous ways. Some relationships are complicated by the intrusion of ideology. In order to enlist support, proponents of some particular form of organization often try to demonstrate that it is necessarily closely tied to another. The identification of decision making through free markets with the system of private property is one such instance; here, typically, the defenders of private property, feeling somewhat on the defensive, seek to buttress their case by claiming that it is an essential condition of democracy and decentralized decision making, which many people favor. It is useful to take a look at some of the combinations that history has in fact produced.

Examples of countries that have combined democracy, a market system, and private ownership of the means of production are, of course, very frequent. Most of the developed countries of the West can be counted in this category. Some of them, however, may be in a process of change. In Western Europe, for instance, various countries have reduced the degree of private ownership. Some countries have reduced the degree of market orientation, substituting a usually mild degree of central planning.

Examples of countries with predominantly private ownership and a high degree of central planning, accompanied by an authoritarian form of government, also have been known. Germany under Hitler represented an extreme case of this form of organization. Under that regime, the market was largely stripped of its functions, economic as well as political, control passing to the government, while private ownership remained unimpaired.

Another quite different combination that is frequently observed involves central planning and authoritarian government but public ownership. This is the situation in most of the socialist countries of Eastern Europe. In a few instances, however, some degree of market-oriented decision making has been introduced. In Yugoslavia, for instance, the market system has been employed in major sectors of the economy. Plants owned and managed by workers operate in a decentralized environment comparable, in some respects, to that of western countries.

Examples of authoritarian government combined with private ownership and a system of relatively free markets can be found in some of the developing countries of Latin America and Africa. It is clear, of course, that these markets usually are free in the sense of an absence of effective control, rather than in the sense of an absence of market imperfections. In short, of the eight combinations of the three dimensions that are theoretically conceivable, the world's passing scene allows us to observe quite a few in actual or historical operation.

Skepticism Is Helpful

The big question is: To what extent are any of these combinations typical, perhaps unavoidable? Given that there are so many, the astute observer will be reluctant to accept the claim that any one combination is indeed essential. This wholesome skepticism will be helpful in examining conflicting claims. Perhaps the claim most persistently made, already referred to, is that of the necessary unity of democracy, the market system, and private property. It rests on the assumption that individuals conducting their economic affairs in a system of free markets will tend to acquire property, that these assets will, in turn, favor the development of the economy, and that the entire process is aided by a democratic government. The democratic form of government, in turn, is believed to draw strength from the fact that economic power is diffused. This diffusion of economic power rests on the division of assets into a large number of individual holdings.

This analysis does not lack a certain degree of persuasiveness. Nevertheless, there is nothing about it that is absolutely compelling. As Berle and Means have pointed out, the nexus between decision making and private property can wear thin with time. Owners may cease to control, ownership may pass to government, yet the enterprises continue to be administered in ways entirely consistent with free markets. This is a decision which each nation can determine in one way or another.

A theory exists which holds that, as the economy grows, individual enterprises will come to be excessively large and will lose all identification with stockholders—and, in that condition, it will be easy for government to take them over. Indeed, it is often argued, government will have to do so, because enterprises of great size become a threat to democratic government itself. This theory has been heard for many decades. Evidence of a trend of events in the directions it indicates, however, is largely lacking. In the United States, enterprises have grown larger—but not significantly larger in relation to the size of the economy. Nor have they grown in relation to the government itself, if the size of the government is measured by its budget. Neither does the federal government seem to have felt much inclination to acquire enterprises from private owners or to start new ones in competition with the private sector. Moves toward public ownership, at the federal or other levels, have originated mainly in the need to deal with bankrupt private institutions such as subways and railroads. The symbiosis of free markets, private ownership, and democratic government seems to have functioned reasonably well.

On the other hand, there is no compelling reason to think that this combination is immutable. While it does not seem likely, the possibility could be envisaged that the government might acquire a much stronger role in planning and guiding the economy, with a corresponding reduction in the role of markets. During the 1930s, trends in that direction seemed to get under way in the United States, but were reversed later. It has been argued that a growing dominance of the government over the economy must lead to an end of democracy itself. But, so far, there is no historical evidence that it must be so. Countries such as the United Kingdom and Sweden have gone quite far at times in a direction of central planning. This does not seem to have raised a serious question about the continuance of their democratic institutions.

An alternative theory, whose origin is on the left rather than on the right, holds that there is a natural affinity between private ownership of the means of production and an authoritarian government. This combination must come about, it is argued, because, in the normal evolution of society, private ownership finds itself increasingly threatened. The final recourse of the wealthy, then, is to establish a repressive government that protects their interests. The classical example frequently cited is that of fascism during the 1930s.

Historical research has produced mixed evidence concerning this interpretation of the German and Italian fascist regimes. They seem to have had many more roots than those that can be traced to the interests of their wealthy supporters. Also, after the advent of those regimes first gave support to the theory, very little more happened during the following forty years to strengthen it.

The effort to identify capitalism with a right-wing dictatorship is matched, at the other end of the political spectrum, by the identification, under the name of socialism, of public ownership, centralized planning, and an authoritarian government. It is evident that the term "socialism" is just as undescriptive as is "capitalism." Does socialism connote the form in which the means of production are owned? Does it refer to the form in which economic decisions are made? These two dimensions, as was discovered by Berle and Means, are separable in the case of capitalism; the same presumably applies in the case of socialism. The additional assumption that these conditions will be accompanied by an authoritarian government is also gratuitous. It is derived from the pattern set by some of the Eastern European countries, but western dread that a move along any one of these dimensions must necessarily mean a move in the other two has as yet received no historical verification.

Other Questionable Associations

These misleading associations, dictated by ideology, can be matched by examples of other associations that are equally questionable. Typical are some supposed cause-and-effect sequences that are attributed to the social organization of countries when, in all probability, they reflect quite different causal factors. One such set of misconceptions, of particular interest to developing countries, has to do with the causes of economic growth. In the United States, there is a tendency to attribute the high standard of living to the special virtues of the U.S. economy—free markets, unhampered private enterprise, a large flow of saving, the absence of central planning and of government interference. The fact is that the growth rate of the U.S. economy has not been particularly high. The U.S. economy is rich because it has grown for a very long time at a moderate but fairly stable rate. Free markets, private enterprise, and a democratic system of government no doubt have contributed to this but have not been totally responsible for it.

A similarly questionable association is constructed by those who attribute the rapid growth rate of the economy of the Soviet Union to the system of centralized economic planning practiced there. The Soviet economy has indeed grown at a faster rate than that of the United States. But an examination of the growth rates of a larger number of countries does not support the belief that central planning was responsible for rapid Soviet growth. The most outstanding case of economic growth has been that of Japan, which has had neither a completely market-oriented economy nor a centrally planned one. From this point of view, Japanese experience casts doubts on ideological assertions concerning both the United States and the Soviet Union. Japan's outstanding strength has been the high rate of saving in her economy, in some years reaching 40 percent of gross national product (GNP). An examination of other countries suggests strongly that it is the rate of saving and investment that determines economic growth. In the United States the rate of saving, equal to about 17 percent of GNP, has been quite low in comparison with the rates in other industrial countries. In the Soviet Union, the rate of saving probably has been above 30 percent, but the level of saving is not necessarily the result of centralized planning. In the United Kingdom, for instance, a moderate degree of planning has been unable to raise the rate of saving, and low British savings have held down the rate of growth. In Japan, saving has been high because of what appeared to be a natural propensity to save on the part of consumers and business. In the Soviet Union, saving has been high because an authoritarian government can control the level of consumption. Here is another case where an ideological interpretation of economic events leads to the wrong conclusions.

A last instance of this kind concerns the belief that ownership of the means of production is somehow the essence of the matter when it comes to evaluating and comparing forms of socioeconomic organization. In the United States, certainly, the role of private property as a determinant of income distribution is in retreat. The means of production, in the sense of business assets, in 1967 amounted to only 41 percent of total national wealth, as against 46 percent in 1929. The share of durable consumer goods, including all forms of housing, had reached 37 percent against 31 percent in 1929. The distribution of ownership, both of homes and of common stocks, is spreading.

No one can demonstrate that any one of the great dimensions of socioeconomic organization is more important than the others. This remains a matter of the preferences of individuals and nations. Certainly, there will be no agreement as to what location along any one spectrum is to be preferred. The best that can be done is to be careful and precise about defining the differences and to avoid assigning to them implications and consequences that they do not possess.

42 The Case for Social Responsibility of Corporations

Views about social responsibility of corporations have deep roots. The widespread belief that corporations have a special responsibility to society draws nourishment from the assertion that corporations are creatures of the state, originally created by act of the sovereign. The other side, which views corporations as instruments simply of their stockholders, rests its case on the origin of the corporation in contract. The acts of the state connected with incorporation have become routine, the powers expressed in charters are very broad, and owners choose between conducting their business in the form of a corporation or a partnership depending largely on tax considerations and the advantages of limited liability. The very term "corporation" is no longer descriptive of the uncorporeal shell that is being brought into the world, in contrast to the much apter Spanish term "*sociedad anónima*."

The ideological fronts are curiously inverted on this issue. The conservative side, usually willing to pay tribute to tradition and history, here leans on the abstract reasoning of the law of contract. The liberal side, usually no great admirer of the paraphernalia of the past, acknowledges a line of reasoning that has strong historical overtones. I shall try to steer clear of both approaches, and base my case for the social responsibility of corporations on what seem to be functional considerations. Specifically, I shall argue that this case is supported by:

1. The analysis of the relationship between goals and instruments;
2. the theory of decision making under uncertainty;
3. the diversification prevailing in the portfolios of most stockholders, which makes stockholders' interest broader than their interest in any one corporation;
4. the continuing character of unregulated corporations today, which are no longer identified with the life cycle of any one product, but seek to become ongoing entities by updating their product mix; and
5. possible advantages accruing to corporations, to their executives and stockholders, and perhaps to society, from carrying out social programs efficiently and financing them by raising prices, that is, with the equivalent of a sales tax, as contrasted with similar programs conducted inefficiently by a centralized bureaucracy and financed with progressive income taxes.

This chapter was a debate with Henry G. Manne and was originally published in: *The Modern Corporation and Social Responsibility* (Washington, D.C.: American Enterprise Institute for Public Policy Research, 1972), pp. 37–62.

Today the issue is sharpening. pressure on the environment and the demand for social betterment widens the area of economic policy where the market, at least as presently constituted, is not obviously the best solution. Some would say that for some of these objectives the market is a totally inappropriate solution. On the other hand, the use of the market as a guidance mechanism seems to encounter somewhat less ideological opposition, as indicated by the experience of socialist countries. Likewise, there seems to be a mounting receptivity to the use of public corporations as means of protecting certain business-type operations of governments, for instance the post office, against the antieconomic effects of the political process.

In any event, the issue is not whether the private corporation can or cannot legitimately be required by society to perform certain functions. In an age when the corporate income-tax rate is 48 percent, it should be obvious that society can make corporations do anything it wants. The incidental fact that nobody knows, and nobody seems urgently interested to discover, who really pays these corporate taxes—stockholders, consumers, or workers—throws a peculiar light on efforts to be extremely precise about the rights and obligations of corporations in other respects. It is worth noting at this point that, thanks to the corporate tax and to the deductibility of charitable contributions (up to 5 percent of income) even when unrelated to business expenses, it is cheaper for the taxpayer to meet such "responsibilities" from corporate pretax income than from dividend income. This happens to be a peculiarity of the American tax system. It does not bear on the broader issue of corporate responsibility but it cannot be ignored as a practical consideration.

The Meaning of Corporate Responsibility

Corporations today are being asked to do a host of things. They are to turn out useful products, at a reasonable price, that give reliable service, do not damage the environment, and are easy to dispose of. In producing these goods and services, corporations are to treat their workers well, avoid discrimination, avoid pollution, conserve resources, pay taxes, and observe a variety of laws covering these and other matters. They are to contribute to society's goals in areas outside or only marginally related to their own business, such as education, urban renewal, and good government. In what sense, and under what conditions, can these inherently desirable objectives be considered "corporate responsibilities," and who or what makes them so?

I take "responsibility" to mean a condition in which the corporation is at least in some measure a free agent. To the extent that any of the foregoing social objectives are imposed on the corporation by law, the corporation exercises no responsibility when it implements them. Even so, compliance with the law can be generous or niggardly; there are borderlines and grey areas where the corporation can make decisions and exercise responsibility.

In the areas of production, of relations with labor, suppliers, and customers, the corporation is under the control of the market. In a fundamental sense, it cannot freely determine the kind of product customers are to buy, or its price, or the wages to be paid. Again, there are ranges of discretion. The larger the corporation, the greater its freedom to vary product, price, and wages. Opinions differ as to the extent to which a corporation, by advertising, can condition its customers and achieve acceptance of socially undesirable products. Nevertheless, it seems clear, for instance, that an advanced-type car that met maximum safety and antipollution standards would not be a commercial success if it had to be sold in competition with ordinary cars at a price covering the extra costs. Neither could a corporation obtain labor at wage rates substantially below what other firms in the same industry are paying.

It is frequently said that power implies responsibility. It is then concluded that, because corporations are supposed to have great power, they must be held accountable in a very far-reaching sense. It is true, of course, that corporations take actions that influence large numbers of people decisively. These actions, however, do not imply a commensurate use of power. Assuming the corporation wants to stay in business, its action is severely constrained by the law and by the market. Power exists only at the margin.

Three basic activities seem to be involved in the exercise of corporate responsibility:

1. The setting of objectives,
2. the decision whether or not to pursue given objectives, and
3. the financing of these objectives.

For instance, the government may set a specific objective, offer a reward to corporations pursuing it, and leave it up to the corporation to accept the offer or not. This is exemplified by a government decision to increase the rate of growth or the competitiveness of American industry by means of an investment tax credit. The responsibility of the corporation, in accepting or rejecting, is a fairly narrow one. Alternatively, the government may establish some kind of tax preference for a much broader objective, say, research and development. In that case, the corporation not only decides on acceptance or rejection of the offer, but also chooses the goal of the research. It exercises a much wider responsibility. In either case, however, the financing comes from the government. As a third possibility, the corporation may freely decide to pursue some social purpose, and do so out of its own resources. It is in this area that most people find the core of responsible corporate action.

This enumeration shows that, in relation to the full range of corporate activities, the exercise of this kind of responsibility has fairly narrow limits. It shows also that, where there is a strong consensus that corporations should engage in certain activities, the most straightforward procedure is either to require them to do so by law, or to induce them through compensation, be it in the form of tax subsidies or penalties, or of an outside government contract. Corporate responsibilities that have not been backed by law or financial inducements may lack the support of a broad consensus, either as to the desirability of a goal or the moral obligation of corporations to pursue it.

To act in compliance with a law or in response to financing offered by government does not downgrade the importance of the action. On the contrary, the absence of a wide range of discretion and hence responsibility for the corporation is likely to be an index of the importance that society attaches to the activity. Government's decision to delegate the function to a corporation simply implies that the corporation appears to be the most appropriate instrumentality.

The corporation may have a comparative advantage in carrying out the activity, as contrasted with the government itself or some other agency, as for instance in on-the-job training. It may be the only candidate, as in building safety devices into products. Corporate intervention may be preferable on grounds of decentralization, of more economic or less political operation. Nevertheless, important as these activities may be, and desirable as the employment of corporations as instrumentalities of the government may be, I would not regard this range of activities as falling under the general heading of "corporate responsibility."

Areas of Responsibility

In order to give concreteness to the argument, it may be helpful to draw up a list of some of the major areas in which corporations are exercising responsibility or in which social critics have held them to have responsibilities. Obviously such a list is bound to be incomplete, and to contain activities of widely varying importance, both to the corporation and to society. Among these areas of responsibility are:

1. Efficiency in the use of resources,
2. adequate expansion to provide growth of output and jobs,
3. research and development,
4. safe and economical product design,
5. socially desirable location of new plants,
6. protection of the environment,
7. conservation of resources,
8. employment and training of minority and handicapped labor,
9. civil rights and equal opportunity,

10. urban renewal,
11. medical care,
12. education, and
13. cultural pursuits.

The degree of responsibility for any of these social objectives depends, in the first place, on the amount of discretion that the law and the market offer to the corporation. It depends, second, on the comparative advantage that the corporation may have in dealing with any particular objective. And it depends, third, on how far the market falls short of meeting social objectives.

The question therefore is to what extent these objectives should be pursued by government action, left to the market, or left to corporate responsibility. None of these approaches precludes any of the others. Where the government takes the principal role, a subsidiary one may still remain for corporate responsibility. In some areas, the corporate contribution is bound to be marginal, because the corporation has little to do with objectives such as education, medical care, and cultural pursuits. In evaluating the role of the market, the critical issue is not only "how perfect" it is in a technical sense. Externalities need to be considered. And even in their absence, the workings of the market may not be what society considers optimal, for instance with respect to the distribution of income. Through the political process, people may establish a hierarchy of values different from that which their market behavior brings about. To take another example, the valuation placed on the future may not be correctly expressed by the market rate of interest, which, employed as a discount factor, would make the world of our great-grandchildren worth a great deal less than we may intuitively believe it to be. Some comments on how to approach problems of this kind will be found in the concluding section of this chapter.

One way in which corporations may discharge their responsibility is to request government to tax or otherwise regulate them when competition makes voluntary action impossible. The complementary case—a request for subsidization—stands in no special need of recommendation.

The questions posed here can be clarified by an examination in more technical terms, to which we now turn.

Targets and Instruments

The respective roles of government and of corporations in helping to attain society's objectives can be examined in terms of the familiar framework relating the number of targets to the number of instruments. At the expense of some abstraction, the community can be viewed as having two sets of objectives: (1) the production of goods and services at minimum costs, and (2) the protection of the environment and the achievement of social equity. The community has two instruments: (1) the government and (2) corporations. Both instruments affect the attainment of both targets, although each instrument affects each target in different degree. If the strength of the two instruments is known, this gives a simple system of two equations with two unknowns, the latter being the degree of target achievement. With two equations and two unknowns there is a solution.

A use frequently made of this framework envisages the existence of "dilemma situations." Such a dilemma exists when the pursuit of one objective does injury to the attainment of the other. For example, the effort to increase production may injure the environment and create social inequities. The effort to protect the environment and establish social equity may hamper production. Under such circumstances, it becomes important to assign each respective objective the instrument that has a comparative advantage in attaining it. If we are prepared to assume that corporations have a comparative advantage in producing goods and services, and that government has a comparative advantage in protecting the environment and social equity, it would then be a mistake to let government look after production, and corporations after environment and equity. The reverse assignment will give superior results. That superior assignment is of course the way in which society has largely organized itself.

It would nevertheless be a mistake to conclude that their unquestioned comparative advantage entitles government or corporations to ignore the objective with respect to which they have a comparative disadvantage. The proponents of the corporate social responsibility believe that these relationships of goals and instruments are not immutable. The trade-off between the impact of corporations on production and on the environment and equity is not linear. Efforts to move in either direction are subject to diminishing returns. Given increases in production can only be bought at more rapidly mounting damage to environment and equity. On the other hand, corporate efforts to pursue environmental protection and equity, carried far enough, will result in losses to production at an increasing rate. The same changing trade-off can be traced on the government's side.

The function of social policy is precisely to guide government and corporate activity so that the comparative advantage of either vanishes. The activities of both must be shifted to the point where the two objectives have the same trade-off for government and corporations. The opponents of a corporate policy deliberately aimed at social objectives claim that corporations are beset by an immutable comparative disadvantage with respect to these objectives. Proponents, on the other hand, believe that the trade-off can be altered. The pursuit of higher production need not be carried on at the neglect of environmental and social values. If it is, society will be failing to get optimal use from the two instruments at its disposal.

The foregoing analysis of the proper use of policy instruments in attaining the objectives of society rests on the assumption that the effects of employing a particular policy instrument are known. As a first approximation, this is a reasonable assumption. The unquestioned fact, however, that the effects can never be known with complete precision has interesting consequences that can be further analyzed. This takes us into the area of decision making under uncertainty.

Theorems in this area acquire particular importance when it can be assumed that the decision maker is averse to risk. When the decision maker is the community at large, the assumption of risk aversion seems plausible. For each individual, risk aversion follows logically from the familiar observation that rising income has diminishing returns, that is, every additional dollar of income adds a little less than its predecessor to the total utility enjoyed by the recipient. A community composed of such individuals should also be risk averse.

Given this characteristic, society can reduce its risk of failing to achieve any one objective by employing the two available instruments simultaneously. In pursuit of a healthy environment and social justice, it will rely only in part on government, placing some trust also in the voluntary action of corporations. This does *not* mean that the government employs corporations as its agents in addition to acting directly. It implies that society relies on the social consciousness of corporations independently of what the government may do to guide corporate action in this regard.

This procedure will pay off provided that the success of government and corporations in achieving the objective is less than perfectly correlated. In other words, if adequate performance by government always means equally inadequate performance by corporations, and vice versa, then society really has but one instrument rather than two. It cannot reduce its risk by employing both simultaneously. What reason is there for assuming that society's trust in government and in corporations, respectively, will not always be disappointed or rewarded in exactly the same degree? If, for instance, government fails to do its proper job in this respect, does that increase or reduce the likelihood that corporations will also ignore the environment and social equity? Or should one expect that concern or neglect by one agent is likely to be associated with the reverse on the part of the other?

There is no general answer. The fact, however, that there is disagreement about whether corporations should have a role in the pursuit of social objectives suggests that there is uncertainty over what can be expected of government. There is no particular reason to expect negative correlation, that is, that government will perform well whenever corporations perform badly, and vice versa. Some degree of independence can reasonably be assumed, however, with regard to government and corporate performance—either may perform well or badly regardless of how the other performs. Hence, the rule that diversification pays seems to apply also in the case where society must decide whether to pursue its objectives with one instrument or two.

Externalities

The presence of externalities, positive and negative, causes the allocation of resources by the market to deviate from the social optimum. If the production of electric power causes air pollution, failure of this negative externality to be included in the price paid by the user causes the private cost of power to fall short of the social cost. Too much power will be produced as a result. If the firm beautifies its plant, the social return on the investment will exceed the private return that the firm can appropriate. This positive externality causes private return to fall short of social return. Not enough beautification will be undertaken in consequence.

The remedies for positive and negative externalities are familiar: tax power, and subsidize beautification. Given today's increasing pressure on the environment, the frequency and magnitude of gaps between social and private cost or return are probably increasing. Actions which, in a richly endowed and not fully used environment, were innocuous, now produce damage. This creates problems for the market economy, and gives new scope to its critics.

Under these circumstances, public action to internalize externalities becomes increasingly urgent. This is one of the main planks in a constructive program to involve corporations. But to the extent that such a program rests on government initiative, we are not here concerned with it. In such programs, corporations simply respond. They do not exhibit social responsibility.

There are, nevertheless, ways in which corporations can take the initiative to achieve internalization. These are: (1) pressure on government to pass appropriate legislation, (2) cooperative action by groups of corporations and (3) recognition by corporations that the interest of stockholders with diversified portfolios goes beyond the profit maximization of any one corporation.

Pressure on Government

Suppose a firm found that a general antipollution campaign in its industry or neighborhood would so improve working conditions and labor supply that the investment would pay off, in financial terms, provided other firms participate. Alone, it cannot influence the environment sufficiently to make a difference from which it could adequately profit. One possible approach would be for this and like-minded firms to request the authorities to impose by law an investment that would benefit them all financially. This is one form of exerting social responsibility.

The firms would be better off if the depollution ordinance took the form of a tax instead of regulations determining maximum admissible pollution. Different firms may encounter different costs in cleaning up. An equal standard for all would be expensive to achieve for some, inexpensive for others. A tax on pollution would cause those firms which could afford it to stop polluting altogether. The rest could choose to pay the tax. If the tax is set at the proper level, that is, at a level that in the aggregate would motivate a sufficient degree of depollution, its objective will be achieved at minimum aggregate cost.

Responsible corporate action therefore can take the form of promoting not only action by government in general, but also action of the most economical kind. The use of antipollution taxes is not at present popular with environmentalists, who regard such a tax as a "license to pollute," which indeed it is. The price is the essence. Business also seems to be skeptical of a tax as opposed to regulation. But where there are significant differences in cleanup costs, the high-cost polluters clearly will find it in their interest to be subjected to a flexible tax rather than to an inflexible ceiling.

Cooperative Action

In the situation described, the firms involved may also consider the possibility of forming an agreement. The content of this agreement might be that all firms would establish equal standards of depollution, or that all would incur equal or proportionate costs. The latter would be the more economical solution. Both solutions, however, raise questions under the antitrust laws.

Under these laws, trade associations and related activities among firms of an industry are of course permissible. They must not, however, facilitate anything in the way of a restraint of trade, including joint price setting. Action that would increase costs, such as a cooperative cleanup campaign, might be interpreted as having the effect of raising prices. In a competitive market, a single firm could not charge an increase in costs to the customer. All firms in the industry could, however. If success attends the effort to reduce pollution and thereby improves working conditions and the labor supply, costs and prices would not increase. But evidently some subtle questions of antitrust policy are involved. A court decision, like that in the case of *A. P. Smith* v. *Barlow,* which opened the door to large-scale corporate giving to educational institutions, might clear the way here.

The Diversified Stockholder

Recognition that the stockholder with a diversified portfolio has a broader range of interests than the maximization of the profits of any one corporation represents a third avenue toward the internalization of externalities.

Suppose a firm finds that investment in the training of unskilled labor would pay off, provided the workers acquiring new skills would stay with the firm permanently. If they leave and go to a competitor, the firm does not realize any return on its investment. But the competitor does, and if the stockholder owns stock in both firms, he will get his return from one firm or the other. The first firm would deprive the stockholder of a feasible return if it failed to make the investment in training, regardless of whether it or the competitor reaps the benefits.

Two assumptions underlie the analysis here summarized. In the first place, the benefits from socially oriented expenditures must be ''appropriable'' by the corporate sector, that is, they must show up somewhere on business income statements as an increase in profits. (Externalities that cannot be appropriated, such as better quality of life not expressed in higher productivity or improved labor supply, however desirable, pose a different problem.) The second assumption requires all stockholders to have shares in all corporations. In this limiting case, it can be shown that even the presence of corporations that refuse to engage in socially oriented expenditures and that thereby steal a march on their competitors does not alter the conclusion that each stockholder's financial interest requires each corporation to engage in socially oriented expenditures so long as there is an appropriate net return to the corporate sector as a whole.

For unappropriable externalities—''better quality of life''—the matter is more complex. Of course stockholders benefit, along with others, from the better quality of life, but as individuals, not as stockholders. Consequently, whether social expenditures by a corporation in which they own stock put them ahead or not depends on the amount of stock they have in each operation. With respect to externalities of this kind, therefore, stockholders will disagree as to whether particular socially oriented expenditures should be undertaken or not. Moreover, the treatment of hold-outs that refuse to engage in such expenditures becomes more difficult.

Dropping the second assumption—all stockholders owning some part of every company—further reduces the precision of the analysis. We then must consider the degree of risk aversion of individual stockholders, greater risk aversion requiring a more complete degree of diversification. Different stockholders accordingly will find themselves differently situated with respect to these broad externalities.

The analysis assumes that corporations act in the interest of their stockholders, which they recognize to be broader than the interest of any single corporation. Stockholder instructions to the corporation may be required to make corporations properly responsive to stockholder interest. The present widespread effort of some stockholders to alert corporations to their moral concerns is an instance of such stockholder behavior, although it is concerned typically with moral issues rather than with maximizing stockholders' return on utility.

The Continuity of Corporations

In textbook economics, a firm produces a product over whose demand it has no control. When the demand disappears, the firm presumably closes up shop.

This picture may not be altogether unrealistic with respect to railroads and other regulated industries, whose regulatory authorities do not permit diversification. But the ordinary unregulated firm, particularly when it is large and not a "one-man" firm, seeks continuity. Stockholders come and go, but the corporation goes on forever.

Greater continuity implies two things. First, the interests of the corporation become more oriented toward the long run. Short-run profit maximization may be harmful to long-term survival. Recognition of social responsibilities may give the corporation the kind of acceptance in the community that it needs if it plans to be an ongoing operation.

A second implication is the expectation of the community that a corporation will have to act more along the lines of the community's interests if it wishes to have continued existence independent of its function as supplier of some product that the community may cease to want. While this expectation of the community is not compelling, I find it persuasive.

One way of expressing this is to say that the corporation's enlightened self-interest has changed. The "enlightened-self-interest" concept has given rise to a great deal of fuzzy thinking, and, therefore, I do not want to employ it here. The enlightened self-interest of a corporation should require it to do certain things that pay off in dollars and cents. Of course this computation usually is very difficult to make. As a result, enlightened self-interest tends to become a catchall phrase for a lot of things that redound to the benefit of the corporation but which have no basis whatever in a cost-benefit calculation. That is not the enlightened self-interest here referred to. Though the computation may be vague, it must make plausible that the rate of return is adequate. Whether the community's desire to have corporations engage in socially oriented activities is justified is of course a question as yet not fully resolved. It is the question we are debating today. I would argue, however, that the mere fact that the community desires it makes a strong prima facie case. The contrary case would have to be very compelling to overcome this presumption.

"Stockholders' Money"

Discussions of social expenditures by corporations habitually run in terms of the appropriate use of "stockholders' money." It is taken for granted that the stockholder bears the cost and that this could constitute a legitimate objection to this kind of corporate spending.

It was already pointed out above that this view is highly misleading, at least as far as the effects of the corporate-income tax are concerned. At a 48 percent corporate rate, the federal government matches the corporation's funds almost dollar for dollar. The government in fact contributes massively while leaving to the corporation the decision over the use of funds. As a means of decentralizing the administration of social programs, and of strengthening a pluralistic society, this arrangement has much to commend it. And it just happens to make 48 percent nonsense out of the claim that corporate social expenditures are financed with stockholders' money.

How about the other 52 percent? If the corporation is the only one in its industry to engage in these expenditures, or engages in much larger expenditures than its competitors, it probably cannot shift the cost. It is then operating with stockholders' money. If, through cooperation, government requirement, well-understood stockholders' interest, or in the corporations' own long-term interest, all or most of the firms in an industry engage in similar expenditures, the cost curve rises, and the cost of doing good becomes a cost of doing business. Contrasting this situation with the alternative, in which the government performs the same socially oriented actions out of taxpayers' money, it is clear that the stockholder may find corporate responsibility a highly rewarding way of getting the nation's social work done.

The Role of Executives

Unlike the stockholder, the executive does not benefit from a diversification of interests. Nevertheless, the social involvement of his corporation holds out many attractions for him, too. He is now called on to make judgments that go far beyond the task of allocating resources in the interest of profit maximization. Instead of being the employee of the stockholders or directors, he becomes an arbiter among competing interests—stockholders, customers, workers, society. This is a heady combination, and it would be surprising if executives did not find it attractive. In particular, young people who look askance on business jobs may find that this kind of orientation suits them.

The arrangement has the political advantage of shifting from the public to the private sector activities that should be performed with maximum economy rather than maximum bureaucracy. It fits into the design of a pluralistic society seeking a high degree of decentralization. On the other hand, it bestows considerable uncontrolled power on corporate executives. The line of accountability becomes unclear. The question of the competence of corporate executives in handling social tasks must be raised. To judge by the great interest that executives have shown in the development of corporate social responsibility, it seems clear that they find the attractions outweighing the disadvantages.

Methods of Implementation

It is evident that large parts of the community today expect corporations to shoulder some social responsibilities. The classical reply that business best discharges its responsibilities by maximizing profits under conditions of competition is unconvincing to many people. In part, to be sure, this reflects erroneous conceptions about corporate profits that fail to take account of the role of profits as a measure of performance and as a source of necessary investment. But on the other hand, these are not the only aspects of profit. Somebody benefits in a more direct sense.

The argument cited in this chapter concerning the role of the diversified stockholder demonstrates that even at the theoretical level profit maximization by the individual firm is an inadequate principle. The issue is not how wide a gap this analysis opens between maximization on behalf of the corporation and maximization on behalf of a diversified stockholder. The fact that there is such a gap—regardless of its size—is important. Nor need one assume that the market will quickly bring about a corporate reorientation in the interest of the diversified stockholder. The fact that in the long run such a tendency should exist justifies corporate efforts to bring about the results more quickly. It also justifies, of course, stockholder activism in persuading corporations of the need to face up to their responsibilities toward diversified stockholders at a minimum.

Consider the mundane consequences of corporate noncompliance. Business today is under critical scrutiny. A refusal to be responsive, however sincerely or adroitly supported by the classical defense of profit maximization, would be hard to sell. The result might well be legislation in the form of taxes and regulation, that in effect would be punitive. A strong antibusiness movement in the country would indeed provide evidence that social involvement would serve the long-run interests of business. One might add that, in an age which demands more than goods and services, the insistence of corporations on being nothing but producers of goods and services threatens to force corporations increasingly out of the main stream of American life and into irrelevance.

The means for injecting relevance into the corporate scene, by the wrong route, already are on social reformers' drawing boards. This proposal for federal incorporation is one such device. Such a law would make corporations the creatures of the state with a vengeance. It would be a bad approach, because it would give the state enormous power without clearly specifying the purposes. As far as the achievement of particular objectives is concerned, it would mismatch instrument and objective. But this is the approach that corporate recalcitrance may provoke.

Many aspects of corporate impact on the environment and on society can indeed best be handled by legislation. Corporate management would be well advised to give support to well-designed legislation. (To be sure, corporations cannot and should not be expected to support extremist legislation of this type.) Appropriate support would be one form of discharging its responsibility.

Cooperation among business firms as a means of reducing the competitive impact of socially oriented expenditures raises the question of relaxation of the antitrust laws. In the abstract, such a question is difficult to answer. Concrete applications and particular cases are needed to facilitate judgment. It should not be difficult for business to pose issues and develop possibilities in these terms, and give the public an opportunity to express its opinion.

For the stockholder, the social responsibility issue promises a real rejuvenation. Since Berle and Means, the stockholder has been regarded as basically functionless, a condition that does not bode well for the survival of private enterprise. In recent years, the cult of performance investing has made the relationship between the stockholder and his company even more tenuous. The new activism exhibited by some stockholder groups, on the other hand, promises a new lease on life.

This new activism, which has been in evidence at the stockholders meetings of many large corporations, is noteworthy as a form of social criticism that works within the system instead of trying to modify, if not to destroy, the system from the outside. It reflects the view, expressed above, that the interests of the stockholder are not necessarily those of the corporation and that the corporation ought to heed these interests. In many cases, to be sure, the pressure of activist stockholders has not been solely or primarily toward socially oriented expenditures that could be appropriated by the corporate sector and that consequently would enhance aggregate profits. Very often, it has aimed at objectives that would enhance the well-being of the entire community, stockholders included, without showing up positively on earnings statements. But some rationale for this type of activism clearly exists in terms of the theory of the diversified stockholders' interest.

This activism contrasts sharply with Wall Street's traditional attitude toward stockholder criticism of management. "If you don't like the management, get out," has been the traditional reaction. This is purely defensive advice. Selling a stock is not a means of penalizing and thereby perhaps reforming the management. So long as a socially recalcitrant management makes money for its stockholders, there will be plenty of people willing to pick up the stock sold by social activists. There is little to be gained from an effort to create pariah corporations.

Nor is much to be gained from an attempt to influence corporations by mere token stock ownership. Groups of young people buying one share apiece in order to gain admission to stockholders' meetings are futile. Their well meant, but not always demonstrably rational, proposals merely strengthen the resolve of more substantial stockholders to send their proxies to the management instead of throwing them in the waste basket. As pointed out above, the interests of particular stockholders may differ on social activities not appropriable by the corporate sector. Small stockholders will tend to be more favorably inclined toward them than large stockholders because all get approximately the same benefits, along with the rest of the community, without all making the same financial sacrifice. But corporate law here seems to give exactly the right answer: The rule is not one man–one vote, but one share–one vote.

The movement to influence corporations by placing representatives of consumers, minorities, and other watch dogs of all kinds on corporate boards, or by opposing and possibly overturning managements, clearly creates certain risks. Board meetings may become unproductive, management may be side-tracked in futile battles, and corporate efficiency may suffer. But a careful and reasonable activation of the potential power of the stockholder need not lead to such consequences. Large institutional investors, in particular, are unlikely to be swayed toward unreasonable action while they have all the more reason—because of their broader interests—to take action of some kind.

Whether based on the principle of diversified stock ownership, or simply a deepened sense of the responsibilities of ownership and trusteeship, stock-holder activism has a strong economic rationale. At the same time, it augurs well for the adaptability of the corporate system to a more demanding world.

43 No Talent for Planning

To question planning is like questioning common sense. We all plan as individuals. Why then fail to make the fullest use of this commonsensical procedure at the national level?

We are not likely to settle this issue in the abstract. Theory tells us that under ideal conditions planning can generate efficient solutions to economic problems. Theory also tells us that under certain conditions markets can fail to provide efficient solutions to the economic problem. In the United States the role of planning, except in war time, has been limited largely to patching up what are perceived to be market failures. In my remarks today I would like to develop the thesis that aside from judgments concerning the efficiency of an ideal planning process this limited role for planning in the U.S. economy is partly accounted for by the fact that our political process and our national character make planning especially difficult.

In particular, I would like to draw upon the planning experience of the two economies that perhaps have been most successful in the postwar period—Germany and Japan. The Germans, who operated a tightly planned economy during most of the 1930s, backed away very deliberately from that system after the war. This is not to say that there are no traces of public planning in the German economy. A systematic and orderly people would have a hard time not engaging in such activities to some degree. But the ideology and, in good measure, the reality have been market oriented. One is tempted to attribute this decision in good part to the historic association of central planning with an obnoxious political regime. But it is worth noting that the Germans explain their preference for the market not only in terms of insurance against a political relapse, but quite specifically also on the grounds of the favorable performance characteristics of the market system. The results achieved, as we know, do not contradict that view.

Japan, despite the small size of its public sector, can be regarded as a country where public planning plays a very considerable role. Whether we think of the policy of doubling GNP in ten years, or of the pervasive influence of the Ministry of Industry and Foreign Trade (MITI), or of the deliberate means employed by the Ministry of Finance and the Bank of Japan in channel-

---

The views expressed herein are my own and do not necessarily reflect those of the Board of Governors of the Federal Reserve System or the Board's staff. This chapter was originally published in *Vie et Sciences Economiques,* April 1976, pp. 1–3; it is the text of a speech to the American Economic Association in Dallas, Texas, on December 29, 1975.

ing financial flows, the ubiquitous role of the public planner is very apparent. By methods very different from those of Germany, a postwar economic performance even more impressive has thus been realized.

As in Germany, the political context of the Japanese orientation toward public planning is important. In this case, however, it is not Japan's political history, but its political process that is the key to understanding Japan's planning. Students of the Japanese way of life refer to Japan as a consent society. That is to say, the predominant mode of group decision making, both public and private, is through consensus rather than confrontation or competition. The interest and opinions of all parties are taken into account. A great effort is made to avoid overruling or outvoting anybody. This pattern seems to prevail both in private corporations and in the bureaucracy. The process often is slow, conveying to the outsider an impression of hesitancy and indecision. But once everybody has signed off on a decision, action is general and forceful.

The environment in which Japan found itself after World War II has favored effective planning for rapid growth. One must suppose that, even if market forces had been allowed to hold sway unmitigated by public planning, Japan would have found itself moving rapidly in the direction of big-industrial-power status. What the Japanese did was to accelerate considerably this nearly inevitable trend. This tendency to plan along the grain of market forces, rather than against it, seems to have been characteristic of Japan's public policies in both the real and the financial sector. Thus, during the postwar period, the Japanese technique of group decision making and the economic opportunities which Japan encountered helped to make economic planning effective.

For the United States, the salient facts of the matter seem to be that neither our political processes nor the general condition of the country favor effective public planning. Compared to the highly structured and closely knit world of Japan, ours is wide open. As contrasted with the principle of consent in Japan, our public decision making proceeds by competition and confrontation. It is a familiar dictum, of course, that politics is the art of compromise. But compromise, in the American framework, often comes only after bruising battles, and it need not carry any further than the point where one side manages to get 51 percent of the vote. The winner takes all; the loser's consent is not solicited.

This, I submit, is a process that makes effective public planning difficult. Confrontation, the effort to achieve a majority, absence of a need to consult the wishes of the minority, suggest severe strains. In the effort to assemble a majority, the competing sides are compelled to make extreme promises. Expectations are likely to be created that exceed possibilities of fulfillment. Demands made on resources tend to exceed the supply. The hallmark of a planned economy under a decision-making system such as ours is likely to be excess demand.

Inflationary propensities of this kind are likely to be enhanced by the technology of planning. Efficiency, getting the biggest bang for a buck, is bound to be the dominant motivation of competent technicians. Good technocrats abhor waste. But a free economy requires a degree of slack, some unutilized supply elasticity, if prices are not to be always rising. Directing a larger share of productive capacity toward planned activities in the American environment, therefore, is likely to lead, first to inflation and later on perhaps even to price and wage controls.

Other features of our political life tend to enhance these propensities. Our political framework has a very short time horizon. All members of the House, one-third of the Senate, face reelection every two years, the president every four. By most international comparisons, these are short periods. Our public attention span also seems to be short. A review of our rapidly shifting public concerns over the last fifteen years readily documents this—with growth, the environment, consumerism, energy independence, and others following and often superseding one another. When the time span during which a national goal can command nationwide attention falls short of the time required to install the corresponding technology, planning, as opposed to more flexible private decision-making processes, in response to rapidly shifting goals will produce disorder and waste.

Finally, and once more in contrast to postwar Japan, the United States today confronts a set of circumstances not conducive to effective economic planning. In Japan, planning essentially was for production. Resources were withheld from consumption and channeled into productive investment. Consumption was allowed to take care of itself as income grew rapidly.

Planning in the United States, I suspect, would be principally for use. Ours has always been a high-consumption and low-investment economy, in comparison to other leading industrial countries. Today, if I read the signs right, consumption even more than in the past outranks production as a national concern.

Production does not rank high in our national scale of values. It is pretty much taken for granted, as concepts like "postindustrial" and maybe "post-economic" society indicate. Our principal concerns are with the old, the young, the unemployed, the welfare recipients, the sick, the consumer—all of them having in common that they are nonproducers. The producer pays.

His job of producing, moreover, is made more difficult by rapidly mounting regulations favoring the environment, health and safety, and a variety of other highly desirable and most worthwhile purposes, all of which have in common the unfortunate feature that they burden the producer. The adversary role in which he is cast is matched by the diminished public esteem in which business is held. The picture of "Japan, Inc.," the intimacy between government and business in France and Germany, contrasts distinctly with the business-government relationship prevailing in the United States.

These circumstances support my hypothesis that planning in the United States would be oriented more toward use than toward production. This orientation would enhance the tendency toward excess demand, with the ensuing probable consequences of inflation and controls.

In summary, proposals for planning in the United States seem to me to propose the wrong thing in the wrong country at the wrong time. Given the American way of making group decisions, given our excessive emphasis on short-run objectives that shift frequently, and given the unsympathetic treatment meted out to the producer, I see little good coming from intensified public planning. It is not surprising that, until recently at least, Americans have tended to favor the free market as a solution to the problem of deciding what is to be produced. The market turns competition into a constructive force, while in politics it becomes a divisive one. The market avoids confrontation by substituting anonymous decision making by the consumer. Private processes of profit and utility maximization help to reconcile competing and shifting objectives with technological and financial limitations.

Market processes, rather than planning, have been appropriate to the American environment, except in wartime. Other countries may be better suited for the application of planning techniques. In the United States, an effort at comprehensive planning is likely to lead to severe political conflict, to excessive demands on the economy, and to inefficient use of resources as divergent and shifting demands fail to be reconciled.

44 The Economist in Government—Relations with Administrators, Technicians, and Academics

The economic profession in the United States can derive satisfaction from the role that it has achieved in the American government, if that role is measured by the importance and the number of the positions occupied by professional economists (rather than by the state of the economy at the present time). Looking at the Cabinet, we see, to be sure, that its senior member, the secretary of State, is a professor of political science from Harvard. The secretaries of the Treasury and of Defense, however, are professors of economics from the Universities of Chicago and Virginia, respectively. The secretary of Agriculture is a former professor of agricultural economics from Purdue University. The chairmen of the Federal Reserve Board, of the Cost of Living Council, and of the Council of Economic Advisers all are, have been, or are about to become professors of economics at Columbia, Harvard, and Virginia respectively. In the ranks next to the top, the number of economists becomes far too extensive to trace across the government. In the Treasury, where I once instituted an inquiry, there were at one time six full professors employed in the Office of the Secretary alone and some sixty to seventy persons in that office who at some time of their lives had taught in institutions of higher learning.

The compilation of full-dress statistical data on the employment of economists in the U.S. government runs into a difficulty not experienced to the same degree in European countries. The U.S. educational process, after sixteen years of elementary, secondary, and higher education, and at an approximate age of 22, produces a young man or woman technically known as bachelor of arts. This college graduate may have majored in economics, in which case very roughly one-third to one-half of total study time would have been devoted to economics. This does not make the graduate a professional economist. The graduate's counterpart in Germany and England has focused exclusively on economics for probably three years and in England may have attained a B.A., and in Germany he or she may be within one or two years of a *Diplom Volkswirt* degree. The German and the English student probably should be regarded as professional economists; the U.S. student is more nearly a liberally educated person with a concentration in economics, prepared to go to graduate school to receive a professional education proper.

This chapter was originally presented at the Conference on "The Role of the Economist in Government," Royaumont, France, April 19–21, 1974.

Before World War II, a B.A. with a major in economics very often was sufficient for good part of the not very numerous government slots for economists, although university teaching has always required a PhD. Increasingly, however, standards have escalated. Today many economics jobs in government are accessible only to PhD's. Some are open to M.A.s, typically PhD candidates who for one reason or another did not complete their dissertations. Very few B.A.s are hired in positions calling for a professional economist.

There are, nevertheless, numerous older government economists who began their careers at a less demanding time and who today do good and responsible work even though they never completed their PhD or even M.A. degree. Academic classifications, therefore, are not a good guide to professional standing in government. Job classifications, on the other hand, are sufficiently flexible as to academic qualifications so that a count of slots in tables of organization also does not say anything very precise about the number of economists employed. An impressionistic figure can be derived from the membership of the American Economic Association, which for the most part includes persons regarding themselves as professional economists, although by no means all of those who do. A survey of the membership shows that, of approximately 14,500 domestic members, 18 percent give government as their principal occupation, 68 percent list academic, and 10 percent list business as their affiliation.

Role, Approach, and Function

Three concepts are implicit in the term *role* when used in discussing the role of the economist in government. An economist's *role* refers to the activities of the economist—economics is what economists do—*approach* refers to the methods that an economist brings to his activities, and *function* refers to the orientation that, in their role as economists and by the use of the economic approach, economists have imparted to government policy.

Role of Economists

The activity of economists in the U.S. government runs the gamut from humble data collection to top-level policymaking. In my own limited experience, the most interesting dichotomy in this area has been that between research and operations. The young PhD entering government typically is concerned both with preserving his professional qualifications and with making an immediate impact on policy. As he discovers that the second is difficult, he is apt to value particularly an opportunity to accomplish the first, preferably by means of turning out publishable research. Government staffers have learned that they must respect this desire if they are to have access to top talent coming out of the universities. This gives rise, from time to time, to "special projects divisions," "research groups," and whatever other descriptions administrators employ to push this kind of candidate through the budget-making process.

Then the pressures of government go to work. In some emergency or other, the head of the agency or division looks for a bright young man who can deliver what is needed. In one agency, in fact, the able members of the staff used to rate the incumbent secretary by how long it would take him to discover them. From then on, the researcher is increasingly drawn into operations, until some years later he discovers that he has lost the capacity, or the taste, for research. The move from (relatively) pure economics to operations is a crucial one in the evolving role of the economist at the staff (civil-service) level.

At the level of presidential appointees, almost all economists find themselves involved immediately in operations. The range of these appointees—who usually arrive with an incoming administration and usually, although by no means always, depart when the party in control of the executive branch changes—appears to be wider than it is in many other countries. Typically, it embraces four echelons—secretary, under (or deputy) secretary, assistant secretary, and deputy assistant secretary.

It is this group that principally deals with the politicians, if that term is employed to denote the members of the Congress. In the U.S. system, heads of departments are not members of the legislature and hence often, perhaps usually, are not professional politicians even though they are political appointees.

The problem of economists dealing with administrators has, in my limited experience, largely disappeared. Twenty years ago it would indeed have required effort for an economist to achieve an adequate hearing and even more to put across some of the technical concepts of his discipline. I know of an agency staff that invented the slide-show performance for economics data, since widely popularized, to focus the attention of the secretary on such esoterica. Today, the use of GNP and balance-of-payments jargon, multipliers, full-employment budgets, and the Phillips Curve has become routine within executive departments and with many members of the Congress. Now it is the businessman in government who feels out of his depth if he has not received some grounding in fundamentals from his own staff or in groups like the Committee for Economic Development, the National Planning Association, or the Council on Foreign Relations.

Approach

Economists, equipped with the "hardest" of the "soft" disciplines, have been interdisciplinary empire builders. Economics, both through its rigorous analytical techniques and through its use of econometric methods, has been able to make contributions in fields such as political science and sociology. At the same time, economists have turned to new areas, such as urban and medical economics. Currently, the applicability of economics analysis to legal problems is increasingly being explored.

These methodological approaches are particularly fruitful in government. A great deal of decision making in government takes the form of yes-or-no decisions. The same is true, of course, of legal decisions. The nature of economics is marginalism. A little more of this is traded off against a little less of that. A closer approach to welfare maximization will be achieved if the inevitable yes-or-no decisions of the politician and of the lawyer can be filled with a quantitative content and with a marginalist approach. By plying their incrementalist method, economists are injecting an approach into government decision making that is helpful.

Function

The function, as here defined, of economists in government has been to institute and help attain a variety of economic objectives. In the United States, these have been made explicit by the Employment Act of 1946, which calls for maximum employment, production, and purchasing power, commonly interpreted as full employment, rapid growth, and price stability. Economists have been highly successful in impregnating the consciousness of administrators, politicians, the press, and the general public with at least two of these objectives—full employment and growth. Without benefit of an Employment Act mandate, they have also done much to alert their listeners to the importance of social objectives, such as a fair distribution of income, elimination of poverty, and general improvement of social conditions.

An observer of the contemporary scene nevertheless is bound to ask himself whether the goals for which economists stand have not in good part been bypassed by events. The overriding importance of economic growth has been questioned effectively by the environmentalists. The desire for price stability, or at least for freedom from severe inflation, which economists have never taken very seriously, now threatens to trigger popular reactions that may damage both the market system and democracy. The economist's emphasis on maximizing short-run output has reinforced the politician's necessarily short time horizon. It thus has led to a neglect of long-run considerations that would stress the conservation of the economic machinery, possibly at some sacrifice of immediate output.

It would seem that the economist could and should extend his sphere of interest to these broader and longer-run concerns. If it should turn out that his professional predilections prevent him from doing so, one must fear that the public will regard his function in government as insufficiently responsive to needs. The economist may then find his role encroached on, perhaps superseded, in the same manner in which he encroached on the role of the lawyer, by who-knows-what new breed of more broadly gauged technician—social scientist, environmentalist, technocrat, or representatives of more esoteric disciplines waiting in the wings.

Professional Identity and Esprit de Corps among Government Economists

One does not become a banker by running an elevator in a bank. Many, but probably by no means all, economists feel the same way about working for the government. They think of themselves as professional economists first and as civil servants second. For political appointees from the universities and elsewhere this applies of course even more.

Various processes may erode this identification and may turn the economist into a professional civil servant. Inability to maintain academic qualifications, through lack of publication and lack of time to keep up with the literature, the sense of doing a worthwhile job, of being close to important decisions, may produce these effects. Identification with an agency may be enhanced by intra-agency rivalry. But there is enough job shifting among departments to prevent identification from becoming universal.

A society of government economists exists. It certainly is not now a union in the collective-bargaining sense. In a time of rapidly advancing public-service unionism, a growing sense of professional identity and esprit de corps can be expected. Its present significance I find difficult to evaluate.

A very different kind of political grouping is that which brings together professional economists in and out of government. All technicians and specialists have their groups and associations, with meetings as part of the annual convention of the Allied Social Science Associations, or sponsored by research organizations and universities, or organized by academic entrepreneurs with foundation support.

Among these numerous groups there is an unstructured nucleus, not very well defined, consisting of leading economists who may now be playing significant roles in government or have done so in the past. Some of these could be described as "fashionable economists," who are in demand for popular lectures, articles in newspapers or popular magazines, or talks to businessmen. They meet haphazardly but frequently in consulting groups of different agencies, the "ins" mingling with the "outs" on terms of professional equality. They all know each other's views, watch each other's work, and enjoy the human warmth created by long association that often goes back to student days. The U.S. political system does not produce a shadow cabinet or its equivalent at the economic level. Nor is there much sense in referring to this group, which continually coopts new blood mainly from the universities, as a power elite. But there is among this group a sense of community that blunts the sharp edges of political or professional disagreement.

Effects of Changes in Government on the Demand for and Uses of Economists

When control of the executive branch changes from one party to another, many members of the group just described find themselves exchanging places. The previous ins return to their universities, research institutes, or business offices; the outs, with some admixture of newcomers, take over. Quantitatively the demand for economists does not change, but its orientation does change.

The public service is protected, of course, against political changes. Replacements are limited, in general, to the presidential appointees, covering something like the top four echelons, as mentioned earlier. Usually there are holdovers, especially in the international area, where some degree of bipartisanship is preserved. Many changes occur with a lag of years and are indistinguishable from normal turnover.

Professional Ethics

The code of professional ethics that binds government economists imposes different constraints on different groups. Civil-service economists are expected to act in a nonpartisan manner, as are all other civil servants. The Hatch Act prevents all civil servants from undertaking political activity. Naturally most economists have convictions, and naturally many of them, and among them probably the best, may find it difficult to live with a regime whose policies they detest. It is my impression that top administrators, where they encounter such attitudes, have regarded them as a problem of cooperation rather than of ethics.

Reasonably severe ethical standards are imposed on political appointees. Government agencies typically require conflict-of-interest statements involving data, among other things, on income and assets of a qualitative, although usually not quantitative, kind. Senate committees examining the president's appointees with a view to their confirmation by the full Senate also want to be satisfied concerning the absence of conflicts of interest. Remunerated outside activities, including directorships, or fees for writing and speaking, are ruled out.

These matters pertaining to all political appointees are simple compared to the issues posed for professional economists with presidential appointments.

The problem presents itself with particular severity for members of the President's Council of Economic Advisers. A summary of a recent discussion of this old and much-argued problem, at the 1973 Convention of the American Economic Association, was distributed at a conference on the role of the economist in government. It is noteworthy that, despite the very different operating styles employed by various council chairmen and members of the past and the present, no strong disagreements as to principles emerged at that meeting. The general conclusion was that the members of the Council of Economic Advisers, as professional economists, are subject to considerable constraints in developing political support for the president's programs before congressional committees and before the public, without being altogether precluded from such activities. The common denominator for professional conduct was found to be honesty. This, however, begs the question whether honesty is enough if the adviser's views are highly subjective.

In the United States, and perhaps not only there, the problem of professional ethics and political involvement is complicated by the difference between the distribution of political views among academic economists and among the population in general. A precise assessment of this difference is, of course, impossible. The appearance of a massive predominance of liberal (left) orientation among the entire universe of economists—academic, business, government—may even be misleading. It could be the result of a selection process that causes economists of less liberal persuasions to become business economists or even civil servants, leaving the more liberal in the universities. Nevertheless, the minority status of economists broadly sympathetic to a Republican administration creates problems of staffing, of nonpolitical conduct, and of relations with the profession. These may cause a code of conduct that is equal in principle for both sides to work out rather differently in practice.

Freedom of Publication

Every government agency can offer one attraction to potential employees that gains in strength with the quality of the candidate: opportunity to publish. Every government agency employs this bargaining instrument at a double risk. The candidate, once employed, may embarrass the agency by what he writes. He may also waste the agency's time and money by working on problems that are publishable rather than useful to the agency. In my experience, the second problem is more frequent than the first. Against publications that are critical of the agency's policy there is a built-in restraint. The writer knows that he endangers not only his own career with the agency but also the publication prospects of all his colleagues. An agency with a sufficiently large staff, moreover, may be able to encourage publication of different and perhaps conflicting orientations, thus gaining a reputation for fairmindedness while diffusing criticism.

Ability to produce a piece acceptable to a professional journal is an essential test of an economist's professional caliber, although certainly not of his usefulness to the agency. An agency will be able to attract better people, and to hold them longer, if it is liberal in its publication policy. The issue, in my view, is far more one of personnel policy than of freedom of speech or other professional ethics.

Recruitment

Given the student population and within it the annual supply of PhD's (in 1971: 32,000), the government's ability to recruit professional economists is a function of several variables. Among these are the interest of students in economics some five to seven years ago, the current willingness of those who then decided to become professional economists to enter government service, the demand for economists from alternative employers, principally universities and business, and the pay scales of these three competing groups.

Over the years the competitive situation of government has fluctuated. As a very broad generalization, however, it can probably be said that the ability of government to attract the cream of the academic crop has diminished over the years. Among today's leading economists, in the universities and in research institutions, an impressive number are graduates of government agencies, in my personal experience particularly of the Treasury and of the Federal Reserve System. Some first-rate people are still going from government to universities or research institutions. My impression is, however, that either their period of service typically has been shorter or their integration with the work of the agency less close. Quite probably the government is handicapped by its pay scale, which tends to be generous at the lower end and less so at the upper. Although at almost all levels government pay compares favorably with university pay, the outside opportunities open to most economists weight the scale sometimes very heavily in favor of academic employment.

Of course, recruitment of recent graduates should be, and to the best of my knowledge is, independent of political orientation. There may be a built-in selection process working in favor of a nonradical but certainly nonconservative orientation where public-service employment is concerned.

The selection of economists for presidential appointments presents a greater difficulty. Here, too, there are opportunities for nonpartisan selection, especially in the international area. Opinions differ as to how far a nonpartisan selection process can be pushed in the areas of domestic micro- and macroeconomics. Policy choices in both areas may have political implications. Microeconomics often implies income redistribution among sectors of the economy. Macroeconomics may involve redistribution via its effect on inflation and unemployment, respectively. The selection process is further complicated by correlations between factors such as political orientation, market versus control preferences, monetarist versus Keynesian leanings, and members of one set of university departments and their students versus another set.

The Use of Part-Timers and Consultants

Many top-notch economists, available to government as consultants, would not come on a permanent or even temporary basis. The difficulty lies in making optimal use of them. In a continuous operation, the consultant rarely is of great value. He misses critical meetings, does not get the papers on time, and becomes an outsider and ineffectual. The same applies when the development of a government initiative, such as a piece of legislation, has moved from the stage of broad planning to the working out of details. Economic expertise in this regard differs from legal expertise, which can indeed be useful down to the final drafting stage.

Consultants are most effective on a special job, particularly if it can be carried out at the consultant's home base. Consultants can also be highly useful in the brain-storming stage of a project, when new ideas are welcome. Periodic meetings with consultants can serve as a valuable check on the progress of some continuing operations. Finally, periodic contact with consultants who are experts and innovators in their own field keeps the government administrator and economist abreast of current thinking. In this age of slow publication and rapid changes of opinion, he could not even do this by reading the journals, assuming he had the time. Discussions with experts convey the comforting and not-altogether-wrong feeling to the government administrator or economist that he knows about developments at the frontier of knowledge.

Maintenance of Value

Expertise obsolesces rapidly. The government economist who does not keep up with his discipline by reading the journals and preferably participating in discussion and circulation of drafts is falling behind. Economists with a strong interest in the development of their discipline will sense the danger and will tend to stay in government only for short periods. Those who stay longer are natural candidates for the process of obsolescence. Daily chores make systematic reading difficult. The urgent always comes before the important. The quality of staff memoranda, usually done on request and under deadline, naturally cannot match that of journal articles. The government economist falls into the habit of accepting lower standards in what he reads and writes. The need to explain complex matters to administrators and politicians contributes to lowering the level of discourse. Contact with practical men and with the realities of life induces skepticism of theorizing, which may widen the gap between the government economist and the top-notch professional.

The nature of the process is obvious to all, and many first-rate government economists struggle desperately to keep it from affecting them. Both government and economist have a strong interest in obviating the process of obsolescence. Although employers, public and private, frequently have programs for rotating employees within the organization, they seem far less inclined to rotate them outside. Thus, there is only a limited amount of retooling of technicians by rotating them through the universities. Perhaps the reason is that when a man is temporarily sent outside the organization, a body is missing somewhere, which is not the case with an in-house rotation method. A strong case can be made, therefore, for sabbatical leaves from government.

The U.S. government has been fairly generous, in my limited experience, as regards leaves without pay for economists. A man of sufficient standing to persuade a university or research institution to finance him for a year can thus retool. By definition, unfortunately, he is the man who least needs it. For the less high-powered economist who does indeed need it, the difficulties are immense—financing, moving the family, finding a replacement in the organization.

There is also the problem of a conflict of interest between the economist and the sponsoring government agency as regards the kind of activity to be pursued in the infrequent event that the government helps the economist to spend a term or a year at a university. Typically, the economist will feel tempted to do some writing, which is a natural urge under the circumstances, since it immediately enhances his professional status. The sponsoring government agency is more interested in retooling, often of a rather pedestrian kind, such as acquiring some econometrics.

It should be realized that for a senior government economist, the acquisition of technical capabilities may not be an optimal use of retooling time. Even if he should become as proficient as his subordinates, his comparative advantage will almost certainly continue to be in areas requiring experience and judgment rather than technical expertise. A broadly gauged approach to retooling programs would therefore be desirable.

There can be no doubt, however, about the importance of periodic retooling as a general practice. So long as taking a government job means, to an ambitious graduate student, a kind of surrender to an intellectually undemanding career, however erroneous this view may be, the government lacks access to the great majority of able students. Only by offering an opportunity to the bright young person to maintain his or her professional quality can broad access to the best products of the universities be assured for government.

Index

About the Author

Henry C. Wallich has been a member of the Federal Reserve Board since March 1974. For twenty-three years previously, he was professor of economics at Yale University, the last four years as holder of the Seymour H. Knox chair. He has also been Assistant to the Secretary of the Treasury, member of the President's Council of Economic Advisers, and consultant to numerous government agencies and foreign central banks.

Dr. Wallich graduated from the Bismarck Gymnasium, Berlin, attended Munich and Oxford Universities, and received the Ph.D. from Harvard University. He initially worked in Argentina in the export business and later on Wall Street as a security analyst. For ten years he was on the staff of the Federal Reserve Bank of New York, the latter half of that time as chief of the Foreign Research Division.

Dr. Wallich has been an editorial contributor for the *Washington Post* and a columnist for *Newsweek* magazine, sharing a column with Milton Friedman and Paul Samuelson. He is author of four books and numerous articles. His list of speeches, articles, and congressional testimony since he joined the Federal Reserve Board includes some 225 items.